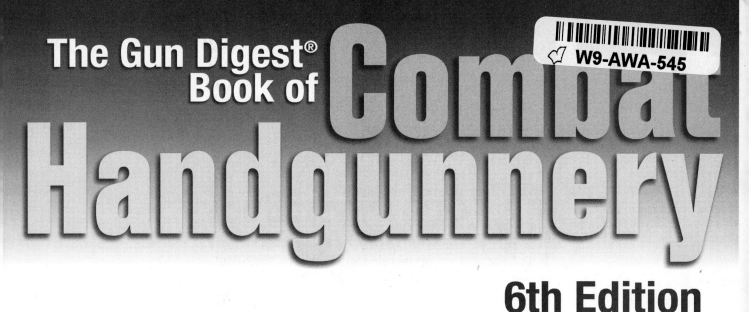

# The Gun Digest® Book of Combat Handgunnery

## 6th Edition

## How to Defend
- Your Family
- Your Home
- Yourself

**Massad Ayoob**

© 2007
by Krause Publications

Published by

**Gun Digest® Books**

*An imprint of F+W Media, Inc.*

700 East State Street • Iola, WI 54990-0001
715-445-2214 • 888-457-2873
www.gundigestbooks.com

Our toll-free number to place an order or obtain a free catalog is (800) 258-0929.

The views and opinions of the author expressed herein
are not necessarily those of the publisher,
and no responsibility for such views will be assumed.

In regard to the mechanical and safety aspects of the guns covered in this book,
it is assumed that the guns are in factory original condition with the dimensions of
all parts as made by the manufacturer. Since alteration of parts is a simple matter,
the reader is advised to have any guns checked by a competent gunsmith.
Both the author and publisher disclaim responsibility for any accidents.

Library of Congress Control Number: 2007923008

ISBN 13: 978-0-89689-525-6
ISBN 10: 0-89689-525-4

Designed by Patsy Howell
Edited by Ken Ramage

Printed in the United States of America

# Introduction

## About The Author

Since publishing his first firearms article in 1971 (*GUNsport* magazine) Massad Ayoob has authored thousands of articles in firearms, law enforcement and martial arts journals, and written more than a dozen books including *In the Gravest Extreme*, widely considered the authoritative text on the use of deadly force by private citizens in self-defense. His life achievement awards include Outstanding American Handgunner of the Year, National Tactical Advocate, the Roy Rogers Award for promotion of firearms safety and the James Madison award for authorship promoting the Second Amendment.

Ayoob served twenty years as chair of the firearms committee for the American Society of Law Enforcement Trainers (including several years on ASLET's ethics committee) and four on the advisory board of the International Law Enforcement Educators and Trainers Association. He has taught at regional, national and international seminars for the International Association of Law Enforcement Firearms Instructors, and has taught the investigation of justifiable homicides at venues ranging from the DEA Academy in Quantico to the International Homicide Investigators Seminars. Mas also served two years as co-vice chair of the forensic evidence committee of the National Association of Criminal Defense Lawyers, one of the very few non-attorneys to ever hold such a position with that organization.

For most of his adult life, Mas has worked full time studying violent encounters, teaching how to survive them, and writing about same. He founded Lethal Force Institute (PO Box 122, Concord, NH 03302, (www.ayoob.com) in 1981. Part-time, he has been testifying as an expert witness since 1979, and has spent 33 years as a part-time, fully sworn law enforcement officer, most of that time as a supervisor with command authority over full-time personnel. At this writing he is handgun editor of *Guns* magazine, law enforcement editor of *American Handgunner*, and associate editor of *Combat Handguns* and *Guns & Weapons for Law Enforcement*. The first five-gun Master in IDPA, Ayoob presently holds the New Hampshire State, Florida State, New England Regional and Florida/Georgia Regional Champion titles with the stock service revolver.

## Dedication

Live long enough, and you can write enough books to dedicate some to your mom and dad, your spouse, your kids, your colleagues, and your mentors. Been there, done that.

This book is respectfully dedicated to my graduates, from Lethal Force Institute and many other programs, especially those who used what they learned to survive. Some of you were kind enough to credit me with saving your lives.

It was good of you, but I have to say you were wrong. You saved your *own* lives… but, in so doing, you validated mine.

Massad Ayoob
July 2007

*Patrolman Massad Ayoob, 1978. Privately owned, department-approved service revolver is his Moran Custom Colt Python .357 Magnum. Photo credit: Dick Morin, Manchester (NH) Union-Leader newspaper.*

*Captain Massad Ayoob, 2006. Service pistol is department issue Ruger P345 .45 auto. Photo credit: Grantham (NH) PD.*

# Contents

CHAPTER ONE

# The Defensive Combat Handgun: An Overview

It is an honor to have been asked to write this edition of *The Complete Book of Combat Handgunnery.* Whomever steps into this authorship has several big pairs of shoes to fill.

This topic has been, literally, a life-long study for me. I grew up around guns, in part because my father was an armed citizen who survived a murder attempt because he knew how and when to use a handgun. He had learned that from his father. My grandfather, the first of our family to come to this country, hadn't been on these shores long when he had to shoot an armed robber. I grew up with a gun the way kids today grow up with seat belts and smoke detectors. It was simply one more common-sense safety measure in a sometimes-dangerous world.

The day came when what I had learned from my forebears, in terms of having defensive weapons and learning skill at arms, saved my life, too, and the lives of others I was responsible for protecting. I passed the skill on to my daughters. My eldest got her license to carry concealed when she was 18. A year or so later, the Smith & Wesson 9mm in her waistband saved her from two would-be rapists. She represented the fourth straight generation of my family in the United States to be saved from violent criminals by a lawfully possessed firearm.

Life takes us down unexpected paths. If, during my somewhat rebellious teen years, you had asked me what I was least likely to become, I would probably have answered, "Cop or teacher." Before long, I had become both. Pausing for a 25-month breather in the early 1980s, I've been a police officer since 1972, and have been teaching about guns during that entire time. My first article in a gun magazine was published in 1971.

There have been a lot of books and thousands of articles under the dam since then, and enough training to fill seven single-spaced résumé pages. Competitive shooting has been good to me; I've earned several state championships, a couple of regional wins, two national champion titles, and three national records. Only a couple of state championships still stand today. I've spent 15 years as chair of the firearms committee for the American Society of Law Enforcement Trainers, a few of those also as a member of their ethics committee, and a couple of years as co-vice chair of the forensic evidence committee for the National Association of Criminal Defense Lawyers.

We live in interesting times for armed citizens. On the one hand, our rights to protect our loved ones and ourselves are constantly attacked by people, often rich and powerful and articulate, who just don't have the first clue. On the other, so many states have passed "shall issue" concealed carry laws that more law-abiding citizens can carry hidden handguns in public today than at virtually any time in the last century.

Researching these things, studying how they happen, and how to prevail and survive if they happen to you, has become my life's work. I founded the Lethal Force Institute in 1981, and it has been a labor of love ever since. The on-scene management of violent criminal threat is a life study, and a multi-dimensional one that goes far beyond the gun itself. We cannot cover them all in one book. No one can. The laws that encompass these things and more, are all dynamic and fluid and subject to change.

The purpose of this book is to transmit a working knowledge of the current state-of-the-art of defensive handgun technology and its corollary topics, of how to effectively use them and how to find out how better to use them and more importantly, *when* to use them. Every effort will be made to explain where certain recommendations and trends came from.

Our guns, ammunition, and holsters are better than ever. So are state-of-the-art techniques that have been developed from modern and "post-modern" studies of what happens to the human mind and body under life-threatening stress. Better than ever also is our understanding of courtroom dynamics as they apply today in the often terrifying aftermath of the justified use of deadly force.

These skills are needed today. Since September 11, 2001, many experts believe they will be needed more than ever. The continued ability to choose to develop these skills, and exercise them if we must, is constantly under attack. It will be a long, hard fight, perhaps a never-ending one, but in the last analysis, that is the nature of the human experience.

I hope you find this book useful. If something seems new and radical compared to older "doctrine," try it yourself before you decide. I can promise you that there is nothing recommended in this book that has not been proven where it counts.

Stay safe.

*Massad Ayoob*
Live Oak, Florida
2007

# CHAPTER TWO

# Enduring Classics

## The Single-Action Autos

### The Model 1911

Roald Amundsen reached the South Pole behind a team of 17 Huskies. The most popular song of the year was "Alexander's Ragtime Band," by Irving Berlin. Ty Cobb was the dominant baseball star. Marie Curie won the Nobel Prize for chemistry. Milk was 17 cents a gallon, two bits would get you 10 pounds of potatoes and three pennies change, and 18 cents bought a pound of round steak. Louis Chevrolet and W.C. Durant introduced the former's automobile. Born in that year were Lucille Ball, Mahalia Jackson, Vincent Price, Ronald Reagan, Tennessee Williams, and the Colt Government Model .45 caliber "automatic pistol."

The year, of course, was 1911. The prices (including that of the Colt) have multiplied. The Chevrolet is vastly changed. The people, for the most part, have passed into

*Gen. William Keys, USMC (ret.) has revitalized Colt's commitment to the 1911 since he became CEO of the company.*

history. Only the 1911 pistol remains with us largely unchanged, and still going strong.

Today, if the covers of gun magazines are any indication, the 1911 is the most popular handgun design of its time. A scan through the catalogue pages of *Gun Digest* shows it is also the most influential. It seems that every year brings at least another 1911 "clone" to the marketplace.

Little has changed in the pistol's core design, but many subtle evolutions have taken place. The first wave came after WWI, when the American military began a study of how small arms had performed in the most recent conflict. The study was rather leisurely, it appears, as the list of complaints wasn't announced until about 1923. About half of the doughboys thought the trigger of the 1911 was too long. Many said the grip tang bit their hands. Most found the front sight post and rear notch so tiny as to be useless. It was also noted that when soldiers missed with it, they generally hit low.

About 1927, answers to these concerns were implemented, creating the 1911-A1 model. The grip tang was lengthened to prevent bite to the web of the hand. The trigger was shortened dramatically, and the frame at the rear of the trigger guard was niched out on both sides to further enhance finger reach. Believing that the low hits were a function of the pistol "pointing low" as opposed to the operators jerking their triggers, the designers gave the A1 an arched mainspring housing that sort of levered the muzzle upward and made the gun "point higher."

*The 1911 is a classic that remains in service. This officer wears his Kimber stainless .45 to work today.*

*The 1911's ergonomics are timeless. The author used this 1991-A1 Colt tuned by Mark Morris to place 2nd Master in the 2001 New England Regional IDPA Championships.*

*Para-Ordnance pioneered the high capacity 1911. The author used this one frequently at the National Tactical Invitational, where its extra firepower (14 rounds total) came in handy.*

Finally, a slightly better and more visible set of fixed sights was mounted to the pistol.

Gun companies and steel foundries were also making advances in metallurgy. It is generally accepted today that early 1911s are made of much softer steel than the 1911-A1 and later commercial Colts. This is why pistolsmiths have historically recommended against tuning early guns for accuracy. They felt the soft steel would not "hold" the fine tolerances required in precision accurizing, a process that became popular among target shooters in the 1930s and has remained a cottage industry within the gunsmithing business ever since.

The 1950s brought the epoch of Jeff Cooper who, writing in *Guns & Ammo* magazine, almost single-handedly re-popularized the 1911. Its one-third firepower advantage over the revolver, eight shots to six, plus its rapid reloading was but one advantage. The short, easy trigger pull – particularly when the gun had been worked on – delivered better hit potential under stress than the long, heavy pull of a double-action revolver. Though it appeared large, the Colt auto was flat in profile and easy to conceal, particularly inside the waistband.

The resurgence of the 1911's popularity had begun. By the 1970s, copycat makers were coming out of the woodwork. Through the 1980s, it at last occurred to makers to furnish the guns at the factory with the accoutrements that were keeping a host of custom pistolsmiths in business. These included wide grip safeties to cushion recoil, with a recurve to guide the hand into position and speed the draw, and a "speed bump" at the bottom edge to guarantee depression of the grip safety even with a sloppy hold. This part was also available "cut high" to allow the hand to get even higher on the grip. A low bore axis had always been one reason the pistol felt so good in the hand and was easily controlled in rapid fire by someone who knew the right techniques. Now, even the folks at the Colt factory began relieving the lower rear of the trigger guard, in hopes that the hand could ride still higher for even better performance. Now too, at last, 1911s were coming out of the factories with heavy-duty fixed sights that offered big, highly visible sight pictures.

There were also high-capacity versions, first with metal frames and then with polymer. Once, it had been standard procedure to send your Colt to a gunsmith to have it "throated" to feed hollowpoints and semi-wadcutters; now, Colt and Springfield Armory and Kimber and many more were producing the guns "factory throated."

By the dawn of the 21st century, the 1911 still ruled, though Colt did not. Kimber had become the single largest producers of 1911 pistols, offering a variety of sizes and formats. Springfield Armory was close behind in sales and equal in quality. Customized target pistols still ruled the bull's-eye firing lines, as they had for decades, but now competitors were showing up and winning with factory match 1911s from Les Baer and Rock River. Since the International Practical Shooting Confederation was founded at the Columbia Conference in 1976, the 1911 had ruled that arena, but now the

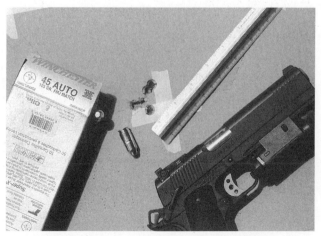

*1911s are capable of awesome accuracy. Springfield Armory TRP Tactical Operator pistol, mounting M3 Illuminator flashlight, put five rounds of Winchester .45 Match into this 1-inch group, hand held with bench rest at 25 yards.*

*Colt collectors will spot the WWII-vintage ejection port and sights on "retro" Colt 1911A1, reintroduced in 2001.*

*Four top-quality manufacturers and styles of modern 1911s, all .45s. From top: Compact Colt Lightweight CCO. Service Kimber Custom II. Hi-Cap Para-Ordnance P14.45. Tactical Springfield TRP with extended dust cover and M3 light.*

winning gun in IPSC was less often the old Colt than a high-capacity variant like the STI or the Para-Ordnance.

Over the years, the 1911 has been produced in a myriad of calibers. The .38 Super 1911s and hot 9mm variants win open class IPSC matches in the third millennium, and fancy inside, ordinary outside 1911s in caliber .40 S&W rule Limited class in that game. The 9mm 1911 is seen as the winning gun in the Enhanced Service Pistol class of the relatively new International Defensive Pistol Association contests, but the .45 caliber 1911 is much more popular, known in IDPA circles as a Custom Defense Pistol. However, in IDPA, even more shooters use Glocks or double-action autos, making the Stock Service Pistol category even more populous than the 1911 categories. The overwhelming majority of 1911s in serious use today are .45 caliber. No one has yet made a more "shootable" pistol in that power range.

Thus, with timeless continuity, the 1911 has outgrown the Colt brand with which it was once synonymous.

### The P-35

"Porgy & Bess" opens in New York, and Steinbeck's "Tortilla Flat" is published. The hot dance is the Rhumba. Milk is up to 23 cents for half a gallon (delivered, of course). Boulder Dam, Alcoholics Anonymous, and the Social Security Act all come into being. It is the birth year

for Woody Allen, Elvis Presley, Sandy Coufax, and the Browning Hi-Power pistol. It is 1935.

The P-35 was the last design of John Browning, who also created the Colt 1911. Many would also consider the Hi-Power his best. Known in some quarters as the GP or *grand puissance,* the pistol may owe more of its ingenuity to Didionne Souave than to Browning. In any case, it was the first successful high-capacity 9mm semiautomatic, and for more than a quarter of a century was the definitive one. It remains today the standard-issue service pistol of Great Britain and numerous other countries.

For most of its epoch, the P-35 was distinguished by a tiny, mushy-feeling thumb safety and by sights that were not the right size or shape for fast acquisition. In the 1980s Browning fixed that at last with its Mark II and later Mark III series pistols, which reached their high point in the Practical model. Good, big sights...a gun at last throated at the Browning factory to feed hollowpoints...big, positively operating ambidextrous thumb safety...legions of Browning fans were in heaven. That the guns by now were being manufactured for Browning in Portugal instead of at the Fabrique Nationale plant in Belgium mattered only to the most rigid purists.

Like the Colt 1911, the P-35 is slim, easy to conceal, and comfortable to carry. The 13+1 magazine capacity seemed to be its big selling point. But if people bought it for firepower, they kept it because it had a more endearing quality: It simply felt exquisitely *natural* in the human hand.

Before people used the word "ergonomics," John Browning clearly understood the concept. No pistol is as user-friendly. Col. Cooper, who has been called "The High Priest of the 1911," once wrote that no pistol had ever fit his hand better than the Browning. What a shame, he added, that it was not offered in a caliber of consequence.

Produced for the most part in 9mm Parabellum and occasionally in caliber .30 Luger, the Browning got a boost in popularity stateside during the 1990s when it was introduced in .40 S&W. The bigger caliber feels rather like a 1911 slide on a P-35 frame, but it shoots well. There were early reports of problems, but the factory quickly squared these away. The 9mm Browning has always been a rather fragile gun when shot with heavy loads. I've seen baskets of broken Browning frames in English military stockpiles and in Venezuelan armories. The hammering of NATO ammo, hotter than +P+ as produced by England's Radway Green and

Venezuela's CAVIM arsenals, was the culprit. Fed the hot loads only sparingly, and kept on a practice diet of low-pressure standard American ball ammo, the 9mm Browning will last and last. The massive slide of the .40 caliber version, along with its strong recoil spring, is apparently enough to keep the guns in that caliber from breaking epidemically.

The Browning's mechanism does not lend itself to trigger tuning in the manner of the 1911, that is one reason it has never been popular with target shooters. For most of its history, its magazines would not fall free unless the pistol was deprived of one of its trademark features, the magazine disconnector safety. The latter, when in place, renders a chambered round unshootable if the magazine has been removed. In the 1990s, Browning came up with a magazine with a spring on the back that positively ejected it from the pistol.

The timeless styling of the Browning made it a classic, but make no mistake: Its easy "carryability," and especially its feel in the hand, have made it an enduringly popular defense gun. From petite female to large male, every hand that closes over a Browning Hi-Power seems to feel a perfect fit. One caveat: Though it will hold 13+1, serious users like the SAS discovered that it wasn't very reliable unless the magazine was loaded one round down from full capacity. Just something to think about.

### Classic Double-action Autos

Some gun enthusiasts would argue whether the words "classic" and "DA auto" belong in the same sentence. Can there be such a thing as a "classic" Mustang? Only to the young, and to fans of the genre. Ditto the DA auto.

Surely, in terms of firearms design history, there were at least a couple of classics. The Walther designs of the 1920s and 1930s are a case in point. There is no question that the P-38 dramatically influenced duty auto designs of the future, though no serious gun professional ever made that pistol his trademark if he could get something else. European soldiers and police dumped them at the first opportunity for improved designs by HK, SIG-Sauer, and latter-day Walther engineers. South African police, who stuck with the P-38 for decades, told the author they hated them and couldn't wait to swap up to the Z88, the licensed clone of the Beretta 92 made in that country.

The Walther PP and PPK have timeless *popularity* that comes from small size and ease of concealed carry, splendid workmanship in the mechanical sense, and a

cachet more attributable to the fictional James Bond than to genuine gun experts who shot a lot, though the great Charles "Skeeter" Skelton was a notable exception who actually carried the PP and PPK in .380. By today's standards, the ancient Walther pocket gun is a poor choice. If it is not carried on safe, a round in the chamber can discharge if the gun is dropped. If it is carried on safe, the release lever is extremely awkward and difficult to disengage. The slide tends to slice the hand of most shooters in firing. Walther .380s often won't work with hollow-points, and though inherently accurate thanks to their fixed-barrel design, often require a gunsmith's attention to the sights to make the guns shoot where they are aimed. There are not only better .380s now, but smaller and lighter 9mm Parabellums!

In the historical design and "influence on gun history" sense, one could call the Smith & Wesson Model 39 a classic. But it, too, was a flawed design, and it would take Smith & Wesson almost three decades to really make it work. The S&W autoloader was, by then, a redesigned entity and a part of the new wave, rather than a true classic like the 1911 or the Hi-Power.

### S&W Service Revolvers

In 1899, President William McKinley signed the treaty that ended the Spanish-American War, the first of the Hague Accords were drafted, and Jim Jeffries was the heavyweight-boxing champion of the world. Born in that year were Humphrey Bogart, Gloria Swanson, James Cagney, Fred Astaire, and the Smith & Wesson Hand Ejector .38 revolver that would become known as the Military & Police model.

The Smith & Wesson double-action was the "Peacemaker" of the 20th century. As the M&P's name implied, it was the defining police service revolver for most of that century, with many thousands of them still carried on the streets today. S&W revolvers fought with American troops in both world wars, Korea, and Vietnam. There are doubtless still some in armed services inventories to this day.

One of the first of many small modifications to the design was a front locking lug that, many believed, made the Smith & Wesson a stronger double-action revolver than its archrival, the Colt. While the Colt had a better single-action cocking stroke and trigger pull for bull's-eye target shooting, the S&W had a smoother, cleaner double-action trigger stroke for serious fast shooting. It was largely

*Here is a circa 1930s production 6-inch S&W M&P with factory lanyard loop and instruction guide.*

*Markings show that this pre-WWII S&W M&P was worked over by Cogswell & Harrison of England.*

*S&W's Military & Police Target model .38 Special predated the K-38 Masterpiece series.*

*The author at 25 with Bill Jordan. Bill is demonstrating the S&W .41 Magnum he helped bring into existence.*

because of this that, by the end of WWII, S&W was the market leader in the revolver field. It remains there to this day, though at this writing Ruger exceeds S&W in total firearms production.

The most popular by far was the .38 frame, now known as the K-frame. One thing that makes a classic handgun is perfect feel. The average adult male hand fits the K-frame perfectly. Larger hands can easily adapt. Smaller hands adapt less easily. In 1954, Border Patrol weapons master Bill Jordan convinced Smith & Wesson to beef up the Military & Police .38 and produce a gun of that size in .357 Magnum. This was done, and another classic was born: S&W's .357 Combat Magnum, a staple of the company's product line to this day.

The same mechanism was adapted to a .44/.45 frame gun, known today as the N-frame. In 1917, S&W engineers created half-moon clips to adapt rimless .45 auto cartridges to revolver cylinders, to fill the Army's need for more handguns during WWI. This concept lives today in S&W's Model 625 .45 ACP revolver, a gun all the more practical since more recent full-moon clips allow the fastest possible six-shot reload. The first of the classic N-frames was the exquisitely crafted .44 Special Triple Lock. 1935 saw the next giant step, the first .357 Magnum revolver. That gun lives today as the practical, eight-shot Model 627 from the Smith & Wesson performance center. The N-frame was also the original home of the mighty .44

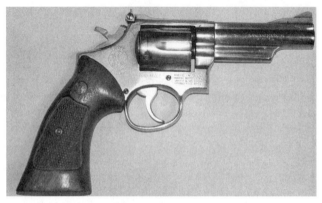

*In the 1970s, the S&W Model 66 became a modern classic.*

*S&W created clips for .45 ACP cartridge, and the 1917 revolver was born. The series reaches its zenith in the Model 625 revolver, this one was tuned by Al Greco and is wearing Hogue grips.*

*Tapered barrel (upper right) was standard configuration of S&W M&P until the late 1950s. Never discontinued, it was overshadowed by the more popular heavy barrel configuration, below.*

*America's most popular service revolver before WWII, the Colt Official Police .38 Special was subsequently pushed into second place by the S&W. This Colt wears a Pachmayr grip adapter, a common accessory.*

*State-of-the-art equipment at the end of the police revolver era: A Colt Python with Hogue grips in Bianchi B-27 holster, with speedloaders in a Safariland quick-release carrier.*

Magnum cartridge in the legendary "Dirty Harry" gun, the Model 29.

In the 1970s, it became the habit of police to train extensively with the hot .357 Magnum ammunition they were carrying on duty, with the particularly high-pressure 125-grain/1,450 fps load being their duty cartridge of choice. This was too much for the .38 frame guns, which began exhibiting a variety of jamming and breakdown problems. S&W upscaled to a .41 frame gun, which they dubbed the L-frame. This turned out to be a much sturdier .357 Magnum, the most practical version of which is probably the seven-shot Model 686-Plus.

There were some growing pains, including L-frames that broke or choked. S&W got that fixed. By the time they were done with it, the L-frame was utterly reliable and deadly accurate…but by that time, police departments were trading to auto pistols *en masse*,

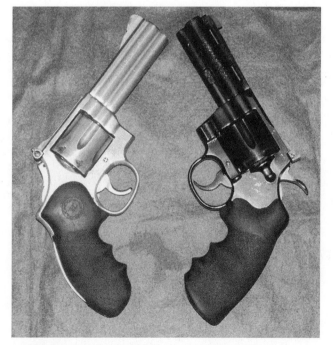

*Here are two classic .357 Magnum service revolvers. Left, S&W 686; right, Colt Python. Both of these wear Hogue grips.*

sounding the death knell for what many believed was the best police service revolver ever made.

## Colt Service Revolvers

Colt's service revolvers, like S&W's, trace their lineage to the 1890s. The Colt was the dominant police gun until the beginning of WWII, with S&W pulling ahead of their archrival in the post-war years and achieving near-total dominance in that market by 1970. Thereafter, Smith service revolvers were challenged more by Ruger than Colt.

The early Army Special and its heirs, the fixed-sight Official Police and the Trooper, were slightly larger and heavier than their K-frame counterparts. While the medium-build S&W was constructed on a true .38 frame, the Colts were actually built on .41 frames. Tests in the 1950s indicated that the Colts were stronger and better suited for hot loads like the .38-44, which S&W only recommended in their .45-frame guns.

Some gunsmiths felt the Colt would stay accurate longer, because its design included a second hand (cylinder hand, that is), which snapped up to lock the cylinder in place as the hammer began to fall. Others said it was less sturdy, because the primary hand seemed to wear sooner than the S&W's. Certainly, there was little argument on trigger pull. Virtually all authorities agreed that the Colt had the crisper trigger pull in single-action and the S&W, the smoother stroke in double-action.

In 1955, Colt introduced what would be their ultimate classic in this vein, the Python. Originally intended to be a heavy barrel .38 Special target revolver, it was chambered for .357 Magnum almost as an afterthought, and that changed everything. The full-length underlug and ventilated rib gave not only a distinctive look, but a solid up-front hang that made the gun seem to kick less with Magnum loads. At the time, the best factory craftsmen assembled the premium-price Python with extra attention lovingly added to the action work. Though he chose to carry a Smith & Wesson as a duty gun, NYPD Inspector Paul B. Weston, an authority of the period, dubbed the Python's action "a friction free

*S&W's Centennial Airweight is a classic snub. This original sample from the 1950s has a grip safety, a feature absent on the modern incarnation.*

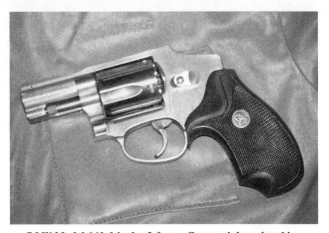

*S&W Model 640-1 is the J-frame Centennial rendered in .357 Magnum. These Pachmayr Compac grips help to cushion the substantial recoil.*

environment." Few challenged the Python's claim as "the Rolls-Royce of revolvers."

The underpaid cop of the time carried one as a status symbol if he could afford it. Three state police agencies issued them. A few went out to selected members of the Georgia State Patrol, and more than that were issued to the Florida Highway Patrol, while the Colorado State Patrol issued a 4-inch Python to every trooper. Today, no department issues this fine old double-action revolver. All three of the above named SP's have gone to .40 caliber autos: Glocks in Georgia, Berettas in Florida, and S&Ws in Colorado.

### The Classic Snubbies

Up through the middle of the Roaring Twenties, if you wanted a snub-nose .38 you were stuck with a short .38 caliber cartridge, too, the anemic little round that one company called .38 Smith & Wesson and the other called

.38 Colt New Police, in their Terrier and Banker's Special revolvers, respectively. (As late as the early 1970s, the Boston Police Department still had a few Banker's Specials issued to detectives. By then, the gun was a true collector's item.)

Then, in 1927, Colt took 2 inches off the barrel of their smaller frame Police Positive Special revolver and called the result the Detective Special. The rest, as they say, is history. A six-shot .38 Special small enough for the trouser or coat pocket, and easy to carry in a shoulder holster, was an instant success. "Detective Special" became a generic term, like "kleenex" or "frigidaire," for any snub-nose .38.

Late in 1949, Smith & Wesson entered the small frame .38 Special market with their Chief Special, so called because it was introduced at an annual conference of the International Association of Chiefs of Police. It only held five shots, but was distinctly smaller than the Colt. Immediately, it became a best seller among both cops and armed citizens.

After *that* little ace trumping, Colt was quick to respond. Both firms had built ultra-light revolvers for the USAF's Aircrewman project, and Colt was first to market with the Cobra, a Detective Special with a lightweight alloy frame. The alloy in question was Duralumin, aluminum laced with titanium, Alcoa #6 or equivalent. The company also came up with a bolt-on device aptly called a "hammer shroud." It covered the hammer on both

*The shrouded hammer makes S&W Bodyguard snag-free while retaining single-action capability. This is the stainless version in .357 Magnum.*

*Colt's .38 Detective Special is absolutely a modern classic. This sample is the popular 1972 style.*

*Taurus CIA (Carry It Anywhere) effectively copies the established styling of the S&W Centennial series. It's available in .38 Special and .357 Magnum.*

sides to keep it from snagging in a pocket or coat lining. Paul Weston had correctly described the Colt hammer spur as being shaped like a fishhook. The Shroud covered the hammer, left the tip exposed to allow single-action thumb-cocking if necessary.

S&W threw a two-fisted *riposte.* Their aluminum-frame snubby, being smaller, was also a tad lighter. A Detective Special weighed 21 ounces, and a Cobra, 15.5 ounces. S&W's Airweight revolver in the Chief Special was listed as a feathery 12.5 ounces compared to 19 ounces in all-steel configuration. Also introduced (first in Airweight, in fact) was their Bodyguard model with built-in hammer shroud. Sleeker than the shrouded Colt, it was also more pleasant to shoot; the rear flange of the screw-on Colt shroud had a tendency to bite the web of the hand. However, the S&W was more difficult to clean in the area of the shrouded hammer, which proved to be a dust-collector with both brands.

Next came a true "once and future" classic, the Centennial. Smith & Wesson took the configuration of the

*Shown with his firm's CIA, Taurus CEO Bob Morrison is proud that his firm's snub-nose .38s are among the most popular.*

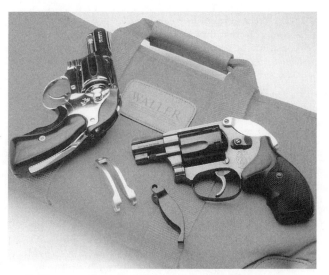

*Colt hammer shrouds for D-frame guns (left) and a new variation for J-frame S&W's (right) are available through W.W. Waller & Son.*

*Bob Schwartz at Waller offers a hammer shroud for the S&W Chief Special that turns it into the Bodyguard configuration.*

old New Departure Safety Hammerless top-break and grafted it onto the .38 Special Chief, creating what had to be the sleekest revolver of the genre. It even had the antique gun's signature "lemon squeezer" grip safety, the only solid-frame S&W ever so equipped. Ironically, because few shooters had yet mastered the double-action shooting concept and most felt they needed the crutch of cocking the hammer to hit anything, sales of the Centennial were mediocre and the gun was discontinued. As soon as it became unavailable, the Centennial became a much sought after "in-gun" among the cognoscenti. It was reintroduced, *sans* grip safety, and has been a best-seller ever since.

By the end of the 20th Century, the classic .38 snub had evolved further. The Colt had been given a heavy barrel treatment in 1972. Even before then, serious shooters tended to prefer the Colt over the Smith in a small snubby. The sixth shot had been the least of its advantages. Most found that with its bigger sights and longer action throw – the one comparison between Colt and Smith in which the Colt would likely be voted to have the better DA pull – the littlest Colt would outshoot the littlest Smith. Now an ounce and a half heavier, with a lot more weight up front, it kicked even less than the S&W and tended to shoot like a 4-inch service revolver. In the latter 1990s, the action was updated and stainless versions were produced, including a splendid .357 Magnum version called the Magnum Carry. The gun then went out of production, though at this writing, was high on the list of "old favorites" to be reintroduced by Colt under the new management regime of retired Marine Corps General Bill Keys.

The baby S&W, meanwhile, had been in stainless and Airweight, and even lighter AirLite Ti (titanium) and SC (scandium) models. Calibers included .22, .32 Magnum, .38 Special, 9mm, and .357 Magnum. A "LadySmith" version had also been marketed successfully. The firm had made larger versions in .44 Special.

During that period Taurus had come up from a cheap alternative to a genuinely respected player in the

*Classic combat revolvers are far from obsolete. These StressFire Instructor candidates at Lethal Force Institute learn to shoot and teach the wheelgun.*

quality handgun market. Their Model 85, resembling a Chief Special, was particularly accurate and smooth, dramatically underselling the S&W and becoming the firm's best seller. The new millennium saw the CIA (Carry It Anywhere) hammerless clone of the S&W Centennial. The first to produce a "Total Titanium" snubby, Taurus made their small revolvers primarily in .38 Special and .357, with larger snubbies available in .44 Special, .45 Colt, and even .41 Magnum.

Rossi also sold a lot of snub-nose revolvers. So did Charter Arms in its various incarnations from the 1960s to the 21st Century. Charter's most memorable revolver was the Bulldog, a five-shot .44 Special comparable in frame size to a Detective Special.

### Beyond Classic

Each of the combat handguns described above remains in wide use today in many sectors of armed citizenry, and/or security professionals, and/or police and military circles. Some consider them still the best that ever existed; others put them in second rank to the guns of today. Certainly, those classic revolvers remain in the front rank for those who prefer that style, but in autoloaders, there are many more modern choices. Who is right about what's best today? Let's examine "the new wave" of combat autoloaders, and see for ourselves.

# Purchasing Used Handguns

Buying a used handgun isn't as fraught with peril as buying a used car. It's a smaller, simpler mechanism. If it has been well cared for, you'll be able to tell.

Buy from people you can trust. It's a sad commentary on human nature that so many people will deal with a

lemon product by simply selling it to someone else. Most reputable gun dealers will stand behind the guns in their second-hand showcases. They may not be able to give you free repairs, but if something goes drastically wrong with it, someone who makes his living from the

*Though pitted and ugly with its badly worn finish, this S&W Model 15 was clean inside and tight. It would shoot 1-inch groups at 25 yards with match ammo.*

goodwill of the gun-buying community will take it back in trade and apply what you paid for it to something else you like better.

Some gun shops have a shooting range attached. With a used gun, you can normally pay a reasonable rental fee, take the gun right out to the range, and give it a try. If you don't like it, you paid a fair price to try a gun. If you do buy it, most such dealers will knock the gun rental off the price, though it's not fair to ask them to knock the range fee off, too.

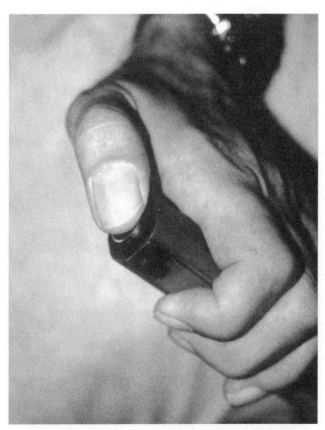

*The thumb rotates against the muzzle of an empty 1911 with the slide closed to check for sloppy fit.*

*Checking the bore without bore light. A white card or paper is held at the breechface and a flashlight is shined on the white surface, lighting up the bore so the interior can be easily seen from the muzzle end.*

### Universal Examination Points

As a general rule, a gun in pristine condition outside has *probably* been well cared for internally. This is not written in stone, however. Accompanying this segment are photos of a vintage Smith & Wesson Model 15 Combat Masterpiece .38 Special. It was found for sale among several others in a North Dakota gun shop in 1998, bearing a price tag of $130. Externally, what blue hadn't been worn off had been pitted. It looked as if someone had left it out in a field for the last couple of years. However, when the buyer examined it, he found the bore to be perfect, and the action so smooth and in such perfect tune it felt as if it had just left Smith & Wesson's Performance Center. He cheerfully paid the asking price, took it home, and discovered that it would group a cylinder of Federal Match .38 wadcutters into an inch at 25 yards.

It can go the other way, too. One fellow left the gun shop chuckling that he'd bought a fancy, premium brand .30/06 rifle, without a scratch on it, for at least $300 less than what it was worth. Then he got it to the range, and

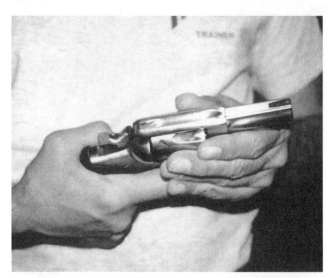

*Testing a revolver's timing. With the free hand thumb applying some pressure to cylinder as taking a radial pulse, the trigger finger starts a double-action stroke…*

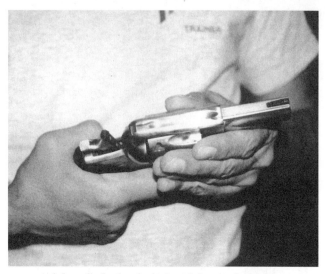

*…and the cylinder has locked up tight even before the hammer falls, showing that this Ruger Service-Six is perfectly timed, at least for this particular chamber.*

discovered it was less accurate than a Super-Squirter. Only then did he check the bore, to discover it rusted to destruction. The previous owner had apparently burned up some old, corrosive WWII surplus ammo in the expensive rifle and neglected the necessary immediate cleaning chores. The gun needed an expensive re-barreling job.

Before you do anything else, triple check to make sure the handgun is unloaded. I have seen people work a firearm's action at a gun show and freeze in horror as a live round ejected from the chamber. Don't let your natural firearms safety habits grow lax because the environment is a shop or show instead of a range.

Have a small flashlight with you, and perhaps a white business card or 3x5 card. (The Bore-Lite made for the purpose is, of course, ideal.) With the action open, get the card down by the breech and shine the flashlight on it, then look down the barrel; this should give optimum illumination.

If the bore is dirty, see about cleaning it then and there. The carbon could be masking rust or pitting. What you want to see is mirror brightness on the lands, and clean, even grooves in the rifling.

Watch for a dark shadow, particularly one that is doughnut shaped, encircling the entire bore. This tells you there has been a bulge in the barrel. Typical cause: someone fired a bad load that had insufficient powder, and the bullet lodged in the barrel, and the next shot blew it out. The bulge created by that dangerous over-pressure experience will almost certainly ruin the gun's accuracy. Pass on it.

Try the action. If everything doesn't feel reasonably smooth and work properly, something is *very* wrong with the action, and unless home gunsmithing is your hobby, you probably want to pass on it.

Now, let's branch into what you need to know about function and safety checks for revolver versus auto.

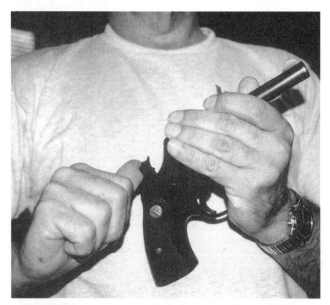

*Testing for "push-off" with cocked Colt Official Police. Hammer stayed back, passing test.*

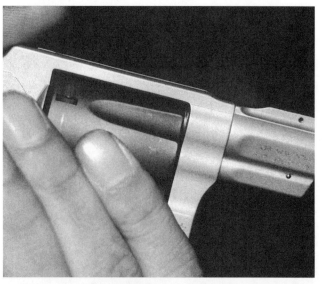

*Drawing the trigger or hammer back slightly to release the cylinder locking bolt, slowly rotate the cylinder to analyze barrel/cylinder clearance.*

### Checking the Used Revolver

Double check that the gun is unloaded, and keep the muzzle pointed in a safe direction. Check the bore and action as described above.

If it has both double- and single-action functions, cock the hammer. Keeping fingers away from the trigger, push forward on the cocked hammer with your thumb. If it snaps forward, you've experienced "push-off." This means either that the gun has had a sloppy "action job" done on it, or was poorly assembled at the factory, or has experienced a lot of wear. Since most experts believe a combat revolver should be double-action only anyway, and a good plan is to have the single-action cocking notch removed after you've bought it, this may not matter to you. Keep in mind, however, that it's an early warning sign that something else might be wrong with the gun.

With the cylinder out of the frame, spin it. Watch the ejector rod. If it remains straight, it's in alignment. If it wobbles like the wheels of the Toonerville Trolley, it's not, and there's a fairly expensive repair job in its immediate future.

Close the cylinder. Looking at the gun from the front, push leftward on the cylinder as if you were opening it, but without releasing the cylinder latch. Watch the interface between the crane or yoke, the part on which the cylinder swings out, with the rest of the frame. If it stays tight, the gun is in good shape. If there's a big gap, it tells

*The author drops a pencil, eraser-end first, down barrel of cocked and empty S&W 4506. Note hammer is back, and decocking lever up…*

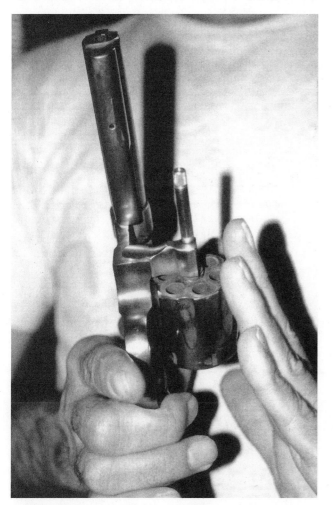

*The cylinder of S&W 686 is opened, then spun. Watch the ejector rod. If it wobbles, it's out of line and may need replacement.*

*…when the decocking lever on the left side is depressed the pencil stays in place. This shows that the decocking mechanism is working properly.*

you that some bozo has been abusing the gun by whipping the cylinder out of the frame like Humphrey Bogart. This will have a negative effect on cylinder alignment and will mean another pricey repair job. A big gap in this spot always means, "don't buy it."

With the cylinder still closed and the muzzle still in a safe direction, take a firing grasp with your dominant hand. Cup the gun under the trigger guard with your support hand, and with the thumb of that hand, apply light pressure to the cylinder. Use about the same pressure you'd use to take your pulse at the wrist. This will effectively duplicate the cylinder drag of cartridge case heads against the frame at the rear of the cylinder window if the gun was loaded.

Now, slowly, roll the trigger back until the hammer falls. Hold the trigger back. With the thumb, wiggle the cylinder. If it is locked in place, then at least on that chamber, you have the solid lockup you want. If, however, this movement causes the cylinder to only now "tick" into place, it means that particular chamber would not have been in alignment with the bore when an actual shot was fired. Armorers call this effect a DCU, which stands for "doesn't carry up." You want to repeat this check for every chamber in the gun.

When the revolver's chambers don't lock into line with the bore, the gun is said to be "out of time." The bullets will go into the forcing cone at an angle. This degrades accuracy, and causes lead shavings to spit out to the sides, endangering adjacent shooters on the firing line. As it gets worse, the firing pin will hit the primer so far off center the gun may misfire. With powerful loads, it will quickly lead to a split forcing cone. It definitely needs to be fixed. (When you get an estimate, if the armorer or gunsmith says you need a new ratchet, get a second opinion. Maybe five out of six times, all the gun needs is to have a new cylinder hand stoned to fit. Replacing an extractor is at least four times as expensive.)

Do all that again, and this time, once each chamber locks into place, wiggle the cylinder. If there's a lot of slop and play, there's a good chance that perfect chamber/bore alignment will be a chancy thing, and

*In a test that will make you cringe, unloaded pistol begins at slidelock with finger on slide release lever…*

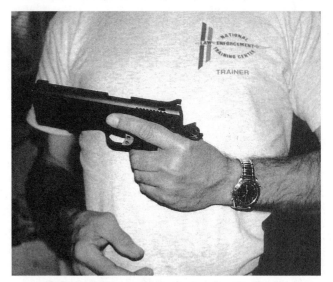

*…and the hammer remains cocked as the slide slams forward. This shows Kimber Custom .45's sear mechanism to be in good working order. However…*

*With magazine removed, hammer cocked, and safety off, the trigger is pulled on an empty Browning Hi-Power. Hammer does not move, demonstrating that magazine disconnector safety is functioning as designed.*

*…if the hammer had "followed" slide to the half-cock position as replicated here, gun would need repairs before being worthy of purchase.*

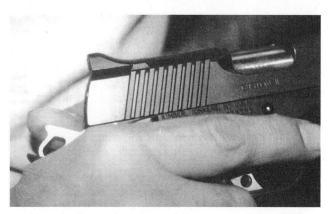

*A less abusive test for hammer-follow on an auto is to hold it as shown and repeatedly flick the hammer back with the free hand thumb.*

accuracy will suffer. This is generally a sign of bad workmanship in a cheaply made gun, and excessive wear in one of the big-name brands.

Push the cylinder back and forth; front to back and vice versa. A lot of slop means excessive headspace. Particularly with a big-bore or a Magnum, it may be a sign that the gun has been shot so much it's approaching the end of its useful life. A good gunsmith can fix this with some cylinder shims, however.

*Check to see if magazines insert and drop out cleanly. This HK USP40 Compact passes the test.*

Get some light on the other side of the gun, so you can look through the gap between barrel and cylinder. Hold the hammer back with your thumb until the bolt drops, and then rotate the cylinder, watching the gap. If you examine enough guns, you will find some that actually touch the forcing cone of the barrel. This is unacceptable; the cylinder will bind, the trigger pull will become uneven, hard, and "grating" as your finger works to force the cylinder past the bind point, and eventually the gun will lock up and stop working. On the other end of the spectrum, you may see a barrel/cylinder gap so wide that you could probably spit through it without touching metal. You can expect poor accuracy and nasty side-spit from such a gun. Reject it unless the seller is willing to pay for the repairs to bring it up to spec.

If the cylinder comes closer to the barrel on some chambers than others, the front of the cylinder is probably not machined true. Most experts would pass by such a revolver.

### Autoloaders

With any autoloader, double check that it is empty and keep the muzzle in a safe direction. Try the action a few times. When you rack the slide, everything should feel smooth. The slide should go all the way into battery – that is, all the way forward – without any sticking points that require an extra nudge. If the gun binds when it's empty, you *know* it's going to bind when the mechanism has to do the extra work of picking up and chambering cartridges. If the gun is clean and is binding, pass it by.

Make sure magazines go in and out cleanly. Some guns (1911, for example) are designed for the magazines to fall completely away when the release button is pressed. If the test gun won't do this with new magazines that you know are in good shape, there could be some serious warpage in the grip-frame or, more probably, something wrong with the magazine release mechanism.

Some guns (early Glocks, most Browning Hi-Powers, any pistol with a butt-heel magazine release) can't be expected to drop their magazines free. However, the magazine should still run cleanly in and out of the passageway in the grip frame.

You want to check the sear mechanism with a hammer-fired pistol to make sure there won't be "hammer follow." The test itself is abusive, and you want to make sure it's OK with the current owner before you do it. Insert the empty magazine and lock the slide back. Making sure nothing is contacting the trigger, press the slide release lever and let the gun slam closed. Watch the hammer. If the hammer follows to the half-cock position or the at-rest position, the sear isn't working right. Either it has been dropped and knocked out of alignment, or more probably, someone did a kitchen table trigger job on it, and the sear is down to a perilously weak razor's edge. Soon, it will start doing the same with live rounds, which will keep you from firing subsequent shots until you've manually cocked the hammer. Soon after *that*, if the malady goes untreated, you will attempt to fire one shot and this pistol will go "full automatic."

Because the mechanism was designed to be cushioned by the cartridge that the slide strips off the magazine during the firing cycle, it batters the extractor (and, on 1911-type guns, the sear) to perform this test. However, it's the best way to see if the sear is working on a duty type gun. (Most target pistols have finely ground sears and won't pass this test, which is yet another reason you don't want a light-triggered target pistol for combat shooting.) If

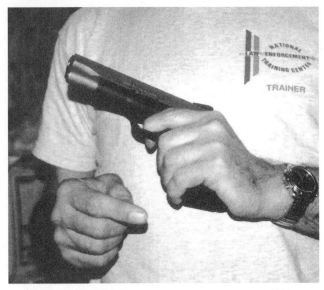

*Checking the manual safety/sear engagement on a 1911. First, cock the empty gun, put the manual safety in the "on safe" position, and pull the trigger firmly as shown...*

this test is unacceptable to the gun's owner, try the following. Hold the gun in the firing hand, cock it, and with the thumb of the support hand push the hammer all the way back past full cock and then release. If when it comes forward it slips by the full cock position and keeps going, the gun is going to need some serious repair.

If the pistol has a grip safety, cock the hammer of the empty gun, hold it in such a way that there is no pressure on the grip safety, and press the trigger back. If the hammer falls, the grip safety is not working.

If the gun has a hammer-drop feature (i.e., decocking lever), cock the hammer and drop a #2 pencil or a flat-head Bic Stik pen down the bore, with the tip of the writing instrument pointing toward the muzzle. With the fingers clear of the trigger, activate the decocking lever. If the pencil or pen just quivers when the hammer falls, the decocking mechanism is in good working order. However, if the pen or pencil flies from the barrel, that means it was hit by the firing pin. You're holding a dangerously broken

gun, one that would have fired the round in the chamber if you had tried to decock it while loaded.

Now, to test the firing pin, we'll use the Bic Stik or the #2 pencil again. This time, we'll pull the trigger. If the writing implement is launched clear of the barrel, you have a healthy firing pin strike. If it isn't, either the firing pin is broken or the firing pin spring is worn out.

*Caution: In both of the last two tests, wear safety glasses and have a clear "line of fire" with no one in the way! That sharp-tipped pen or pencil will come flying out of the barrel with enough force to cause a cut or nasty eye damage! Also in both of these tests, you'll need an empty magazine in place if the pistol has a magazine disconnector safety.*

To make sure that the magazine disconnector safety is operating, remove the magazine from the empty pistol, point it in a safe direction, and pull the trigger. If the hammer falls, the disconnector device either is not working or has been disconnected.

A sloppily fitted auto pistol is not likely to deliver much in the way of accuracy. Bring the slide forward on the empty gun, put the tip of a finger in the muzzle, and wiggle it around. If it's tight, it bodes well for accuracy. If it slops around a lot, the opposite can be expected. With the slide still forward, bring a thumb to the back of the barrel where it is exposed at the ejection port, and press downward. If it gives a lot, that tells you that the rear lockup isn't as solid as you'll need for really good accuracy. In either of these measurements, it's hard to explain how much play is too much. Try this test with some guns of known accuracy, and you'll quickly develop a "feel" for what is and is not what you're looking for with that particular make and model.

### Summary

Well-selected "pre-owned" handguns are an excellent value. Firearms are the ultimate "durable goods." How many people do you know who drive their grandfather's car or keep the family food supply in their grandmother's ice box? Probably not too many. But if you start asking, you'll be amazed how many people you know still cherish their grandparents' firearms.

It's no trick at all to find a perfectly functional combat handgun, revolver or auto, on the second-hand shelf at half the price of a new one. That leaves you more money for ammo, training, skill-building...and enjoying the life and the people you bought that gun to protect.

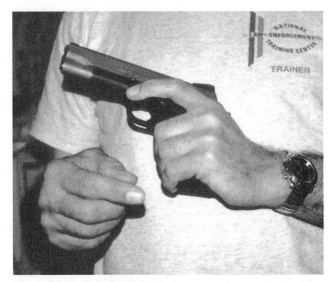

*...now, remove finger from trigger guard...*

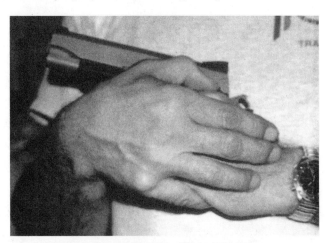

*...and release the thumb safety. If hammer stays motionless as shown, that portion of the mechanism is in good working order. If hammer falls at this point, gun is DANGEROUSLY damaged!*

# CHAPTER THREE

# Modern Paradigms

## The Glock

Gaston Glock had made a fortune producing assorted polymer items at his factory in Austria. His reputation was such that more than one firearms company soon approached him to make a polymer pistol frame. Being (a) a manufacturer, (b) a businessman, (c) a designer, and (d) smarter than hell, it occurred to him that he could design his own gun to manufacture. He set his design team to work, giving them a clean sheet of paper.

In the early 1980s, there was little new under the sun in the form of handguns. The most high-tech auto pistols were largely refinements of older designs. For example: take the 1950 Beretta service pistol, add on a 1930s vintage Walther-type hammer-drop safety and a 1908 vintage Luger magazine release, and you had the "new" Beretta. But what came off the Glock drawing board was something new indeed.

It looked like something out of Star Trek. It was sleek, with a raked back grip angle that could be compared to a Luger or a Ruger only in the angle, not in the shape. It was square at front and back. It had no hammer, inside or out; the pistol was striker fired. The polymer frame, plus a design created from the ground up for economy of manufacture, ensured under-bidding of the competition. The other makers' guns carried 14 to 16 rounds of 9mm Parabellum, but this one carried 18. The trigger pull was very controllable, and consistent from first shot to last. More importantly, the thing worked with utter reliability and survived torture tests.

It wasn't the first "plastic gun." Heckler and Koch had pioneered that more than a decade before, with plastic framed P9S and VP70Z lines, only to be met with poor sales. No one predicted success, figuring that the Austrian army's adoption of the pistol was merely a sign of chauvenism.

It is doubtful that any greater underestimation was ever made in the world of the handgun.

The Glock's entry into the American handgun marketplace was nothing less than stunning. The American branch of the firm, Glock USA, was established in Smyrna, GA. A couple of guys who knew the marketplace were on board: Bob Gates, late of Smith & Wesson, and Carl Walter.

*In the Glock light-weight, compactness, controllability and power come together in the author's favorite of the breed, the .45 caliber Glock 30. This one holds the short 9-round magazine designed for maximum concealment.*

*Author appreciates "shootability" of Glocks. He used this G17 to win High Senior and 2nd Master at 1999 New England Regional IDPA Championships, placing just behind national champ Tom Yost.*

A number of signs in the marketing heavens were in alignment, and this confluence of the stars would make Glock the biggest success story in firearms in the latter half of the 20th century.

American police chiefs still clung tenaciously to their service revolvers. Unique among police equipment, the revolver had not changed materially since the turn of the century. Uniforms were better, the cars had modernized along with the rest of America, communications were state of the art, and even handcuffs had improved and been streamlined. But if you went to a police museum, you would find that only two things had gone basically unchanged since the dawn of the 20th century: the police whistle, and the police service revolver.

Patrolmen's unions and well-versed police instructors were clamoring for autoloaders. For years, the chiefs had put off these requests with stock answers. "Automatics jam." "Our guys won't remember to take the safeties off when they draw to fire in self-defense." "They're too complicated." "Automatics cock themselves and go off too easily after the first shot."

Meanwhile, instructors were chanting the old military mantra, "Keep it simple, stupid." Any auto adopted by most of them would have to be simple, indeed.

Enter the Glock.

It endured torture tests for thousands of rounds. Buried in sand and mud and frozen in ice, it was plucked out, shaken off, and fired. It worked. Sand and mud and ice chips flew along with the spent casings, but the guns worked. One adventuresome police squad deliberately dropped a loaded Glock from a helicopter at an altitude of 300 feet. The gun did not go off. When it was retrieved, though one sight was chipped, it fired perfectly.

Safety? There was no manual safety per se. All safeties were internal and passive. "Point gun, pull trigger," just like the revolver. When BATF declared the Glock pistol to be double-action only in design, the argument about cocked guns being dangerous went out the window, too.

The first pistol was the Glock 17, so called because it was Gaston Glock's 17th specific design. It became the flagship of a fast-expanding fleet. Though Glock would later describe it as "full size," it was actually smaller than a Model 1911 or a Beretta 92, more comparable in overall length to a Colt Lightweight Commander, and it weighed even less.

Next came the even smaller Glock 19 with its 4-inch barrel. The 16-shot 9mm was roughly the overall dimensions and weight of a Colt Detective Special with 2-inch barrel that held only six rounds of .38 Special. At the other end of the size spectrum, Glock introduced a target model in the late 1980s, the 17L with 6-inch barrel. This gun had a light 3.5-pound trigger pull, a pound and a half lighter than the standard gun. Other trigger options were also made available. New York State Police said they'd adopt the gun, but only if Glock made it with a heavier trigger. Thus was born the New York Trigger, which brought the pull weight up to roughly 8 pounds. NYSP adopted the Glock 17 so equipped, and their troopers carry it to this day.

1990 was a pivotal year for Glock. They announced their big-frame model, the Glock 20 in 10mm, the caliber expected to sweep law enforcement after the FBI's recent announcement of adopting the S&W Model 1076 in that caliber. The gun was quickly adapted to .45 ACP. In January of that same year at the SHOT Show in Las Vegas, Smith & Wesson and Winchester jointly announced the development of the .40 S&W cartridge. Gaston Glock returned home with ammo samples and very quickly the standard Glock was reinforced to handle the more powerful cartridge with its faster slide velocity. Within the year, the South Carolina Law Enforcement Division had adopted the full size Glock 22 in that caliber and proven it on the street, and others were ordering the compact Glock 23.

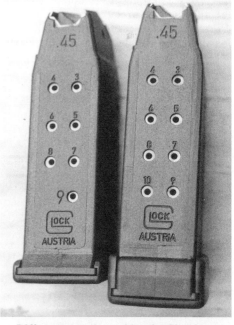

*Different magazines add to the Glock's versatility. Left, a short-bottom nine round magazine for maximum concealment; right, 10-round mag with little finger placement support. Both are for the Glock 30 .45 auto.*

*The Glock 17 holds 18 rounds of 9mm Parabellum in a pre-ban magazine. This specimen has Glock's oversize slide release and Heinie sights.*

In 1993, after a gunman with a 9mm murdered a young NYC cop while he was reloading his mandated six-shot revolver, the Patrolman's Benevolent Association at last prevailed over management and NYPD reluctantly went to the auto. All new recruits would have to purchase a 9mm instead of a .38, and in-service officers could buy one if they wanted. NYPD had always required their personnel to buy their own guns. Three double-action-only 16-shooters were authorized: the SIG P226 DAO, the S&W Model 5946, and the Glock 19. The Glock was by far the lightest and most compact for off duty and plainclothes carry, and by far the least expensive; it became first choice by such an overwhelming margin that many observers around the country thought NYPD had standardized on the Glock.

In the mid-1990s, the company found another huge success with their baby Glocks. The size of snubby .38s with twice the firepower and more controllability, the babies shot as well as the big ones. They were dubbed G26 in 9mm and G27 in .40 caliber. Slightly larger compacts were offered in 10mm Auto and .45 Auto, the Glocks 29 and 30 respectively. When a groundswell of popularity emerged in police circles for the powerful and accurate .357 SIG cartridge, Glock offered that chambering through the line as Model 31 (full size), Model 32 (compact) and Model 33 (subcompact).

The company didn't stop there. Integral recoil reduction ports were offered, creating a factory compensated gun in either compact or full size. These kept the same model numbers as the base guns, but with the suffix "C". The firm also introduced the "Tactical/Practical" series. Midway in length between full size and long-slide, they were exactly the length of the old Colt Government Model. This suited the .40 caliber G35 well for the Production class in IPSC shooting (where that caliber barely "made major"), and the 9mm G34 perfectly for Stock Service Pistol class in IDPA, where Dave Sevigny has used one to win repeated national championships. A number of departments from Nashua, NH to Kerrville, TX have made the Glock 35 the

standard issue duty pistol, usually with a retrofit of a New York trigger.

By the turn of the 21st century, the Glock pistol dominated the American law enforcement market to the tune of roughly 65 percent.

### Modifying the Glock

The pistol comes from the factory with what the company calls a "standard" trigger, which uses an S-shaped spring to connect the trigger to the unique cruciform sear plate. (The "Tactical/Practical" comes with a 3.5-pound trigger, like the long-slide 9mm 17L and .40 G24 models.) Supposedly delivering 5 pounds of pull, the standard trigger generally weighs out to about 5.5 pounds. Most civilian shooters leave it as is, as do many police departments including Washington, D.C. Metro, the Illinois State Police, and the FBI.

Many, including this writer, have followed the lead of the NYSP and gone with the original weight New York Trigger, now known as the NY-1. The intention of this design was to mitigate accidental discharges caused by human error. There is some three-eighths of an inch of travel from when the Glock trigger is at rest and ready to when it reaches its rearmost point and discharges the pistol. On the standard set-up, it feels like a Mauser military rifle trigger with a long, light take-up and then about a tenth of an inch of firm resistance before the shot is fired. When human beings are in danger, their inborn survival mechanism triggers a number of physiological changes, one of which is vasoconstriction. That is, blood flow is shunted away from the extremities and into the body's core and the major muscle groups. This is why frightened Caucasians are seen to turn ghostly pale, and it is why frightened people become clumsy and lose tactile sensation in their fingers under stress. In such a situation, it is feared that if the finger has erroneously strayed to the trigger prematurely, the shooter won't be able to feel it taking up trigger slack until too late.

The advantage of the NY-1 trigger is that it offers a very firm resistance to the trigger finger from the very beginning of the pull, a resistance so strong it probably *will* be palpable to the shooter even in a vasoconstricted state. This means a lot more than merely 3 pounds additional pull weight. (The NY-1 increases the pull to a nominal 8 pounds, which usually measures out to more like 7.75 pounds.) This, plus excellent training, allows NYSP and other departments to have an excellent safety record with these guns.

New York City Police Department initially put some 600 Glocks in the field among specially assigned personnel, ranging from Homicide detectives to the Missing Persons unit. These first guns had the standard 5-pound triggers, and after a spate of accidental discharges, the Firearms Training Unit

*Top, the Glock 27 holds 10 rounds of .40 S&W ammo; bottom, NAA Guardian holds 7 rounds of .380 ACP. Which would you choose?*

mandated an even heavier trigger than the State Police had. Thus was born the NY-2 trigger module, also called the New York Plus. This brought the pull up to a stated 12 pounds, which usually measures about 11.5 pounds on a well broken-in Glock.

This writer personally thinks the NY-2 passes the point of diminishing returns by making the trigger harder to control in rapid fire. Like many, I actually shoot better with the NY-1 at 8 pounds than with the standard pull. The reason is that the different design gives a cleaner "trigger break" as the shot goes off, and the heavier spring better resists "backlash."

Finally, I've found as an instructor that the little S-spring on the standard trigger system is the one weak link in an otherwise ingenious and robust mechanism. I see several break a year. The NY module that replaces that spring is much sturdier and I've personally *never* seen one break. For all these reasons, I have the NY-1 in every Glock that I carry, and strongly recommend it for any Glock carried for duty or defense.

Atop some models sits the other weak link: plastic sights. Retrofit steel sights (the Heinie unit is particularly good) or metal night sights with Tritium inserts that can be ordered on the gun from the factory solve this problem. There is the rare breakage of locking blocks, but that is no more common than cracked locking blocks on Berettas or cracked frames on SIGs, Colts, etc. The finest machines can break when they are used hard and long, and it is no reflection on the product. Outfit your Glock with an NY-1 trigger and good steel sights, and there's nothing left on it that's likely to break.

### The Appeal of the Glock

This gun is simple. Most armorer's courses (in which you are taught by the factory to repair the guns) take a week. Glock's takes one day. The pistol has only 30- some components. Almost all armorer's operations can be done with a 3/32-inch punch. You do need a screwdriver to remove the magazine release button.

*There is no easier pistol to learn to shoot well!* No decocking lever to remember; that's done automatically. No manual safety to manipulate; the safeties are all internal and passive. If your gun was made prior to 1990,

*Contrary to popular belief, Glock was not the first auto pistol with a polymer frame. This Heckler & Koch P9S which pre-dated the Glock considerably with a "plastic frame," was not a huge marketing success.*

call the factory with the serial number and see if it should have the no-charge new-parts update. Then, like every Glock produced for more than a decade, it will be totally impact resistant and "drop-safe."

Insert magazine. Rack slide. That's it. Now shoot it like you would a revolver, taking care to keep your thumb away from the slide and your firing wrist locked, as you would with any semiautomatic pistol.

If you want a manual safety for weapon retention purposes, or because it just gives you peace of mind after a lifetime with some other brand of pistol carried on-safe, an excellent right-hander's thumb safety can be installed at very reasonable cost by Joe Cominolli, PO Box 911, Solvay, NY 13209.

The Glock is an extraordinarily reliable and long-lived pistol. It is light, fast-handling, and very controllable. The polymer frame can be seen to flex in high-speed photography as it fires, and this seems to provide a recoil-cushioning effect that is enhanced by the natural "locked wrist" angle of its grip-frame. The Hybrid Porting conversion, which reduces recoil by sending several gas jets up through the top of what used to be the slide, will vampire as much as 100 feet per second of velocity and create a louder report, but allows amazing shot-to-shot control. While it seems to take a master gunsmith to make Hybrid-porting work reliably on a 1911, the Glock seems to function perfectly with it installed.

The Glock is southpaw-friendly and lends itself to ambidextrous shooting. A growing cottage industry offers useful accessories for it. Laser sights are available from Laser-Max and Crimson Trace. Models made in the last few years, compact size and larger, have an accessory rail that will accommodate a flashlight. The company has always been scrupulously good about customer service in terms of parts and repairs.

Accuracy is adequate at worst and excellent at best. The only Glocks that seemed to be really inaccurate were the very first runs of the Glock 22, and the company squared that away quickly. I have a Glock 22 that, out of the box, will stay in 2.5 inches at 25 yards with good ammunition; this specimen was produced in 2001. The baby Glocks are famous for their accuracy. This is because the barrels and slides are proportionally thicker and more rigid on these short guns, and also because the double captive recoil spring that softens kick so effectively also guarantees that the bullet is out of the barrel before the mechanism begins to unlock. Modifying a Smith & Wesson auto to have that same accuracy-enhancing feature costs big bucks when done by the factory's Performance Center; it comes on the smallest Glocks at no charge.

The .45 caliber Glocks also seem to be particularly accurate. First, the .45 ACP has always been a more inherently accurate cartridge than the 9mm Luger and particularly the .40 S&W. Second, the .45 barrels are made on different machinery than the other calibers at Glock, and seem to be particularly accurate. The "baby .45," the Glock 30, combines both of these worlds and may be the most accurate pistol Glock makes. My Glock 30, factory stock with NY-1 trigger and Trijicon sights, has given me five-shot, 1-inch groups at 25 yards with Federal Hydra-Shok and Remington Match ammunition.

There is a good reason for the Glock pistol's predominance in the American law enforcement sector and, to a slightly lesser extent, the armed citizen sector. Quite simply, the product has earned it.

# Today's Double-Action Autos

Walther popularized the double-action auto with a de-cocking feature in the 1930s. It was seen at the time as a "faster" auto, the theory being that with a single-action auto like the Colt or Browning, you had to either move a safety lever, or cock a hammer, or jack a slide before firing. With the DA auto, it was thought, one could just carry it off safe and pull the trigger when needed, like a revolver.

At the time, most of America felt that if they wanted an auto that worked like a revolver, they would just carry one of their fine made-in-USA *revolvers,* thank you very much. In the middle of the 20th century, 1911 flag-bearer Jeff Cooper applied an engineer's phrase that would stick to the double-action auto forever after. The concept was, he said, "an ingenious solution to a non-existent problem."

Whether or not that was true at the time, a problem later came up to fit the solution. America had become, by the latter 20th century, the most litigious country in the world. With more lawyers per capita than any other nation, the United States became famous for tolerating utterly ridiculous lawsuits that, had they been brought in a country that followed the Napoleonic Code, would probably have ended up penalizing the plaintiff for having brought an unmeritorious case. Two elements of this would have impact on handgun selection in both police and private citizen sectors.

Gun control had joined abortion as one of the two most polarized debates in the land. Prosecutors were either elected by the same folks who elected the politicians, or appointed by elected politicians. Some of them found it expedient to "make examples" of politically incorrect shootings of bad guys by good guys. For this, they needed a hook.

Contrary to popular belief, prosecutors don't get big occupation bonus points for winning a conviction for murder instead of manslaughter. If they get a conviction, they get credit, period. If they bring a case and lose, they lose credibility and political capital. This is why a good chance of a win on a lower charge beats a poor chance of conviction on a higher charge. To convince a dozen people

*Ruger's P90 beat every other double-action .45 tested and became the issue weapon for author's police department in 1993, along with Safariland SS-III security holster.*

with common sense sitting in a jury box that a good cop or a decent citizen has suddenly become a monstrous murderer is a pretty tough sell. But to convince them that a good person could have been careless for one second and made a mistake is an easy job, because every adult has done exactly that at some time. A murder conviction requires proving the element of malice, but a manslaughter conviction requires only proving that someone did something stupid. Thus, it came into vogue to attack politically incorrect justifiable homicide incidents with a charge of manslaughter.

It is common knowledge that a light trigger pull – what a lay person would call a "hair trigger" – is more conducive to the accidental discharge of a firearm than a long, heavy trigger pull that requires a deliberate action. Cocking a gun, or pointing an already cocked gun at a suspect, could therefore be seen as negligence. Now, the key ingredient of a manslaughter conviction was in place.

It reached a point where prosecutors would actually manufacture a "negligent hair trigger argument" even in cases where the gun was never cocked. One such case, *State of Florida v. Officer Luis Alvarez,* is mentioned elsewhere in this book. Alvarez' department responded by rendering all the issue service revolvers double-action-only. Some saw this as a weak concession to political

*A relic of the early 20th Century, the slide-mounted safety/de-cock lever of Walther PPK inspired designs of S&W, Beretta, and others much later in the "wondernine" period.*

correctness. It must be pointed out, however, that if the double-action-only policy had been in place before the shooting, the prosecution never would have had that false hook on which to hang the case, to begin with.

And that was just in criminal courts. On the civil lawsuit side, something similar was happening. Plaintiffs' lawyers realized that the deep pockets they were after belonged to insurance companies, not individual citizens who got involved in self-defense shootings. Almost everyone who shot an intruder had homeowner liability insurance, but such policies specifically exempt the underwriter from liability for a willful tort, that is, a deliberately inflicted act of harm. The lawyers could only collect if the homeowner shot the burglar by accident. Thus was born the heavy thrust of attacking guns with easy trigger pulls, and of literally fabricating the "cocked gun theory of the case." Private citizens who kept guns for self-protection and were aware of these things began to see the advisability of double-action-only autos as well as revolvers for home defense and personal carry.

A two-pronged concern was now in place. Fear of accidental discharges of weapons with short trigger pulls, and fear of false accusation of the same. Police chiefs who had once authorized cocked and locked Colts and Brownings for officers now banned those guns. Detroit PD and Chicago PD are two examples. Many private citizens who carried guns and followed these matters saw the trend, and decided that a design that was double-action at least for the first shot might have an advantage.

Thus was born the interest in DA pistols. The compactness of the Walther .380 had already made it a popular concealed carry handgun. Smith & Wesson's double-action Model 39, introduced in the mid-50s, had captured the attention of gun buffs. It was a good looking gun, slim and flat to carry in the waistband, with a beautiful feel in the hand, and it was endorsed by such top gun writers of the time as Col. Charles Askins, Jr., George Nonte, and Jan Stevenson.

The 1970s saw the development of high-capacity 9mm double-action designs, and of hollow-point 9mm ammo that got the caliber up off its knees. With expanding bullets, the 9mm Luger's reputation as an impotent man-stopper in two world wars was rehabilitated to a significant degree.

These guns became known as "wondernines," a term that was coined, I believe, by the late Robert Shimek. Known to gun magazine readers as an expert on handgun hunting and classic military-style small arms, Shimek was known only to a few as a career law enforcement officer who wore a 9mm SIG P226 to work every day.

These "wondernines" worked. In the late 70s and early 80s, the manufacturers refined the designs to meet the virtually 100 percent reliability requirements in the JSSAP (Joint Services Small Arms Project) tests that would determine the service pistol that would replace the ancient 1911 as the U.S. military sidearm. As a result, they were thoroughly "de-bugged." The prospect of a giant, lucrative government contract proved to be a powerful incentive to "get the guns right."

They would become the platforms of the .40 S&W cartridge in 1990, and of the subsequent .357 SIG cartridge. They would be enlarged, keeping the same key design features, to handle the .45 ACP and the 10mm Auto.

These were the guns that would change the face of the handgun America carried.

## Beretta

Beretta snatched the gold ring when the ride on the JSSAP merry-go-round was over, winning the contract as the new primary service pistol of the U.S. armed forces. There were a few broken locking blocks and separated slides. Though some of these involved over-pressure lots of ammo that would have broken any gun, and others involved sound suppressors whose forward-levering weight didn't allow the locking blocks to work correctly, jealous manufacturers who lost the bid amplified the "problem" to more than it was. Almost without exception, military armorers and trainers who monitor small arms performance in actual conflicts have given the Beretta extremely high marks for its performance in U.S. military service.

It has also stood up nobly in the U.S. police service. For many years now the issue weapon of LAPD (almost 10,000 officers) and Los Angeles County Sheriff's Department (some 7,000 deputies), the Beretta 92, 9mm has given yeoman's service. Thanks to its open-top slide design, it is virtually jam-free, and one of the very few pistols that can equal or exceed the Glock in terms of reliability.

The glass-smooth feel of the action as you hand-cycle the Beretta is the standard by which others are judged. The 92F series, with combination manual safety/decocking lever, may have the single easiest slide-mounted safety to operate. Two large departments, one East Coast and one West, mandate that their personnel carry the Beretta on-safe. Each department has logged numerous cases in which the wearers' lives were saved by this feature when someone got the gun away from an officer, tried to shoot him or her, and couldn't because the safety was engaged.

The Beretta is also a very accurate pistol. Five rounds of 9mm commonly go into 1-1/2 inches at 25 yards from the standard Model 92. The Model 96, chambered for .40 S&W, passed the demanding accuracy tests of the Indiana State Police and was adopted as that agency's standard issue sidearm. The state troopers of Rhode Island, Florida, and Pennsylvania joined Indiana and issue the

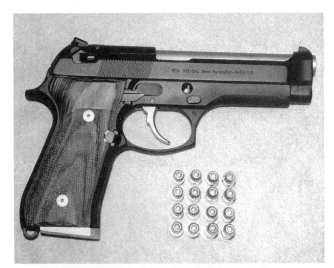

*A new wave classic, to mix a metaphor, the Beretta 92 proved to be an utterly reliable 16-shot 9mm, winning the U.S. Government contract and arming countless U.S. police agencies. This is a G-model, customized by Ernest Langdon, who won national championships with such guns.*

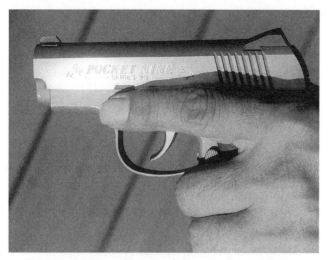

*Colt's Pocket Nine, a 9mm Parabellum the size of a Walther PPK but lighter, was the company's high point in double-action auto manufacture. For reasons explained in the text, it is no longer produced at this writing.*

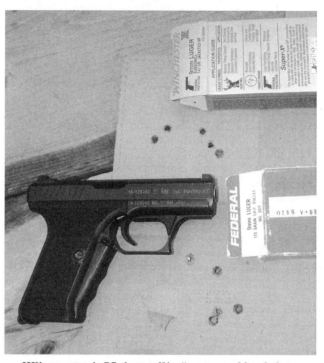

*HK's ergonomic P7 shows off its "guaranteed head-shot accuracy" at 25 yards with two of the most accurate 9mm rounds available, 115-grain Federal 9BP and Winchester's Olin Super Match 147-grain, both with JHP projectiles.*

96 at this writing. The city police of San Francisco and Providence also issue the 96.

In .40 S&W, my experience has been that the Beretta is a notch below its 9mm cousin in reliability. For this reason, Ohio state troopers dumped the 96 for the SIG equivalent.

Beretta's updated Cougar is a good gun. It is the issue weapon of the North Carolina Highway Patrol (in caliber .357 SIG) among others. The latest version, the polymer-frame 9000 series, is not particularly ergonomic and has not been so well received.

### Colt

America's most famous producer of single-action autos has not fared well on the double-action side of that table. Their first, the Double Eagle, misfired constantly in its original incarnation. When I broke the story on that, Colt was gracious enough to recognize the problem and correct it. The pistol, however, still looked like what it was: a Government Model with a double-action mechanism cobbled together in a fragile way to get past the Seecamp Conversion patent. It did not fare well and is no longer in production.

Colt's All-American 2000 was a sad and ugly thing. Jams. Misfires. Pathetic accuracy and a horrible trigger pull. Heralded by the newsstand gun magazines as a great leap forward in technology, it soon died a well-deserved death.

Colt's only good double-actions were their last, both DAOs. The little Pony .380 worked, and the Pocket Nine 9mm *was* a breakthrough: a full power, seven-shot 9mm Luger exactly the size of a Walther PPK .380 but 5 ounces *lighter,* utterly reliable, and capable of 2-inch, five-shot groups at 25 yards. While the triggers were heavy, they were controllable. Alas, only about 7,000 Pocket Nines were produced before a patent infringement suit by Kahr Arms shut down production.

### Heckler & Koch

HK's 1970s entries in the double-action auto market, the VP70Z and the P9S, did not succeed. The former

worked well as a machine pistol and poorly as a semiautomatic. The latter, exquisitely accurate, was before its time. It needed its chamber throated to feed hollow-points reliably, and its decocking mechanism, which involved pulling the trigger, was enough to make police firearms instructors wake up in the middle of the night screaming.

The P7 was much more successful. With an ingenious combination of gas operation and a squeeze-cocking fire control system that the company called Continuous Action, it created a cult following among handgunners. The gun was either loved or hated with no middle ground. A fixed barrel made it deadly accurate, with sub-2-inch groups at 25 yards more the rule than the exception. The squeeze-cocking came naturally and the pistol was super-fast to draw and fire. A low bore axis, plus the gas bleed mechanism, made it the lightest-kicking of 9mm combat pistols. Widely adopted in Germany, it became the issue service pistol of the New Jersey State Police in 1984 as the P7M8, with American style mag release and eight-round magazine. The double-stack P7M13 was subsequently adopted by Utah state police.

Its strength was that it was easy to shoot; its weakness was that it was easy to shoot. Many instructors associated the design with a likelihood of accidental discharge. Cost of manufacturing plus the changing balance of dollar and Deutschmark soon rendered it unaffordable for most civilians and almost all police. Still produced in the M8 format, this unique and excellent pistol is fading from the scene, but still cherished by a handful of serious aficionados, all of whom seem able to shoot it extremely well.

HK tried to get back into the police service pistol market with the gun they sold to the German armed forces, the USP. A rugged polymer-framed gun, it is available in several variants: lefty, righty, double-action-only, single-action-only, safety/decock or decock-only lever, and assorted combinations of the same. Available calibers are 9mm, .40, .357 SIG, and .45 ACP. It was the USP that introduced the now widely copied concept of the dust cover portion of the frame being moulded as a rail to accept a flashlight attachment.

I've found the USP conspicuously reliable, except for occasional jams in the 9mm version. It is also extremely accurate. Though competition versions are available, the standard models, particularly in .45, are tight shooters in their own right. Starting with probably the heaviest and "roughest" double-action only trigger option in the industry, they now have one of the best in their LE module, developed in 2000 for a Federal agency and offered to the civilian public in 2002. The HK USP is approved for private purchase by Border Patrol, and is the standard issue service pistol of departments ranging from San Bernardino PD to the Maine State Police.

### Kahr

Brilliantly designed by Justin Moon, the Kahr pistol is slim and flat, comparable in size to most .380s, and utterly reliable with factory 9mm or .40 S&W ammo. The double-action-only trigger is smooth and sweet, and the guns have surprising inherent accuracy. My K9 once gave me a 1-3/8-inch group at 25 yards with Federal 9BP ammo.

The only real complaint shooters had about the Kahr was that, being all steel, it seemed heavy for its size. This was answered with the polymer-framed, P-series guns. Whether the polymer-framed P9 and P40 will last as long as the rugged little K9 or K40, or their even smaller MK (Micro Kahr) siblings, is not yet known. NYPD has approved the K9 as an off-duty weapon for their officers, and Kahrs sell quite well in the armed citizen sector.

The Kahr's controls are so close together, given the small size of the pistol, that a big man's fingers can get in the way a little. By the same token, the gun tends to be an excellent fit in petite female hands.

Improving on the Kahr is gilding the lily, but a few gunsmiths can actually make it even better. One such is Al Greco at Al's Custom, 1701 Conway Wallrose Rd., PO Box 205, Freedom, PA 15042.

### Kel-Tec

In the early 90s, noted gun designer George Kehlgren pulled off a coup: the Kel-Tec P-11. With heavy use of polymer and a simple but heavy double-action-only, hammer-fired design, he was able to create a pocket-size 9mm that could retail for $300. At 14-1/2 ounces it was the weight, and also roughly the overall size, of an Airweight snubby revolver, but instead of five .38 Specials it held 10 9mm cartridges. One California law enforcement agency hammered more than 10,000 rounds of Winchester 115-grain +P+ through it with very few malfunctions and no breakage during testing.

The magazine is a shortened version of the S&W 59 series. This means that hundreds of thousands of pre-ban, "grandfathered" 14- and 15-round S&W 9mm magazines exist to feed it. This is handy for spare ammo carry and for home defense use where concealment is irrelevant.

Kel-Tec has made the same gun in .40, but not enough are in circulation for the author to have a feel of how they work. Numerous Kel-Tec P-11s have been through our classes, and the only problem with them is that the heavy

trigger pull becomes fatiguing during long days of shooting. However, any competent pistolsmith can give you a better pull for only a small portion of the money you save buying a P-11. Early problems with misfires in the first production runs were quickly squared away.

Perhaps Kehlgren's most fascinating design is his tiny P-32, which will be discussed two chapters subsequent.

### ParaOrdnance

When the sharp Canadians who popularized the high-capacity 1911 brought out their double-action-only model, they called in the LDA. The shooting public automatically assumed it stood for Light Double-Action, even though ParaOrdnance never called in that per se. They didn't have to. The assumption was correct. The pull stroke feels so light that your first thought is, "Will this thing even go off?"

It will. There were some minor problems with the very first LDAs, but the company got them squared away in a hurry. The ones we've seen since, in all sizes, have worked great. Factory throated with ramped barrels and fully supported chambers, they have the slimness and quick safety manipulation of the standard 1911, and in the single-stack models take the same magazines. This .45 is an excellent choice for the 1911 devotee who thinks it's time to go to something in a double-action.

### Ruger

Ruger's P-series of combat auto pistols, scheduled to debut in 1985, did not hit the marketplace until 1988. Bill Ruger had shown me the blueprints and rough castings of his original design, an affordable 9mm auto, in the early 1980s and had sworn me to secrecy. Early tests showed some jamming problems with some departments, though the ones we tested were perfectly reliable, but accuracy was sloppy with 4-inch to 5-inch groups being common at 25 yards. The P85 was not a success.

Stung by this, one of the few failures in the history of his company, Bill Ruger and his engineers set to work with a vengeance to correct the problems. The P85 Mark II and later the P89 had total reliability and better accuracy. There would be excellent medium- to service-size .40s and more compact 9mms to come. For my money, though, the triumph of the P-series was the P90 in .45 ACP.

*Accuracy is a hallmark of the Ruger .45. The author's department-issue P90 has just scored 597 out of 600 points on a PPC course.*

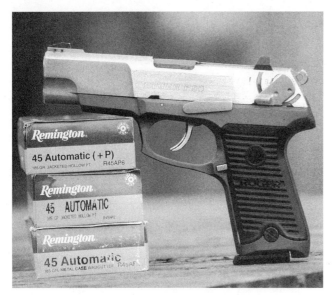

Unlike most 1911s, the "new wave" Ruger P90 feeds reliably with everything from light target loads (bottom) through standard .45 ACP (center) to the hottest +P with 10mm auto power level (top).

Adopted and proven by Huntington Beach (CA) PD, the SIG P220 popularized the double-action .45 auto among America's police and armed citizenry. This is the latest version, all stainless, with 9-round total capacity.

Designed at a time when it looked as if the 10mm would be the best-selling law enforcement round, the P90 was engineered to take a lifetime supply of that powerful ammo. Ironically, it was never chambered for that cartridge commercially, but in .45 the gun was "over-engineered," meaning it could take unlimited amounts of hot +P ammo with impunity. Moreover, thanks to some input from Irv Stone at BarSto, the P90 was the most accurate duty auto Ruger ever produced. One and a half inches for five shots at 25 yards is typical, and with the best ammo, I've seen these guns produce groups under an inch at that distance. There is no more accurate "modern style" .45 auto, though the Glock, SIG, and HK USP may equal, but not exceed, the Ruger in this respect.

The P90 is also extraordinarily reliable. In testing for the 1993 adoption of a duty auto, my department found that the Ruger P90 outperformed two more famous big-name double-action .45s, and adopted the P90. It has been in service ever since and has worked fine. Gun expert Clay Harvey tracked .45 autos of all brands used intensively for rental at shooting ranges, and found the Ruger undisputedly held the top spot in terms of reliability. In the latter half of the 1990s, Ruger introduced the P95 9mm and P97 .45 with polymer frames. These allowed production economy that made these guns super-good buys at retail, and both had superb state of the art ergonomics and fit to the hand.

San Diego PD bought large numbers of Ruger 9mm autos and reported excellent results. Ditto the Wisconsin State Patrol, which issued Ruger 9mm autos exclusively for many years.

### SIG-Sauer

Originally imported to the U.S. long ago as the Browning BDA, the SIG P220 .45 was adopted by the Huntington Beach, CA PD. Numerous other agencies followed after learning of HBPD's excellent experience with the gun. And, after decades of ignoring their home-grown 1911 pistol, numerous police departments looked

at swapping .38 revolvers for .45 autos. A trend was emerging. When the P226 16-shot 9mm didn't make it out of the finals for the military contract, the police community welcomed the pistol with open arms.

The SIG fits most hands well, and soon there was a short-reach trigger available for those with smaller fingers. The trigger action was deliciously smooth, and the SIG was easy to shoot well. Straight-line feed meant that it fed hollow-points from the beginning. Texas and Arizona troopers went from revolvers to SIGs early, and though both have changed calibers since, neither has changed brand. One of the first auto pistols approved for wear by rank and file agents, the SIG has been a popular FBI gun ever since. It has long been the weapon of Secret Service and Air Marshals. The troopers of Connecticut, Delaware, Massachusetts, Michigan, Vermont, and Virginia have joined Texas and Aarizona troopers in adopting the SIG. This writer has carried the P226 and P220 on patrol for many a shift and always felt totally confident in the weapons.

With the early P226 and P220, the springs on the side-mounted magazine release tended to be too light,

"New wave" combat handguns deliver accuracy users of some of the classics could only dream about. Here are three five-shot groups at 25 yards with different .45 ACP rounds from SIG P220 stainless double-action.

resulting in an occasional unintended drop of a magazine. This was fixed some time ago. One runs across the occasional cracked frame, but SIG is good about fixing them, and the guns are so well designed they keep running even if the frame is cracked. The most annoying problem is a tendency for the grip screws to work loose.

SIGs tend to be very accurate pistols. I've seen more than one P220 group five shots inside an inch at 25 yards with Federal Match 185-grain .45 JHP, and the P226 will go around 1-1/2 inches with Federal 9BP or Winchester's OSM (Olin Super Match) 147-grain subsonic. The side-mounted decocking lever is easy to manipulate, and the SIG-Sauer design is more southpaw-friendly than a lot of shooters realize. Your experience, if you buy a SIG, is unlikely to be sour.

### Smith & Wesson

The company that introduced the American-made "double-action automatic" took a while to get it right. There were a lot of feed failures and breakages in early Model 39, 39-2, and 59 pistols. Moreover, those guns were not drop-safe unless the thumb safety was engaged. Illinois State Police made them work by having their Ordnance Unit throat the feed ramp areas of all 1,700 or so pistols in inventory.

The second generation was drop-safe, and designed to feed hollow-points. These were characterized by three-digit model numbers without hyphens: the 9mm Model 459, for example, the Model 469 compact 9mm that the company called the "Mini-Gun," and the first of the long-awaited S&W .45 autos, the Model 645.

Ergonomics, however, still weren't great. The trigger pull suffered by comparison to the SIG, and the grips felt boxy and square. The introduction in 1988 of the third-generation guns with four-digit model numbers (5906, 4506, etc.) cured those problems. The only remaining source of irritation on S&W's "conventional style" defense autos is the occasional badly placed sharp edge.

From CHP to the Alaska Highway Patrol, S&W's 12-shot .40 caliber Model 4006 is the choice. S&W .40s are also worn by the troopers of Iowa, Michigan and Mississippi, while Idaho has the double-action only S&W .45 and Kentucky State Police issue the 10mm S&W Model 1076. A number of S&W autos are found in the holsters of FBI agents and Chicago and New York coppers, and S&W 9mm and .45 pistols are the only approved brand in addition to the Beretta for LAPD officers. The Royal Canadian Mounted Police use the S&W 9mm auto exclusively, in DAO models.

In concealed carry, two S&W autos stand out above all others. One is the accurate, super-compact, utterly reliable Model 3913 9mm. Endorsed by every leading female firearms instructor from Lyn Bates to Gila Hayes to Paxton Quigley, the 3913 works well in small hands and its safety features, like those of its big brother, make it ideal for those at risk of disarming attempts. Not only does the standard 3913 have a slide-mounted manual safety, but like the Browning Hi-Power and its own traditional siblings, it has a magazine-disconnector safety. This means that if someone is getting the gun away from you, you can press the release button and drop the magazine; this will render the cartridge in the chamber "unshootable" unless pressure was consistently applied to the trigger from before the magazine was dropped. This feature has saved a number of police officers in struggles over service pistols. It makes sense to security-minded private citizens, too.

*The double-action-only version of SIG P226 (note absence of de-cocking lever) is in wide use by Chicago PD, NYPD, and numerous other agencies.*

The other standout, a genuine "best buy" in the compact .45 auto class, is the Model 457. Compact and light in weight, this 8-shot .45 auto has controllable recoil, delivers every shot into about 2.5 inches at 25 yards, and is a stone bargain because it has S&W's economy-grade flat gray finish. The action is as smooth as that of its pricier big brothers. A whole run of these were made in DAO for the Chicago cops, and they were snapped up immediately. Cops know bargains.

### Taurus

In the last two decades of the 20th Century, the Brazilian gunmaker Forjas Taurus doggedly rose from an also-ran maker of cheap guns to establish a well-earned reputation in the upper tiers of reliability and quality. Much of the credit belongs to their PT series of auto pistols. Originally these were simply licensed copies of the early model Beretta 9mm. Over the years, Taurus brought

*John Hall, right, then head of the Firearms Training Unit of FBI, shows the author the Bureau's new S&W Model 1076 10mm in Hall's office at the FBI Academy, Quantico. The year is 1990. Photo courtesy Federal Bureau of Investigation.*

in some design features of their own, notably a frame-mounted combination safety catch and de-cocking lever similar to the one that would later be employed on the HK USP.

We see a lot of Taurus pistols at Lethal Force Institute. The PT-92 through PT-100 models in 9mm and .40 S&W come in, shoot several hundred rounds, and leave without a malfunction or a breakage. Accuracy is comparable to the Beretta, but cost is hundreds of dollars less. Finish may not be quite so nice, nor double-action pull quite so smooth, but these guns are definitely good values. Some find the frame-mounted safety of the Taurus easier and faster to use than the slide mounted lever of the modern Beretta, particularly shooters who come to the double-action gun after long experience with Colt/Browning pattern single-action autos whose thumb safeties are mounted at the same point on the frame.

Taurus has also introduced a high-tech polymer series called the Millennium, aimed at the concealed carry market. This gun has not yet established the excellent and enviable reputation for reliability that the Taurus PT series has earned.

There are many other double-action autos on the market. These listed above, however, constitute the great majority of what American armed citizens carry, and almost the totality of what American police carry. These were the guns that shaped the double-action auto cornerstone of the new combat handgun paradigm.

# Super-Light Revolvers

Combat handguns with lightweight aluminum frames have been with us for more than half a century. Smith & Wesson's Airweights immediately followed the introduction, circa 1950, of the Colt Cobra and lightweight Commander. The aluminum frame became standard a few years later on S&W's 9mm. The 1970s would see Beretta and SIG follow S&W's lead with aluminum-framed duty autos, and of course, Glock popularized the polymer frame in the 1980s.

Great leaps were made in the latter 1990s, however, as Smith & Wesson introduced Titanium and then, at the turn of the century, Scandium to create a generation of light and strong revolvers unseen until this time. Taurus followed immediately with their Ultra-Lite and Total Titanium series. Today, we have medium-sized revolvers in easy-to-carry weights that fire .38 Special, .357 Magnum, .44 Special, .45 Colt, and even the mighty .41 Magnum.

For each such gun that finds its way into the field, there are several small-frame "super-lights" that are being carried in .22 Long Rifle, .32 Magnum, .38 Special, and even .357 Mag. The majority of these are .38s.

The reason the little super-lights are so much more popular than the big ones doesn't have much to do with the fact that they've been around just a little bit longer.

It's a convenience thing. There is a huge market among civilians with CCWs and cops already overburdened with equipment. People want small, powerful handguns that don't drag and sag when worn on the body. Let's examine some of the weight standards we're talking about.

Smith & Wesson's Centennial "hammerless" revolver is a case in point. I own them in all four of the different weight configurations. It's interesting to see how they "weigh in," in more ways than one.

### Model 640 all-steel

This is one of the first of the re-issued Centennials, produced circa 1990 with the frame stamped +P+. I've always carried mine with the 158-grain +P FBI loads. It shoots exactly where the sight picture looks. It is very accurate, and head-shots at 25 yards are guaranteed if I do my part. Recoil with the +P is stiff; not fun, but not hard to handle either. Shooting a 50-round qualification course with it is no problem. It weighs 19.5 ounces unloaded.

### Model 442 Airweight aluminum-frame

As with the 640, this gun's barrel and cylinder are machined entirely from solid ordnance steel. This gun shoots where it is aimed. It is reasonably accurate. A

*A seven-shot L-frame snubby is a good "envelope" for the ultra-light .357 concept.*

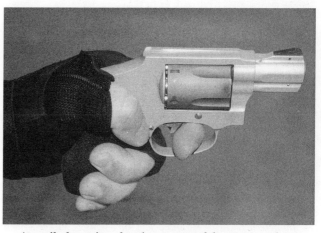

*A recoil-absorption glove is a most useful accessory when shooting the lightest, smallest-frame revolvers!*

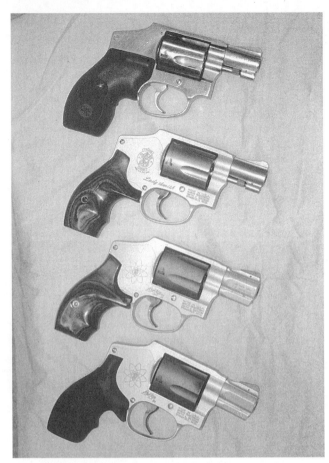

*Here are the four S&W Centennials discussed in this chapter. From top: all-steel, Airweight, AirLite Ti, and AirLite Sc.*

*Top, a factory brushed nickel Model 442 Airweight, and below, an AirLite Ti. Both have Crimson Trace LaserGrips. The lower gun is one third lighter, but feels twice as vicious in recoil. The author prefers the Airweight for his own needs.*

perfect score on the 50-round "qual" course may not be fun with the now distinctly sharper recoil, but it is not my idea of torture, either. A perfect score on the qualification isn't that much harder to achieve. The more visible sight configuration on the newest Airweights helps here. Weight is 15.8 ounces unloaded.

### Model 342 AirLite Ti

This gun's barrel is a thin steel liner wrapped inside an aluminum shroud, and its cylinder is made of Titanium. Like most such guns I've seen, it hits way low from where its fixed sights are aimed. I cannot shoot +P lead bullets (the "FBI Load") in it because the recoil is so violent it pulls them loose. Jacketed +P is the preferred load. The one qualification I shot with this was with jacketed CCI 158-grain +P. Recoil was so vicious I was glad I had a shooting glove in the car. When it was over, I was down two points. Rather than try again for a perfect score, I took what I had. It was hurting to shoot the thing. This gun is not as accurate as the all-steel or Airweight, putting most .38 Special loads in 3-inch to 7-inch groups at 25 yards. Weight, unloaded, is 11.3 ounces.

### Model 340 Sc Scandium

Chambered for .357 Magnum, this gun manages not to tear up the FBI load in the gun's chambers, but doesn't shoot it worth a damn for accuracy. Admittedly, this isn't the most accurate .38 Special cartridge made, but the load gives me about 5 inches at 25 yards in my Airweight, versus 15 inches of what I can only call spray out of this gun, with bullets showing signs of beginning to keyhole. This gun also shot way low. Recoil with Magnum loads was nothing less than savage. The little Scandium beast was somewhat more accurate with other rounds, but not impressively so. After five rounds, the hands were giving off that tingling sensation that says to the brain, "WARNING! POTENTIAL NERVE DAMAGE." When passed among several people who shoot .44 Magnum and .480 Ruger revolvers for fun, the response was invariably, "Those five shots were enough, thanks." I didn't even try to shoot a 50-shot qualification with it. Unloaded weight is 12.0 ounces.

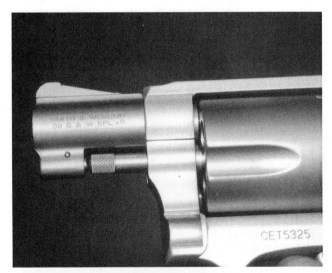

*The little notch at the tip of ramped front sight is an improvement on current S&W J-frame snubbies with all-steel barrels. This is the LadySmith Airweight.*

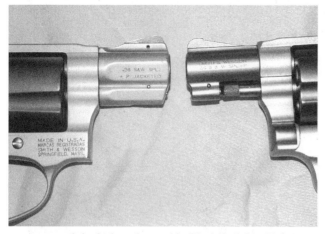

*Accuracy is in the barrel assembly. The 342 AirLite Ti, left, has a thin barrel within a shroud, and a too-high sight that makes shots print low. The conventional one-piece steel barrel of Airweight LadySmith, right, delivers better groups and proper sight height puts shots "on the money."*

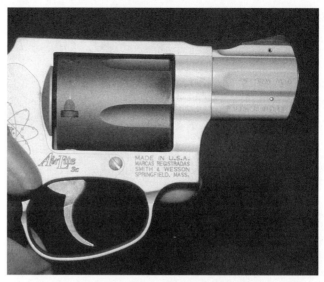

*A warning on the barrel shroud of AirLite Sc: it reads, 357 S&W MAG/NO LESS THAN 120 GR BULLET.*

The thin steel barrel sleeves of the Ti and Sc guns just don't seem to deliver the accuracy of the all-steel barrels of the Airweight and all steel models. All four guns are DAO, so it wasn't the trigger. The same relatively deteriorating accuracy was seen in the super-lights with mild .38 wadcutter ammo and big Pachmayr grips, so it wasn't the recoil. To what degree this is important to you is a decision only you can make.

Now, let's put all that in perspective. In the 1950s when all this ultra-light gun stuff started, Jeff Cooper defined the genre as meant to be "carried much and shot seldom." Alas, the days when we can do that are over, at least in law enforcement. Any gun we carry on the job is a gun we are required to qualify with repeatedly. As I look at my 340 Sc and 342 AirLite Ti, it occurs to me that if I'm deliberately going to do something that hurts like hell, I should go to Mistress Fifi's House of Pain and at least get an orgasm out of the deal.

This is why, for my own small backup revolver needs, I tend toward either the Model 442 or the Ruger SP-101. While the latter gun is even heavier than the Model 640, it fires the .357 Magnum round with very controllable recoil. A qualification with the SP-101 using full power 125-grain Magnum ammo could be called "exhilarating." The same qualification with the same ammo in the baby Scandium .357 qualifies absolutely as torture, at least in my hands.

Different people have different abilities and needs. My fellow gunwriter Wiley Clapp admits that the 342 Sc kicks like hell, but it's his favorite pocket gun nonetheless, even when stoked with Elmer Keith Memorial Magnum ammo. As you look at our differing preferences, note two things. First, Wiley is a big, strong guy. I, on the other hand, resemble the "before" picture in the Charles Atlas ads. Second, Wiley is retired from law enforcement and no longer required to qualify at regular intervals with

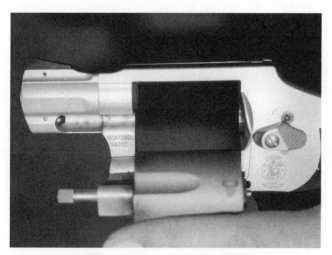

*The Model 340 Sc 12-ounce "baby Magnum" was among the first S&Ws to receive integral lock treatment; note keyway above cylinder latch.*

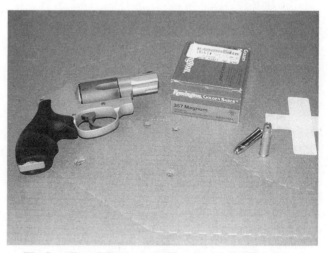

*The Scandium J-frame gave 100 percent reliability with Golden Saber medium-velocity .357 Magnum, but uninspiring accuracy.*

*The grimace on the face of this shooter after firing his first full Magnum round from the Scandium J-frame says it all.*

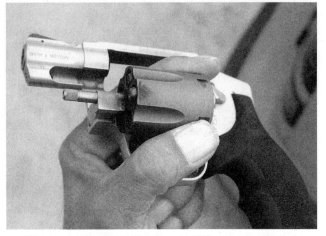

*Here's what happens when you use full-power lead bullets in a Ti or Sc S&W. Inertia from the violent recoil pulled the bullet nose of the 158-grain Magnum forward, "prairie-dogging" out of the chamber and preventing rotation.*

backup guns and their carry ammo. Those repeated qualifications are something I'm still stuck with.

For me, the balance of the super-light versus the Airweight comes out in favor of the Airweight for two reasons. At least in .38 Special, I can use my favorite load, that +P lead hollow-point that would pull loose in the chambers of the lighter guns. Moreover, in my career as an instructor I've seen a whole lot of people conditioned to flinch and jerk their shots because their gun hurt their hand when it went off. I don't want that situation to develop with me especially when I'm into the last layer of my safety net, the backup gun in my pocket. That's why, since I have to shoot a lot with any gun I carry, I want to carry a gun I'm comfortable shooting a lot.

We have more choices than ever, choices that fit some of us better than others. That's a good thing.

There are a great many people who can benefit from the super-light small-frame revolvers. Before you choose, check out the Taurus line. Some are equipped with integral recoil compensators that make them distinctly easier to shoot than a Smith & Wesson of equivalent weight with the same ammo. In fact, the comps take enough oomph out of the kick that the lead bullet +P rounds *don't* start to disassemble themselves in the chambers of Taurus guns so outfitted.

Another option is caliber change. My colleague Charlie Petty recommends the .32 Magnum in these guns. The recoil is much more controllable and the power level will still be more debilitating to an opponent than a mouse-gun. And, speaking of mouse-guns, a considerable number of the AirLite Ti revolvers have been sold as the Model 317, an eight-shot .22 that weighs only 9.9 ounces unloaded.

Let's think about that last concept. No, I'm not *recommending* a .22 for self-defense. But if the person is only going to carry a 10-ounce .25 auto anyway, they're far better served with a top quality eight-shot, 10-ounce .22 revolver. The Model 317 will go off every time you pull the trigger, which is more than you can say for most .25 autos. Unlike most small auto pistols in .22 Long Rifle, this revolver will work 100 percent with the hot, hypervelocity .22 rimfire ammo typified by CCI's Stinger, the cartridge

*The Model 340 Sc jammed after the third shot. Note how the bullets of Remington 158-grain SWC .357 cartridges have pulled forward from recoil inertia. At right is a properly sized round from same box for comparison.*

that began that concept long ago. Perhaps because the .22 doesn't generate enough heat to affect the thin steel barrel sleeve, the AirLite .22 will generally group better than the .38 and .357 versions. It will outshoot most any .25 auto going.

### More Wattage for the Lite

The super-light revolver comes into a different perspective when you look at the larger models. In the Taurus line, I've found all the Ultra-Lites and Total Titanium models I've fired to be good shooters. The larger frame models come with the company's unique Ribber grips, for which I give great thanks. They soak up recoil better than anything S&W currently offers. Add to that the option of the integral recoil compensator, and you have a much more shootable gun.

Alas, as with the Smiths, all is not perfect with these guns, either. I've run across several Taurus revolvers of this genre whose cylinders were simply too tight and were rubbing against the forcing cone of the barrel, mucking up the trigger pull and binding the action. A quick trip back to the plant to widen the barrel cylinder gap fixes this, however. I've also seen several that didn't shoot to point of aim.

Groups, however, were consistently good. I recall one snubby .41 Magnum Taurus that put five shots into 2-5/16 inches at 25 yards. The ammo was PMC 41A, a full power 170-grain .41 Magnum hollow-point. If the late, great Elmer Keith, the father of the .44 Magnum and co-parent of the .41 Mag, still walked among us, I suspect this little Taurus is what he'd carry for backup.

Both S&W and Taurus have produced L-frame .357 Magnum super-lights. They weigh in the range of 18 ounces, which is about the heft of the old six-shot K-frame Model 12 Airweight .38 snubby. But instead of six .38s, these sleek shooters give you seven rounds of .357 Magnum. Recoil can be snappy, but nothing you can't handle. Use the Ribber grips on the Taurus, and get a pair of K-frame round-butt Pachmayr Decelerator Compac grips for the S&W to take the sting out. These are comfortable holster guns and conceal well under a light jacket, or in a good inside-the-waistband holster under a "tails-out" shirt.

S&W has also sold a number of their Model 396 revolvers, hump-backed L-frames that hold five rounds of .44 Special. The shape of the grip-frame forces you to have your hand low on the gun, and this puts the bore at such a high axis that the gun has a nasty upward muzzle whip. Personally, I can't warm up to this gun. Accuracy is mediocre, in a world where even short-barreled Smith & Wesson .44 Specials have historically shot with noble precision. I tested one next to a Glock 27 on one occasion. The auto pistol was smaller, roughly the same weight, and held 10 rounds compared to the wheelgun's five, in roughly the same power range. The Glock shot tighter groups faster and was actually easier to conceal.

All these guns have a place. The light .357s and the little Taurus .41 make good sense when you're in dangerous animal country and want something very powerful for up-close-and-personal defense, but want to keep the backpack as light as you can.

The big contribution of the super-lights to combat handgunnery is found, nonetheless, in the smallest ones. Easier to conceal on an ankle or snake out of a pocket than a square-backed auto pistol, easy to load and unload

*The finger points to where sights were aimed at 25 yards. The 340 Sc hit far below that, with a poor group.*

*This federal agent experiences the recoil of a .357 Mag round in S&W 340 Sc.*

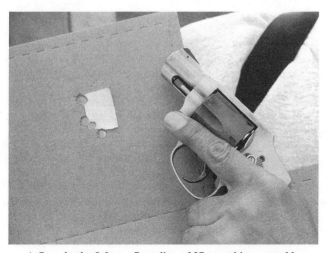

*At 7 yards, the J-frame Scandium .357 gave this acceptable head-shot group.*

*Here is the Taurus CIA (Carry It Anywhere), that firm's answer to the S&W Centennial.*

*Trainer Michael de Bethancourt shows the aggressive stance required to control "baby Magnums" such as this 340 Sc.*

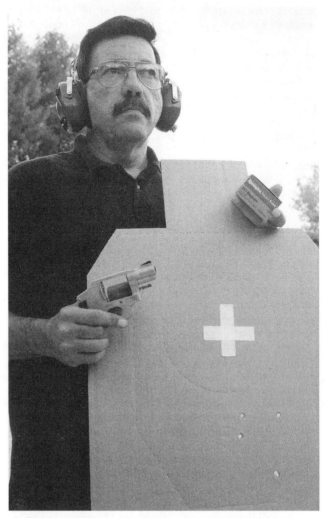

*The five gut-shots were aimed at the center of the chest from 25 yards. Ammo was medium-velocity Remington Magnum fired from the 340 Sc. The author is about as pleased as he looks.*

and utterly reliable, these little revolvers make up for their vicious recoil with their reassuring presence: being so easy to carry and to access, they're always *there*.

When Bert DuVernay was director of Smith & Wesson Academy, he made the very good point that while revolvers were indeed becoming a thing of the past as mainstream police service weapons, the small-framed revolver with a 2-inch barrel seemed assured a spot in the law enforcement armory as a backup and off-duty weapon. He seems to have called it right.

In states where "shall-issue" concealed carry has only recently been instituted, armed citizens are learning all over again how handy the "snub-nose .38" is as a personal protection sidearm. Many of the permits are going to law-abiding civilians who use these as their primary carry guns. For many of them, the option of the super-light models makes carrying a gun easier. For some, the super-light guns make carrying a gun *possible*. For that reason alone, I am grateful that these good guns exist.

# Micro Handguns

First, let's define our terms. How small is small? Smith & Wesson dubbed their 13-shot 9mm pistols of the 1980s, the Model 469 (blue) and 669 (stainless), "Mini-Guns," but they were substantial enough that a number of cops wound up wearing them as uniform holster weapons. Glock's smallest models have been known as the "mini-Glocks" and the "baby Glocks." Kahr Arms dubbed their smallest series with an MK prefix, for "Micro Kahr."

How small is mini, baby, or micro? We can start smaller than that in the world of the combat handgun.

For many years, the tiny .25 auto was considered the quintessential "ladies' gun" and the "gentlemen's vest pocket pistol." There has been the occasional save of a good person with one of these guns because they simply had a gun, and might not have had anything bigger when the attack came. However, we'll never know how many people have been killed or crippled by attackers who weren't stopped in time by the feeble bite of these tiny sub-caliber guns. As the streetwise martial artist Bill Aguiar put it, "A .25 auto is something you carry when you're not carrying a gun."

Sometimes a .25 is all you can handle. A psycho was beating a single mom in California to death when her little boy, pre-school age, grabbed her Raven .25 auto and screamed, "Get away from my mommy!" When the man did not, the child carefully shot him in the head, killing him instantly and saving his mother's life. I doubt he'll grow up troubled by the act. In Washington, an elderly man with an invalid wife fended off the attackers with the only weapon available, his wife's little .25 auto. As the attackers broke down the door and came at him, he fired once and the men fled. One died a few steps from the back door from a tiny bullet wound in the carotid artery. The other was captured within a few blocks. The grand jury almost instantly exonerated the old gentleman, and probably considered chipping in to buy him a bigger gun.

*Comparable in size are the Colt Pony Pocketlite .380 (left), Beretta Tomcat .32 (center) and Seecamp LWS –32, (right). Author picks the .380 for deep concealment.*

*Both at 14.5 ounces, S&W Airweight .38 Special at left is only slightly larger than Beretta Tomcat .32, right. Author chooses the .38 hands down.*

Since the 1970s we've had tiny, single-action, spur-trigger revolvers that harken back to S&W's No. 1 revolver of Civil War vintage, only smaller. They range in caliber from .22 Short through .22 Long Rifle to .22 Magnum. These guns are so tiny they are awkward to manipulate. A fellow on the range recently handed me one to fire. I pointed it downrange too casually, and when I triggered a shot, the gun jumped right out of my hand. I had only been holding it with part of one finger. Embarrassing? Yes, but not nearly so embarrassing as if it had happened in a fight.

Let me be the first to say that there are people who owe their lives to these little guns. In Los Angeles, a woman carrying one was savagely attacked. She pressed the muzzle into her assailant's chest, pulled the trigger, got him just right, and killed him where he stood. The slaying was ruled justifiable. In the south, a police officer was disarmed of his .41 Magnum revolver. The resolute lawman drew his mini-revolver from his pocket and laid into the attacker, who decided that rather than be shot with *anything,* he would give the revolver back. In South Africa, a gang of armed thugs set upon a man outside his suburban house. Rather than let them get in to attack his family, he drew his miniature single-action .22 revolver and opened fire on them. It was rather like sending a Chihuahua to attack a wolf pack, but he pulled it off. He managed to wound one or two of them. Deciding that being shot even with tiny bullets was not nearly as much fun for them as terrorizing helpless people, the attackers fled.

Yes, there are people who have used tiny guns with tiny bullets successfully for self-defense. There are also people who have jumped out of airplanes with non-functional parachutes and survived. It is respectfully submitted that neither is a promising model for the rest of us to follow.

Next up on the handgun ballistics food chain is the humble .32 ACP cartridge. There is no credible authority who will recommend this gun as a primary weapon, but everyone in the business admits that it's a quantum leap beyond .22 or .25 caliber. Evan Marshall's research into actual shootings indicates a significant number of one-shot stops with this cartridge. However, a review of the cases synopsized in his books shows a disproportionate number of these were either gun-against-knife or disparity of force cases. Disparity of force is the legal term for when one or more unarmed men attack someone with

such force that likelihood of death or great bodily harm becomes imminent. The attacker's greater size, strength, skill, or force of numbers is treated as the equivalent of a deadly weapon that warrants the use of a genuine deadly weapon in lawful self-defense.

The Winchester Silvertip, the CCI Gold Dot, and the Federal Hydra-Shok are hollow-point .32 rounds developed in hopes of getting the .32 caliber up off its knees. They get all the power out of the round that is probably possible. The problem is, there isn't that much there to start with. We've tested these in the slaughterhouse on smaller hogs and goats. The bullets usually deform. Sometimes they expand and sometimes they don't and sometimes the hollow cavity just turns into a little fish-mouth shape. However, unlike some .380 rounds, they don't seem prone to ricochet. If they don't get the caliber up off its knees, they at least get it up off its belly and onto its knees, and that's *something.*

Jeff Cooper once said that people buy .45s for the powerful cartridge, and buy 9mms because they like the design features of the guns. It follows that people buy tiny guns so they can have some sort of firearm without being inconvenienced by a significant weight in the pocket or by wearing a concealing garment.

*Tomcat with tomcat, Beretta on left and Scottish Fold on right. Some have job descriptions more suitable for "mouse-guns" than others.*

The brilliance of the Seecamp design, the pistol that re-popularized the .32 auto in our time, was that Louis Seecamp was able to conceive a pistol the size and shape of a Czech .25 auto that would fire the larger cartridge. The Seecamp is all the more brilliant in that it *works*. Now, this is the gun of Jeff Cooper's nightmares: double-action for *every* shot, no sights, and only a .32. The mission parameter was for a pistol that would be used at arm's length. Famed officer survival instructor and gunfight survivor Terry Campbell used to call these little pistols "nose guns," because the only way you could count on stopping the fight was to screw the muzzle up the attacker's nose and then immediately pull the trigger.

The supply of Seecamp pistols has never caught up with the huge demand in the marketplace. Other companies entered the field with "Seecamp clones": Autauga Arms, and North American Arms with their Guardian pistol. I never did test the former. The latter wasn't quite as reliable as the Seecamp but was easier to hit with because it had at least vestigial gunsights.

Next up was the gun that quickly became the best seller of its *genre*, the Kel-Tec P-32. One of several ingenious designs from the fertile brain of George Kehlgren, the P-32 weighs an incredible *6.6 ounces* unloaded. No bigger than the average .25-auto and almost wafer-thin, it has tiny little sights that you can more or less aim with, and a surprisingly nice double-action-only trigger pull. Polymer construction is what reduces the weight. By contrast, the NAA Guardian 13.5, and the Seecamp, 10.5 ounces. Each of these guns holds six rounds in the magazine, and a seventh in the firing chamber. All are DAO. The Kel-Tec is the lightest, the least expensive, and has the easiest trigger pull.

I have seen the occasional Kel-Tec that malfunctioned, usually when it was dirty or had at least gone a lot of rounds between cleanings. I've also shot some whose owners swore they had never jammed. Kel-Tec takes good care of their customers if they have a problem.

### Perspectives

The young lady in Los Angeles who killed the rapist was in a situation where she simply could not afford for it to be known that she was armed. From undercover cops to private citizens with gun permits who work in anti-gun environments, the same holds true for a lot of people. Yeah, I know, I'm the guy who said "Friends don't let friends carry mouse-guns." But for some people it's that or nothing.

Let me tell you about one of my clients. He was a hunter and target shooter who owned some fine rifles and shotguns. The only handgun he owned was a gift from a friend, a Smith & Wesson .22 Kit Gun. He took it on hunting trips. He would while away the slow times plinking at tin cans from the porch of the hunting cabin, and the little .22 also allowed him to quickly dispatch a downed deer without damaging the skull for mounting. The night came when a burglar alarm went off in his home, telling him a flower shop he owned was being broken into for the umpteenth time.

If he had gone intending to kill someone, he would have loaded his .30/06 auto rifle or one of his 12-gauge shotguns. Thinking about protection, he grabbed his only handgun, the little .22, and loaded it on the way to the shop. Given the lateness of past police responses in this community in which the cops were heavily burdened with calls, it was his intent to frighten away the intruders. But

*Relative sizes, different power levels. Clockwise from noon, S&W Model 3913 9mm, Kahr K9 9mm, S&W Sigma .380, S&W M/640 .38 Special. In the center is Walther PPK .380.*

*The NAA Guardian .380, center, is barely larger than FN .25 auto, above, or Beretta Jetfire .25 ACP, below. The .380 would be the definite choice here; the Guardian is among the smallest available.*

when he got to the scene he was attacked. He fired two shots and the attacker fled.

It reinforced both sides of the issue. *If the guy ran, he wasn't incapacitated.* Yes. I know. That's why I don't recommend .22s. *That guy ran a mile before he bled to death!* Yes. I know. That's why I don't recommend .22s. *If that guy had gone into fight mode instead of flight mode he could have still killed your client!* Yes. I know. That's why I don't recommend .22s. *Then why are you talking about this as if his having a .22 was a good thing?* Because the circumstances were such that a .22 was the only gun he would have had with him…and it saved his life. End of story.

### Perspectives

It's all well and good to say, "If you don't carry a .45 or a Magnum, you're a wimp." But there is idealism, and there is what Richard Nixon called *realpolitik*. We have to face reality. I'm fortunate enough that my job, the place I live, and my dress code allow me to carry a full-size fighting handgun almost all the time. Not everyone is that fortunate.

There's another argument in this vein that goes one tier up. I know a lot of cops who are proud of how they look in their tailored uniforms, and don't want the unsightly bulge of a big gun for backup. Shall I tell them if they don't carry a chopped and channeled .45, they deserve to have no backup at all?

*The Guardian .380 is a late-arriving "hide-in-your-hand" pistol barely larger than some .25 autos. A definite "new paradigm" combat handgun.*

I know a lot of armed citizens who already realize what a commitment it is to carry a gun all the time, period. If they're going to carry a second gun – a good idea for civilians, too – their wardrobe may not allow the small revolver or baby Glock I favor. For them, the backup weapon might be a Kel-Tec .32, or nothing at all.

When you demand all or nothing, history shows us, you're generally likely to end up with nothing. A tiny, small-caliber handgun is not what you'd want to have in your hand if you knew you were going to get into a fight to the death with an armed felon. But it's at least something. And something is better than nothing.

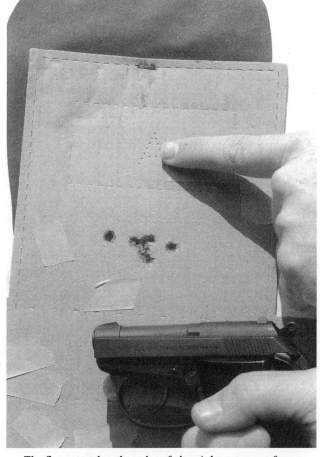

*The finger touches the point of aim. A decent group from the Beretta Tomcat .32 went extremely low at only 7 yards.*

*The Guardian .380, top, is only the tiniest bit larger than the .32 version (below) that preceded it. Nod goes to the .380.*

# CHAPTER FOUR

# A Blueprint For Learning The Combat Handgun

I was reading the deposition of a man who was being sued for shooting a contractor who showed up at his house early. He thought the man was a burglar. When asked why he shot him, he replied he didn't mean to; he intended his shots to warn, he said under oath. Did he aim the gun? No, he just pointed it. Had he been trained with his home defense gun, or even fired it before the day in question? No, he snapped indignantly, it wasn't like hunting where you needed a training course…

That man ended up paying a great deal of money to the man he shot, to that man's attorneys and to his own. Firing guns at human beings is not something you want to be ill prepared for in a moment of crisis. How does that preparation begin?

Some states have made training mandatory before issuance of a concealed carry permit. A few have even put together specific courses that must be taken. Two of the best are found in Arizona and Texas. Neither lasts long enough to give you anything close to all you need, but they give a solid foundation.

There are doubtless people reading this who have been shooting and carrying handguns longer than I, have forgotten more than I know, and could outshoot me on demand. They and I will both, however, be teaching others who are completely new to this discipline, some of whom are going to buy this book for that very reason. Therefore, let's address this progression beginning at new shooter level.

### The Basics

Don't leave the gun shop without having a professional show you how the gun works. Loading and unloading, manipulation of safety devices, even field stripping. Make sure you have an owner's manual with it. Once you have it…READ the owner's manual before going any farther.

If you are new to the gun, don't go out shooting by yourself. It's like a new pilot starting solo, or trying to learn to swim all alone. Find someone who knows this stuff.

Focus at first on safety…and keep that focus for as long as you own firearms. We bought a combat handgun to provide safety for ourselves and those we're responsible for. Whether or not we ever have to draw that gun on a dangerous felon, we know that we will spend the rest of our lives with that gun. Putting it on, wearing it, taking it off…loading it, unloading it, checking and cleaning it…sometimes when we're distracted or tired or stressed…*in proximity to the very*

*Match sponsors have the wherewithal to set up more complicated scenarios than most of us can on our own. Here a range officer follows a shooter through a complex stage at the S&W Mid-Winter IDPA Championships, 2002.*

*Police Chief Russ Lary tries his hand with his off-duty compact S&W .45 at the IDPA Mid-Winter National Championships, 2001.*

*The author awaits approval of the range officer (back to camera, wearing body armor) before ascending the stairs in Jeff Cooper's "Playhouse" simulator at Gunsite.*

*Left to right: Cat Ayoob, Peter Dayton, and Mas Ayoob pause between stages at the National Tactical Invitational, 1996. This event has always been a useful training experience.*

*Shooting under the eye of experienced shooters is a fast track to improved skill. This is an LFI class in progress at Firearms Academy of Seattle.*

*people we bought the gun to protect.* The price of gun ownership is like the price of liberty: eternal vigilance.

It's always a good idea to start with a basic handgun safety class. The National Rifle Association has tons of instructors all over the country. Check locally – your gunshop will know where you can get training. This is one reason to buy your gun at a dedicated gunshop instead of a Big Box Monster Mart where today's gun counter clerk is yesterday's video section clerk. Another excellent source of information is your local fish and wildlife department, which generally has a list of basic firearms safety instructors as well as hunter safety instructors.

You may not be ready yet to compete, but you're always ready to learn from the best. Find out from the gunshop what local clubs are running IPSC or IDPA matches. Contact those clubs. See about joining. *Ask about safety classes offered by the IPSC and IDPA shooters!* These will focus on important elements like drawing and holstering that might get short shrift at a basic firearms safety class. Find out when they're having matches, and go a few times to watch. Remember to bring ear and eye protection. Watching skilled practitioners handle their handguns gives you excellent early role models.

### Be A Joiner

Definitely join a gun club. You'll like the people, you'll enjoy yourself, but more importantly, you'll now be exposed to a whole group of seasoned shooters who have ingrained good safety habits. Never be afraid to ask questions. These folks enjoy sharing a lifestyle they love, and are always ready to help a new shooter get started.

*This shooter puts his 1911 to work from behind a realistic barricade during an IDPA match at the Smith & Wesson Academy.*

Another good thing about joining a club is that on practice nights, there's usually an opportunity for people to try one another's guns. Finding out that the Mark II Master Blaster Magnum isn't nearly as controllable as the gun magazine said it would be is much more painless at the gun club trying a friend's, than after you've shelled out a thousand bucks for your own. This factor alone can more than make up the cost of your membership and range fees.

### Formal Training Begins

I truly wish that shooting schools like the many available today existed when I was in my formative years. It would have saved me a lot of wasted time learning as I went. Unfortunately, the boom in concealed carry permits has drawn out of the woodwork a swarm of get-rich-quick artists who smelled a fast buck, took a few courses, and declared themselves professional instructors. As Jeff Cooper once commented on the matter, "There are a great many people teaching things they haven't learned yet."

When you inquire for particulars at a shooting school, request a resume of the person who will be the chief instructor at your course. If he gets indignant and refuses, he's told you all you need to know. Keep looking. Once you get the resume, do what you would do with any other prospective employee's resume, and check it out to make sure he's been where he says he's been, and has done what he says he's done. (You're hiring him to perform a service for you, right? Of course, he's a prospective employee.)

*Local police officers experience role-playing training set up by Lethal Force Institute students, who are playing the bad guys and bystanders in this scenario.*

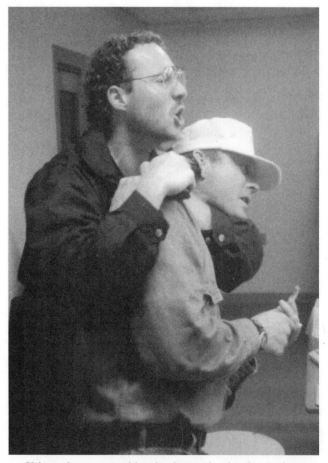

*Using a dummy gun, this role-player takes another student hostage in live-action scenario training at LFI.*

If in the early stages the prospective instructor is patronizing or condescending, move on. One of the truly great officer survival instructors, Col. Robert Lindsey, makes a profound point to his fellow trainers. "We are not God's gift to our students," Lindsey says. "Our students are God's gift to us."

Nationally known schools may be more expensive, but they are generally worth it. If a cadre of instructors has been in business for 15 or 20 years, it tells you that there aren't too many dissatisfied customers. Particularly in the time of the Internet, word gets around. The various gun chat rooms on the 'Net are also a good source of customer feedback. The best, however, is advice from someone you know and can trust who has already been to the school in question.

Once you get there, *be a student.* Soak up all you can, paying particular attention to the explanation of why the instructor recommends that a certain thing be done a certain way. Litmus test: If he says, "We do it that way because it is The Doctrine," add more than a grain of salt to whatever you're being asked to swallow. Try it the instructor's way; you're there to learn what he or she has to teach. You wouldn't throw karate kicks at a judo dojo; don't shoot from the Isosceles stance if the instructor is asking you to shoot from the Weaver.

Don't be afraid to ask for a personal assessment or a little extra help. Any instructor worth his or her title will take it as a compliment that you asked, not as an imposition.

## Journeyman Level

You have progressed. You're into this stuff now. You want to get better. *Yes!*

Remember at this stage that revelatory, life-changing experiences tend to come one to a customer. After you've become a reasonably good shot, further improvement will probably be incremental. In your first few schools in a discipline, you're trying to absorb it all and wondering if you're a bad person because you might have missed some small point. As time progresses and you get more courses under your belt, some of what you hear at successive schools will sound familiar. That's OK. It never hurts to reinforce and validate something positive that you've already learned. You'll be all the more appreciative when you do pick up something new, and all the more insightful when you put that new knowledge to use.

The instructor can't do it all for you. Skill maintenance is the individual practitioner's job. Martial artists and physiologists tell us that it takes 3,000 to 7,000 repetitions to create enough-long term muscle memory that you can perform a complex psycho-motor skill, such as drawing and firing a pistol, in the "automatic pilot" mode that trainers call Unconscious Competence. One intense week a year at the gym, and 51 weeks as a couch potato, won't keep your body in shape. That kind of regimen won't keep your combat handgun skills in shape, either.

By now you should have found at least one gun/holster combination that works well for you. Stay with it for a while. Don't try to buy skill at the gunshop. Buy ammo or

*Self-defense training goes beyond shooting. Do you know self-treatment for a gunshot injury if you're alone and wounded? Paramedic and LFI Staff Instructor Bob Smith demonstrates for a class.*

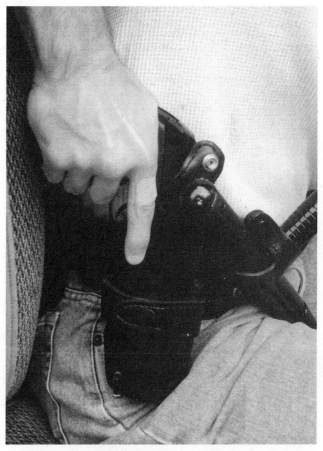

*Learn to draw from compromised positions. This officer clears an issue DAO Beretta Model 8040 from a Safariland 070 security holster while seated in vehicle.*

*Sometimes intense training can hurt. Allan Brummer takes a full power hit of OC pepper foam...*

*...and proves he can "fight through it," drawing a dummy gun and issuing commands while carrying out tactical movement.*

reloading components there instead, to better reinforce and enhance the skills you already have.

This is a good time to be thinking about some sort of practical shooting/action shooting/combat shooting competition. Doing well gives us motivation to get better. Being exposed to others who've been to different schools and shoot with different styles will broaden your horizons and give you new ideas you can put to good use. Sometimes even more importantly, this will introduce you to a new circle of friends and acquaintances who have the same self-defense values as you. Even if the thrill of the competition wears off, the pleasure and value of the friendships you make there will stay with you.

Remember as a journeyman that safety still has to come first. You're shooting enough now to be a high profile potential victim of the "familiarity breeds contempt" syndrome. Avoid that at all costs. The carpenter is more skilled with a hammer than the home craftsman, but he can still hit his thumb. The reason is that he uses it more, and is that much more exposed to that danger. So it is with us. Remember...eternal vigilance.

### In The Land Of The Experts

When you get really deep into this, and really good at it, improvement comes even more slowly. When Mike Plaxco was the man to beat in combat competition, he told me, "I get slumps just like everybody else. When I do, I change something in my shooting style. It makes me focus again, makes things fresh again, and makes me work at it again." Good point.

*Can you draw weak handed if your dominant hand is taken out? Here the author clears a Glock 22 from Uncle Mike's duty rig.*

*Here the author rinses out his teenage daughter's eyes after she has taken a hit of pepper spray.*

*Ambush waiting! The Beamhit system uses guns modified to non-lethal function and vests to carry the sensors which register only stopping hits.*

*Wearing protective gear and using Code Eagle modifications of S&W revolvers that fire only paint pellets, these students act out a car-jacking scenario.*

We're not going to preach here, but there are a great many people in this country who need to know these things, and not all of them can afford to travel to shooting schools to learn them. There comes a time when giving back is almost a moral obligation, like courtesy on the road. Consider teaching. Helping at a course at your local club, or volunteering to help someone who has once trained you, is a good place to start.

When you teach something, it forces you to see the forest for the trees. I can remember taking classes in things I didn't care about, but needed the course credit for. It was as if my mind was a tape recorder that held the information long enough to play it back on the final exam, and then erased the tape once the chore was done. That wasn't "life learning," and I regret it now. There were times when I took a class just for myself, saw something I liked, kept it, but didn't really get into the details of why I did it that way. If we don't understand why we're doing what we're doing, even if it works for us, we don't truly command the skill. I regret those learning experiences now, too.

I learned that I didn't really command a body of knowledge until I had been certified to teach it. "Hey, wait a minute, people are going to be asking me why we do it this way, and why we don't use technique X instead? I have to explain that? Hey, Coach, brief me on that one more time..."

Teaching not only ensures that we have it down, it puts the final imprimatur of understanding on our own performance in that discipline, sharpening us like the double-stamping of a coin. Since the inception of ASLET, the American Society of Law Enforcement Trainers, I've been chair of its firearms committee. ASLET's

*Have you learned how to return fire from disadvantaged positions if wounded? Here, LFI-II students go through one of several such drills.*

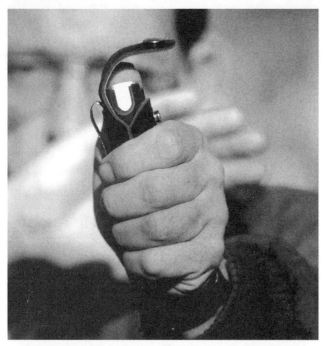

*Make sure your self-defense training is not confined to just the gun. OC pepper spray requires training to use to its best advantage.*

motto is *qui doscet, disket*. Translated loosely from the Latin: "He who teaches, learns." Thousands of my brethren and I have learned the truth of that through ASLET and similar organizations such as IALEFI, the International Association of Law Enforcement Firearms Instructors.

*On qualification day at an LFI-I class, the instructor's target...*

You're not comfortable with public speaking or perhaps some other element of formal teaching? That's fine, but if you look around there will be people in your family, your neighborhood, your workplace or somewhere else in your ambit who are interested in acquiring a defensive handgun or have already done so, and desperately need to know these things. Take those people to the range. Be patient. Be supportive. Give them what you wanted to get when you began in this discipline.

If nothing else, you'll make a good deposit in the karma bank and you won't come back as a dung beetle.

### Final Thoughts

Read on the topic. Watch the new generation of combat shooting videos. It's one thing to read about it, and another to actually see masterful speed shooting in action. One thing videos can do that even experience cannot is deliver instant replay in slow motion, showing subtleties of technique frame by frame.

Learn from your mistakes. Losing a match or a having bad day at the gun class doesn't mean you're a bad person and you need therapy. Winning gives you warm fuzzy strokes, and it also gives you positive reinforcement, validating that you're doing it right. But losing is where you learn. Think about it: How many of life's lessons did

*...has become the traditional award for the most-improved shooter. The staff, whose collective vote determines the recipient, signs it. Here John Strayer waits his turn to sign as Steve Denney pens some words of encouragement to the winning student.*

*Training should give you fallbacks for worst-case scenarios. Here, author drills on weak-hand-only with his Glock 22.*

you learn by messing something up? Sometimes, that's the strongest reinforcement of the learning experience. On days when you win, you can say to yourself, "A day well spent. I'm on the right track." On days when you lose, you can say to yourself, "A day well spent. I've learned a lesson, and I will *not* repeat the mistake I made today." Sometimes, the "instructional days" are a lot more valuable than the "positive reinforcement days."

It has been said that experience is the collected aggregate of our mistakes. But wisdom, said Otto von

Bismarck, is learning from the collected aggregate of the mistakes of others. That's why we read and study and reach out beyond our own experiences.

How do you best practice? This way: Stop practicing! This doesn't mean that you don't shoot or drill in your movement patterns or perform repetitions of tactical skills. It means that if before you practiced, now you *train!*

Practice can easily turn into just hosing bullets downrange. Often, you wind up reinforcing bad habits instead of enforcing good ones. Training, on the other hand, is purpose-oriented. Where practice can easily degenerate into "just going through the motions," training sharpens and fine-tunes every motion. If practice was going to be a couple of hundred rounds downrange, training might be as little as 50 rounds, but all fired with purpose. You, the box of ammo, and the electronic timer (one of the best investments you can make in your own skill development) head to the range. Instead of creating 200 pieces of once-fired brass, your goal is 50 draws to the shot. Each will be done in a frame of time that satisfies you and results in a good hit, or you'll analyze the reason why not and correct what's going wrong.

Shoot in competition. It hones the edge. A gun club that's enthusiastic about IDPA or IPSC (see the chapter on Combat Competition) will be able to set up complicated and challenging scenarios that you or I might not have the time or the money to construct. You'll get to watch top shooters in action and pick up subtle lessons from how they handle various tactical problems.

If there's no competition near you, or not as much as you like, shoot with a buddy or a loved one. Personally, I find I put forth my best effort against someone who shoots about the same as I do. When I shoot against world champions, it's exciting, but I know I'm not really going to beat them. When I shoot against someone who's had a lot less opportunity to develop skill, I'm not challenged. Someone who's at the same level seems to bring out the greatest internal effort.

Go ahead and side-bet with each other. That's a good thing, too. It conditions you to the reality that every time you pull that trigger, something rides on the outcome. You'll pay for a bad shot and be rewarded for a good one. Soon, shooting under pressure becomes the norm.

Your partner is not as good a shot as you are? Pick a course of fire and each of you go through it a couple of times and determine an average score. Subtract the one from the other, and give the difference to the lower scoring shooter as a handicap.

*Don't assume that statistics are right, and you'll only be in a gunfight at point-blank range. Here bodyguard Lars Lipke deploys his HK P7M13 at 50 yards, from standing position…*

*…and from the more effective Chapman Rollover Prone.*

*Learn to make tactical movement as thoroughly ingrained as stance and trigger press. Here Justine Ayoob, 15, performs a tactical reload while moving behind cover at the New England Regional IDPA championships.*

*Be able to shoot effectively from non-standard positions. National IDPA champ Ted Yost shows his form with a "cover crouch," which gets him down behind the rear of a car faster than conventional kneeling.*

Let's say it's a course of fire with 300 points possible. You average 299 and the partner averages 230. Give the partner 69 bonus points as a handicap. Now he or she is challenged: beating you is within striking distance, where before it seemed hopeless. This will encourage the partner to really focus and put forth his or her best effort. Before, you weren't challenged, but now you know that the newer shooter with the faster learning curve only has to get a little better to beat you. You, in turn, are now motivated to shoot a perfect score, the only thing that will keep you from losing the bet.

At Lethal Force Institute, we have the instructors shoot what we call a pace-setter drill on the last day. Just before the students shoot their final qualification test, the staff will shoot the same course of fire as a demonstration. This does several good things. First, it lets the students see what's expected of them. Second, watching us do it

helps them "set their internal clock" which in turn helps them make the times required for each string of fire. Third, it gives them a mental image of what they are supposed to be doing.

Bob Lindsey, the master police officer survival instructor, noted in the 1980s that a number of cops who were losing fights would suddenly see in their mind's eye an image of an instructor performing a technique. They would act out that image, make it work, and prevail. He called it "modeling." This is the main reason we do the pace-setter drill. Until then, I had followed the advice I'd been given in firearms instructor school. "Don't shoot in front of the students," I had been told. "If you're as good as you're supposed to be, it will make some of them despair of ever reaching your level. And if you blow it, you lose your credibility."

That had made sense. If a student asked me back then, "When do we get to see *you* shoot," my standard answer was, "When you go to Bianchi Cup or Second Chance. You're not here to see how well I can shoot. You're here to see how well *you* can shoot."

Lindsey's research changed my opinion on that. It was after hearing Bob's presentation on modeling that we started the pace-setter drills at LFI. Since we've been doing it, the scores of the students have gone up, and fewer of the students have had problems getting all their shots into the target before the cease-fire signal.

One thing we added was an incentive. Whatever score I shoot, if the student ties me he or she gets an autographed dollar bill with the inscription, "You tied me at my own game." If the student beats me, it's an autographed $5 bill that says, "You beat me at my own game." It's the cheapest investment I can make in their shooting skill, and it pushes them to do their best. It's natural for a student to want to exceed the instructor...and frankly, accomplishing that is the highest compliment a student can pay to a dedicated teacher.

My favorite award to give out is "most improved shooter." This award is the instructor's target, signed by all the staff. Often, the student who has accelerated "from zero to 50" has accomplished more than the already-skilled student who came to class at 100 miles an hour and was only able to get about 5 miles an hour faster.

In the end, it's up to you. Your skill development will be proportional to how much time you're prepared to spend training yourself, and acquiring training from others.

*"Simunitions" has ushered in a new dimension in reality-based training. This Glock has been factory modified to fire only the Simunitions paint pellet rounds.*

Getting good training is cost-effective, because despite tuition and travel expense, it saves you re-inventing the wheel. Yes, it takes a lot of years to get a Ph.D. in nuclear physics, but it would take you a helluva lot longer to figure out nuclear physics by yourself. Shooting isn't nuclear physics, but you don't need years in the university to learn it either. A few well-chosen weeks, backed up by your own commitment to a training regimen of live fire when you can and dry fire the rest of the time, will be the best investment in skill development you can make.

I do this for a living, as a full-time teacher and part-time cop, part-time writer, and part-time everything else. I'm supposed to have "arrived." But it's never wise to kid oneself. This sort of thing, at its greatest depth, is a life-study. As soon as you think you've "arrived," you stop moving forward. That's why I budget a minimum of a week a year for myself to take training from others. It keeps me sharp, and keeps the mind open. The old saying is true: Minds, like parachutes, work best when they're open.

# The Heart Of The Beast:
# Mastering Trigger Control

Agreed: What kind of bullet we're firing doesn't matter unless the bullet hits the target.

Agreed: The bullet doesn't have to just hit, it has to hit something vital.

Agreed: The bullet doesn't have to just hit something vital, it has to hit something so immediately vital that the person can no longer continue to attack.

Agreed: We'll have a very short time frame in which to accomplish this.

Agreed: As much as we might rather have a rifle, a shotgun, or a submachinegun to deal with this problem, the tool we're most likely to have with us is a handgun.

If we can agree that all these things are predicates to stopping a deadly fight with a combat handgun, then we are agreed that accuracy is extremely important. It's like high school Logic 101: If A is true and B is true, then AB must be true.

A lot of things will impact our ability to deliver accurate shots rapidly while under stress. Will you use a one-hand or two-hand hold on the gun? Two-hand is more accurate, but one-hand is sometimes more expedient. Will you use Weaver or Isosceles stance? There are times when it can matter, but they are relatively rare. Any basic marksmanship instructor will tell you that once you've brought your gun on target, there is one key element to

making the shot fly true: *You must pull the trigger in such a way that the gun is not jerked off target.*

We know that because the bullet flies in a relatively straight path, any deviation of the sight alignment is magnified in direct geometric progression. If your trigger pull jerks the muzzle off target by the tiniest fraction of an inch, the shot may hit in the white of the target, but not the black of the center scoring area at 25 yards. "Hah," say the clueless. "That's a target shooter talking! Those increments don't matter in a close-range gunfight!"

Ya think? Then, consider this.

You and I start the fight at the distance of only *one yard,* 36 inches torso to torso. You have drawn to shoot from the hip so I can't reach your gun. Let's assume further that your pointing skills are perfect today and your gun is dead center on my torso. You now jerk your trigger, moving the gun muzzle a mere inch to your strong-hand side. *Only one yard away, your shot will miss my main body mass.* It might go through the "love handle" and give me a .45 caliber suction lipectomy, or it might even hit my arm if it's hanging to the side, but it won't do anything to effectively stop me from harming you.

That's why, in real world combat shooting and not just match shooting, trigger control is so important. *The trigger is the heart of the beast! If you don't control the*

*Trigger control need not sacrifice speed. Here, Marty Hayes is firing four rounds in a fraction of a second from a prototype Spectre pistol. Note two .45 ACP casings in mid-air above the gun, a third below, and the muzzle flash of the fourth round.*

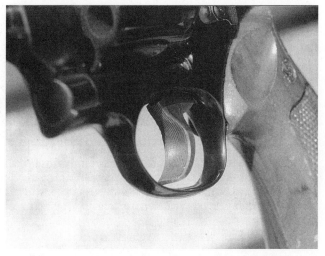

*S&W's wide, serrated "target trigger" is the best type for single-action target shooting, but the worst choice for double-action combat shooting.*

*trigger, you don't control even what should have been the most perfectly aligned shot!*

How can we hope to control the trigger under extreme stress? By being trained and conditioned to do it beforehand. Is it easy? No, and that's why we've devoted a whole chapter to the concept.

### Understanding The Mission

Too much combat handgun training has been borrowed from the world of target shooting. While some of the concepts survive the translation from range to street, some don't. One that doesn't is the *targeteer's* concept of trigger activation.

We are told that we should contact the trigger with the tip or the pad of the trigger finger. When asked why, we are told that this is the most sensitive portion of the finger and therefore the part most suited to this dextrous task. That makes sense as far as it goes, but let's analyze the target shooter's task versus the defensive shooter's.

In bull's-eye pistol matches, the core event is shot with the .22 caliber. You have, let's say, a High Standard .22 match pistol. It weighs 48 ounces, more if you have it scoped, and it has a crisp 2-pound trigger pull that needs to move only a hair's breadth. The gun is loaded with standard velocity (read: low velocity) .22 Long Rifle, which kicks with about as much force as a mouse burp. In this course of shooting events, "rapid fire" is defined as five shots in 10 seconds. All well and good.

But let's put ourselves somewhere else, perhaps a darkened parking lot. Our 260-pound assailant, Mongo, is coming at us with a tire iron. We are armed with a baby Glock, the G33 model that weighs only about 19 ounces. Its New York trigger gives us a pull weight of almost eight pounds over 3/8 of an inch. The power of its .357 SIG cartridge is that of some .357 Magnum revolver rounds, generating significant recoil. For us, "rapid-fire" has just become five rounds in *one* second, before Mongo reaches us with the tire iron.

Let's see, we have a few things to think about: a 3-pound gun with a 2-pound trigger, versus a 1-1/4-pound gun with an 8-pound trigger. We have 1/10 of an inch of movement versus 3/8 of an inch. We have almost no recoil versus sharply noticeable and palpable recoil. We have five shots in 10 seconds versus five shots in one second. Have the mission parameters changed for the trigger finger?

Obviously, the answer is yes. We're going to need a stronger finger, a finger with more leverage, to achieve the necessary results.

### Placement And Fit

You'll find that you have much more control of a longer, heavier combat trigger pull if you contact the trigger with *the palmar surface of the distal joint* of the index finger. It is at this point that the digit has the most leverage to draw the trigger rearward with the most speed and the least effort.

At LFI, we developed a simple test to allow you to see and feel this for yourself. Open this book and set it down where you can read it with your hands free. Take your non-dominant hand, turn its palm away from you, and extend the index finger. Stiffen it up: this finger is going to be a trigger with a heavy pull.

Now, with the index finger of your shooting hand, try to pull that "trigger" back, using the *tip* of your trigger finger. You'll have to use great effort – enough effort to probably distract you from focusing on much else – and when the finger does start to give, it will move in fits and starts.

*S&W's "Ranger" trigger has smooth surface so the finger can glide across it during fast double-action work without pulling the muzzle off target.*

Now try it again, making contact with the *pad* of your trigger finger. The pad is defined as the center of the digit, where the whorl of the fingerprint would be. You won't feel much difference.

Now, for the third and final portion of the test. With your "finger/trigger" still rigid, place your trigger finger at the same spot. Make contact with the crease where the distal phalange of the finger meets the median phalange, as shown in accompanying photos. Now, just roll the stiffened finger back against its force. Feel a huge difference? This is why the old-time double-action revolver shooters called this portion of the trigger finger the "power crease." It is here that we gain maximum leverage.

Of course, for this to work the gun must fit your hand. In the early 1990s, when gearing up to produce their Sigma pistol, Smith & Wesson paid some six figures for a "human engineering" study of the hands of shooters. It turned out my own hand fit exactly their profile of "average adult male hand." Not surprisingly, I found the Sigma to fit my hand perfectly.

Gaston Glock did much the same. However, he went on the assumption that the shooter of an automatic pistol

*In the old days, shooters tried to "stage" double-action revolvers, especially Colts like this snub Python. Today's more knowledgeable shooters use a straight-through trigger pull. Note the distal joint contact on the trigger.*

*This is the hand of a petite female on a gun that's too big for her, a Model 625 from S&W Performance Center. Note that she has been forced to use the "h-grip," in which the hand and forearm are in the shape of lower case letter h. One can get better trigger reach with this method, but at the expense of weakened recoil control.*

*Many prefer the short-reach trigger on a 1911, particularly those with small hands or those who use distal joint contact on the trigger as the author does. This is a 10mm Colt Delta Elite customized by Mark Morris.*

would be using the pad of the finger. When I grasp the Glock properly in every other respect, my finger comes to the trigger at the pad. To make it land naturally at the distal joint, I need the grip-shape slimmed and re-shaped, as done by Robar (21438 N. 7th Ave, Suite E, Phoenix, AZ 85027) or Dane Burns (700 NW Gilman Blvd, Suite 116, Issaquah, WA 98027). On a K-frame S&W revolver whose rear grip strap has not been covered with grip material, my trigger finger falls into the perfect position. Ditto the double-action-only S&W autos, and ditto also the Browning Hi-Power with standard trigger and the 1911 with a short to medium trigger.

Proper grasp means that the web of the hand is high on the back of the grip-frame, to minimize muzzle jump and stabilize an auto's frame against the recoiling slide. The web should feel as if it is pressing up into the grip tang on the auto, and should be at the very apex of the grip frame of the revolver. The long bones of the forearm should be directly in line with the barrel of the gun. This properly aligns skeleto-muscular support structure not only with the handgun's recoil path, but also with the direction of the trigger pull. The trigger finger, we mustn't forget, is an extension of the arm.

*Although the Glock was designed to be shot using the pad of the trigger finger; the author finds he has better control in extreme rapid fire with his finger deeper into the trigger guard.*

When the gun doesn't fit and the finger can barely reach the trigger, it will tend to pull the whole gun inboard. That is, a right-handed shooter will tend to pull the shot to the left. If the gun is too small for the hand and the finger goes into the trigger guard past the distal joint, the angle of the finger's flexion during the pull will tend to yank the shot outboard, i.e., to a right-handed shooter's right.

This is why gun fit is critical. The key dimension of determining the fit of the gun to the hand is "trigger reach." On the gun, it is measured from the center of the backstrap where the web of the hand would sit, to the center of the trigger. On the hand, it is measured from the point of trigger contact (distal joint suggested) to the center of the web of the hand in line with the radius and ulna bones of the forearm.

Avoid if possible the expedient hand position called the "h-grip," intended for adapting a too-small hand to a too-large handgun. In it, the hand is turned so that, with the hand at the side, hand and forearm would resemble a lower case letter "h." This brings the backstrap of the gun to the base joint of the thumb and brings the index finger forward far enough for proper placement on the trigger.

While this can work with a .22 or something else with light loads, it's a matter of robbing Peter to pay Paul. What is gained in getting the trigger forward is lost by a weakened hand grasp on the gun. Recoil now goes directly into the proximal joint of the thumb. Doctors tell me that this is a quick short-cut to developing artificially-induced arthritis in that joint. Such a grip was one of the "remedial" techniques employed by FBI instructors in the late 1970s for small-handed female agent recruits firing +P ammunition. It not only failed to work, it beat up their hands. It was one reason that in the landmark case of *Christine Hansen, et. al. v. FBI* we won reinstatement and compensation for a number of female agents who had been fired because they couldn't qualify with the old-fashioned bad techniques. The same court ordered FBI to "revise and update its obsolete and sexist firearms training."

Distal joint contact works well even for single-action autos. Even when the pull weight is relatively light, "leverage equals power, and power controls the pistol."

*With DA-to-SA pistol, like this Beretta 92G, placing finger at distal joint will give good control with both types of trigger pull.*

*Trigger control is all the more important with more difficult tasks like one-handed double-action work with a light gun, such as this Colt Magnum Carry .357 snub.*

This placement of the finger eliminates the old shibboleth of double-action first shot pistols that said one had to change finger position between the double-action first round and the single-action follow-up shots. Place the distal joint on the trigger for the first heavy pull, keep it there for subsequent shots, and all will be well.

### Rolling Pace

From here on, it's a matter of pace. Learn trigger control as you would develop any other physical skill. Remember what I call "Chapman's Dictum": Smoothness is 5/6 of speed. Crawl before you walk, and walk before you run.

Start slowly. Do lots of dry fire. Watch the sights as they sit silhouetted against a safe backstop. *Do not let the sights move out of alignment at any point in the trigger stroke, particularly when the trigger releases and the "shot breaks."* Then, gradually, accelerate the pace.

Generations of combat shooters can tell you: accuracy first, speed second will develop fast and accurate shooting skills much more quickly than a curriculum of speed first and accuracy second. If you stay with it for several thousand repetitions, you will find that you can roll the trigger back as fast as your finger will go, without jerking your sights off target. Put another way, we can learn to hit as fast as we were missing before.

The key to trigger manipulation under stress is to *distribute the trigger pressure.* A sudden 4-pound jerk will inevitably pull a 2-pound gun off target. Smooth, evenly distributed trigger pressure done at the same speed will fire the gun just as quickly, but without moving the alignment of bore to target. The key words here are *smooth* and *even.*

Generations of shooters and gunfighters have learned to talk themselves through the perfect shot. They chant it to themselves like a mantra. "Front sight! Squeeze the trigger. *Squee-e-eze...*" One instructor says "squeeze," another says "press"; this writer uses "roll." To me, the word "roll" connotes the smooth, even, uninterrupted pressure that I want. The word doesn't matter so much as the concept.

Don't try to "stage" or "trigger-cock" the pistol. This is fine motor intensive, and our fine motor skills go down the drain when we're in danger and our body instinctively reacts. Such skills just won't be with you in a fight. Learn from the beginning to keep the stroke smooth and even, executed in a single stage.

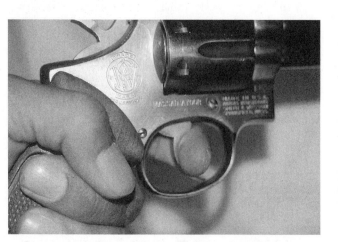

*Proper trigger finger placement for DA work with K-frame S&W .357.*

*A smooth double-action trigger stroke is bringing the next .357 round under the hammer of this S&W Bodyguard.*

*A workable solution. This Colt Python has a serrated trigger, usually undesirable for double-action work, but the ridges between the serration grooves have been polished glass smooth, solving the problem.*

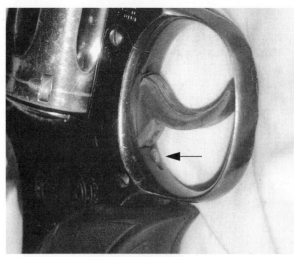

*Note S&W's internally adjustable trigger stop, coming down into trigger guard at a point behind the trigger. Because there is a remote chance it can come out of adjustment and block the trigger…*

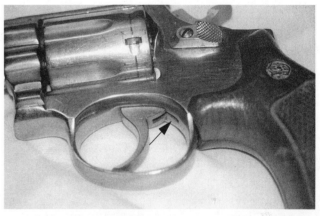

*…it is usually removed from a duty gun, as it has been from author's S&W Model 66.*

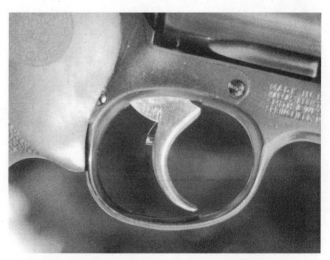

*Here's a true combat trigger stop. It is welded in place. It can't move and cause problems, yet it cures aim-disturbing trigger overtravel. Installed on author's S&W Model 25-5, in .45 Colt, by Al Greco.*

A word on "surprise trigger break." Marksmanship instructors tell us to let the trigger go off by surprise so we don't anticipate the final release and jerk the gun. However, if you say in court that the shot went off by surprise, it sounds to anyone without your training as if you didn't mean for it to go off. That can turn a justifiable, intentional shooting into a negligent act of manslaughter. *We don't begin pressing the trigger back – we don't even **touch** the trigger – until the intent to immediately fire has been justifiably formulated!* The only surprise should be in what fraction of an instant the deliberate shot discharges.

### Trigger Mechanicals

A light trigger pull is, more than anything else, a crutch for bad trigger technique. It is also "plaintiff's counsel's guaranteed employment act" in the civil liability sense. On a defense gun, you don't need a *light* trigger pull, you need a *smooth* trigger pull.

The surface of the trigger should be glassy smooth, with rounded edges. Grooves, serrations, or checkering on the trigger will trap the flesh of the finger and translate any lateral finger movement to undesirable lateral gun movement. As the finger moves back, it may change its exact contact point with the trigger very slightly, and if that happens, we want the finger to be moving smoothly and easily across the frontal surface of the trigger. On revolver triggers in particular, it's also a good idea to round off the rear edges of the trigger, to keep the flesh of the finger from being pinched between the trigger and the back of the trigger guard at the end of each firing stroke.

Beware of "backlash." This is the movement that occurs in the instant between when the sear releases, and when the rear of the trigger comes to a stop. Because spring pressure resisting the finger has just been released, there is a tendency for the finger to snap back against the rear of the trigger guard, possibly jerking the muzzle off target. An "anti-backlash device" or "trigger stop" is a good idea, *if* it is constructed in such a way that it cannot come out of adjustment, move forward, and block the trigger from firing. This problem was known to occur in the old "built-in" trigger stops of Smith & Wesson's target and combat-target revolvers (K-38, Combat Magnum, etc.) and it got to the point where departments ordering such guns would specify that the trigger stop device be left out entirely. A good pistolsmith can weld up a stop on the back of the trigger or the back of the trigger guard, then grind or file it to a point where the trigger will always be operational.

*Power stance in action. Dave Sevigny, National IDPA champion, shows winning form with a Glock 34 at the New England Regional Championships.*

*Smaller people need the power stance more than big bruisers. Justine Ayoob is 15 in this photo as she wins High Novice in the enhanced service pistol class at the New England Regional IDPA championships. Note power stance as she delivers head-shots with a Novak Custom Browning 9mm.*

# Lost Secrets Of Combat Handgun Shooting

Evolution of doctrine is a strange thing. Sometimes, we do something after we've forgotten why we started doing it. Sometimes, we forget to do things we should be doing.

There are secrets the Old Masters of combat handgunning knew, secrets that have been lost to most because they weren't incorporated into this or that "doctrine." Just because they are lost doesn't mean they don't still work. Let's look at a few of them.

### Lost Secret #1: The Power Stance

In true *combat* handgun training, as opposed to recreational shooting, you are preparing for a fight. This means you should be in a fighting stance. Balance and mobility can never be compromised in a fight. Accordingly, your primary shooting stance should be a *fighting* stance.

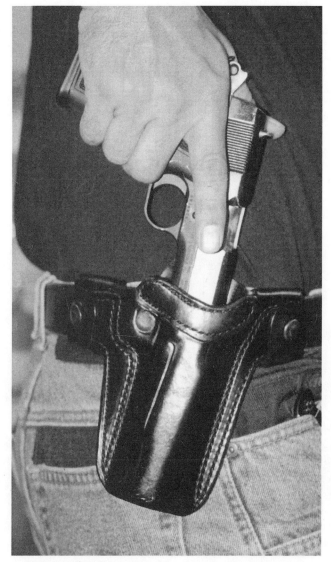

*A high-hand grasp is best taken with the gun still in the holster, as shown here pulling a Para-Ordnance .45 from Alessi CQC holster.*

When the body has to become a fighting machine, the legs and feet become its foundation. You can expect to be receiving impacts: a wound to the shoulder, a bullet slamming to a stop in your body armor, and certainly the recoil of your own powerful, rapidly fired defensive weapon. Any of these can drive you backward and off-balance if you are not stabilized to absorb them and keep fighting.

The feet should be at least shoulder-width apart, and probably wider. Whether you're throwing a punch or extending a firearm, you're creating outboard weight, and your body has to compensate for that by widening its foundation or you'll lose your balance.

We have long known that humans in danger tend to crouch. It's not just a *homo sapiens* thing, it's an erect biped thing. The same behavior is observed in primates, and in bears when they're upright on their hind legs. In his classic book "Shoot to Live," Fairbairn observed how men just on their way to a dangerous raid tended to crouch significantly. Decades before Fairbairn had noticed it, Dr. Walter Cannon at Harvard Medical School had predicted this. Cannon was the first to attempt to medically quantify the phenomenon called "fight or flight response" as it occurs in the human. While we know now that Cannon may have been incorrect on some hypothesized details, such as the exact role that blood sugar plays in the equation, we also know that on the bottom line he was right on all counts.

When threatened with deadly danger, the erect bipedal mammal will turn and face that danger, if only to observe and quantify it before fleeing. Its torso will square with the thing that threatens it. One leg will "quarter" rearward. This is seen today in the boxer's stance, the karate practitioner's front stance, the Weaver stance of

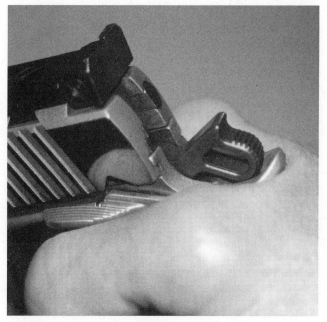

*A high-hand grasp on a Kimber Gold Match .45; note the "ripple of flesh" at the web of the hand.*

pistol shooters, and the "police interview stance" taught at every law enforcement academy.

The head will come forward and down, and the shoulders will seem to hunch up to protect it. The knees will flex, lowering the center of body gravity, and the hips will come back, coiling the body for sudden and strenuous movement. The feet will be at least shoulder-width apart laterally. The hands or paws will rise to somewhere between waist and face level.

This, and not the exaggerated "squat" of the ancient FBI training films, is the true and instinctive "combat crouch." The body is balanced forward, rearward, left and right, its weight forward to both absorb and deliver impact.

There is no good reason for the combat shooter not to stand like this. Indeed, there is every reason for him or her to do it.

A key element of the power stance as we teach it at Lethal Force Institute is the application of the *drive leg*. In the martial arts, you generate power in a punch by putting your whole body behind it. Whichever leg is to the rear is the drive leg. Beginning with the knee slightly flexed, the practitioner digs either the heel or the ball of the foot into the ground, straightening the leg. This begins a powerful turn of the hips. The hips are the center of body gravity and the point from which body strength can most effectively be generated. The punch and extending arm go forward along with the hip. The forward leg has become the weight-bearing limb; it needs to be more sharply flexed than the rear leg because as force is delivered forward, it will be carrying well over half of the body's weight.

### Lost Secret #2: The High-Hand Grasp

It's amazing how many people come out of shooting schools and police academies not knowing the most efficient way to hold a handgun. The primary hand's grasp, which some instructors call "Master Grip," needs to be able to stand by itself. In a shooting match that calls for a two-handed stage, we know we'll always be able to achieve the two-fisted grasp. In the swirling, unpredictable movement that occurs in close-range fights, however, we can never be sure that the second hand will be able to get to its destination and reinforce the first. It might be needed to push someone out of the way, to ward off the opponent's weapon, or simply to keep our balance. That's why the initial grasp of the handgun with the dominant hand must be suitable for strong control of one-handed as well as two-handed fire.

The hand should be all the way up the backstrap of the grip-frame. With the auto, the web of the hand should be so high that it is not only in contact with the underside of the grip tang, but pressed against it so firmly that it seems to shore up a ripple of flesh. On the revolver, the web of the hand should be at the highest point of the grip-frame's backstrap. There is only one, easily fixed potential downside to a high hand grip. If the grip tang has sharp edges, as on the older versions of the 1911, this can dig painfully and even lacerate the hand. Sharp-edged slides on very small autos, like the Walther PPK, can do the same. Simply rounding off sharp edges or installing a beavertail grip safety fixes that.

Now let's count up the many advantages of the high-hand grip. (1) It lowers the bore axis as much as possible, giving the gun less leverage with which to kick its muzzle up when recoil hits. (2) It guarantees that the frame will

*A high-hand grasp on a revolver. Note that the top edge of the gripframe is higher on the "hammerless" S&W Centennial (AirLite version shown), affording the shooter more control than a conventionally styled revolver. Note also the white-nailed "crush grip."*

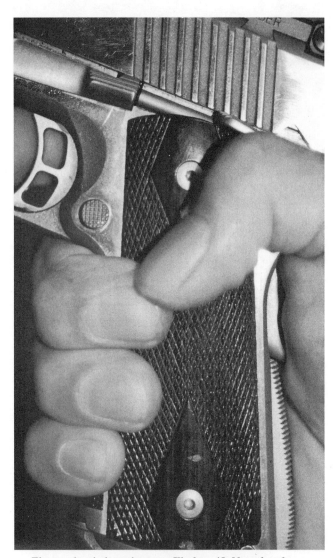

*The crush grip in action on a Kimber .45. Note that the fingernails have turned white from max-force gripping pressure.*

be held as a rigid abutment for the auto's slide to work against. With too low a hold, the whipsaw recoil that follows moves the frame as well as the slide, dissipating some of the rearward momentum needed to complete the cycle. The result is often a spent casing caught "stovepiped" in the ejection port, or a slide that does not return fully to battery. (3) On most handguns, this grasp allows a straight-back pull of the trigger. If the gun is grasped too low, a rearward pull on the trigger becomes a downward pull on the gun, jerking its muzzle – and the shot – low. Draw is hastened because (4) the grip tang of the auto is the easiest landmark for the web of the hand to find by feel.

Pick up a gun magazine with one or more stories on action shooting championships, and watch how the winners hold their guns. The webs of their hands will be riding high. Now you know why. The champions know what so many other shooters have missed.

### Lost Secret #3: The Crush Grip

In target pistol shooting, light holds are in vogue. The bull's-eye shooter is taught to let her pistol just rest in her fingers with no real grasp at all as she gently eases the trigger back. The IPSC shooter is taught to apply 60 percent strength with the support hand and 40 percent with the firing hand (occasionally the reverse, but 50 percent of available hand strength in any case).

Common sense tells us this will not do for a fight. For one thing, it is dexterity intensive, and dexterity is among the first things we lose in a fight-or-flight state. For another, the genuine fight you are training for always entails the risk of an opponent attempting to snatch your gun away. We know that action beats reaction. If you're holding your handgun lightly or with only half your strength and it is forcibly grabbed or struck, it will probably be gone from your grasp before you can react. But if you have conditioned your hand to always hold the gun with maximum strength, you have a better chance to resist the attack long enough to react, counter with a retention move, and keep control of your firearm.

A third tremendous advantage of a hard hold, one that world champion Ray Chapman always told his students, is that it's the ultimate consistency in hold. "40 percent hand strength" is one thing in the relatively calm

environment of the training range. It's something else when you're at a big match shooting for all the marbles, and it's something a league beyond that when you're fighting for your life. One effect of fight or flight response is that as dexterity goes down, strength goes up precipitously. Even in target shooting, marksmanship coaches agree that a consistent hold is a key element of consistent shot placement. There are only two possible grasps that can be guaranteed to stay truly consistent: no pressure at all, or maximum pressure.

A fourth big advantage for the crush grip is that it prevents "milking." When one finger moves, the other fingers want to move with it. The phenomenon is called "interlimb response." As the trigger fingers tighten, so do the grasping fingers, as if they were milking a cow's udder, and this jerks the shot off target, usually down and to one side. But if the fingers on the gripframe (NOT the trigger finger!) are already squeezing as hard as they can, they can't squeeze any more when the index finger separately pulls the trigger, and milking is thus made impossible.

Finally, the hard hold better controls recoil. If you had me by the throat and were holding me against a wall, and I was struggling, would you relax your grip or hold harder? The harder you hold me against the wall, the less I can move. Similarly, the more firmly you grasp your gun, the less *it* will move in recoil, in terms of both overall gun movement and the stocks shifting in your hand.

Detractors of the concept call this "gorilla grip," and warn that it interferes with delicate movement of the trigger finger and can cause small tremors. Those of us who advocate crush grip answer, "So what?" Delicate manipulation of the trigger disappears once the fight is on. The hands are going to tremble under stress anyway, and the shooter might as well get used to it up front in training. If the sights are kept in line, the gun's muzzle won't tremble off a target the size of a human heart.

### Lost Secret #4: Front Sight

Every marksman who is accomplished with open sights remembers the day he or she experienced "the

*The front sight is the key to good hits. In close, even an image like this, well above the rear sight, will put the shot where it needs to go.*

*The most precise, almost surgical, accuracy comes when the eye focuses on the front sight, with the rear sight in secondary focus and target in tertiary focus.*

epiphany of the front sight." The phrase "watch your front sight" doesn't mean just have it in your field of view. It doesn't mean just be aware of it. It means focus on it as hard as possible, making sure it's on target, and that it's not moving off target as you stroke the trigger. Pistol champions and gunfight survivors alike have learned that this is the key to *center* hits at high speed under pressure.

*A smooth roll of the trigger becomes more critical as the shooting problem becomes more difficult. With the 11-ounce .357, double-action, and weak-hand-only, you can be sure the author is focusing on this trigger stroke.*

As discussed in the chapter on point shooting, you don't need the perfect sight picture of the marksmanship manual. But remember that the handgun is a remote control drill, and it must be indexed with where we want the hole to appear, or the hole will appear in the wrong place. The sights, at least the front sight in close, will be the most reliable such index.

### Lost Secret #5: Smooth Roll

A smooth, even, uninterrupted roll of the trigger, as discussed in the last chapter, is critical if the shooter is going to break the shot without jerking it off target.

Note that the last two elements, "front sight" and "smooth trigger roll," are not listed as "to the lines of secrets four and five, prior." This is because it's debatable whether they are really lost secrets, and if so, who lost them. Every competent instructor will teach the students how to use the sights and how to bring the trigger back. The problem is, these things are very easy to forget until the student develops the discipline to first think about doing them, and then finally ingrain the concepts through repetition so they are done automatically.

Power stance. High hand. Crush grip. Front sight. Smooth roll. I try to go through it in my mind like a pre-flight checklist before I even reach for the gun.

You don't even have to think about it all at once. As soon as you know there may be a stimulus to draw the gun, slip into a power stance. It might be a thug giving you the bad eye as you wait for a bus, or it might be that you're on the range awaiting the "commence fire" signal. If you're in the position to start, you don't have to think about it any more.

Condition yourself to always begin the draw by hitting the high hand position. Once it's there, it's done and you don't have to think about it any longer.

Crush grip? I tell my students to think of the eagle's claw. When the eagle sleeps, it does not fall from its perch because its claws automatically clutch it with a death grip. If we condition ourselves to do this whenever we hold the gun, it'll happen on its own when we need it without us having to think about it.

Power stance...high hand...crush grip...front sight...smooth roll. Recover these "lost secrets" and apply them...and watch your combat handgun skill increase.

*Power stance, high hand, crush grip, front sight, smooth roll. The author, foreground, brings it all together as he wins a shoot in the Northwest. Note that spent casing is in the air above his STI, but gun is already back on target despite recoil of full power .45 hardball. Photo by Matthew Sachs.*

# CHAPTER FIVE

# "Maxing" Qualification And Competition

The master gunfighters of the 20th century – Bill Jordan and Elmer Hilden of the Border Patrol, Jim Cirillo and Bill Allard of the NYPD Stakeout Squad – all felt that shooting in competition sharpened your ability to shoot under stress in defense of your life. If you haven't tried it, you should.

Just in case you haven't competed, let's see what it's like. Come with me and shoot a match. I can't make it up for you. I don't do fiction. The only way to do it is for you and I to "channel" together, as the Yuppies say. It's June 5, 2001. We're at the Cheshire Fish & Game Club, the host range for the event, sponsored by the Keene, NH Police Department. The occasion is the annual conference of the New Hampshire Police Association, and the combat shoot that accompanies it is the *de facto* state championship in police combat shooting for cops in the Granite State.

*You want a gun and ammo that you know will work. With the Glock 22 (NY-1 trigger, Meprolight fixed sights) and Black Hills EXP ammo, you have both.*

## Getting Ready

Bad news: you're stuck doing it with me, a "geezer cop" in his fifties. Good news: this particular geezer knows this particular beat, and you and I are prepared to compete on a level playing field.

Rules are that you have to compete with the gun you carry on duty. No tricky recoil compensators or optical sights. Holsters must be suitable for police wear, with retaining devices not only present but fastened before each draw. Ammunition must be suitable for law enforcement use.

My department issues a traditional-style double action .45 auto that is justly famous for both its accuracy and its reliability, two things I appreciated when I won this match with my issue weapon last year. For the whole second quarter, I've been in plainclothes – actually allowed to wear a beard, which I can't in uniform – because I'm a captain who handles primarily administrative and training tasks. These include test and evaluation of new equipment, etc. I've been assigned to test two new uniform security holsters that are about to come into the field. Since the Glock pistol is by far the most common in law enforcement today, it is what these new holsters were initially made to fit. My chief has given me permission to carry one on duty for testing purposes. It's the Glock 22, .40 caliber, the single most popular Glock thanks in large part to police sales, and at the same time, the single most popular police service handgun in the U.S. today. It is as it came from the factory: bone-stock, equipped with the 8-pound New York (NY-1) trigger and Meprolight fixed night sights.

The new security holsters haven't come in yet, so my gray whiskers and I have a reprieve for a while yet in plainclothes, but I'm carrying the G22 to get bonded with it beforehand. It's a good little pistol, particularly with the ammo my department issues for off-duty or plainclothes wear with that caliber, the Black Hills EXP. It sends a 165-grain Gold Dot hollow-point out of the barrel at an honest 1,150 feet per second, a .357 Magnum power level, and it is loaded to match-grade quality specifications. When we sighted in this gun/ammo combo for the first time at 50 yards, aiming for the head of a silhouette target, we jerked one shot down into the neck and didn't count it. But the other four shots were in the head in a *one and seven-eighths inch group*. Is *this* gonna be accurate enough for the B-27 target with competition scoring rings, where the tie-breaking center X ring measures 2 inches by 3 inches? *Oh,* yeah!

We're wearing what we wear to work these days. BDU pants (loose, comfortable, lots of pockets, great for

*Each shooter finds his own pace. The hands of the shooter in the background are beginning to separate as he prepares to reload his Beretta while transitioning from standing to left-side kneeling; the officer at right is already in a kneeling position and has just fired the first shot from that position with his Glock.*

strenuous things like going prone and running, which we'll have to do here.) Polo shirt with the department patch logo on it, one size large to help conceal the bullet-resistant vest. (We wear the vest on duty; we'll wear it here.) Handcuffs in a Galco quick-release plainclothes carrier. The dress gun belt is by Mitch Rosen, as are the first magazine pouch and the holster. The rig fits us perfectly, as it should; it's the one Rosen called the ARG for Ayoob Rear Guard. It rides comfortably inside the waistband behind the strong side hip, secured by a thumb-break safety strap. Backing up the Rosen pouch with its 15-round Glock "law enforcement only" G22 mag are two more pouches, both Kydex, one by Blade-Tech and one by Ky-Tac. This match will have some stages where two reloads are necessary, and then we'll have to reload

*Firing prone from 50 yards. Note that each officer has a slightly different technique.*

to "hot" condition before refilling magazines, etc. Hence, the need for four magazines on the person, including the one in the gun.

Let's get our head right. We're going for the title of top dog, or in this case, top law-dog. That engenders pressure. There's a little more of that on you and me than on most of the others. One person has to be the defending champion from last year, and that raises the price of the ego investment bet on the table. That person, right now, is us.

We get the briefing on the course of fire. There has been a last-minute change in rules. At the barricades, we cannot touch the wall with either gun or hand to stabilize for the shot. OW! Particularly at 50 yards, this hurts accuracy: we're firing free-hand instead of with support. The good news is everyone has to do the same. It's fair, a level playing field. We are *awfully* glad, you and I, that we have a lot of experience shooting at long range with a pistol held in unsupported hands from the standing position.

## 50 Yards

We'll have exactly 60 seconds to go prone, fire six, reload, stand, fire six from one side of the barricade (no support, remember), reload again, and fire six more from behind the wall on the other side without actually touching that wall. We MUST be effectively behind cover or we'll be penalized.

We load the Glock 22, holster, fasten the safety strap, and stand by, hands clear of the holster. On the signal, we draw and drop into the rollover prone technique you and I learned from world champion Ray Chapman so many years ago. AAUUGGHH! There's grass between us and the target, obscuring aim! We scoot to the side, get a clear shot, and begin shooting. The readjustment of position has put us behind the other shooters from the get-go.

We fight the urge to hurry. Front sight is dead in the center of the target. We carefully press the trigger back until the shot breaks. Then again. And again.

Those six are done, and the clock is ticking. We feel the shots went right in where we wanted them. A review of the target in a couple of minutes will prove us right. But now, as we leap to our feet, our right thumb punching the Glock's magazine release as our left hand snatches a fresh mag from behind the left hip and snaps it home, the left thumb pressing down on the slide lock lever to chamber a fresh round, there is a sense that we are behind the others in time. This is a quick stage. Normally in police combat shooting, 24 shots are fired from this 50-yard distance, all of them supported either by the barricade or in the sitting or prone position, and you have two minutes, 45 seconds. That works out to 6.875 seconds per shot. We've just fired the only *six* shots where we'll have support, that of the ground in the prone posture, and we're firing at a rate of 3.33 seconds per shot, faster than double speed.

The first shot from standing feels perfect. But on the second we feel ourselves jerk the trigger, actually *see* the front sight dip in the notch as the shot breaks. The sight hasn't gone down that much, but there's a geometric progression here. The slightest drop of the front sight means a bullet *way* low by the time it reaches its mark half a football field away.

*Fifty yards seems a long way off, even when firing prone.*

Brain cells front and center! We have to tighten up! Consciously, we harden our hold to better stabilize the gun (since there's nothing but our bare hands to stabilize it at all) and dig our rear leg into the ground to drive our body forward. This will let our body weight help better to snap the gun down out of recoil and back into line with the target, giving us fractions of a second more time per shot to "hold and squeeze."

Those six are done. Speed reload. We're back on target with not a lot of time left, standing just behind the cover on the other side of the barricade. We chant to ourself consciously but silently, "Power stance! High-hand grasp! Crush grip! Front sight! Smooth ro-o-oll of the trigger."

We finish about 10 seconds ahead of that unforgiving clock. We reload and holster, set about refilling our magazines, and then prepare to go forward to score. Jerry St. Pierre of the Keene Police is leading the host team. He knows how easily the whole target can be missed from this far away. He's going to score and mark the 50-yard hits before we go any further.

As we approach the targets, we see something in the pelvis of our silhouette target. Oh, *please,* let that be a staple or something! No such luck. The shot we jerked would have been a take-down hit on a man, and would have been worth three out of five points if the target was scored in the police qualification fashion. But this is the police *competition* scoring system, and that shot is counted as a miss. Ten points gone for one bad shot!

In a regular PPC match, that would ruin you. The master class shooters here get 580 and 590 out of 600 scores routinely with their match guns at standard time, and 10 points gone for one of the 60 shots would tank you out of the match for good. Fortunately, here *everyone* is shooting at double speed and using service guns. The playing field is still level…*but you and I can't afford any more mistakes!*

### 25 Yards

We start with six shots kneeling. Then fire, six from the left side of the barricade, standing, and six more from the right, the same way, with a mandatory reload between each stage. The latter is done to level the playing field for any shooter who has a revolver or a low-capacity auto. This is the first year I've been here where not a single wheelgun is in evidence. In this state, the transition to the service pistol is virtually complete. You usually have 90 seconds for this stage in a Police Combat match, and can stabilize your support hand on the barricade. Here, we can't use anything to steady on, and time is only 60 seconds. Only two-thirds the time, and at least double the difficulty.

The timer sounds. We draw first, then drop to kneeling – even at speed, we don't cross a bent lower leg with the muzzle of a loaded gun – and lock in our front sight. The gun was sighted to hit dead on at 50 yards and this means we have to hold a tad low in close, taking a 6 o'clock sight picture that balances the "X" on top of the front sight.

We are thinking "front sight, smooth roll…front sight, smooth roll" for each shot. The reloads, practiced so many times, seem to happen on automatic pilot. There is just time enough to "ride the link" of the Glock trigger, to fire each shot, let the trigger come back forward just enough until we feel the click of the mechanism resetting, and then we draw the trigger back again, feeling the smooth subtle movement of the Glock pistol's cruciform sear plate until each subsequent shot is released.

*Officers fire over the barricade at 25 yards, and also from around both sides. Duty pistols are Glock in the foreground, Beretta 9mm at left.*

*Rather than brace an elbow at the knee, these officers use "speed kneeling" around replicated cover at 25 yards.*

We make the time. That's no sweat. Under pressure, things go faster than you think. Glance downrange. There are a very few shots out in the 9-point ring, but the rest have gone true to center. Life is good.

Now comes what, for some, is the toughest stage. You stand at 25 paces facing the target, hands at your side. On the signal, you draw and fire six shots…in ten seconds, including reaction time. Getting the shots off is no problem. Making the hits in that tiny center ring is the problem.

You and I breathe deeply as we hear the command sequence begin, holding the air in and letting it hiss slowly out. It's the internalized version of that "breathe into the paper bag" trick we cops always use with people in crisis who are hyperventilating. Ya can't do the bag on the range or in a fight, though. Some call it "crisis breathing." You and I learned it decades ago in a karate dojo where they called it *sanchin* breathing.

The signal comes. We draw, lock in, get the front sight on target, and roll the Glock's trigger back. Our head is forward and down, like a vulture's, the way humans stand when in the grip of "fight or flight" response. This helps us stay focused on the front sight ("target identified, missiles locked on target, launch, maintain target lock for next missile…"). We finish a good second before the cease-fire

*On signal, officers sprint forward from 25-yard line…*

*…to 15 yards, where they draw and fire. Note safety officer moving in behind the firing line.*

*Note individualized versions of the low ready positions as officers await command on the firing line…*

*…to react, bring up the gun, and score two hits at 15 yards, all in two seconds.*

signal is sounded. We glance downrange as we reload. There aren't any more errant hits outside the 10/X rings than there were before.

### 15 Yards

Reloaded, we begin standing at the 25-yard line. On the signal, we have to run forward to the 15-yard line, draw, and fire two shots, all in only six seconds. The horn sounds. We lunge forward. Time slows down. As we approach the line we use a trick we learned from World Champion Ray Chapman: a little jump in the air, then land at the finish point on flexed and coiled knees as the gun comes out, as is only now allowed. There isn't much time left. We snap it to line of sight in an Isosceles hold, and instead of using the usual post in notch sight picture, we just align the three big dots of the Meprolight fixed night sights that came on our service Glock, and roll the trigger back, fighting the urge to hasten the shot. Bang, bang, *beep!*

We've made the time. Not everyone else has been so fortunate.

Now we go to a low ready stance. Three more times, the signal will come to shoot, and each time we'll have only two seconds to raise our service weapon, align it, and get two shots into that heart-sized center ring. We must start with our finger outside the trigger guard. Most are holding it straight on the frame: safe, but slower than it needs to be. Not all of them make the time. Many are starting with their fingertip on the front of the trigger guard. Fast, but tricky: under stress, this position holds the trigger finger taut, and when it snaps into the trigger it hits with impact, often breaking the shot prematurely. That's tragedy on the street, and it's a bad hit here on the line. Some others learn that today the hard way.

You and I start with our trigger finger flexed, the tip of the finger touching the takedown niche on the side of the Glock frame. Now, on the signal, as we raise the gun we can thrust the finger swiftly into the trigger guard *across* the trigger, until we find that sweet spot where the distal joint of the finger feels virtually centered on the trigger so we have maximum leverage for a fast, straight-back pull that won't move the muzzle off the target. BAM-BAM! We're in! And again, BAM-BAM. We're doin' OK.

*The officer at left is down on his right knee behind left side cover; the officer on right has chosen the left knee for better balance with slight leftward lean.*

*One-hand-only stages at 7 yards are the cruncher for time.*

With the six-round magazines that are demanded (to level the playing field between the different service guns styles), we're at slidelock, and we quickly reload. Some of our brother and sister officers have come to grief at this point, and they're out of the running. Their guns jammed. When you have only two shots left, and two must be fired, and your pistol locks up in the middle of that, two seconds simply isn't time enough to recognize the malfunction, clear it, reload, and fire another round. Fortunately, you and I have a Glock with Black Hills ammunition, two exemplars of reliability, and that disaster does not befall us.

## 7 Yards

This is the final stage. The cruncher. The one where cops are most likely to fail to get their shots off in time. In PPC, it's 12 shots in 25 seconds, including the reload, in a two-hand stance. But here in New Hampshire, you draw strong-hand-*only*, fire five shots, reload, then shift the gun to your other hand and fire five more shots weak-hand-*only*, all in only 15 seconds.

We're ready. We've practiced this. We start in a fighter's stance, not a target shooter's stance, and on the start signal we draw and bring the gun into the target like a Shotokan karate fighter throwing a punch. The body weight behind the Glock keeps it on target with the stout recoil of the hot Black Hills load, the three dots already back at center in the time it takes to re-set the trigger. The gun goes to slidelock. Speed-reload, hand change. We sense the clock ticking and, losing our sense of time we fire faster than we should, finishing the whole thing in about 10 seconds. But all ten of those last shots are inside the 10 and 10-X rings, and our job is done.

## It Ain't Over

Now you stand by your target and await the official scorer. Smoke 'em if you got 'em and cope with the stress. It's like waiting for the biopsy to come back from the lab. The stress isn't *nearly* over yet.

We check the target along with the scorer. We don't like it, but he has it right. It's not the best we have ever done. On the other hand, it *is* the best score on the first relay, and we're in the lead.

The match sponsors have announced that each shooter can get one second chance over the course. However, *as soon as they fire the first shot of their second try, their first score becomes null and void.* You and I immediately go over to the registrar, pay an entry fee, and book a slot to shoot again if we have to.

Now comes a war of nerves and ego. You and I don't like that score, particularly the 10 points down shot from 50 yards. We want to try again, strut our stuff, shoot better than we did before. That's understandable. However, ego must come second to The Job. I represent my police department here. My chief wants our department to keep the title from last year. If I get beaten,

*This state trooper is at 7 yards as he draws and fires five shots strong-hand-only with his issue S&W .45 auto...*

*...he ducks down to reload (good survival training in action!) and then...*

*...fires the last five shots weak-hand-only.*

*All draws begin with the safety devices fastened.*

*This is the combination that won the year before: Ruger P90 with fixed IWI night sights and Winchester USA 230-grain .45 hardball.*

I'm ready to shoot again...but if my chief of police ever finds out that I had victory solidly in my hand, then shot again to feed my ego *and lost what I already had locked up,* he is going to start wondering whether I should really keep command authority after making such a stupid decision. Soon I will be walking foot patrol in the sanitary landfill or something.

So we must wait these tension-filled moments, you and I who are shooting together, until the scores are in and "last relay" is called.

Several have tried twice. None have beaten the top score on the board. That score is ours.

The end of the match feels almost anti-climactic. It is announced that you and I have won. We shake hands with the match director, Officer Jerry St. Pierre, and some kind person takes a photo.

You and I have won the state shoot. Our prize is a Glock 27 pistol, donated by Riley's Sport Shop in Hooksett, NH. It's identical to the one that has been strapped to our left leg the whole time in an Alessi ankle holster, a fallback in case something goes wrong with the Glock 22 and we quickly need a gun to finish the match. The Glock 27 will take the Glock 22's magazines that are already on our belt.

But we'll leave with some lessons even more valuable than that excellent Glock pistol.

*Focus on the task, not the goal.* The task was to shoot perfect shots, 60 of them. We dropped our focus on one and blew the shot. Our 59 decent hits turned out to be enough to get us through the "trial." If we focus on the goal, we'll neglect the tasks necessary to achieve it, but if we focus on the tasks, the goal will achieve itself.

*You need a damn good gun with damn good ammo* for something like this. With the Glock 22 and the Black Hills EXP .40 ammo, we had both. Others who might have beaten us failed when their equipment failed. Ours didn't.

*The trigger is the heart of the beast.* When you control the trigger, you control the shot. You and I just experienced living proof that a heavy trigger isn't

*Match director Jerry St. Pierre, right, congratulates the author on winning the title.*

uncontrollable. Those 8 pounds of pressure were manageable enough. In my experience, the New York trigger gives a cleaner trigger break and less trigger backlash. It's a win-win thing, and that's why I have a New York trigger on every Glock I ever carry for anything serious, like this one, which is, for now, my police service pistol.

*One in the hand really is worth two in the bush.* Right brain warring with left brain, I desperately wanted to shoot the course again to get a better score. But logic won out over ego, as it always should. You don't throw away a locked-in victory for a mere *chance* at a more spectacular victory. This is just one example of many of how competition teaches us how to make life decisions.

*Self-coaching works.* Often times, you'll be coaching a friend and watching him miss the plates. You yell, "Front sight!" and then comes, BANG-CLANG, and the hit is achieved. You don't need a separate coach if you're constantly reminding yourself of what to do. Works in a match, works in a fight, works in any life crisis.

Combat competition isn't gunfighting. You know you won't die if you fail. But it's as close to a microcosm of a gunfight as you can come in training as far as pressure is concerned. I've done my share of Simunitions and similar realistic role playing, and I can tell you the stress is more in a big match.

Anything that conditions you to shooting under pressure can help you stay alive with a gun in your hand. Combat competition is the most cost-effective, most readily available avenue to getting used to the pressure.

# Combat Competition

There are those of us who can remember when we shot bull's-eye pistol matches because, in part, we wanted to stay sharp with the guns we carried for self-defense. Why? Because it was the only game in town! Today, things are a lot better.

Let's take a look at the combat shooting competition that is currently available to the law-abiding private citizen in the United States. It's not that any one has it all over the other. Each element will have a piece of the puzzle.

## IDPA

Bill Wilson and some others who felt that available defensive handgun competition had become more of a game than a training tool founded the International Defensive Pistol Association in the mid-1990s. It has been the fastest-growing shooting discipline of its kind since. For the author's money, it's the "best game in town," but it still doesn't have everything.

You need a "street gun" in a "street holster," which in most stages will be concealed when the start signal comes. The holster must ride behind the hip, and hide under the concealing garment. The ubiquitous 1911 .45 auto and its 10mm sister compete in CDP (Custom Defense Pistol) class. A Browning Hi-Power or other cocked-and-locked 9mm, .38 Super or .40 pistol will be used in ESP (Enhanced Service Pistol). A double action auto or a Glock

would enter the single most popular category, SSP (Stock Service Pistol). For wheelgunners, there is SSR (Stock Service Revolver). Even with high capacity guns, the shooter is limited to 10-round magazines in the interest of a level playing field.

A shooter who does not use available cover will be penalized. Just like in a gunfight, only in a match, the penalties aren't nearly as harsh. Often, the shooter is required to move while shooting, and will be penalized if he comes to a stop to fire.

A stage may begin with the practitioner seated in a car, lying in bed, even sitting on a toilet. Don't worry; they'll let you keep your pants up. Failure to neutralize a bad guy target gains a penalty. Hitting a no shoot target is a BIG penalty. In these things, again, IDPA is reflecting real world values.

There will be a penalty for leaving live ammo behind or making a reload on the run. As in real life, IDPA figures it's healthier to stay behind cover and only move if you have a fully reloaded gun already in hand. While I think the emphasis on tactical reloads over speed reloads is a bit excessive, that's just one participant's opinion.

The target is reasonably realistic, a cardboard silhouette with an 8-inch maximum point "A-zone" in the center of the chest. Some targets will be steel knock-downs. I've seen events where the targets were on their sides, simulating a pack of wolves or wild dogs. Protecting yourself from vicious animals is legitimate self-defense too, one too often neglected in the other shooting disciplines.

If you've been to a lot of matches, you've seen chronic whiners and "gamesmen" who aren't there to learn, just there to win, and sometimes they are there to take their insecurities out on others. IDPA has an answer for that. Anything that smacks of cheating or bad sportsmanship earns a "failure to do right" penalty that is so massive it blows the offender out of the match. It has served to keep egos well in line.

To see what it's all about, to find a club offering IDPA events within reach of you, or to see about starting up such matches yourself, check out the website at www.idpa.com

### IPSC

The International Practical Shooting Confederation was founded in the mid-1970s under the direction of Jeff Cooper, who had created "replicated gunfight" matches as early as the 1950s with his "Leatherslaps" and the founding of the Southwest Combat Pistol League in California. Until then, the efforts of Cooper and company were exotica that we read about, but couldn't share unless we moved to the West Coast; now, it was available to all.

*Four flavors of Glock .40. From top, G35, G22, G23, and G27. The author has seen them all used in matches by people who actually carried them on the street.*

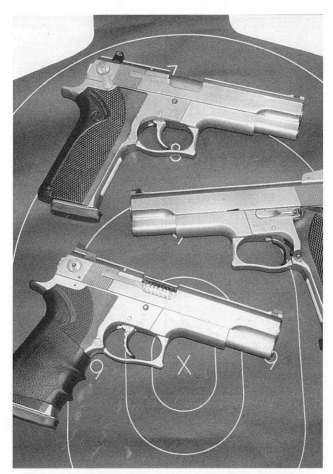

*When he carried the S&W 4506 on duty (top), the author had Wayne Novak make him up a custom single-action version for matches (center), and later had another crafted in .45 Super by Ace Custom (below). However, as time wore on...*

*...experience taught him to just shoot the duty gun in matches. He did OK.*

*These officers shot the Washington State Championships with the .45s they carried on duty. Left, Bill Burris with street-tuned Para-Ordnance; right, the author with his issue Ruger P90.*

The early days of IPSC were much like IDPA today. "Real" guns. "Real" scenarios. I had the privilege of running the first IPSC Sectional Championship in the United States, with Col. Jeff Cooper and section coordinator Jim Cirillo present, in 1976. The event was weighted toward larger caliber guns with "Major/Minor" scoring. A hit in the center ring was worth five points with either a 9mm or a .45, but outside that ring, you lost twice as many points if you were shooting 9mm instead of .45. The Colonel said that this appropriately rewarded the more competent gun handler, who was dealing with more recoil and wielding a "more serious" weapon.

That made sense a quarter century ago, when high efficiency ammunition for medium calibers such as 9mm and .38 Special was just coming in. Today, however, a 115-grain 9mm at 1,300 feet per second will kill a criminal just as dead as a 230-grain .45 ACP at 850, and might actually cause more tissue damage. This is why IDPA chose to avoid major/minor, instead instituting a "power

*Bill Fish shoots an IDPA match with his Glock 34. The skills transfer…*

floor" in each caliber and having like guns shoot against like guns.

I was there over the years when IPSC seemed to change course. The first big switch to the "race guns and space guns" came when John Shaw had pistolsmith Jim Clark build him a Colt .45 auto with forward muzzle weight. The gun was originally for the Second Chance bowling pin shoot, which is why that genre became known as "pin guns," but John quickly found it advantageous in IPSC and promptly won the national championship with it. The race was on: Mike Plaxco, Bill Wilson, and other master shooters with gunsmithing skills soon built expansion chamber recoil compensators to further tame the recoil.

Then Rob Leatham discovered that he could hot-load the .38 Super to make major, and the intense pressure of the red-line-loaded cartridge created more expanding gas for a recoil compensator to work with. Muzzle jump was now nil. Then Jerry Barnhart proved that with an Aimpoint red dot sight, one could see the aiming index and the target on the same visual plane and hit faster. Next thing you knew, every gun had a big "can" on top for the shooter to aim through. Holsters for these guns evolved into super-fast skeletons carried at the front of the belt, with such a precarious hold on the pistol that Barnhart was successful selling a device he called a "walk-through strap." This was a strap that would keep the gun from falling out of the holster while the range officer walked the

*…to the Glock 19 and Glock 26 he carries. In fact, he is known to compete with all three. Note the identical "Glock socks" on each.*

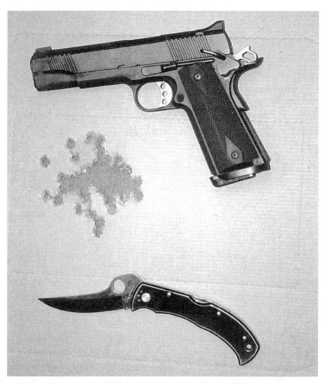

*Many combat handguns are accurate enough for competition yet reliable enough for carry. This out-of-the-box Kimber Custom II has shot a perfect score on a 60-round qualification, in a 4-inch group as measured by the Ayoob Spyderco knife. Ammo was full power .45 hardball.*

competitor through the course! Clearly, the "Practical" element of IPSC was coming into grave question.

Next, pioneered by Para Ordnance, came the wide-body "fat guns" that held huge magazines. I saw .38 Super pistols with extended fat mags that could fire more than 25 shots without reloading. By now shooters were using triggers with as little as 28 ounces of pull – an accident waiting to happen in a real-world stress situation, but a winner's edge in IPSC. Competing against a pistol that didn't need to be reloaded and had a trick sight and no recoil and a telekinetic trigger left a cop with a department issue nine-shot double-action .45 asking himself, "Why bother?"

The sport began to stagnate. People broke off and formed things like IDPA. Gun expert Andy Stanford wrote in *American Handgunner* magazine of what he called "The Lost Tribe of IPSC," people like Bill Wilson and Ken Hackathorn and Walt Rauch and myself who had been in at the beginning, but had become disenchanted with IPSC.

The typical IPSC course is a "search and destroy" assault in which the shooter runs through a maze of targets and shoots the ones who are supposed to be bad guys, suffering only a 10-point penalty for shooting an innocent bystander. It is little wonder that the cops started to back away. That was a shame, because the realism of the early IPSC days had done wonders when grafted into the training of forward thinking police departments like that of Orlando, Florida.

This is not to say that one might not *need* a dollop of "run and gun" as they prepare their training recipe for real-world defensive handgunning. In January 2002, a Palestinian terrorist whipped an M-16 out from under a long coat and opened fire at a bus stop in Jerusalem,

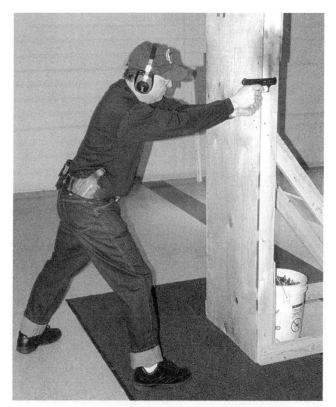

*This shooter fires from behind cover at 20 yards in the IDPA National Mid-Winter Championships at the S&W Academy. The pistol, drawn from thumb-break concealment holster, is his daily carry gun, HK P7 9mm,...*

*...which he reloads tactically behind cover, a hallmark of IDPA, before he continues shooting from opposite side of the barricade.*

Bill Wilson, founder of IDPA (center) explains the target's scoring system to the author and an unidentified IDPA member.

The owner of this target grade HK P9S 9mm has carried it on police patrol, worn it concealed, and shot it at the Bianchi Cup.

killing two innocent women and wounding at least 14 more people. Nearby, a plainclothes Israeli police sergeant named Hanan Ben Naim, dressed in jeans and tennis shoes, drew his Jericho and gave chase. At the end of the foot pursuit Naim faced the terrorist at a range of 20 feet and fired with the Jericho, a 9mm pistol that resembles the Czechoslovakian CZ75, as the terrorist opened up on him with the M-16. The assassin missed. The brave young sergeant didn't, and his pistol fire killed the machinegun-armed terrorist where he stood.

Today, IPSC is trying to return to its roots with a Revolver class, a Production Class, and a class called Limited-10. The latter is an iron-sight pistol with no compensator and a magazine that can hold no more than 10 rounds. Production Class is geared to Glocks and double action semiautomatics. At this writing, it has not taken off like IDPA, but perhaps it needs more time for the word to get out.

IPSC in the United States is governed by USPSA, the United States Practical Shooting Association. For information contact their website www.uspsa.com.

### PPC

Get a bunch of police pistol team types together in a bar after a match, and it's about a two-beer argument whether "PPC" stands for "Practical Police Course," "Practical Pistol Course," or "Police Pistol/Combat." Some of the run-and-gun types suspect it stands for "pretty pathetic crap" because the shooting goes slower than they like.

Going back half a century, this course of fire began with police officers using revolvers and ammo loaded one cartridge at a time out of belt loops or pouches. With speedloaders for revolvers, let alone magazines for semiautomatic pistols, there's no question that the times in PPC may be overly generous. 25 seconds to draw, fire six, reload, and fire six more, two-handed, from 7 yards? Come on. NRA, the governing body of PPC shooting, has brought that down to 20 seconds, which is a start.

NRA has never let civilians shoot this match under their auspices; for reasons of political correctness, they don't want the negative publicity of citizens shooting at "pictures of human beings," as reporters like to call the B-27 silhouette target. Nonetheless, many gun clubs offer PPC shooting matches to civilians.

I started shooting bull's-eye. I went to PPC, known locally as "Police Combat," as soon as I could because it was faster, more relevant, and frankly more fun. I jumped from there to IPSC when it became available. By comparison, PPC was old and slow. Many years later, I came back to it. For one thing, *I* was now old and slow.

It's obsolete in terms of shooting speed, but PPC offers some good things. It puts more emphasis on use of cover than any other kind of combat shooting competition. Consider the microcosm of PPC, Match Five, also known as the National Match Course. You'll fire 12 shots from 7 yards, 18 from 25, 24 from 50 yards, and the last 6 at 25 again, this time standing without cover and support. The

This shooter runs a PPC match from standing right-hand barricade position.

*The Para-Ordnance pistol, top, will kick harder with the same .45 ammo than match Colt Government with D.R. Middlebrooks JetComp compensator, below, but manipulation will be similar.*

The center rings are too low, focusing on the solar plexus area instead of the heart. However, the 10-ring is almost exactly the size of a human heart. The IDPA target with its 8-inch center circle and the IPSC Brussels target with its 6-inch wide by 11-inch high center rectangle are altogether too generous. In either, what in the real world would be a "lung shot" has the same match scoring value as a "heart into spine" shot. That's simply not practical.

Even before IPSC, PPC evolved into an equipment race with "space guns." In open class, the weapons you need to win are "PPC revolvers" with massive barrels and sight ribs, or long-slide autos with similar sights. Both would be impractical to carry. Fortunately, NRA has been emphasizing stock gun classes for revolver, auto, and "off-duty guns," and I think these will be the salvation of the sport. Last year's National Championship in the stock service pistol event, I'm told, was won by a Richmond (VA) cop with the *SigPro* pistol he was issued by the department, and department-issue 125-grain CCI Gold Dot ammo, caliber .357 SIG. This is a good sign.

If you're a full or part-time police officer or security professional or in the military with an MOS in law enforcement, you're eligible for PPC shooting under NRA's auspices. Contact the National Rifle Association and direct your inquiry to the Police Competitions division. If you're a private citizen, you'll have to check around with the gun shops and gun clubs to see who in your area offers PPC shooting to the public.

18 at 25 are all from behind a vertical wall called a barricade: six kneeling strong hand, six standing weak hand, six standing strong hand. At 50 yards, it's six each from sitting, prone, left barricade and right barricade. The low positions replicate taking cover behind something like an automobile. This means that of 60 shots, all but 18 – more than two-thirds – train you for shooting from behind cover.

The cover rules are strict. You'll be penalized if your foot steps past the barricade's edge, because that would have put some of your main body mass out into the field of fire. By contrast, IDPA allows up to 50 percent of your body to be exposed before you're penalized for failure to use appropriate cover. In the real world, the single tactical failure that gets most good guys killed is failure to use cover that was available before the fight started.

Don't write off the 50-yard shooting as irrelevant; the distances at which the cops engaged the gunmen exceeded that in both the North Hollywood bank robbery shootout and the Columbine incident, two infamous case studies in the need for intensive marksmanship training on the part of the good guys. Another good point for PPC is the B-27 target they use.

It's not my favorite target. Originally known as the Prehle target, it came about many years ago when a smart trainer named Prehle superimposed the scoring rings of the Olympic Rapid Fire target over the old Colt silhouette.

*Using guns modified for non-lethality, Chris Edwards and the author shoot each other as the latter opens a closet door during a force-on-force stage at National Tactical Invitational. Ayoob recommends the NTI as a learning experience for any who haven't tried it.*

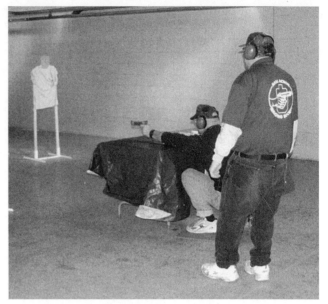

*In this stage, officer Jerry Lashway rushes forward to snatch a "baby" from high chair and pull her to "cover"...*

*...as he returns fire weak-hand-only with his Les Baer .45 auto. The scene was part of the 2002 Smith & Wesson MidWinter Championships.*

### Tactical Shooting

My fellow LFI instructor Peter Dayton and I were the only two men to compete in all six of the first National Tactical Invitational shooting events. It was a concept developed by three well-qualified men, Chuck Davis, Skip Gochenauer and Walt Rauch, to truly test tactical skills in not only shooting but building search and related disciplines. We loved it. Alas, in the mid-90s, it took a different direction. Rauch and Davis were no longer really in the picture. It ceased to be a competitive skill test and became more a learning experience, in which the sponsors were teaching the lessons. That is certainly useful for some people. It was simply no longer what Dayton and I and some others were looking for, so we went elsewhere.

I've been told that the NTI has gotten better since then. It is certainly a good learning experience. Follow *Combat Handguns* magazine for information on how to apply for the next NTI; the group that runs it usually makes their announcements there.

### Pin Shooting

In the late 1960s, armed citizen Richard Davis won a gunfight with three armed robbers. He was hit twice himself during the fracas. As he recovered from his wounds, it occurred to him that there had to be something better to stop bullets with than one's own body. He invented the concealable soft body armor he called Second Chance. By January of 2001, more than 2,500 identified good guys and gals had been saved by the concept, more than 800 by Richard's Second Chance brand alone.

In the early days, he had to overcome the myth that the blunt trauma of a bullet striking the soft armor would render the officer helpless. He needed a visually dramatic target that would show the truth. He set up a table on a dirt firing range in Walled Lake, Michigan, on which he placed a couple of blocks of Roma Plastilena modeling clay (then used to demonstrate bullet effect before the

coming of improved ballistic gelatin). He also set up a few bowling pins.

What happened next, as a home movie camera whirred erratically, was law enforcement history. Davis loaded a Colt .357 Magnum with hot Smith & Wesson brand .38 Special ammo that was the forerunner of today's +P, and he blew up the clay blocks with a couple of rounds.

Then he turned the gun on himself ... and shot himself in the midriff.

Immediately, to show that the impact of the slug had not impaired his ability to fight, he spun back toward the table and with the three rounds left, shot the three bowling pins.

*Practical matches replicate practical situations. This IDPA stage begins with pistol lying on "toilet tank" in "restaurant rest room." Shooter will begin seated on replicated toilet. In the interest of dignity, pants won't be dropped.*

*Match gun? Street gun? Two guns in one! The author used this S&W Model 625 in .45 ACP to shoot a personal best at Second Chance (faster than he'd ever shot a comp gun) and to make Master at the IDPA Mid-Winter National Championships in 1999...and it is the gun he would carry on duty if he was required to switch back to a service revolver tomorrow.*

A few years later, already a millionaire from his invention, Rich wanted to give something back to the cops who had made him successful. He decided to create the Second Chance Street Combat Shoot, in the mid-1970s. He invited a few friends to the first one for a "test drive," and then opened it up to all cops in 1976.

I was there. I found it a lot tougher than it looked. If you think about it, a bowling pin is a very anatomic target. The neck/head area of the pin roughly duplicates the human cervical spine. The pin widens at the same place and to about the same width as the human heart, and truncates at about where the xiphoid process would be on a human sternum. A powerful bullet that hits the pin anywhere would pretty much do the job on a human antagonist.

Richard's Second Chance match became a regular stop on the "professional tour" of handgunning...and more. If the big shooting matches were rock concerts, Second

Chance was Woodstock. It was a "happening." Free food and barbecues, parties, fireworks, and a smorgasbord of shooting that was sort of like a carnival midway, except that the games weren't cheating you and if you performed well, you won guns. There were people who went to the eight-day festivities who didn't even compete anymore, and just came to be with other like-minded shooters. A few years into the experience, Richard had remembered his roots as an armed citizen and opened it to civilians.

Second Chance, sadly, was discontinued in 1998, a victim of fear of civil liability on the part of the corporate board. But it had left a legacy. There are hundreds and hundreds of "pin matches" held now at local clubs around the country. Check at your gun shop or gun club and find out where they're happening near you.

The range is close, 25 feet. However, just as in real life, only center hits count. The object is to blow each bowling pin all the way back off its 3-foot-deep table. Whoever gets all the pins off fastest, wins. If you hit more than an inch off center with a powerful bullet, the pin will spin sideways instead of falling back, and you'll have to shoot it again. It will roll in unpredictable directions and you'll have to track it carefully to shoot it once more and finally blow it away. But if you hit it dead center, it's "out of the fight."

Richard and I got together some years ago and wrote a book on how to do this, called "Hit the White Part." The joke went around that it was my combat shooting book for black guys. In fact, the title came from the single most common question/answer sequence Richard had to go through with new shooters. They would ask arcane questions like, "Where on the bowling pin should I aim?" Richard would reply, "Don't overcomplicate it. Just hit the white part." The book is available for $11.95 +$4.90 shipping from Police Bookshelf, PO Box 122, Concord, NH 03301, or you can order from the website, www.ayoob.com.

### Advice in General

I went through the whole thing with the race guns and space guns and PPC guns. They're still in my gun safe. They hold pleasant memories, and they're good investments, but I never seem to shoot them anymore. I retired from the "pro tour" in 1981, and have since shot matches just to keep my hand in. The matches are my personal "pressure laboratory," to see how well a given technique works under stress, and to constantly keep testing myself for self-defense ability.

How deeply you get into it is up to you. Even when I was into it deeply, I made a point of shooting a gun that was analogous to what I carried. When my department issued the K-frame S&W Combat Magnum, I shot a K-frame S&W PPC gun that had been tuned by Ron Power. I won my share of matches and trophies and guns with it, and every stroke of the trigger in competition was pretty much the same as what I had with the revolver I carried on police patrol.

When my match gun was a Plaxco or Middlebrooks Custom .45 tricked out with a recoil compensator, my carry gun on duty and off, and the gun I kept by the bed, was a Colt Government Model or Commander .45. The same feel, the same trigger, the same manual of arms.

In a time when I could carry my Colt Python on duty, I had Austin Behlert put a heavy match barrel and sight rib on a Colt that I shot in open PPC matches. I used the

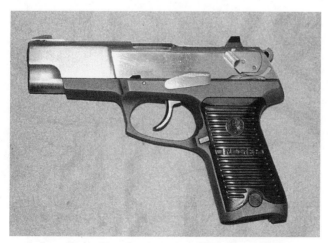

*So inexpensive it's a best buy, the reliable Ruger P90 is accurate enough to win combat matches.*

4-inch duty gun in NRA Service Revolver, a 6-inch Python in the NRA's Distinguished event, and a 2-1/2-inch Python tuned by Reeves Jungkind (who also did my PPC gun's action) for the snubby events. I won the state championship in police combat two or three times with the 4-inch Python, which had been slicked by Jerry Moran, and once with the snub-nosed Jungkind gun shooting against the 4-inch revolvers. I never felt handicapped when I didn't have the crutches of the heavy barrel and the massive sight rib.

When my department issued the S&W 4506, I dedicated myself to that gun. Bob Houzenga slicked up my personal duty pistol, and I bought another 4506 and sent it to Wayne Novak, who made it single action and put in a Model 52 match trigger for competition. I shot that for a year or two, and then realized the trigger wasn't the same and I was kidding myself, so I just competed with the 4506. One year at Second Chance I shot the target version in the Pin Gun event and the duty gun in the Stock Gun class, won a gun with each, and discovered to my surprise that I had shot a faster time with the gun I carried on duty than with the target pistol. Not long after that, my team won the four-man state championship in a bowling pin event called "Rolling Thunder." One contestant shot a rifle, one a pistol, one a pump shotgun, and one an auto-loading scattergun. I anchored on pistol with my duty 4506, double-action first shot and all, and we took home the big one.

The lesson is this: *compete as much as possible with the gun you actually carry.* This way, you'll maximize the effect of "shooting the match as training." If you think about it, one definition of "training" is the LFI definition: "authentically replicated experience." The more you shoot matches with the gun you're likely to actually have in your hand if you have to fight for your life, the more each of those matches becomes a true, relevant training experience.

A lot of times, I'll shoot a match with whatever gun I'm testing for a gun magazine at the time. Testing guns is part of my job. How it works in human hands under stress is one of the things I test for, and that's why when the scheduling permits I'll shoot a match with whatever handgun I'm writing up. I don't do that for myself. I do it for the readers of the test.

There are also times when I'm shooting a match to win, and I know I'm up against stiff competition who are all equipped with the best guns, and I'd be a damn fool not to have the best gun myself. In those events, I might indeed use a high tech, state-of-the-art custom match pistol if one is allowed.

But the ones I like most are the matches where you *have* to use the gun you carry. Our state championship for cops is like that where we live. I've found that whether you carry a K-frame or a Python, a Ruger .45 auto or a Glock, doesn't make that much of a difference. If you've bonded to the gun, as you should with the weapon you carry to defend your life and the lives of the innocent, you'll do OK with it.

Competition with the defensive handgun is one of the strongest avenues to developing the skills that will save your life. It has been my experience that the only people who say otherwise are those that haven't tried it, and therefore don't have a right to the opinion, or those who shot so badly in competition that they're desperately trying to deny the future they saw when they failed on the range that day.

*These two S&W target-grade .38s complement one another. Top, Combat Masterpiece Model 15 for carry; below, 6-inch Model 14 with BoMar sight rib, for PPC shooting. Identical frames, actions and Hogue grips allow strong skill translation from match gun to duty gun.*

*This shooter tests his skill with his Glock carry gun against the ringing targets of the Steel Challenge.*

# CHAPTER SIX

# Combat Handgun Controversies

## Revolver Versus Auto

They've never stopped arguing about this one…and they've rarely made the most cogent points for either side!

In days of yore, gun magazine editors who ran out of fresh ideas could always get another few pages out of the "revolver versus auto" thing. The auto guy would write about "wave of the future" and "firepower!" The revolver guy would warn about the hazards of untrustworthy jam-amatics compared to "our trusted friend, the six-shooter" and point out that since most gunfights were supposed to be over in 2.3 rounds, if you couldn't do it with six you couldn't do it at all.

What happened? Basically, things changed. In those days, about the only reliable autos were the Colt .45 and the Browning 9mm, and then only if you fed them ball ammo. Round-nose, full-metal-jacket was an adequate stopper in .45, though it didn't optimize the cartridge's inherent potency, but it was woefully inadequate in 9mm. When loaded with hollow-points, most of the autoloaders of the mid-20th century *did* jam, if not epidemically then at least enough to worry about.

In the 1970s, when police departments and armed citizens started switching to 9mm high-capacity pistols, someone coined the term "wondernine" for this new hardware. There was nothing wondrous about a 9mm auto with a double-stack magazine; the classic Browning

Hi-Power had been around since 1935. What was wondrous was that this new breed – Beretta, Heckler & Koch, SIG-Sauer, second-generation Smith & Wessons – actually *worked* with JHPs. In 1985 came the Glock, just as reliable and even simpler to operate, and the dominance of the modern auto became a *fait accompli*.

The revolver remains the choice of handgun hunters, who but rarely go after game with their .44 and .50 Magnum Desert Eagle and .45 Magnum Grizzly autos, but that's a topic for a different book. The wheelgun is by no means dead in the combat handgun world. Bert DuVernay, the master instructor who once ran the Smith & Wesson Academy, said that the revolver would remain strong as a backup and off-duty gun among police. The years have proven him correct on that.

The cylinder gun also remains the choice of most experts when outfitting novices who won't necessarily be getting the structured training and in-service refresher time that a cop will get with his duty automatic. That's a good place to start when listing the real-world attributes of each design concept.

*Better hit potential under stress seems to be a cardinal advantage of the self-cocking auto pistol with its short, light trigger stroke, such as this Beretta 9mm.*

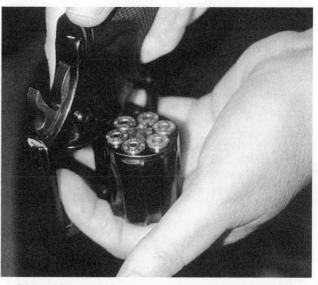

*It's easy for a new shooter or someone with weak hands to open the cylinder of a double-action revolver like this Colt Detective Special and check to see if it's loaded or not.*

## Revolver Advantages

**Ease Of Administrative Handling.** The routine loading, unloading, checking, and cleaning that a combat handgun demands is more easily accomplished with the revolver. That's particularly true if the user is debilitated or injured, or lacking in strength in the hands and upper body. There's no tough recoil spring to muscle a slide against, and no hidden firing chamber where a live cartridge can secrete itself while an amateur thinks the removal of the magazine has unloaded the gun. Even a little old lady with osteoporosis can activate a cylinder release latch, push a cylinder out of a frame, and check to see if the revolver is loaded or not.

**Simplicity Of Function.** No magazines to worry about. Nothing that you need to run a revolver can get separated from it except for the ammunition. Load gun, point gun, pull trigger. If cartridge misfires, pull trigger again. That simple.

**Reliability.** Yes, revolvers can jam, and yes, some of our modern autos are splendidly reliable. That notwithstanding, if you take *all* auto pistols currently in defensive use and compare them to *all* modern revolvers, the autos are at least slightly more likely to malfunction. The auto requires maintenance, particularly lubrication. The auto's magazine springs can take a set after being kept loaded for too long. A Smith & Wesson hand ejector model of 1899, if kept in a cool dry place for more than a century and then loaded with fresh ammunition, would undoubtedly fire. Few of us would want to stake our lives on the functionality of a 1911 pistol whose magazine spring had been fully compressed since before WWI.

*A wide mouth guarantees these Federal 125-grain Magnum loads will expand when fired from this S&W 686 revolver, but few auto pistols would feed such ammo reliably.*

**Ammo Versatility.** Your revolver will run blanks, snake-shot or rat-shot, light target loads, standard service rounds, or Monster Magnum cartridges. No alteration is required when you change ammo. Your auto, however, was designed with a slide mass/spring compression rate geared for a certain range of duty ammunition. Too light a load won't run the gun. Too hot a load may actually cycle the slide so fast it closes again on an empty chamber because the magazine spring didn't raise the next cartridge fast enough to be picked up. A bullet profile with

*Street cop and six-time national champion Bob Houzenga carries a department issue Glock .40 as primary duty gun...*

*...but prefers a revolver, specifically this S&W Model 642, for backup for reasons explained in the text.*

*Most autos are easier to shoot well under stress than most revolvers. In this qualification shoot, Tracy Wright (left), the author, and Bob Smith (right) have all shot perfect scores with 1911 Tactical .45s tuned by Mark Morris, standing at rear.*

No guarantees, but if something even *might* work to your advantage, it's worth considering.

**Barricade Advantage.** When you have to fire from behind cover, you want to maximize that cover. With an auto pistol, the gun has to be out away from the wall or its slide can jam from friction. This means your head has to come out that much more from behind cover to aim, and where your head goes, your body follows. With the revolver, you can lay the barrel right against the barricade. This also steadies your aim somewhat (though it also increases felt recoil), but mainly, it brings you in deeper behind protective cover.

**Low Maintenance.** Unless you've rusted it shut or crapped it up so much there's a layer of carbon binding the cylinder's rotation past the forcing cone of the barrel, or debris built up under the ejector star, your revolver will probably do OK without a cleaning. An auto, even if pristinely cleaned after its last firing, should be lubricated regularly. The long bearing surfaces of slide and frame require lubrication for reliability. When the gun is carried in a holster, the liquid lubricant drains out. It can also evaporate. This can lead to a jammed-up pistol. The revolver, in my opinion and that of many experts, actually shouldn't be lubricated inside. Doesn't need it. That means a person who doesn't clean and lube his revolver regularly is not susceptible to gun lock-up when they need their handgun most, but the auto shooter most certainly is in danger of that.

**Deep Concealment Access.** When you carry in a real hideout location – ankle rig, pocket, belly band, or Thunderwear – the gun is pressed tightly against your body. The flat sides of the small auto's grip frame will be so close to your flesh that, in a fast-draw emergency, your fingers almost have to claw to gain a solid drawing grasp. But the rounded profile of a small revolver's grip-frame guides the firing hand right into drawing position. Deep concealment is slow to draw from anyway; using a revolver there minimizes that problem.

For those who wear ankle holsters, there's something else to consider. The gun is inches above the ground, with dirt and grit being kicked up around it with every step. This is why an "ankle gun" is generally covered with a fine film of grit after you've been out and about wearing it for a few days. The finely-fitted moving parts of most small auto pistols won't take that. We've had cases from California to Florida where the good guy drew a small auto from an ankle holster, got off a couple of shots, and suffered a malfunction at the worst possible time. A quality revolver, by contrast, will shoot even if it has dust bunnies in it.

**Cost/Value.** Look in the catalogs of companies that produce both revolvers and

too flat a nose or too short an overall cartridge length may compromise your auto's feed reliability, too. None of that compromises the turning cartridge wheel from which the revolver draws its nickname.

**Intimidation Value.** When a homeowner points an automatic pistol at an arrogant intruder, he may believe it's a toy. He might convince himself it's your grandfather's war souvenir with cobwebs instead of cartridges in the chamber. If that makes him go for his gun, or for yours, he might get lucky. But if you're pointing a revolver at him, he will almost certainly see something else: the heads of live cartridges pointing right at him. The sight of these missiles poised for launch may make the difference in convincing him that you're not running a bluff, and result in his deciding not to attack.

*Shooting from right to left, John Lazzaro smokes a table of pins with his modified S&W 1917 .45 revolver. With only five pins, a shooter this good won't need more than six shots.*

*Even the finest auto pistols can jam. This is a failure to eject with the Kahr P9.*

*Though complicated for a novice to handle, the HK P7 pistol is extremely easy for most people to shoot fast and straight once they are familiar with it.*

semiautomatic pistols. Taurus and Smith & Wesson are good examples. You'll generally find, grade for grade, that the revolvers are significantly less expensive.

**Accuracy.** As noted elsewhere in this book, accuracy can be more important in a combat handgun than many traditionalists believe. We can get by with the accuracy of any of the auto pistols recommended in this book, but more never hurts. The revolver, by and large, is more accurate than an auto pistol of similar quality grade.

In 1988, the department I then served became the fourth in the nation to adopt Smith & Wesson's third-generation .45 automatic, the Model 4506. It was a splendid gun. Ours averaged about 2.5-inch groups from the bench at 25 yards. However, the S&W Model 13 .357 Magnum revolvers we traded in for them were capable of holding the same size group at twice the distance.

## Autoloader Advantages

**High Hit Potential Under Stress.** When the Illinois State Police adopted the Smith & Wesson Model 39 semiautomatic in 1967, they were ahead of their time. They and other cops with revolvers of the period were hitting bad guys with about 25 percent of the bullets they fired in action. With the adoption of the 9mm auto, hit ratio skyrocketed to somewhere around 65 percent.

The auto pistol is more ergonomic. Most revolver users who knew their stuff put after-market grips on their wheelguns as soon as they bought them. In the 1990s, S&W and Colt wised up and put the after-market grips (Uncle Mike's and Pachmayr, respectively) on their own guns at the factory. "If you can't beat 'em, join 'em."

The auto's lower bore axis reduced recoil. Most autos have a shorter trigger pull, at least after the first double-action shot, which means that shooter panic is less likely to muscle the gun barrel off target as the defender jerks at the trigger. It is significant that ISP noted a lot of those 35 percent misses were the first double-action shot.

It should also be noted that the best hit potentials in the field have been with *single-stack* (8- or 9-shot) pistols. With high-capacity guns – especially when the cops were told the new pistols had been bought for "firepower" – the firepower seemed to become a *raison d'etre* that led to a "spray and pray" mentality. Significantly, ISP troopers' hit percentages in the field reportedly went down when they went from single-stack Model 39s to higher capacity guns.

**Proprietary Nature To The User.** We have case after case on record of suspects getting the gun away, trying to shoot the officer, and failing because the snatched weapon was a semiautomatic pistol carried "on safe." Most tests on this over the last 20 years (the first was published circa 1981 in

*There's that firepower thing. An auto will still be shooting when revolver is reloading and, with both starting empty, the auto will be shooting sooner than the revolver, all other things being equal.*

*Not every .45 auto will handle this broad range of ammo without a malfunction, though this SIG P220 stainless passed the test.*

*Police Chief* magazine, the journal of the International Association of Chiefs of Police) have resulted in the unfamiliar person taking an average of 17 seconds to figure out which little lever "turned on" the pistol.

Many auto pistols don't have this feature. Many double-action models are in the hands of people who don't choose to use this feature. This feature *can* be retrofitted to some revolvers: the Murabito safety catch conversion, and the "smart gun" conversion called MagnaTrigger. That said, the ability to serve as proprietary to the user is primarily a function of the semiautomatic pistol.

**Firepower.** Purists will tell you that you can't call it "firepower" until you get into belt-fed weapons. Realists know that since the first two cavemen started throwing rocks at each other, whoever threw the most rocks the fastest and straightest had an advantage.

The degree of advantage varies from gun to gun. If you go from a five-shot .38 revolver to a seven-shot Micro Kahr 9mm, it's a 40 percent increase. When California Highway Patrol went from six-shot .38 service revolvers to 12-shot S&W Model 4006 autos, they doubled their firepower. When any department went from six-shooters to the 18-shot Glock 17 in 9mm, they had 300 percent the firepower they had before. And that's just the in-gun reservoir of ammo. The auto pistol is also faster to load (in case a gun is kept unloaded for home defense), and faster to reload, especially under stress.

You can get awfully fast at refilling a wheelgun with speedloaders. You may get to where you can reload a revolver faster than I can reload an auto pistol. But you'll never get to where *you* can reload a revolver faster than

*you* can reload an auto pistol, assuming the same amount of practice with each gun.

Times have changed. We're seeing more multiple offender assaults, more and more perpetrators involved in professional armed robberies. In the horror of September 11, 2001, we saw hijack teams of up to six terrorists. If hit potential might be as low as one out of four shots in the stress of combat, and multiple opponents are increasing, you don't need to be a math major to see the advantage of a defensive weapon with more firepower.

Add to that the fact that the bad guys are using small-unit guerrilla tactics (fast movement, and cover) and are more likely than ever to be wearing body armor. Both of these factors mean you're likely to have to fire more shots before one takes effect. Firepower is more important today than when revolvers ruled.

**Relative Compactness.** A semiautomatic is flatter than a revolver of equal power. That makes it easier and more comfortable to conceal discreetly. That goes double for spare ammo: speedloaders for revolvers have as much bulge as another whole revolver's cylinder, but flat spare magazines for autos "carry easier."

**Relevant Training.** That "takes any ammo that fits its chamber" thing is sometimes an advantage for the revolver, but it became a disadvantage under the old paradigm of cops training with .38 wadcutters that kicked like mouse farts, yet actually carrying Elmer Keith Memorial Magnum rounds for serious business. Revolvers are gone from the police scene now for the most part, and toward the end of their reign police instructors made officers qualify with the same rounds they loaded for work, but you still see that "practice with light loads, carry with heavy loads" thing with armed citizens.

Ya can't do that with an auto pistol, gang. Go below the threshold of what the gun was designed for, and your auto pistol won't work. That means the auto forces you to use ammo that's at least reasonably close to the power of what you'd carry on the street. That means its design enforces more relevant training.

**Lower Muzzle Flash.** Large-bore auto pistols generally have less muzzle flash than large-bore revolvers. The .357 SIG auto round doesn't flash as much as the .357 Magnum revolver round, and most 9mm auto

*This Colt 1911A1 .45 auto is locking open after the last shot. A shooter can reload it faster than a revolver.*

ammo flares less at the muzzle than does equivalent .38 Special revolver ammo. We are in the time of low flash powders for premium ammo for both types of gun, so this is not as huge a difference as it was in the old days...but the difference is still there, and it favors the auto pistol. A gun whose muzzle flash blinds you when you fire it at night is not conducive to your being able to see the sun rise the next morning.

### Conclusions

There are still very real revolver advantages versus auto advantages. As Bruce Lee said, each practitioner of the given martial art must assess her own strengths and weaknesses, and choose what she will fight with accordingly.

When in doubt, carry one of each. For most of my adult life, I've carried two guns. The primary was usually (but not always) a service-size semiautomatic pistol. The backup was usually (but not always) a small frame snub-nosed revolver. The main fighting weapon gave me improved hit potential and all the other factors when it was an auto. The backup revolver gave me fast access and certain function from deep concealment, and also allowed me to arm a compatriot with a gun whose manual of arms I wouldn't have to explain when there wasn't time.

I always figured if I carried a revolver *and* an auto, when I got to the Pearly Gates I'd be covered, whether Saint Peter turned out to be a Jeff Cooper fan *or* a Bill Jordan fan.

# DAO Versus DA/SA

The double-action auto pistol in its conventional style – i.e., self-cocking itself after the first DA shot and becoming single-action for each shot thereafter until de-cocked – at first seemed hugely logical for police and armed citizens. Many think it still does.

Later came DAO, or double-action-only. This, in effect, was a mechanism that allowed the gun to "de-cock" itself after every shot. Some, especially in the higher echelons of law enforcement, believed this was safer for the rank and file. It has become hugely popular in policing, somewhat less so among the private citizenry.

Jeff Cooper said that *any* double-action auto was "an ingenious solution to a non-existent problem." He considered double-action-*only* autos to be anathema to good shooting as he knew it, and at one point forbade such guns from his famous shooting school, Gunsite. A gunwriter once remarked, "Double-action-only is so stupid, they're making jokes about it in Poland." Meanwhile, three of our six largest law enforcement agencies mandate DAO auto pistols: NYPD, Chicago PD, and the Border Patrol.

Who's right? Let's hash out the arguments and decide.

In 1990 I found myself teaching a class for the DEA Academy at Quantico. DEA shares the same facility as the FBI Academy. They call each other "the guys down the street." I took some extra time to spend with John Hall, then the chief of the FBI's Firearms Training Unit. They

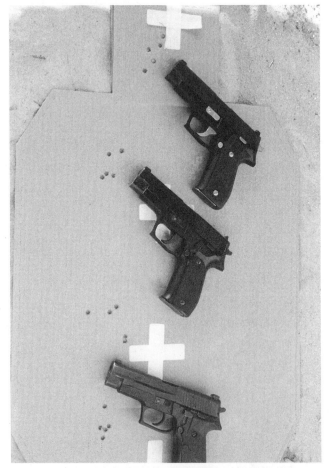

*The DAO SIG E26 fired the top group at 25 yards. An older DAO P226 fired the second group down. A DA first shot with four SA follow-up rounds from a conventional P226 delivered the third group, followed by the bottom group, the same gun fired single-action for all five shots.*

*If you've already fired a shot under stress, and aren't deeply familiarized with your weapon, you may not remember to de-cock. In such circumstances, this lady is well served with DAO Kahr K9 as she covers the threat zone from behind cover while calling 9-1-1.*

*Bill Laughridge lines up the DAO auto that may be the easiest of all to shoot well, the Para-Ordnance LDA.*

*Don't tell a seasoned shooter that a good DAO auto isn't controllable. The author shot this 60-round qualification group with Beretta 96D Centurion and full power .40 S&W ammo. The "D" suffix after a Beretta model number means double-action for every shot.*

were in the news big time because they were then in the process of implementing the adoption of a gun they had designed with Smith & Wesson, the Model 1076 10mm. 10mm Auto was the hot ticket during that period.

Some departments were already going over to the DAO concept. I asked John why he and his agency didn't buy into that. The reply was clear and succinct. The rationale of the double-action trigger with its long, heavy pull, John explained, was to reduce the likelihood of accidental discharges under stress. He and the Bureau accepted that. This was why it was only DA first shot autos that were approved for the Bureau's then approximately 7,000 agents. Only the *crème de la crème,* the elite Hostage Rescue Unit, was allowed to carry single-action autos. At the time the HRU had Browning Hi-Power 9mms customized by Wayne Novak, and local-office FBI SWAT teams had the DA/SA SIG P226 9mm.

Hall continued his explanation. "Almost all accidental discharges are one-shot events," he said. "After the first shot, if he needs to continue shooting, the agent is in a gunfight." Hall and company wanted that agent to have the easiest possible job of making those subsequent shots count under stress. The self-cocking trigger was deemed the best way to achieve that obviously worthwhile goal.

This made sense to me. I had always been an advocate of a broad weapons policy that let officers pick, within reason, the guns that worked best for them. As the motorcyclists say, "Let those who ride, decide." I still believe that. But, two years before, my new chief had decided that we would all carry the same gun, and all I had left to say about it was what gun it would be. I had been instrumental, in 1988, in selecting an issue gun very much like what Hall came up with: the Smith & Wesson 4506.

The reasons Hall had cited were there. So was the fact that our people had to patrol in some nasty winters, and for a third or more of the year would have to manipulate guns with hands impaired by either numbing cold or feel-blunting gloves. With the gloves, a lot of double-action-only guns – including the S&W .357 Magnum revolvers we issued up until then – could have their trigger return blocked by the thick glove material on the trigger finger. This could turn the six-shot .357 into a single-shot. With the DA/SA Smith auto, once they fired the first shot, the trigger would stay in a rearward position until all further necessary shooting was done. Then, with the trigger finger removed from the guard, the officer's thumb could easily manipulate the slide-mounted de-cocking lever. It seemed the safest and most practical method.

Frankly, it still does. Well over a decade later, I now serve another department. We've had similar guns, the Ruger P-series .45 autos, as standard issue since 1993. The previous department, last I knew, still had their conventional style S&W autos. I note a point: *neither department, in all those years, had an accidental discharge with those "traditional style" DA/SA semiautomatic pistols!*

### Genesis of DAO

In the early 1980s, police chiefs became increasingly aware of accidental discharges caused by the "hair trigger" effect created when officers cocked their service revolvers. LAPD started what became a trend, an alteration of the revolver's mechanism (the simple removal of the cocking notch of the hammer) that rendered the gun double-action only. Sure enough, when no one could cock the gun, cocked gun "accidentals" disappeared. Miami PD, NYPD, and Montreal PD soon followed suit.

I can tell you the inside story on two of those last three. Miami made their S&W Model 64 .38 revolvers DAO after the controversial killing of Nevell "Snake" Johnson in an inner-city video arcade by Officer Luis Alvarez. It was a cross-racial shooting that triggered the second largest race riot in the city's history. Janet Reno was then the State's Attorney (the chief prosecutor) for Dade County, which encompasses Miami. The city needed a scapegoat. Alvarez was offered up. He was charged with manslaughter. The prosecution's theory was that Alvarez had cocked the hammer of his gun to show off as he arrested Johnson for possession of an illegal weapon, and that the resultant hair-trigger effect had caused the gun to accidentally discharge because Johnson, while turning to surrender, unexpectedly startled Alvarez. Since it was against regulations to cock the gun for a routine arrest, this theory created the element of negligence, a necessary ingredient to the state's formula for manslaughter conviction.

There was one small problem. The story was all BS. Alvarez never cocked the gun. His defense lawyers, Roy Black and Mark Seiden, retained me as an expert witness. We were able to *prove* that he had never cocked the gun. The jury learned that Johnson had spun toward Alvarez and his rookie partner and had reached for the stolen RG .22 revolver in his waistband, with the obvious intention of killing both cops. At that moment, Luis Alvarez had instantly and intentionally done the right thing: he shot and killed the gunman.

The trial lasted eight weeks, the longest criminal trial in Florida history. It ended with an acquittal after only two hours of jury deliberation, including dinner. The acquittal triggered the *third* largest race riot in Miami history, but that's another story. This trial comprises one fourth of famed defense lawyer Roy Black's superb book, *Black's Law*, if you want to read more about it.

*"New" doesn't always mean "progress." The author found in testing of these two Berettas that the newest Model 9000-D, below, didn't hold a candle to older Model 96D, above. Both are DAO in caliber .40 S&W.*

The point is, the city had all their revolvers rendered DAO between the shooting and the trial. The local cops called them "Alvarized" guns. Though it was nothing more than a concession to political correctness, it's entirely possible that later, down the road, this alteration did have some positive safety benefits. I can't say either way. If nothing else, it kept unscrupulous prosecutors from throwing any more innocent cops to the wolves with the bogus "cocked gun" theory.

The Montreal decision to go DAO came after the case of *Crown v. Allan Gossett*. Canadian firearms training of the period was at least 20 years behind that of the U.S., and Gossett had become a constable of the Montreal Police when they were still taught to shoot a revolver by cocking the hammer and squeezing off single-action shots at bull's-eye targets. The night came when he was in pursuit of a felony suspect, and had to draw his issue S&W Model 10 .38 caliber service revolver. As the suspect spun toward Gossett, the constable was seen to jerk as if startled, and his gun fired. The violent jump of the gun with mild .38 recoil, and the look of shock on Gossett's face as it discharged, were noted by witnesses and tended to confirm the fact that it was an unintentional discharge.

It was believed that the gun was cocked. Gossett didn't remember cocking it. I believed him and so, in the end, did those who tried the facts, the only ones whose beliefs counted. The Crown, as the prosecution is known up there, charged him with manslaughter on the same grounds as Reno had charged Alvarez. It was their theory that negligence (intentional cocking of the gun), plus death (which obviously took place) equals manslaughter.

I testified for Gossett, too. Like Alvarez, he was ultimately acquitted. We believe that one of two things happened: he went back to his original training reflexively and in those high-stress moments cocked the gun without realizing it, or the hammer had become cocked by accident. We'll never know which. At the time, Montreal issued a crappy holster that appeared to be living proof that you could tan the hide of a chicken and make gunleather out of it. The safety strap went over the back of the trigger guard instead of over the hammer. The unprotected hammer could thus snag on seat belts, coat sleeves, or just about anything else and become cocked while still in the holster, unnoticed by the constable wearing it.

After Gossett's ordeal, Montreal got some decent gunleather and ordered the Model 10s made DAO.

What does all this have to do with auto-loading pistols? Glad you asked. It *is* a long story.

Shortly after the Alvarez trial, the Miami street cops and their union went to the chief in Miami and asked for high capacity 9mm autos to replace their .38 six-shooters. They were confiscating an increasing number of high-cap autos from dopers – their city was then the illegal drug capitol of the nation – and they sought parity. Sure, the chief said, you can have hi-cap autos…*if* you can find one that's double-action for every shot!

The union (and the city firearms instructors) pleaded with Beretta, SIG, and S&W to make a 9mm auto that was double-action for every shot. The companies thought the idea was stupid and blew them off. At about that time, the Bureau of Alcohol, Tobacco, and Firearms declared the Glock pistol's mechanism, which its inventor designated Safe-action, to be "double-action only."

It was delicious. The chief who hadn't wanted autos for his troops was "hoisted by his own petard." In desperation, seemingly impossible torture tests were ordered for durability. The Glock passed them. To cut to the chase: Miami became the first really big, high-crime city to adopt the Glock. They were the flagship of the fleet, and soon Glock was outselling all the rest combined. Beretta, SIG, and S&W *now* felt the impetus to come out with DAO guns…but they were too late to stop the huge momentum Glock had developed in the police market.

Today, Miami PD still issues the Glock, having upgraded from the 9mm to the .40 S&W caliber. Montreal, when they went to autos, went DAO too, as did virtually all of Canadian law enforcement. While most provincial and municipal agencies in Canada chose the .40 caliber, the Royal Canadian Mounted Police and the Montreal PD went with DAO Smith & Wesson pistols in 9mm.

### The Decision Today

There are shooters who prefer DAO because having only one trigger pull to work with for every shot is easier for them. I won't argue the point. I've seen too many shooters for whom that was true. If you anticipate the shot and jerk the trigger when you're working with a gun that has a short, light pull, the DAO is something you should try.

There are departments that can't devote as much time and money as their instructors would like to train the rank and file with handguns. NYPD (40,000 officers) and Chicago PD (13,000 cops) are well known for being in that situation. Both of them require that all personnel, except for older officers who are "grandfathered" with permission to carry double-action revolvers, carry DAO auto pistols on duty.

I've seen people under stress "lose it" to the degree that after they had fired one or more shots, they forgot to de-cock their conventional DA autos before holstering. In one case in California, an officer did this with his Beretta 92F 9mm after shooting an attacking pit bull. He had not only forgotten to de-cock, he had forgotten to take his finger off the trigger. As he put the gun back in his holster, his finger caught the edge of the leather that was designed to cover the trigger guard, and came to a stop. However, the gun kept going, driving the trigger against the finger. BANG! He shot himself in the leg. Now even more stressed than before, he tried to shove the gun into the holster again. BANG! He shot himself a second time in

the space of only a few seconds. The unique "partially open front" design of his department's trademark holster had allowed the Beretta to cycle while partially holstered.

Some believe this is a training issue. For the most part, it is, but the fact remains that the harder it is to pull the trigger, the harder it is to pull the trigger *accidentally*. When you have a light, easy, single-action trigger, there is good news and bad news. The good news is it's easy to shoot. The bad news is it's easy to shoot. It's the situation that will determine whether a certain type of trigger pull is a good thing or a bad thing.

### Design Features

All DAO handguns are not created equal. The ParaOrdnance LDA (an acronym its users have determined stands for "Light Double-action"; the manufacturer never actually spelled it out) has a deliciously easy trigger pull. Some police departments (such as North Attleboro, Massachusetts) have already adopted it for standard issue. Some others (such as the San Bernardino Sheriff's Department) have approved it for duty if deputies wish to buy their own.

Next up on the "ease of manipulation" ladder are the DAO guns of Kahr Arms and Smith & Wesson. Both are extremely smooth and easy to shoot well. The Kahrs are small, reliable hideout guns; the S&W line encompasses small to large and includes duty-size service pistols.

The DAO Berettas tend to be lighter than the regular Berettas in the big 92 and 96 series guns, but heavier than LDAs, Smiths, or Kahrs. The absence of a single-action sear removes a friction point, and I believe the springs are a bit lighter. On the other hand, Beretta's little Model 9000 polymer gun has a nasty double-action pull.

The theory is that transitioning to DAO gives you one less manipulation to worry about, that is, de-cocking after the shooting is over. That's true as far as it goes. On the other hand, a great many people find a shorter, lighter trigger pull is less likely to jerk shots off target, particularly when firing under great stress and at great speed.

Beretta's 96D in double-action only (short barrel Centurion model shown) has earned a good reputation in the field.

*Don't say DAO autos aren't accurate. Illinois State Rifle Association president Rich Pearson, right, holds a cutout group he watched the author shoot at 25 yards with hot Triton 115-grain/1,325 fps 9mm ammo from this SIG P226 DAO.*

Personally, I can live with either style. I've explained why I'm partial to the "conventional" style, the DA/SA. That's not a habituation thing, that's an "I've looked at everything I and my people need where we are" thing. But my people and I aren't you and yours, and we may be in two different places in more ways than one, with two distinct sets of needs.

I serve a small police department where we can train intensively. Whether or not we're all likeable, we're all demonstrably competent. What if I had to take responsibility for training 40,000 personnel, most of whom were not interested in spending a minute to develop confidence and competence with the gun if they weren't being paid for it? What if I could only pay for a couple of days a year of that training? In that case, the double-action-only concept would look very good, indeed.

When the police instructors and supervisors pick a gun for their officers, two commandments must be kept in mind. *Know thy specific needs,* and *Know thy personnel.*

When a law-abiding citizen makes that decision between these two common types of semiautomatic pistol, a similar process makes sense. Before you decide whether you want a DAO pistol, or a "conventional" DA pistol, or perhaps something else, there are again two commandments: ***Know thy specific needs*** and, perhaps more important, ***know thyself.***

# On-Safe Versus Off-Safe

Pick up a standard model S&W, Beretta, or Ruger auto pistol. Manipulate that little lever at the rear of its slide. If two typical firearms instructors are standing one on each side of you, ask them, "What *is* that lever?"

On a typical day, one might answer, "It's the safety." The other would be likely to scream, "That's not a safety, it's a de-cocking lever!"

And if a firearms engineer was there, he'd probably sound like the Doublemint Twins. "It's two levers – *two* levers! – two levers *in one!*"

Who's right? In a greater or lesser way, all three.

Popularized on Walther pistols developed in the 1920s and coming to prominence in the 1930s, refined by Smith & Wesson on their first 9mm pistols in the mid-1950s, this dual-purpose lever may be the single most misunderstood piece of equipment that you'll find on any combat handgun. If you look at the patents, Smith & Wesson's for example, you'll find it listed as a "safety/de-cock" lever.

I was very much a part of things when autoloaders began pushing revolvers out of the law enforcement handgun picture in the mid-1980s. I saw some scary things, some of which still exist. A few others and I had been voices in the wilderness crying out in the early and mid-1970s that these "automatics" had some advantages that might make them worthy of replacing our ancient "service revolvers."

Most of the police chiefs back then didn't know from guns. They relied on their firearms instructors for input on that. The problem was most of their firearms instructors only knew the revolver. Such an instructor had a set of pat answers when cops came to him asking why they couldn't carry autoloaders.

"Those autos will jam on you," the instructors would say. "Besides, the revolver is loaded and ready to go when you're in danger! Just draw and shoot! With an automatic, you'd have to slow down and take the safety off – if you remembered!"

Then, in what must have seemed to some of them like a cataclysmic change of worlds, the union guys had won, and the chiefs were giving them the autos they had asked for. Groping desperately to catch up with technology they had spent their firearms training careers trying to pretend didn't exist, a lot of these instructors had no *clue* how to manipulate the slide-mounted safety on firearms coming into service. Some examples included the Ruger auto the Wisconsin state troopers had adopted, the Beretta that had been chosen by LAPD, and the Smith &

Wesson chosen by the Illinois State Police before any of the rest.

Rather than teach its manipulation, it was easier to pretend that it didn't exist. "It's not a safety catch, it's a de-cocking lever" became the mantra. Now, had this gone to court, I can say as both a police prosecutor and an expert witness that the argument would probably have been destroyed in less than a minute of cross-examination.

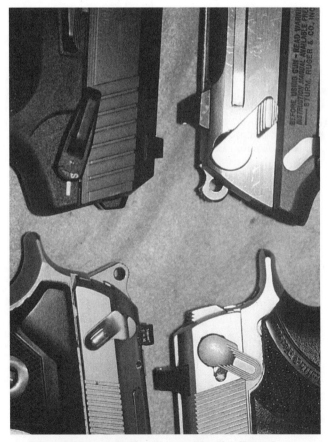

*Four popular combat handguns with safety/de-cock levers. Clockwise from noon, those of Ruger, S&W, and Beretta are slide-mounted, while that of HK USP is mounted on the frame.*

"Sir, you are the department's designated firearms expert, correct?"

"Yes."

"And you say this part is not a safety, it's strictly a de-cocking lever?"

"Yes."

"Sir, I show you these two documents. Exhibit A is the patent for the gun you issue your department. Exhibit B is the nomenclature sheet produced by the factory that manufactured the gun you issue to your officers. Can you tell the jury what the part in question is called by these authoritative sources in these documents?"

"Um, it says 'safety/de-cocking lever'…"

"Nothing further."

You can't say something isn't what it obviously is, just because you want it to be so. That's Stalinist revisionism. It didn't even work for Stalin.

It is possible for departments to lose their own sense of institutional history. When you forget where you came from, it's always a bad thing. Case in point: the Illinois State Police, who in 1967 became the first major police department in the USA to issue autoloading pistols.

Here's the real story. ISP at the time let the troopers buy their own Colt or S&W, .38 or .357 revolvers. They were required to be armed off duty, and virtually all carried small-frame snub-nose .38s. The department wanted them all to qualify with the off-duty guns as well as the duty weapons. The scores with the snubbies were pathetic. Let's face it, guns like that were tough to shoot on courses of fire that emphasized 25-yard shooting at the time. The superintendent tasked Louis Seman, then head of Ordnance for the department, with finding a solution.

The solution was the Smith & Wesson Model 39. Weighing only 26.5 ounces, it was midway in heft between a 19-ounce off-duty Chief Special and a 34-ounce K-frame service revolver. It was flat in silhouette, easy to conceal in plain clothes. It reloaded more quickly – *way* more quickly – than loose revolver shells from the dump pouches of the time. While it lacked the inherent accuracy of the guns it replaced (you were doing well to get a 4-inch group at 25 yards), its beautiful hand-fitting ergonomics made the Model 39 9mm autoloader easy to shoot. Maybe it wouldn't equal the revolvers in a machine rest, but you could *put* all its shots into that 4-inch group at 25 yards, and that meant a perfect qualification score.

A decade or so later, I came to Illinois under the auspices of the Troopers' Lodge 41 of the Fraternal Order of Police, the entity that represented the troopers in bargaining. I did the first poll of the troopers on this gun. Some 87 percent of them wanted to go to something else. These 1,700 or so people resented having an alien concept foisted upon them by what they perceived to be one Ordnance Corporal and one desk-bound superintendent.

But, an interesting thing showed up in all that research. Those troopers had been in a bunch of deadly encounters, and I was given *carte blanche* by the administration to study them. Even though the majority of the troopers at that time wanted to go back to the revolver, there was overpowering evidence that Seman had made the right choice.

I was able to identify **13** troopers who were alive because they'd had the S&W automatic, and would have probably been killed if they'd been armed with six-shot revolvers. I could find **no** case where a trooper armed with the 9mm was shot by a criminal and would not have been shot if the trooper had been armed with a revolver instead.

Everyone thinks firepower is the *raison d'etre* for an auto instead of a revolver. It certainly was a factor, but not the main factor. I found two officers who survived because either the seventh or eighth shot put down the attacker. Trooper Ken Kaas was facing a charging attacker who had a 20-gauge auto shotgun, and a man who had already shot people and was wielding a 12-gauge pump was charging Trooper Les Davis. Both fired their last couple of shots and dropped their would-be murderers. Troopers Lloyd Burchette and Bob Kolowski both ran dry and needed quick reloads to keep up the pace of fire that finally saved their lives in a sustained firefight.

That was four. Of the remaining nine, a few, who were in struggles for their guns were able to hit the magazine release button, and thus activate the magazine disconnector safety. This is the feature seen on the standard S&W auto, the Browning Hi-Power, and some other guns that renders weapon unable to fire, even with a cartridge in the chamber, if the magazine has dropped out of place. In each of those cases, when the suspect finally got the gun away from the trooper, the attempt to shoot the officer failed.

However, the overwhelming majority of those "auto pistol saves" were cases in which the suspect got the gun away from the trooper, pointed it at him, and pulled the trigger…*and the gun did not go off because the trooper had been carrying it on safe.*

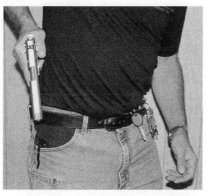

*The draw begins. The S&W 4506 is carried on-safe in an LFI Concealment Rig…*

*…At about the time the gun clears the body, the thumb has pushed the lever into "fire" position…*

*…Since the action was accomplished during the draw, there has been no significant time loss in getting a ready-to-fire .45 up on target. Note that the lever is in the "fire" position with the red warning dot exposed.*

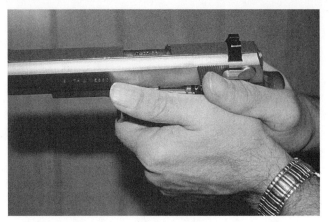

*This ergonomic grasp, widely used by combat champions, is perfectly compatible with disengaging a slide-mounted manual safety.*

From 1967 until well into the 1980s, Illinois troopers were given the option of carrying their gun "on safe" or "off safe." They were shown how to flip off the safety as they drew. The decision was then left up to them.

Then, in the 1980s, some personnel changes took place in the Ordnance Section. Seman was long since retired. Now it was time for the wise senior men who had replaced him, Bob Cappelli and Sebastian "Bash" Ulrich, to take their well-earned retirements too. As transfers, promotions, and retirements would have it, some new people soon flooded into ISP Ordnance. The department thought it best to send them to an outside instructor school.

The school they went to was a famous one that will remain nameless. The instructors were told at that school, "It's not a safety catch, it's a de-cock lever. The gun should be carried off-safe at all times, because it's too awkward to move the lever under stress."

Never mind that in the history of the department, no Illinois State Trooper had ever been hurt because he couldn't get his gun off-safe in time. "The Word From Afar" now became "The Doctrine." Troopers were now *mandated* to carry their S&W autos off-safe. This situation continued until the late 1990s, when the department switched from the S&W 9mms they carried – 16-shot third-generation models by that point – to the Glock 22 pistol, which has no manual safety at all, and requires no decocking lever.

I suppose that's one way to deal with the problem…

### The Lessons of Engineering…

Certain auto pistols *must* be on-safe to shield the user from unintended discharges. No logical, sane, and experienced firearms instructor would argue that a single-action auto pistol should be carried off-safe. There is simply too much danger of its easy, short-movement trigger being unintentionally activated.

The Colt .45 and all the many clones of that 1911 design, the Browning Hi-Power, the Star FireStar, and other such designs, are all carried cocked and *locked* by any professional worthy of the name.

When such guns are drawn, the safety is flicked down into the "fire" position as the gun muzzle comes up into the target, after the intention to immediately fire has already been formulated.

There are also certain double-action autos that are not "drop-safe" if the manual safety is not engaged. These include all Walther PP and PPK series guns, and all first-generation Smith & Wesson double-action autos. Two-digit primary model numbers distinguish the latter. The Model 39, 39-2, 59, etc., do not have internal firing pin locks. This makes them and the previously mentioned Walther designs subject to "inertia firing" if dropped or struck on the muzzle or the rear of slide. The firing pins on these guns are only "locked and/or blocked" if the manual safety is engaged.

An officer with an off-safe Model 59 in his holster was carrying a large box of evidence out of the police department. His hands being full, he tried to activate the bar that opened the front door by hitting it with his hip. His pistol's hammer was the contact point, and – BANG! The pistol fired in the holster.

A couple tried to carry a loaded, off-safe Walther .380 into the house along with several bags from a shopping trip. The gun slipped and fell, landing on the floor on its hammer. BANG! The pistol discharged and struck one of the spouses, producing a grave gunshot wound.

### …and the Lessons of History

Gun retention is the big advantage of on-safe carry. Gun retention is the corollary science to gun disarming. It is the defeating of the disarming attempt.

*Washington:* The suspect jumps a cop, gets his cocked and locked 1911 .45 away from him, tries to shoot him. Nothing. Suspect, still with gun, runs. Cop

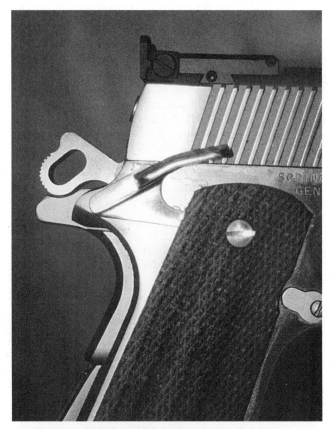

*The many 1911 fans think having to carry their gun on-safe is a tactical advantage. The author thinks they're right. Here's the easily manipulated ambidextrous safety of Ayoob's cocked and locked Springfield Trophy Match .45.*

*Practice plus proper technique equals fast, sure draws to the shot with a double-action pistol carried on safe.*

commandeers passing car, takes suspect at gunpoint with 2-inch .38 revolver, and suspect surrenders. A cop-killing was prevented.

*Indiana:* Armed robbers take a gun shop owner at gunpoint, relieve him of his HK P7 pistol, take him into back room to murder him. The suspect with the P7 tries to shoot: no effect. He has not fully squeeze-cocked what might be called the "safety lever" at the front of the gun. The gun shop owner grabs a secreted .357 revolver, shoots down two robbers and survives.

*Alabama:* A suspect being arrested grabs an officer's S&W 9mm from the holster, aims at him, pulls trigger. Nothing happens; gun is "on-safe." The officer draws a back-up Taurus .38 from his ankle holster. The terrified suspect drops the gun and surrenders. No blood is shed.

*Illinois:* Two suspects attack, disarm, and beat a state trooper. One suspect takes his gun and tries to shoot him. He can't because the S&W Model 39 is on-safe. At this point a second trooper arrives, orders men to stop; suspect points gun at this trooper and pulls trigger. The S&W still won't fire. Second trooper shoots and kills gunman, saving both troopers' lives.

*Utah:* Many witnesses watch as an officer is sucker punched and knocked unconscious. The attacker pulls the gun from the uniform holster, points it at the officer, and pulls the trigger. Nothing. The S&W 9mm was being carried on safe. The suspect jacked the slide, ejecting a live round, aimed and attempted to shoot again. Nothing. The suspect then fiddled with the slide release lever trying to find the safety, aimed at the officer, and pulled trigger. Nothing. The suspect pressed the button behind the trigger guard and the magazine dropped under a car where it was found later. The suspect again tried to shoot the cop. Nothing. Finally finding the safety lever, the suspect tried again to shoot the cop. Nothing. The magazine disconnector safety had been activated, preventing the firing of the round in the chamber. The suspect then threw the gun at the prostrate officer and fled. The officer survived.

*Florida:* A suspect has stolen a Smith & Wesson 9mm auto that is fully loaded with round in chamber, but has been left on-safe. As he robs and attempts to murder cab driver, the gun does not fire. When the cab driver sees the

suspect pulling the trigger, he goes for his own gun, a cocked and locked Colt .45 automatic. Since he owns the gun, the cab driver knows where *his* safety is. He shoots and kills the robber, saving his own life.

The list goes on…

### Know Thy Weapon

The choice is yours. But be sure it is an informed choice. Look at all sides, weigh all the risks, then decide what works for your balance of need versus risk.

It pains me to see cops and law-abiding citizens giving up a life-saving tactical advantage because their instructors don't know how to operate their tools. More than a decade ago, I was at a seminar where one of the instructors who told those Illinois State Police instructors to give up their safety catches was teaching. He chanted the mantra: "It isn't a safety, it's a de-cocking lever."

I just said the truth to him. "On my department, the chief has mandated that we carry our S&W .45 autos on-safe. Show us what you think is the best way to do that."

He stood there for a moment fumbling with an S&W, wiggling the last digit of his thumb off its median joint as if he was trying to shoot marbles. He said, "You can't. See?"

I didn't want to attack him in public, but he was wrong. You *can,* and I *can* see, and so can you.

With the slide-mounted safety, where the lever has to be pushed up, certain guns are awkward. The little Walther is a case in point. Its lever is at the wrong angle for mechanical advantage. It's one of many reasons I don't carry that tiny .380.

But with the S&W, the Beretta, or the modern Ruger, it's a piece of cake. Simply *thrust the firing hand's thumb up, at a 45-degree angle, as if you were trying to reach the ejection port. Unless your thumb is very short or bends outward to an unusual degree, this will pop the safety catch into the fire position.*

With some holsters, the thumb strap or strap paddle may get in the way. While it would be dangerous to off-safe a single-action auto in the holster, I'm comfortable doing that with a double-action; hell, everybody else is telling you to carry it off-safe to begin with! Videos and high-speed photos of me when I'm drawing showed me that I disengage the safety lever at about 45 degrees of muzzle angle as I'm coming out of the holster. I win my

*This 45-degree straight angle thrust of the thumb of the firing hand is the most efficient way to disengage a slide-mounted manual safety.*

share of matches, and have outdrawn my share of scumbags, and all I can say is, "It works for me."

I'm prepared to test this under pressure. I've done it already. Smith & Wesson owns videotape of me in police uniform doing it, in a film made but never released after my old department adopted the 4506 and Tom Campbell, then an S&W staffer, brought me down to do the flick. S&W Academy's great instructors Bert DuVernay, Brent Purucker, and Tom Aveni were all present when I went to an advanced instructor school there and beat everybody else on the draw to accurate shot, using a 4506 carried on-safe. There were lots of witnesses when I won the 2000 New Hampshire state shoot for cops, on a fast 7- to 50-yard combat course using an on-safe Ruger P90 .45 drawn from a fully secured Safariland 070/SSIII holster.

The techniques are there. The safety catch factor in weapon retention is there. If you find the techniques don't fit your hands, so be it, but make your decision of "off-safe" instead of "on-safe" an informed decision, not just a blind acceptance of something you were told by someone who might not have known how to do it.

The life on the line is your own.

# Point Shooting Versus Aimed Fire

For more than a decade, this is a topic that has been guaranteed to not only sell gun magazines, but to generate a flurry of angry letters to the editors. Gun expert Dave Arnold was the first to make a key point about it. "A lot of this argument," Dave said, "is simply a matter of terminology."

As one who has been in or around the center of that debate since 1990, I'll certainly buy *that!* Let's see if we can't quantify our terms at the very beginning so we're all working off the same sheet of music.

Two concepts need to be understood first: *index* and *coordinates*. Index is what lines up the gun with that which is to be shot. Coordinates are the things we have to accomplish to achieve index.

There are perhaps three possible indices by which we can line up our gun with the target or the threat:

**Body Position Index.** This would be the situation where you can't see where the gun is aimed, so you're using a certain body position to align the gun with the target. In the obsolete FBI crouch, the coordinates are backside low, upper body forward, gun punched forward to keep it from going too low. In the speed rock, discussed elsewhere in this book, the coordinates include leaning the upper torso all the way back to bring the forearm lateral as the gun is fired immediately upon levering upward away from the holster. In pure hip-shooting, you are relying on either long-term muscle memory developed through exhaustive practice, or by a degree of talent few of us could ever hope to possess. I would define any type of body position index as "point shooting."

**Visual Index.** This is where you are indexing by seeing the gun or the gunsights superimposed on the target. If you can see the gun is on target, I consider this aimed fire. Whether you are superimposing the silhouette of the whole gun over the target, or looking over the top of it, *or* taking a classic sight picture, the only question remaining is whether it's coarsely aimed fire or precisely aimed fire.

*Firearms instructor Andy Stanford explains the cone of shot dispersal and the importance of indexing the gun on target. In his hand is a Ring brand dummy gun with Ashley Express high-speed sights.*

*Here's a situation where hip-shooting will work. The target is at the height of the driver in an average-size car. If the driver pulled a gun during a traffic stop, the officer's hand already on a backup gun in his pocket could give him a fighting chance with this technique.*

*This is a StressPoint Index. It is almost as accurate at close range, and much faster than a conventional sight picture, especially if eye focus is on the threat instead of on the defense gun.*

**Artificial Index.** This would be something like a laser sight. Let's say you have a ballistic raid shield in one hand, and a gun in the other. It will be awkward and difficult to bend the arm into a position where you can aim through the Lexan view port using the regular sights. If you reach your gun around the side of the shield and see your red dot on target, the artificial mechanism of the projected laser dot has indexed the weapon for you, rather than you visually aligning the gun or aligning it by body position index.

Since the laser sight is by no means universal, this argument of point shooting versus aimed fire really comes down to an issue of body position index versus visual index.

*A gun must "point" for you if you're going to hit with true "point shooting." If the natural hold is center for you with this customized Glock 23...*

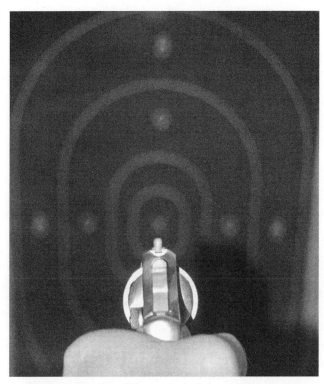

*The front sight doesn't have to be in focus to index the shot when it is sitting up out of the rear notch. The revolver is S&W Model 64.*

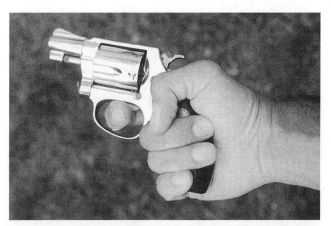

*...then you'll probably shoot high with this slim-gripped S&W Model 60 revolver...*

*...and way low with this Beretta Model 21 pocket pistol.*

The middle road position is, "practice both." That saves controversy, but if you're teaching cops or others with limited time who can't waste even minutes on useless stuff because you don't have as much time as you need to give them key life-saving skills, you can't afford to save controversy any more. A great many police departments have either gotten away from point shooting entirely, or given it very short shrift. The reason is that their cops get into a lot of shootings, and they can quickly find out what works and what doesn't. Departments that have learned to re-emphasize sighted combat fire include LAPD and NYPD, to name but a few. Both saw a significant jump in hit percentages in actual gunfights after renewing their emphasis on visually indexing the duty sidearms.

A book could be written on this topic – some have been, and more will be – but let's cut to the chase. The bottom line is this; a lifetime of studying real-world gunfight dynamics has taught this author that true point shooting simply doesn't work, except for a handful of extremely skilled and highly practiced shooters.

Perhaps the easiest way to proceed directly to the bottom line is to debunk the myths that have developed, particularly in the past 15 years or so, about point shooting.

### Myths of Point Shooting

*"Point shooting worked for Capt. William Fairbairn of the Shanghai Police, who survived over 600 gunfights shooting this way."* **WRONG.** If you read Fairbairn's classic book "Shoot to Live," you'll see that the *entire 1,000 man Shanghai Police force* was involved in some 660 gunfights during the 10-year period in question. While it's entirely possible that in a violent city Fairbairn might have had his gun out of the holster 600 times on the street, he was not in 600 gunfights and never claimed he was. If you think about it, Fairbain would have killed more opponents than were accounted for by Sgt. Alvin York, Audie Murphy, and Carlos Hathcock combined.

*"The great Col. Rex Applegate taught point shooting and quantified statistics showing that it worked for the OSS!"* **MISINTERPRETED.** Col. Applegate was indeed a great man. I knew him. I was there to congratulate him

when he won his long overdue Outstanding American Handgunner of the Year award, and he was there to congratulate me when I won mine a few years later. We both spoke before the Joint Services Small Arms Project on the Personal Defense Weapon project, at Oak Ridge.

Unlike many who quote him, I had the privilege of him showing me his technique. A photo of that experience accompanies this article. You can see that he has brought my Beretta pistol up to arm's length, and you can draw a line from the pupil of his eye to the front sight to the target.

Rex *called* it point shooting to distinguish it from the precise, focus-on-the-front sight concept taught in the traditional marksmanship manuals. But, make no mistake, Rex had the gun up where the eye couldn't miss it, even in the tunnel vision state of fight or flight reflex. That's why his technique worked, and that's why shooting that way still works, as Sgt. Lou Chiodo and the California Highway Patrol have proven. It's just not really "point shooting." Again, we're back to Dave Arnold's point: a lot of this is semantic quibbling.

*"Point shooting can be learned in 50 shots live-fire, or even just by dry firing in the mirror!"* **UNTRUE.** This has been set forth in print by two separate point-shooting advocates, neither of whom to my knowledge has actually ever run a live-fire shooting class. Both have repeatedly turned down invitations to demonstrate their skills in public. One has produced a video in which, if you look carefully, he can be seen to be scattering his shots all over

Ed Lovette demonstrates the Applegate-based point shooting he learned from Lou Chiodo. This style will work, because the gun and its sights intrude into the cone of tunnel vision and the weapon can be visually indexed.

*End of argument. Rex Applegate demonstrates his point shooting technique for Ayoob's camera with Ayoob's Beretta 92. Note that you could draw a line from the pupil of his eye to the front sight to the target. This, the author submits, is coarsely aimed fire, not point-shooting.*

a huge target at close range with his point shooting techniques. The other caused to be published a photo of himself dry-firing at a mirror. If you look carefully at the picture and lay a ruler over the gun barrel, you can see that he is performing the almost impossible feat of missing himself in his own mirror. The shot would have gone over the reflected image's shoulder. Shooting at a mirror is a false approach to learning body-position index shooting anyway, since the eye can see where the mirror image is pointing and automatically correct, which would never happen in real life.

*"Aimed fire was proven useless when NYPD had only 11 percent hits with it."* **WRONG.** That low hit potential figure attributed to aimed NYPD fire is taken from the single worst year in more than 30 years of the department's SOP-9 study. Standard Operating Procedure Number Nine is the intensive debriefing of all officers on that PD who fire a shot with their duty or off-duty weapons other than on the range. The low hit percentage years turned out to be due primarily to officers *not* seeing their sights when they fired. This led John Cerar to institute a "back to basics" training program when he took over NYPD's Firearms and Tactics Unit, which emphasized the use of the front sight. Soon, progressively, hit percentages crept upward and with more officers using their sights when they fired "for real," actual hits in street gunfights tripled over the previously quoted figure. The people who incorrectly applied that statistic obviously never contacted the NYPD. I did. The facts are there, documented with excruciating thoroughness, for anyone who wants to seek the truth.

*"The effects of epinephrine dumping into your body under stress will make it impossible for your eyes to focus on your sights, so you* **have** *to point shoot!* **UNTRUE, and proven so.** In experiments conducted by the Olympic Training Center and the U.S. Army Marksmanship Training Unit (1981) and at Lethal Force Institute (1998), shooters were injected with doses of epinephrine calibrated to equal the "fight or flight state." In all cases, the shooters were able to see their gun sights with crystal clarity, and to hit what they shot at aiming that way.

*"I've read of people who fired and hit and don't remember seeing their sights."* **UNFOUNDED ARGUMENT.** You've also read about people who didn't remember firing, but they did. A large percentage of gunfight survivors didn't hear their shots, but that doesn't mean their guns were silent. Some remember seeing their sights, and some don't. That doesn't mean they didn't see their sights, any more than not remembering consciously pulling the trigger means they didn't pull it.

### Problems With Point Shooting

Dennis Martin, the martial arts and small arms expert who for some time was Great Britain's coordinator for the International Association of Law Enforcement Firearms Instructors, has little use for point shooting. He told me, "When the SAS had as their primary mission the eradication of enemy soldiers in combat, they taught point shooting with a high volume of gunfire. But as soon as their mission was changed to include hostage rescue, they switched from point shooting to Col. Cooper's concept of the 'flash sight picture.' Now they had to shoot through narrow channels between innocent people, and it would have been irresponsible to do that without aiming their weapons."

This is as clear an explanation of the problems with point shooting as I've ever seen. As an expert witness for the courts in weapons and shooting cases for more than 20 years, I realized early on that again and again, point shooting was culpable when the wrong people were hit by the good guy's fire. One case is mentioned elsewhere in this book. The man "pointed" his .38 for a warning shot and hit, crippling for life, a man he said he was trying to miss. More common are people hitting those other than the ones they're trying to hit. I was retained on behalf of one police officer who "point-shot" at the tire of a car that was going toward a brother officer and instead hit in the head and killed a person inside the vehicle. I was retained on behalf of another who, at little more than arm's length from a murderer trying to shoot him, resorted to the point shooting he had been taught and missed with all but one shot. The one hit, almost miraculously, nailed the bad guy in the arm and cut the radial nerve, preventing his attacker from pulling the trigger. But one of his misses struck, and horribly crippled for life, an innocent bystander – one of the potential victims the officer was trying to protect.

You don't need too many cases like that to understand why true

*A shooter attempts point shooting. Note the widely scattered hits even at very close range.*

point shooting, firing without being able to see where the gun is oriented, can quickly pass the point of diminishing returns. Law school students are taught that the exemplar of recklessness is a "blind man with a gun." A person who is firing a gun when they can't see whether or not it's on target is, in effect, a blind man with a gun. It could be eloquently argued in court that, *ipso facto,* firing without being able to see where the gun is aimed creates recklessness. In turn, recklessness is the key ingredient in the crime of Manslaughter and in a civil court lawsuit based on Wrongful Death or Wrongful Injury.

Enough said?

### Point Shooting Alternatives

If there isn't time for a precise, perfect marksman's sight picture, at the closer distances it will suffice to simply be able to see the gun superimposed over the target. As noted earlier, if you can see the gun, it's aimed fire. Now it's just a matter of how precise the visual index is. Let's analyze the precision, from the most precise on down.

A classic marksman's sight picture, with that 1/8-inch-wide front sight visible in the rear sight's notch, level on top and with an equal amount of light on either side, is absolutely "do-able" in combat. Countless gunfight and military battle survivors have proven it. In Jim Cirillo's most famous gun battle, his strongest memory was seeing the front sight of his S&W Model 10 in such stark clarity that he was aware of every imperfection in the tiny grooves machined across its surface. In that gunfight, he shot three men in three seconds, and he shot one of them out from behind a hostage. Bill Allard was the one guy on the NYPD Stakeout Squad who shot more armed criminals in the line of duty than Jim, and he told me he always saw his sights. His strongest memory of *his* most famous gunfight, a pistolero and a rifleman that he took out in a hail of bullets, was seeing the front sight of his handgun so sharply that he could have counted the grooves in it. Ed Mireles, the hero of the infamous 1986 FBI shootout in Miami, told me that among his most vivid memories were the giant white ball that was the front sight of his Remington 870 12-gauge shotgun, and the giant orange front sight of his S&W Model 686 revolver, as he fired the shots that blew away the two cop-killers in question.

*An instructor demonstrates the protected gun position at National Tactical Invitational at Gunsite.*

Next down the list of precision is the "flash sight picture" popularized by Jeff Cooper. The sights are more or less in line, but you're not trying for a perfect image. You just quickly verify that they're on target and break the shot. It can be done at surprisingly high speed.

Ratchet down one more notch on the coarseness level to the StressPoint Index, a concept I developed in the 1970s and published in the 1980s. You're focused on the target – something you always have to be prepared for

*Firearms instructor and combat pistol champ Andy Cannon has just shown an entire class of students that their guns are sighted in close enough...*

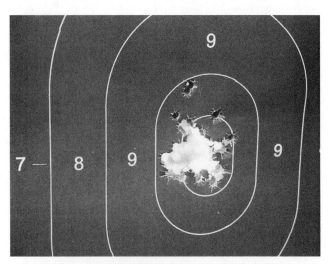

*...by putting six shots from each into this heart-size group. Try that with point shooting!*

because nature makes us look at what threatens us – and over the spot on the threat you want to hit, you see superimposed the image of a front sight sitting on top of a rear sight. Break the shot, and if you're inside 7 yards or so, that spot you're focused on is exactly where you'll see the bullet strike. Todd Jarrett rediscovered this concept later, calling it "shooting out of the notch" to describe the front sight's orientation with the rear, and he won national and world championships with it at super-speed.

One more notch down and you have what master gunfighter Jim Cirillo calls the "silhouette" technique. You see just the silhouette of your gun superimposed over the target. If you know your gun, you can tell instantly from the shape if it's "on." The rear of the cylinder will be round instead of oblong, and the "safety wings" of a Smith & Wesson or Beretta standard model auto will be silhouetted. Don't hesitate, break the shot. You're there.

The better shooting technique systems that have been called "point shooting," the ones that actually work such as Applegate's, all bring the gun up to the line of sight so high that it will intrude into the cone of tunnel vision. As Cirillo has said, you'll see it subliminally even if you don't see it consciously. That will let you hit at close range. That will give you a good chance of getting through the fight.

### Bottom Line

If the gun is where you can see it at close range, you can hit. You're visually indexing your gunfire. You're aiming. Perhaps you're aiming crudely instead of precisely, but you're aiming. If the gun is where you cannot see it, it can be argued that you are not really in control of it. You're relying on a body position index. There are problems with that.

The body position index only works on a static range. You can get yourself set up exactly with the target, then go through the motions and repeat the alignment. But this is false to reality. On the street, the opponent may be above or below you. As soon as he moves laterally, as he undoubtedly will unless he has a death wish or is

terminally stupid, all the coordinates will break and you'll be back to being a "blind man with a gun."

The ultimate boast of shooters is, "If I can see it, I can hit it." This is admittedly a bit over the top. You and I can both see the moon and the sun, but neither of us can hit them with a bullet. But there is a corollary here: *if we can't see the gun in relation to its target, we probably can't hit the target.*

We live in a world where if we fire for real and don't hit the target dead center, it can remain hostile long enough to murder us or those we love. We live in a world where if we launch a deadly bullet when we can't see the predictable course it will take, we can not only expect to perpetrate a tragedy, but expect to pay dearly for it in both criminal and civil court.

That's the problem with point shooting. If you are truly convinced that your main plan of action should be to fire in self-defense without being able to see where your gun is pointing, do yourself a favor and at least equip the weapon with a laser sight.

One rationale the author can see for hip shooting: you've been manacled behind your back with your own cuffs and have sneaked out your backup gun. This is a great argument for a laser sight! Note that one shot has gone low right out of the vital zone.

*Author can point shoot when he has to, as in this required stage on three targets in tight time frames at first National Tactical Invitational. He finished in the top 10. The pistol is a Colt Government Model stainless by D.R. Middlebrooks.*

# CHAPTER SEVEN

# Defensive Handgun Ammunition Selection

## Morgue Monsters And Jello Junkies

Handgun "stopping power" has been a topic of heated debate for more than half a century. The debate shows little sign of fading away.

On one side are those concerned primarily with field results. In their forefront are Evan Marshall, a retired homicide detective and SWAT instructor from the Detroit PD, and his colleague Edwin Sanow, a trained engineer who has been accepted by the courts as an expert on the topic. Marshall's research of several thousand shootings has been compiled in books from Paladin Press including *Handgun Stopping Power* and *Street Stoppers*, co-authored by Sanow. Their research indicates that in certain calibers, medium- or slightly lighter than medium-weight bullets at high velocities have the most immediate effect on felons who are shot. Those calibers include 9mm Luger (115-grain JHP at +/- 1,300 fps) and .357 Magnum (125-grain SJHP at +/- 1,400 fps). They have also found that in some calibers, the heaviest projectiles normally encountered, moving at moderate velocities, did the best job. These include .38 Special (158-grain LHP at +/- 850 fps) and .45 Auto (230-grain JHP at +/- 850 fps).

On the other side of the fence are those led by Dr. Martin Fackler and an organization he created called International Wound Ballistics Association (IWBA). Fackler's theory, based largely on measurement of wound paths in a specific 10 percent formula of ballistic gelatin that he created, is that penetration of at least 12-inches in the human body is essential to hit vital organs. This favors the heaviest available bullet, traveling at moderate velocity. In .45 Auto and .38 Special, both sides are in agreement. In 9mm Luger, they are not, with Fackler and his colleagues recommending the subsonic 147-grain JHP at +/- 970 fps.

Those who follow the street research believe that if lab research isn't proven by what happens in the field, the lab research, by definition, must be flawed. Those who believe in the lab research cite its repeatability, noting that every shooting is at least subtly different from every other.

Who is right? Each side has a piece of the puzzle. The laboratory research can explain to us why certain rounds may work better than others. It can predict a round that will dangerously over-penetrate, or which will break up so soon it won't reach vital organs in time to stop a murder attempt. But field results assembled over time do, quite definitely, point to certain trends. When we ignore what happens in the real world, we do so at our peril.

*Vern Geberth, who wrote the authoritative text on homicide investigation, felt that all 9mm rounds were highly lethal. Shown is SIG P226 with 115-grain hollow-points.*

*Before the bullet matters, it must hit the target. A stock Ruger P90 .45 has just put five rounds of inexpensive Remington-UMC training hardball into about 1-1/4 inches, center to center, at 25 yards.*

## The Scope of the Task

How a gunshot wound causes a violent human being to cease hostilities is a much more complicated question than it sounds. IWBA feels that only three such mechanisms exist, and only two can be reliably counted upon. Disruption of the central nervous system can do it. So can the effect of hemorrhage when it reaches the point that there is insufficient flow of oxygenated blood to sustain consciousness. IWBA indicates that any "stop" not attributable to one or the other of these two mechanisms must be attributable to psychological surrender; basically, the opponent wimped out after he was shot.

Central nervous system (CNS) impairment will certainly work. So, obviously, will massive hemorrhage, though the latter will take time. Most physicians agree that if the brain is fully oxygenated at the moment of the shot, the patient can maintain consciousness and perform physical action for up to about 14 seconds *even if the heart stops completely at the shot.* Thus, the great many instant one-shot incapacitations that we have on record in which the bullet's path never touched brain or spinal cord cannot be explained away by blood loss. Many of these individuals were hard fighters, impervious to fear, and it is most unlikely that a psychological dread of being shot caused them to faint.

Dr. Dennis Tobin, a neurologist, has hypothesized that a mechanism called "neural shock" can cause collapse from a gunshot wound even when vital organs are not permanently damaged. Others believe that the temporary cavitation around the wound track, which becomes larger as velocity increases, has the effect of stunning organs that sustain no permanent, quantifiable damage. This flies in the face of the IWBA theory that only tissue actually destroyed by the bullet's passing will materially contribute to incapacitation. Yet it has happened too many times to ignore.

Chuck Karwan, who wrote *The Complete Book of Combat Handgunnery* two editions ago, did an absolutely excellent essay on this concept in those pages. A military combat veteran and advanced martial artist, he noted that blows to many parts of the body could cause instant incapacitation, yet leave no permanent wound cavity per se. Since many of the men so incapacitated were

*Bullet designer and multiple gunfight survivor Jim Cirillo believes bullet design is critical. Here he shows the importance of a sharp-shouldered bullet when a projectile strikes hard bone on an oblique angle.*

hardened, trained fighters willingly in the ring, it is hard to imagine that they fainted or otherwise experienced a "psychological stop" because someone punched them.

Those who disagree with Sanow and Marshall attack their statistics and their interpretation of them. Statistics can be argued. Reality cannot. During the period the Indianapolis Police Department issued the 125-grain .357 Magnum hollow-points at about 1,400 feet per second, some 220 violent felony suspects were shot with that round by IPD officers. City officials told me there was never an effective return of fire from a felon hit with one of these bullets in the torso. The Kentucky State Police had essentially the same experience with the same load. The Illinois State Police for almost 20 years carried the 115-grain +P+ hollow-points at 1,300 fps velocity. It worked so well in their troopers' many gunfights that it became known as the Illinois State Police load among the nation's cops and gun enthusiasts.

Yet because both rounds are designed to penetrate 9 to 11 inches and stop, after having created a massively wide wound path, both are seen as inadequate by the IWBA because they do not meet IDPA's mandatory 12 inches of penetration in the gelatin used to simulate muscle tissue. One memorable gelatin test of the early 1990s gave the 9mm 115-grain/1,300 fps load a wound value of zero, even though it had caused the wound cavities with the largest volume, because by design none of the projectiles reached the foot-deep penetration mark! The bullets instead averaged between 9 inches and 10 inches of bullet penetration. This is about the depth of the average adult male chest, front to back. That interpretation would have been laughable enough, had it not been for the fact that the same report listed a .380 hollow-point as having a "minus" wound value. Presumably, if you were shot with it you would feel better than had you not been shot at all. Such interpretations destroy any value of the underlying work that went into the testing, which is a shame.

Dr. Bruce Ragsdale at the Armed Forces Institute of Pathology embedded pig aortas in Fackler gelatin. He noted that when a round like the ISP load passed close to the vessel without actually striking it, the stretch cavity was still sufficient to transect the aorta – that is, to tear it

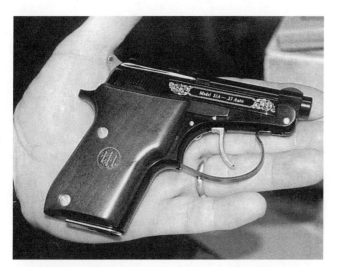

*Both sides of the ammo controversy agree that .25 autos like this Beretta Model 21A are insufficiently powerful for self-defense.*

*Most would agree that the .480 Ruger, a powerful, deep-penetrating cartridge intended for hunting large game, is probably too hard to control and penetrates too deeply for most to consider for self-defense against humans.*

apart. He presented those findings at a bona fide wound trauma conference. A senior IWBA official, who was present, never uttered a peep…but continued to write that, at handgun velocities, only tissue actually touched by the bullet and damaged by it would contribute to incapacitation. Hmmm…

More than a decade ago I sat down in an outdoor café with a physician who is an apostle for the "deep-penetrating bullet" theory. I gave him the names of personnel at the Indianapolis Police Department and the Kentucky State Police who would confirm the real-world performance of the 125-grain Magnum ammunition he said was over-rated and ineffective. He replied that there was no need to do so, because the gelatin told the whole story.

It was this attitude that caused Evan Marshall to coin the term "Jello Junkies" for those who would not venture beyond the laboratory environment to correlate their theories with real-world findings. It was a gun magazine editor who coined the term "Morgue Monsters" for those who felt that only the results of actual shootings would tell the tale. The two sides have remained at odds with one another ever since, with some very acrimonious comments being issued. Interestingly, most of the personal attacks have been by followers of the IWBA dogma attacking Marshall and Sanow. Make of that what you will.

The problem with this dichotomy is that both sides have authoritative backgrounds. When two experts disagree, who is the layman to believe? The person who carries a gun for serious self-defense is now in the position of a juror assessing conflicting expert testimony in a court case. It becomes necessary to compare the arguments and weigh them in light of logic, common sense, and life experience.

That's what we'll attempt to do in the following pages.

# Recommended Loads

There are so many different calibers and loads that we can't cover them all here. That would take a separate book. In fact, Marshall and Sanow have written more than one book on the topic and they still haven't covered all the load combinations! Therefore, let's stick with the most popular and most effective of the self-defense calibers.

We won't be working with .480 Ruger, .454 Casull, or .50 Desert Eagle. These big boomers are hunting rounds and generally too powerful for personal defense. Nor will we work with cartridges so tiny and notoriously impotent that most police departments forbid their officers to carry them even as backup. The .22 and the .25 auto can certainly kill, but they can't always *stop*, which is a different thing altogether. Such small rounds require literally surgical bullet placement, with the primary point of aim being deep brain. However, both are notorious for ricocheting off human skulls, so where does that leave you?

**.32 Auto.** It is a little known fact that NYPD became the first police department to issue semiautomatics early in the 20th century, with a quantity of Colt .32s. They got away from them in part because they were too feeble, and the department standardized on the .38 Special revolvers instead, many of which remain in service. European police departments issued .32s for decades because the sidearm was seen as a badge of office, and these small autos were convenient and had a low-key look. Then terrorism and violent crime struck Europe, and the cops needed real guns; they switched en masse to .38 Special revolvers and 9mm autos.

Today, thanks to the defining Seecamp LWS-32, pistols the size of .25s are now available in this caliber, and it has become an in-thing to carry them. Various hollow-points are available. All open sometimes. None open all the time. The Winchester Silvertip was the .32 cartridge the Seecamp was built around, and has the best track record. The Marshall Study shows a surprisingly high one-shot stop rate, but also includes a disproportionate number of strong-arm robbers and rapists or attackers with clubs

*The Seecamp .32 auto was made to work with Silvertip ammo, which is as good an ammo choice as any in that caliber.*

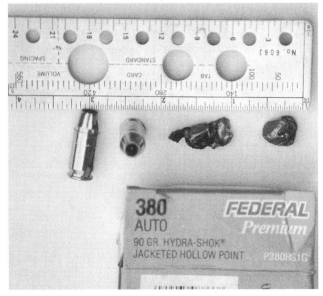

*This is what a .380 Hydra-Shok looks like after being fired into living tissue.*

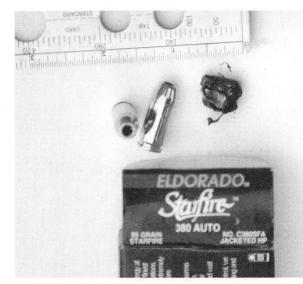

*PMC StarFire's bullet, designed by Tom Burczynski, is as dynamic an expander as you will find in .380 caliber. This one was retrieved from a slaughterhouse test.*

and knives instead of guns, who may have simply given up after realizing they were up against a gun and had already been shot once. Still, the Silvertip has the most established track record, and when I carry my own Seecamp .32, it's the round I choose.

**.380 Auto.** Known in Europe as the "9mm Short," this round seems to constitute the acceptable minimum dividing line in defensive handgun potency. Some experts will say it's barely adequate, and the others will say it's barely inadequate. The ball rounds penetrate too deeply and can ricochet, creating narrow, puckered wounds in the meantime. The hollow-points, when they open, may not go deep enough.

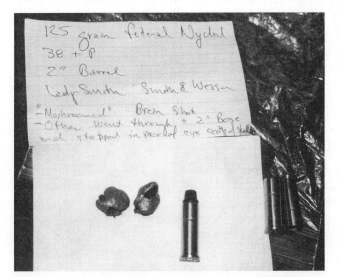

*Federal Nyclad Chief Special load, a standard pressure, nylon-jacketed 125-grain hollow-point, gives the most dynamic bullet performance the author has seen in a low-recoil .38 Special cartridge. Note the significant expansion even when fired from 2-inch barrel into living flesh and bone.*

In some of our advanced classes, we have the student kill a large animal with their carry gun and load, then dissect the wound to see what it did. Seven times now I've seen .380 JHPs either stop in the frontal wall of the skull or ricochet around the skull to the ear. Not impressive. These days, for students with the smaller gun, we use very small swine to prevent torturing the animal. All animals used in this way were destined to be slaughtered for meat on the given day anyway, but a clean and painless death is ethically required here. The .380 doesn't seem to deliver that reliably.

I haven't run across an actual shooting yet with the Remington Golden Saber, which at 102 grains is the heaviest bullet available for the .380. I did shoot a hog with it on one occasion. The bullet just got through the frontal wall of the skull and barely touched the brain. Most JHPs weigh 85 to 90 grains. Winchester Silvertip and Federal Hydra-Shok seem to lead the pack and perform about the same.

**.38 Special.** This is the universally accepted minimum or above-minimum load for self-defense. With certain loads, it's far below minimum. The classic example is the old 158-grain lead round nose. It provides too much penetration and too little stopping power. For most of the 20th century, this round was the police standard, and only the commanders who issued it had anything good to say about it. Street cops called it "the widow-maker" because so many times, an officer would empty it into his attacker, and the assailant would live long enough to still make the cop's wife a widow.

Hollow-points work better, but not all hollow-points are created equal. Where low recoil is imperative – a very light revolver, or a .38 in a very frail hand – the best of the standard pressure, mild-kicking loads seems to be the Federal NyClad Chief Special. As the name implies, it was expressly designed for small, light revolvers. The soft lead bullet begins to deform as soon as it hits. We've never seen it fail on large animals in the slaughterhouse, and it showed up well in the Marshall study. The nylon-jacketed bullet weighs 125 grains.

*There is no more proven .38 Special load, even for snubbies like this Taurus Model 85, than 158-grain lead semi-wadcutter hollow-point at +P velocity.*

Head and shoulders, the best .38 Special is the old "FBI load," developed by Winchester in 1972. It is comprised of an all-lead semi-wadcutter bullet with a hollow point at +P velocity. FBI, RCMP, Metro-Dade Police in Miami, St. Louis, Chicago PD, and a great many others used this round in countless gunfights, out of snubbies and service revolvers alike. They all had excellent results with it. Because there is no copper jacket that has to peel back, a design feature that seems to require considerable velocity to work, the soft lead slug seems to open even when fired at lowered velocity from short barrels and even when fired through heavy clothing.

Recoil is snappy in the small, light guns, but very easy to handle in a service revolver. The "FBI load" is a legendary man-stopper. It delivers the performance ammo makers were hoping for with the 147-grain subsonic 9mm at 970 fps. Alas, the copper jacket of the 9mm round didn't always open up the way the lead slug of the .38 FBI load did.

Most brands give reasonably similar performance, though over the years the Winchester has used the hardest lead and the Remington the softest, with the Federal brand in the middle. Evan Marshall's observation that the .38 Special FBI load hit about like GI .45 hardball seems to have been proven out in 30 years of extensive field testing.

**9mm Luger.** Illinois State Police were not the only ones to prove that the +P+ 115-grain JHP at 1,300 feet per second was the best man-stopper in this caliber. U.S. Border Patrol and Secret Service found the same in extensive study of real-world experience. ISP used mostly the Winchester brand, Border Patrol the Federal, and Secret Service the Remington. There was little difference between the brands, which had one other thing in common: all were sold to police only, and not to the general public.

However, CCI Speer has recently released this load to the law-abiding public with the Gold Dot bullet. An identical cartridge produced with top quality has been available for some time as the Pro-Load Tactical, and the Triton Hi-Vel is very similar.

124-grain "hot loads" at about 1,250 feet per second also have a good track record. The Gold Dot in this format has worked splendidly for NYPD since its adoption in 1999, and is also the 9mm load of choice for the Denver Police Department.

Many older guns won't stand up to these high pressure loads in constant shooting, and some people don't like the little extra jolt of recoil they give. In the same size gun, a +P or +P+ 9mm kicks about the same as a standard pressure .40 S&W load. In a modest recoil 9mm, history has shown us that you can't beat the Federal Classic 9BP, a 115-grain JHP at about 1,150 feet per second. It is standard issue for Philadelphia PD and New Jersey State Police at this time; both have had many shootings with it, and been satisfied with the results.

Most law enforcement agencies that adopted the 147-grain JHP subsonic, as noted above, have gotten away from it after disappointing results in the field. Expansion failures and overpenetrations occurred too often. While some departments, such as Las Vegas Metro and Jacksonville simply went to faster-moving 115-grain JHPs, others simply bought more powerful guns that fired the .40 Smith & Wesson, the .357 SIG, or the .45 ACP. LAPD, LA County and Chicago PD got around the 147-grain subsonic's perceived weaknesses by authorizing privately-owned .45 autos for those who didn't trust the slow-bullet 9mm ammo.

*Federal's 9BP 115-grain load is the most effective standard-pressure 9mm cartridge the author has found. It worked very well for many years for the New Jersey State Police in their HK P7M8 pistols such as the one shown.*

*The Remington 115-grain JHP 9mm proved accurate in this STI Trojan pistol, but higher-velocity versions of the same round have been more dynamic "on the street."*

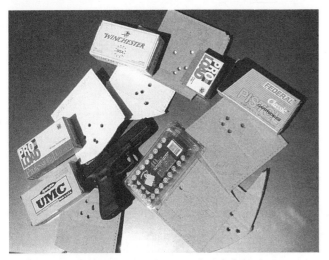

*Accuracy of given load in given gun is a definite factor. These are assorted .40 S&W cartridges, fired from Glock 22 at 25 yards.*

*With 135-grain/1,300 fps ammo for personal defense needs and 165-grain/1,150 fps for police service use, the 16-shot (with pre-ban magazines) .40 caliber Glock 22 is a potent sidearm indeed.*

*Federal's standard 155-grain JHP .40 has proven itself well in the field in pistols like this Beretta 96D Centurion.*

**.40 S&W.** Conceptualized by Paul Liebenberg and Tom Campbell at Smith & Wesson and created by them and Winchester, the .40 Smith & Wesson was simply a 10mm Short. Indeed, the sarcastic called it the .40 Short and Weak when it was introduced in 1990. Intended to be a bridge between the 16-shot 9mm and the 8-shot .45, the 12-shot .40 proved to be a viable compromise. Within a few years it was the most popular law enforcement cartridge as measured by new gun orders.

With its original load of a 180-grain subsonic bullet at 980 fps, it was indeed a viable compromise, and it worked out better than many of us feared it would, though it still had some tendency to overpenetrate. As new loads were developed that performed better, many saw the .40 as upscaling from compromise to optimization.

The 165-grain bullets at 1,150 fps and 155-grain slugs at 1,200 or better, dubbed "cruiserweights" by gun expert Dean Spier, passed all the FBI barricade and gelatin tests and still expanded and created significant wounds. Border Patrol reports excellent results with the 155-grain Remington and Federal JHPs, Nashville has experienced extraordinary performance with the Winchester taloned hollow-point weighting 165 grains The 165-grain Gold Dot bullet as loaded by Speer delivers similar performance, and when the same projectile is loaded as the hot EXP by Black Hills, performance plus match-grade accuracy is achieved.

Dick Kelton conceptualized the 135-grain .40 caliber hollow-point at 1,300 fps in the early 1990s, and I convinced a small ammunition company to manufacture the load after extremely impressive slaughterhouse testing results. When the first field shooting report came in, it was from a coroner's office asking what sort of explosive had been put in the bullet! Striking in the abdomen a man who was attempting to stab a police officer, the 135-grain JHP had flung him back and to the ground. He was clinically dead within 10 seconds, a result not explainable by an abdominal wound, however massive this one was.

The 135-grain/1,300 fps combination is now available with excellent quality control in the Pro-Load Tactical and Triton Hi-Vel lines, using the same well-proven Nosler projectile. Its 10-inch wound depth, however wide the wound, does not excite police who want their ammo to pass FBI 12-inch penetration/barrier protocols, but is ideal for armed citizen self-defense scenarios as they generally unfold.

**.357 SIG.** What is, in essence a .40 S&W cartridge necked down to take a 9mm bullet, the .357 SIG was an attempt to gain .357 Magnum power level in a moderately sized auto pistol. It clearly succeeded. The cartridge is now in use by the state troopers of Delaware, New Mexico, North Carolina, Texas, and Virginia. It replaced the +P+ 9mm ammunition of the Secret Service and the Air Marshals. Simply put, the latter two agencies liked what they got out of a 115-grain 9mm bullet at 1,300 fps, and figured they'd get more of it with a 125-grain 9mm bullet at 50 to 100 feet per second greater velocity.

They were right. With the cartridge in use for several years, uniformly excellent results have been reported. Richmond, VA has had seven shootings at this writing, all very fast stops. In only one was the suspect shot several times, probably because he was attempting to murder a downed officer and brother officers hosed him as fast as they could pull the triggers of their *Sig Pro* pistols. In a Texas shootout, a veteran trooper shot at the gunman ensconced in a semi-tractor trailer, but the bullets from his .45 did not go through. His rookie partner's SIG P-226 spat a .357 SIG Gold Dot through the cab and through the gunman's brain, killing him. Richmond noted that despite 16-inches of penetration in gelatin, all the 125-grain .357 SIG Gold Dots they've fired into men have stayed in the bodies, or in the clothing on the opposite side.

One Virginia trooper told me that what impressed him the most about the .357 SIG was that it dropped offenders instantly even when hit in non-vital areas like the abdomen. Numerous officers noted that it delivered instant one-shot stops on pit bulls, when in the past they'd had to pump round after round of 147-grain 9mm subsonic into similar animals. While 115-grain through 150-grain loads exist, virtually all shootings on record have been made with the 125-grain round. The Gold Dot is the most proven.

The .357 SIG has drawn the wrath of at least one critic, who insisted that it was no better than 9mm subsonic and that its massive temporary wound cavity surrounding the bullet's path was irrelevant. The cops just rolled their eyes, reviewed their dynamic real-world results, and kept carrying their .357 SIGs.

**.357 Magnum:** Amply represented in police gunfights since its inception in 1935, the original 158-grain flat-nose bullet load immediately earned a reputation for excessive penetration that continued when hollow-point bullets of the same weight were introduced. Not until Super Vel introduced a high velocity 110-grain hollow-point did law enforcement have a .357 round that would stay in a felon's body and use its energy effectively. When Remington introduced the 125-grain hollow-point at 1,450 fps, the round hit its stride. With a wound channel 9 inches to 11 inches deep and massively wide, it set the all-time standard for one-shot stops in actual field shootings. The price, however, was a nasty kick, an ear-splitting blast, and a blinding muzzle flash. Nonetheless, the full power 125-grain remains the clear winner of the .357 Magnum defense load sweepstakes.

**10mm Auto.** Touted in the mid-1980s as the long-sought "ultimate man-stopper," the 10mm's popularity got a shot in the arm when the FBI adopted the caliber in the late 1980s. Unfortunately, to make recoil more

*Speer Gold Dot 125-grain .357 SIG has given dynamic street performance in many shootings. The pistol is full-size P226.*

*Winchester Ranger 165-grain high-velocity .40 load has been spectacularly successful for Nashville (TN) Metro Police. Greg Lee of that department demonstrates with an issue Glock 22 service pistol.*

controllable they watered down the power to the level of a .40 subsonic. The FBI load for 10mm was jokingly called a "minus-P". Prior to that, most of the ammo available for the 10mm was hard-jacketed, deep-penetrating stuff better suited to hunting hogs than anti-personnel work. When people were shot with it, it tended to go all the way through without having much immediate visible effect. Interest had waned in the caliber before the really promising anti-personnel ammo, 155 grains at 1,300 fps or 135 grains at 1,450 fps, had a chance to be represented in actual gunfights.

Flat-shooting and accurate, the 10mm like the .41 Magnum never had a chance to prove itself. The author carries one frequently as a personal weapon, generally loaded with 155-grain JHP at 1,300.

**.45 Auto.** All those 20th century gunwriters weren't exaggerating when they called the .45 ACP (Automatic Colt Pistol) round a "legendary man-stopper" even before hollow-point bullets became available for it. Hollow-points just made it more effective and less likely to dangerously overpenetrate.

There are 165-grain JHPs available for it at a screaming 1,250 fps, but to my knowledge no one has ever been shot with one and its real-world ability remains unproven. However, Remington's 185-grain +P at 1,140 fps and similar loads by other makers have been well proven in the field, and are among top choices in the caliber. What you're losing in extra recoil, you're gaining in a flatter trajectory. The +P 185-grain .45 shoots like a full-power 10mm and allows easy hits on man-size targets out to 100 yards and beyond. This would be the load of choice if the mission profile included likelihood of long shots. Because short-barrel .45s lose velocity dramatically, some feel the +P load is a logical compensation when loaded in a "snubby" auto of that caliber.

For typical pistol distances, jacketed hollow-points with the same ballistics as the GI ball round proven for more than nine decades (230-grain bullet at 830 to 850 fps from a 5-inch barrel) have earned undisputed top dog status. With the high-tech hollow-points, more shootings have occurred with the Federal Hydra-Shok than any of the others, but we also get excellent reports on the Winchester SXT, the Remington Golden Saber, and CCI Gold Dot. In one slaughterhouse test, the PMC StarFire outperformed all of them by a slight margin. There are many good loads to pick from here. The high-tech modern bullets mentioned in the last couple of lines were all expressly designed to open even at reduced velocity when fired from short-barreled guns.

Another advantage of the 230-grain standard-velocity round is that once you know the full-price hollow-points will feed in your weapon, practice with relatively inexpensive "generic hardball" gives you the exact same recoil and point of aim/point of impact as the duty load.

These are the rounds this writer would personally recommend. Some go more toward the Fackler side of the house, and some more toward the Marshall/Sanow side. What do you do when you're advising someone who is torn between those two authoritative sources? Why, you find something both sides agree on, and we'll look at that next.

*Federal's 230-grain Hydra-Shok is seen by many as the "gold standard" for .45 auto rounds at regular pressures. This is what one looks like after impacting living flesh and bone. The pistol used was a Springfield Armory, with a 5-inch barrel.*

# Compromise Ammo

When life just isn't black and white, a shade of gray is often the real-world middle ground. Sometimes we just have to compromise.

Let's say it's the early 1990s, and you are the head of firearms training for a 100-officer department. The chief wants to go to one standard pistol for all armed personnel. Half your guys and gals like the firepower of the typical 16-shot 9mm. The other half are more concerned about per-shot power, and want eight-shot .45s. The solution, of course, is the 12 shot .40 S&W. Each side gives a little, gets a little, and can claim to have won the argument. Now everyone is free of the controversy and can focus on what really wins gunfights: mindset and preparedness, proper tactics, and shooting skill.

But what if the caliber has already been selected, and the argument is what load to select? If the troops have

been reading the gun magazines or are on the net, and you have 50 of them in the Marshall/Sanow camp and 50 on the Fackler side, a decision for one side will tick off the other. Far worse, it will leave half your troops with a lack of confidence, and confidence is always one of the cornerstones of competence.

The trick is to find rounds that both sides agree on. Believe it or not, they exist. Let's look at the serious calibers only.

**.38 Special: The old FBI Load.** Previously, we discussed the .38 Special lead semi-wadcutter hollow-point at +P velocity. This is the round recommended for the .38 Special by the group Dr. Fackler founded and leads, the IWBA. It has also been at the top of the Marshall/Sanow list in the caliber more times than not.

*The author's department issues Black Hills 230-grain .45 ACP for their Ruger P-90 duty weapons...*

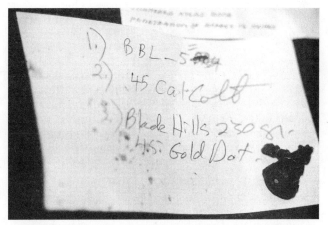

*...and this is one reason why. Massive expansion of the Gold Dot bullet has caused a large wound at the proper depth in living tissue. Both sides of the stopping power argument agree on a 230-grain JHP at 850 fps.*

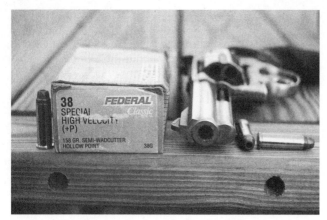

*For a .357 Magnum revolver like this S&W Model 686, the only defense load both sides agree on is the old FBI .38 Special round, a +P all-lead semi-wadcutter hollow-point.*

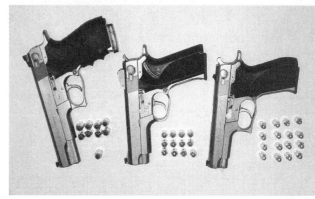

*Caliber is one of the compromise options. You could choose (from the left) a nine-shot .45, a 12-shot .40 or a 16-shot 9mm. The .40 splits the difference. These are all S&W pistols; the 4506, 4006 and 5906.*

There has been the occasional year where lighter, faster bullets seemed to be working better in recently compiled shootings, but over all the years Marshall's work has been published, it has led the pack in .38 Special. This has been true with snub-nose revolvers as well as service-size guns with longer barrels.

When *these* two warring factions agree on something, it's got to be good. The consensus is almost universal among serious professionals. The lead SWCHP +P is street-proven *and* lab-proven as the best .38 Special self-defense load there is.

**.45 ACP: 230-grain JHP.** Both sides find this type of cartridge the top choice in the caliber. They seem to differ only on the brand choice. The Marshall Study has consistently put the Federal Hydra-Shok ahead of other rounds of its type, though not by much. Fackler has stated that he considered the old Winchester Black Talon (which in .45 ACP was a 230-grain at standard velocity) to be the greatest advance in handgun ammo since the hollow-point bullet.

Personally, I've found the Hydra to open a little more consistently than some others, and to be truly match-grade in accuracy, for whatever that's worth in combat ammo selection. But the FBI uses the Remington Golden Saber in 230-grain. I've seen 230-grain Gold Dots dug out of human flesh, and the mushrooming was impressive. My own department issues that bullet in the accurate Black Hills duty round, loaded to hit 850 feet per second from the 4-1/4-inch barrels on our issue guns, and I'm extremely comfortable carrying it. As noted in the previous chapter, one test I performed comparing hi-tech 230-grain .45 ACP JHP in the slaughterhouse resulted in the PMC StarFire showing very slightly more tissue disruption than in any of the others. Really, it's almost a coin toss.

The point is, both sides agree. The issue is resolved. The .45 Auto shooter can now move on to those things mentioned above that will *really* win the fight.

**.40 S&W: 180-grain subsonic JHP.** IWBA recommends the original 180-grain subsonic. Marshall and Sanow list other rounds, notably the full-power 135-grain and 155/165-grain loads, as having slightly more stopping power. However, the Federal Hydra-Shok 180-grain subsonic is very close to the top of their .40 charts, and certainly on the list of recommended loads.

Again, the only difference is in the details. Where Evan and Ed rate the Hydra-Shok tops among the subsonic .40s, Marty seems to clearly prefer the Winchester. While I have to side with Sanow and Marshall on the best 9mm and .357 loads simply because my field research comes out yielding the same top rounds as theirs, I have to go to Fackler's side of the line in brand selection among 180-grain subsonic .40 S&W offerings. I've run across several shootings with Winchester's talon-style Ranger load. All but one stayed in the body. All have opened up exactly like a Winchester publicity photo. All have stopped hostilities immediately. The one that exited the offender involved a slender female who was trying to murder an officer. The bullet that punched through her left a massive exit wound and instantly stopped her attempted cop-killing.

Unfortunately, the Ranger load is currently offered only to law enforcement. Fortunately, there is not all *that* much difference. The California Highway Patrol has

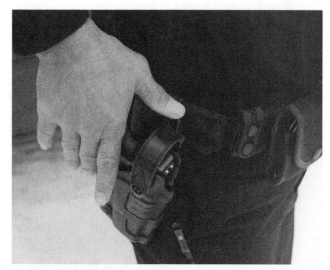

*When you can't decide on a 9mm load you like, reach for a .40 caliber of the same make and model! Both sides of the argument are satisfied with the 180-grain .40 subsonic JHP, though the author loads hotter ammo into his Glock 22, carried here in a Safariland Raptor snatch-resistant duty holster.*

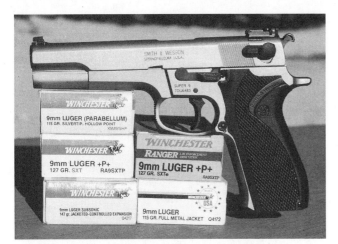

*Which of these 9mm loads is the best? The debate continues. Of those shown, the author would take the 127-grain +P+. The pistol is the S&W Super 9, made for the European market and seldom seen in the U.S.*

issued the ordinary Remington 180-grain subsonic (not the hi-tech Golden Saber version) for most of the time since their 1990 adoption of the .40 S&W cartridge. CHP's thousands of highway patrolmen collectively log a great many shootings. The agency has pronounced itself quite pleased with the performance of that ammunition as well as the performance of their chosen sidearm, the Smith & Wesson Model 4006.

In other calibers, there seems to be no such common ground between the two camps. This is not to say that compromise is not possible.

Let's say your choice of handgun is the .357 Magnum revolver. There is simply no Magnum round on which both sides agree. But any .357 Magnum revolver will fire .38 Special +P ammunition. A logical choice presents itself: Load with the FBI .38 Special formula, and you're good to go.

The 9mm Luger remains one of our most popular caliber choices. There is no 9mm round on which both sides agree; indeed, this caliber has probably been the focus of more argument between the two camps than any other. So, the logical compromise in a 9mm is ... the 180-grain subsonic .40 S&W.

Think about it. Almost any modern handgun you want to buy in 9mm is also available in .40 caliber, sacrificing

only one to four rounds of magazine capacity. Beretta, Glock, Kahr, SIG, Smith & Wesson, Taurus ... even if you prefer the 1911 or the Browning Hi-Power; if the company makes that gun in 9mm they make one identical or almost identical to it in .40 caliber.

Sometimes compromise isn't possible. Sometimes, though, it's a necessity. And sometimes it's a good thing, because it gets us past the small arguments so we can focus on more important matters.

The placement of the shot will be more important than the "wound profile" of the bullet we launch. Tactics that put us where we can shoot the offender more quickly and easily than the offender can shoot us, may be even more important than shot placement. And being alert enough to see danger signs in time to avoid being shot at all might be more important still.

That said, the ammunition in our gun is one of the few variables in a violent encounter that we can control before the fight starts, and we'd be fools not to load the most effective ammunition for the purpose. One thing that is not examined enough is tailoring the ammunition to its "mission profile."

You wouldn't hunt small antelope and moose with the same ammunition. Different jobs require different tools. If you were a police officer on rolling stakeout, tracking armed offenders and pulling them over at opportune times, it would be reasonable to expect that you would often have to fire through auto bodies and auto glass, and you would want ammo with deep tactical penetration. If you were the court security officer in a crowded Hall of Justice designed by an architect who thought marble was the key to structure, you have much greater concerns about over-penetration and ricochet, and this could and should alter your approach to ammunition selection.

Pick something suitable for the task, something that has already been proven on the street as well as tested in the laboratory. Don't be "the first on your block" to get the cool new ammo that is the subject of full page ads in gun magazines, but has never been used for its intended purpose and thus, in real world terms, remains untried. Let someone else be the guinea pig. In this discipline, the price of failure is simply too great.

Getting bogged down in one corner of a multi-dimensional discipline will not serve you well. There is a legal maxim that is on point to this: *De minimus non curat lex.*

The law does not bother with trifles.

# Since The Last Edition

Between the Fifth Edition of this book and this Sixth, forests have possibly been denuded for gun magazine articles and bandwidth sacrificed on the Internet for the discussion of stopping power, but in reality remarkably little has changed.

The fast, medium-weight bullets have further proven their value on the street in 9mm, specifically the Winchester Ranger 127-grain +P+ and the Speer Gold Dot 124-grain +P. The latter was adopted by the Chicago PD after numerous dismal failures with assorted 147-grain subsonic JHPs, and no complaints have arisen since the ammo change. The NYPD, many more shootings later, is reportedly delighted with the performance of the +P 124-grain Gold Dot.

Ironically, the 147-grain subsonic has finally grown into its promise with current iterations of Speer Gold Dot, Winchester Ranger, and Federal's new HST ammunition, but in the last half-decade still more departments have just dumped the 9mm and gone to something bigger, or optionalized something bigger, or gone to faster 9mm rounds as Chicago did. Today's 147-grain high-tech subsonic is the best ever, but still not quite up to the 127-grain +P+, the 115-grain +P+, or the 124-grain +P.

The .357 SIG continues its triumphant march, with a few more state police agencies adopting it after the splendid success it has enjoyed in street shootings in Texas, Virginia and elsewhere. Most are using SIGs in either the full-size P226 or the more compact P229 format

*A 230-grain .45 GAP bullet, from a 5-inch Springfield XDLE, has slightly outpenetrated its .45 ACP equivalent from a 5-inch Springfield 1911A1, above. Both are Winchester Ranger 230-grain JHPs.*

*The 5.7mm FN pistol has generated much controversy, but not yet any substantial confidence. Author does not yet consider it "a player" in the combat handgun world.*

(the latter is also the choice of Secret Service and Air Marshals), but the state troopers of New Mexico and Tennessee and the conservation officers of Pennsylvania tell me they are delighted with their Glock 31 pistols in the .357 SIG chambering. Other manufacturers have offered this caliber as well.

The big cartridge story of the five years between editions of this book has been, I think, the .45 GAP. As noted in more detail in the chapter on the latest handguns, this .45 **G**lock **A**uto **P**istol cartridge is a .45 **A**utomatic **C**olt **P**istol casing shortened and made stronger with scientific sophistication, thanks to a design team led by Ernest Durham. The shorter round equals, and often exceeds, the one that's been around since shortly after the turn of the 20th century, so long as you compare the .45 GAP to standard pressure .45 ACP. +P .45 ACP will outrun the .45 GAP by as much as it outperforms the standard .45 ACP with the same projectile. However, standard-pressure .45 ACP ballistics

have become something of a gold standard for stopping power, so that puts the .45 GAP in good company.

The *raison d'etre* of the .45 GAP is that it puts .45 ACP performance into a 9mm envelope by using a cartridge the same overall length as the 9x19. In 1990, the .40 S&W became the ultimate compromise cartridge because it delivered *close* to .45 ACP ballistics in the 9mm-size pistol envelope; the .45 GAP goes all the way and delivers *true* .45 ACP performance in that envelope, albeit with somewhat fewer rounds.

*The .357 SIG is solidly ensconced and rising in popularity. Here are but a few of the ammo selections that have been offered in this caliber.*

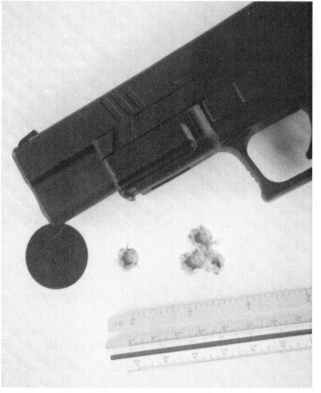

*The .45 GAP has proven to be an accurate cartridge. Author shot this group at 25 yards with Winchester USA 230-grain ball, out of XD45 pistol. Note that 4 of 5 bullet holes are touching.*

*Here are just seven of the assorted loads currently available in .45 GAP.*

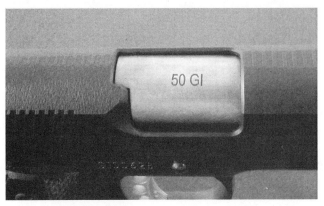

*The new .50 GI cartridge for the 1911 pistol is still a novelty at this time, but may prove to be a player if it becomes a sufficient presence "on the street" to prove itself.*

The world of the gun is a conservative planet, and the .45 GAP was not an immediate bestseller. Fans of the .45 ACP predicted its doom and called it a vanity cartridge because it had the Glock name on it. A few years into its epoch, however, the .45 GAP was adopted by the Georgia State Patrol (eleven-shot G37 model for uniform wear, and a G29 seven-shot subcompact to every trooper for backup and off-duty use). Shortly thereafter New York State Police, disappointed with the effects over many years of 9mm 147-grain subsonic and, toward the end, 124-grain standard pressure JHP, also adopted the Glock in .45 GAP. It is said at this writing that the state police agencies of South Carolina, Pennsylvania, and Kansas may follow. We are probably looking at the beginning of a domino effect, and we don't know yet how far the dominoes will fall.

Ammo for the .45 GAP is now produced by virtually all the big makers and many of the smaller ammunition companies. I've shot guns Springfield Armory has made for it – their short-stroke subcompact 1911 and their standard-size XD, which proved to be deliciously accurate

in the 5-inch Tactical model – and am told that ParaOrdnance is also now making pistols in .45 GAP. Glock, meanwhile, has the standard size G37, the compact G38, and the subcompact G39, all of which seem to work just fine.

To understand why the GAP appeals to law enforcement and some others, listen to the words of a police sergeant in New York State, who wrote me, "I just read your article about the .45 GAP in *Tactical Response*. I chose the G37, G38, and G39 for our department this past spring. You hit the nail on the head when you wrote about the grip frame being a consideration. Our officers favored the G37 frame 10:1 over the G21 frame. We went from a .45 ACP (S&W 4566). The GAP fills our needs: I wanted to keep the .45 ballistics and go to a simpler gun. I just read another article of yours about the problems with the decocking of a pistol. I found this to be true during many Q (qualification) courses. I saw good officers failing to decock or failing to recognize that the decocker/safety had been activated. This was a problem I did not like to see occurring on the range because I know the consequences that could happen on the streets. We went through 85 officers transitioning to the GAP and had no problems attributed to the gun. The guns performed well and were very accurate. We did have some problems with a batch of ammo but Winchester fixed that without any hesitation. All our officers said good things about the Glock and almost everyone shot better than on previous Q courses. Keep up the good work, it is appreciated by the officers." – *Sgt. Dave Iacovissi, Rome, NY Police Department.*

No, this new cartridge won't change the world, and it probably won't outsell Glock's other pistols in more popular and time-proven chamberings. But the .45 GAP has proven itself a real answer to a real problem, and a useful new tool to have on board. I suspect you'll be hearing much more about it several years from now in the next edition of the GUN DIGEST BOOK OF COMBAT HANDGUNNERY. There will be many more investigated shootings with the .45 GAP on file by then. I'm predicting that they'll show just what we're seeing now. In the several gelatin tests I've observed, and in two actual fatal shootings (one with FMJ ball, one with Winchester 230-grain Ranger), the results were instant stop, instant death and penetration and expansion exactly consistent with the same projectiles out of a standard pressure .45 ACP.

*These 230-grain Ranger SXT bullets exhibit near-identical deformation and penetration depth in gelatin. Without the labels, could you tell the recovered projectiles apart? (Photo courtesy Olin)*

# CHAPTER EIGHT

# Defensive Gunleather Today

## Concealment Holsters

Thanks to the enlightened and widespread adoption of "shall-issue" concealed carry legislation, more ordinary American citizens are carrying guns in the 21st century than at any time in the 20th. As determined by Professor John Lott, and others, to a point that can no longer be realistically questioned, this seems to have improved the public safety.

We have more good concealment guns and concealment holsters than ever before. The term "gunleather," once the catch-all for belt, holster, ammo carrier and related accoutrements, must now be expanded to include leather-look synthetics like Uncle Mike's lightweight Mirage, Kydex holsters by countless makers, other related "plastic" technology as exemplified by Fobus, and fabric units ranging from ballistic nylon to Cordura.

Before looking at where the holster goes, let's look at what it's made of.

*Leather* has among its good points tradition, style, and pride of ownership. With the potential for perfect fit, it remains for many the preferred choice. Downsides: requires a modicum of care, may be tight when new and loose when very old, and may squeak if not properly cared for.

*Plastics*, whether Kydex or polymer or whatever, require no break-in. They generally fit perfectly from the start. They are *very* fast, so much so that synthetic holsters now rule all the combat shooting events that include quick-draw. Downsides: they can break, particularly in a struggle for the holstered gun. With rare exceptions like the suede-lined Hellweg, they make a distinctive grating sound when the gun is drawn, which can hamper a surreptitious draw in certain danger situations. They are dramatically cheaper than leather as a rule, quality level for quality level.

*Fabric* "gunleather" is generally the cheapest of all. It rarely offers a perfect fit, but does generally allow silent draw.

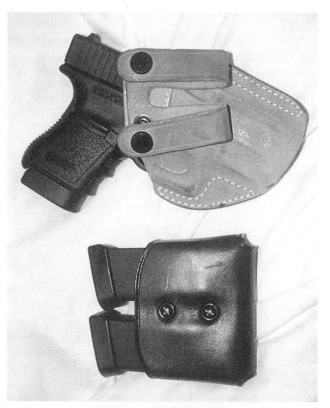

Here a Glock 30 rests in a leather IWB holster, with a double spare magazine pouch, all by Galco.

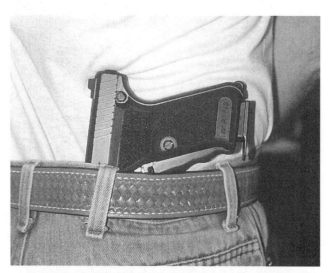

*Carrying a handgun loose in the waistband is never the best idea. This HK P7M8 has shifted position and accidentally released its magazine.*

*Dave Elderton, founder of Ky-Tac, left, discusses his super-fast and super-concealable Kydex holsters with a satisfied customer and national champ, Bob Houzenga.*

Now, let's look at the most street-proven holster styles for lawfully concealed handguns.

### Strong-Side Hip Holsters

For plainclothes police and armed citizens alike, particularly males, this is overwhelmingly the most popular concealment holster site. On the male body, a pistol just behind the hip bone tends to ride very comfortably, and is naturally hidden by the drape of the concealing garment in the hollow of the kidney area. Just behind the ileac crest of the hip is the best location. At the point of the hip, the holstered gun will protrude obviously on one side, and dig at the hip bone on the other. The dominant hand is very close, being on the same side, which is conducive to a tactically sound fast and efficient draw. The dominant-side forearm is in a position to naturally protect the holster.

The higher, more flaring hip of the typical female, plus her proportionally shorter torso, makes the strong-side hip holster work against her. A disproportionate number of females choose to carry their guns in other locations.

### Crossdraw Belt Holsters

Whether you see it spelled crossdraw, cross-draw, or cross draw, it's all the same. We're talking about a belt-mounted holster mounted butt-forward and requiring the dominant hand to reach, to at least some degree across the abdomen for access. Hence, the terminology "crossdraw."

*NRA director and firearms instructor Mike Baker examines the first "tuckable" holster, designed by Dave Workman. The deep area between the belt loop flap and the holster body allows the shirt to be tucked in around a holstered gun. A key chain on the belt loop makes it look harmless. Draw is done with a Hackathorn Rip. This may be the most widely copied of the new concealment holster designs.*

*Uncle Mike's holsters drove the market price downward in Kydex rigs, and work fine. This one holds a Kimber target grade .45 auto with Pachmayr grips.*

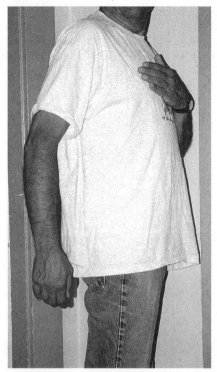

*Untucked T-shirt, one size large, completely conceals…*

*…a 4-inch square butt, Hogue-gripped S&W .357 Combat Magnum in Bianchi #3 Pistol Pocket holstered inside the waistband.*

forward of the hip, which causes concealment problems. In a face-to-face struggle, the butt of the gun in a crossdraw holster is presented to the opponent and may be actually more accessible to him than to you.

### Shoulder Holsters

The gun is suspended under the weak-side armpit by a harness that goes around the shoulders, hence the name of this rig. A shoulder holster draw is a form of crossdraw. Broad-chested, broad-shouldered men may have difficulty reaching the gun, though buxom women don't seem to have the same problem. For a number of reasons, shoulder holsters tend to be more readily

Good news: This is very fast for a seated person, particularly if the gun is forward of the off-side hip. It is particularly well suited to males who have rotator cuff problems or other conditions that limit the mobility of the strong-side shoulder. For reasons discussed above, it also works better for females than for males as a rule. The typical female's arm will be proportionally longer and more limber vis-à-vis her more narrow torso. The crossdraw tends to conceal better for women than for their brothers, and to be more accessible. Bad news: For most males to be able to reach the gun they must have it

*Many female shooters are more comfortable with crossdraw holsters. This one has done well with hers.*

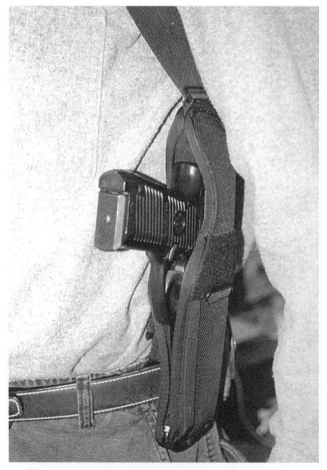

*The upright shoulder holster works particularly well with large guns under heavy winter coats. This is author's Bianchi Ranger, holding a Ruger P97 .45 auto.*

*Unusual, but useful, is this security shoulder system by Strong Holster. From their Piece-Keeper series, it has a unique two-way safety strap release that's easy for the legitimate user to operate, but tough for a snatcher. This one holds the author's department-issue Ruger P90 .45 auto with IWI night sights. In the belt pouches are spare magazines and OC pepper spray.*

---

A particularly useful variation of the shoulder holster is the type of rig that attaches a small handgun to the opposite armpit area of a "bulletproof vest." Noted Officer Survival authority Jim Horan designed the very first of these.

Women seem partial to shoulder holsters. They solve the problem of having to wear a heavy-duty belt that is incongruous with the typical professional woman's wardrobe.

Bad news: Many find shoulder holsters uncomfortable, and as noted, they are not the easiest to keep discreetly concealed. A jacket or some similar garment must be kept on at all times. If the harness is not secured to the belt, the holstered gun and magazines will bounce around and hammer the rib cage mercilessly if you have to run.

### Small of Back Holster

Often called SOB for short, this holster carry is thought by some to earn that nickname in more ways than one. The pistol is carried at or near the center of the lumbar spine. The theory is that even if the concealing garment blows open, it will not be visible from the front. It is reasonably fast with a conventional draw and particularly easy to access with the weak hand, an attribute shared by the crossdraw and the shoulder holster.

Good news: Excellent concealment from the front and fast access when standing. Bad news: Almost impossible to reach from a seated position, especially with seat belts in place. A gun in this position is extremely difficult to defend against a gun snatch attempt. The gun tends to catch the rear hem of the concealing garment and lift it up in such a way that the wearer can't see or feel it, but everyone behind him or her sees the exposed gun. Finally, any rearward fall guarantees the equivalent of landing on a rock with your lumbar spine.

detectable under a supposedly concealing garment than many other types.

Good news: Cops in particular like "shoulder systems," a concept developed by Richard Gallagher, founder of the old Jackass Holster Company and today's gunleather giant Galco. If you are right-handed, the handgun rides under your left arm and pouches containing spare ammunition and handcuffs ride under the right. This provides balance and comfort despite the added weight. More to the point, it allows you to put on all your gear at once as quickly as putting on a jacket, and taking it all off just as easily.

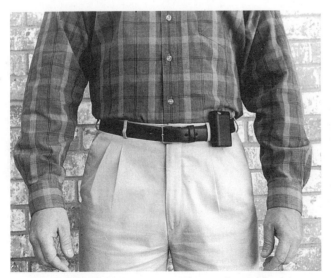

*This individual doesn't appear to be carrying a gun...*

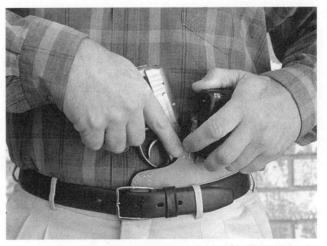

*...until he pulls up his Pager Pal holster with AMT .380 auto. With this draw, be careful the muzzle doesn't cross the support hand. Photos by Pager Pal.*

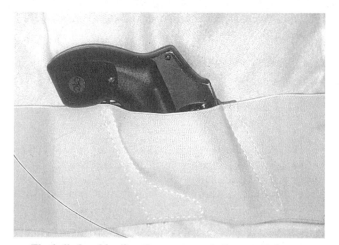

*The belly band is often the most practical concealed carry system in a business environment. This one, by Guardian, holds a Model 442 Airweight S&W .38 Special with Crimson Trace LaserGrips.*

### Belly Band Holster

This is a 4-inch-wide elastic strip with one or more holster pouches sewn in. It is ideal for wear with a tucked-in shirt or blouse and no jacket. The belly band is worn "over the underwear and under the overwear."

Most advertisements for such products show them being worn inefficiently. For the male, these rigs work best at belt level, with the handgun just to the side of the navel, butt forward in what has been called "front crossdraw" carry. To speed the draw, the second button above the belt may be left undone. A necktie will cover this minor lapse of fashion protocol.

Many women prefer to wear the belly band just below the breast line. Natural fabric drape hides it well.

Good news: Unbeatable for discreet carry under business clothing. This holster is faster than it seems and can be combined with a money belt.

Bad news: Some find this carry uncomfortable. The wearer is, practically speaking, limited to a fairly small gun. A small-frame, short-barrelled revolver with rounded edges is particularly suitable for belly band carry.

### Pocket Holster

At this writing, loose-fitting pants of the Dockers and BDU persuasion are in style, and literally cover the wearer in situations from "tie and jacket" to "tailgate party informal." All are well suited for small handguns in the pockets. The larger cuts will allow pistols up to the size of baby Glock autoloaders. Tight jeans, on the other hand, may limit you to the tiniest "pocket autos."

This is not to say that the wearing of a pocket gun is entirely "fashion dependent." Fortunately, certain "timeless" styles lend themselves to pocket carry. These include police and security uniform pants, military style BDUs, and the seemingly eternal men's "sack suit."

Just dropping the gun in the pocket is not enough. It will shift position, often winding up with its grip-frame down and the muzzle pointed straight up, a nightmare if you need a reasonably fast draw. In the pocket, "the naked gun" will also print its shape obviously to the least discerning eye, and will tend to wear holes in the pocket lining.

A pocket gun needs a pocket holster. This product serves to break up the outline, protect pocket lining and thigh alike from chafing, and to assure that the handgun is always oriented in the same, appropriate position. The front side trouser pocket is almost universally deemed the pocket of choice for "pistol-packing."

Good news: The hand can be casually in the pocket and already holding the gun. The draw can be surprisingly fast. A jacket can be removed with impunity if the gun is carried in the pants.

Bad news: The gun can be lost from all but the best pocket holsters when rolling and/or fighting on the ground. It is difficult for the weak hand to reach if necessary and limits the user to a fairly small handgun.

### Ankle Holsters

Since the first horseman stuck a pistol in his boot-top, this method of carry has been with us. It is somewhat fashion-dependent. Peg-bottom jeans or Toreador pants just weren't made for ankle rigs. On the other hand, "boot-cut" jeans, "flares," and the old bell-bottoms were perfect for ankle holsters. Standard cut men's suits and uniform pants adapt to this carry well.

The ankle rig is the holster people are most likely to find uncomfortable. Very few of them fit well. The holster

*A pocket holster is essential for pocket carry. This one, by Alessi, holds a S&W Centennial Airweight with Uncle Mike's affordable version of Spegel Boot Grips.*

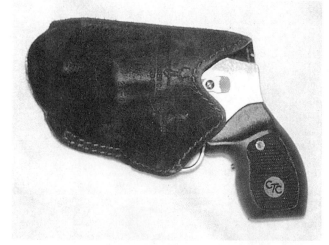

*The author's favorite pocket holster is the Safariland, here holding a S&W Model 640 Centennial with LaserGrips.*

*Fobus ankle holster can conceal this baby Glock .40 if the pant legs are loose enough.*

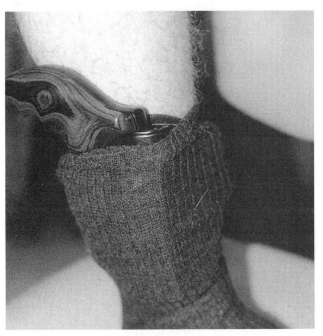

*Pulling a sock up over the ankle holster distinctly enhances concealment.*

body wants to be firm and well-fitted, but the part of the rig that touches the leg needs to be soft and supple. All-wool felt lining seems to be the best interior surface option; even those allergic to wool can cure the problem with hypoallergenic white all-cotton socks under the holster. Some ankle rigs are available with sheepskin lining.

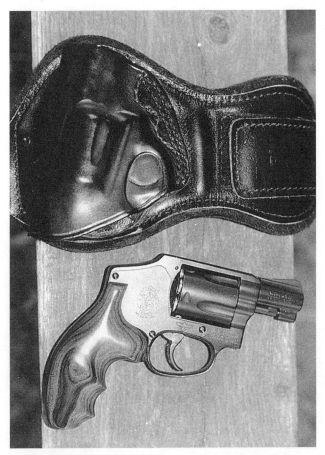

*Alessi is the author's choice in an ankle holster for all-day wear. This one holds a Gunsite Custom S&W Model 442 Airweight with Hogue grips.*

It takes about a week of constant wear to become accustomed to the new weight and constriction at the ankle. Hint: It conceals better if the sock is pulled up over the body of the holster, leaving the butt exposed for a quick draw. Also, because running through brush or simply crossing your ankles can release a safety strap, it is imperative that an ankle holster's scabbard portion fit the gun tightly enough to keep it in place during strenuous activity.

Good news: Ankle rigs are among the fastest holsters to access while sitting and are perhaps *the* fastest to access when you're down on your back. Since the legs no longer bear the body's weight, you can simply snap the ankle up to the reaching hand. Most users find that wearing it on the ankle opposite the dominant hand, butt to the rear, works best.

Bad news: These are among the slowest to draw from when standing and can be uncomfortable. Weight and particularly constriction around the lower leg can aggravate phlebitis and any number of medical conditions where impaired circulation to extremities is a concern.

### Fanny Pack

From the defining DeSantis "Gunny Sack" to the Second Chance "Police Pouch" that opens up into a bullet-resistant shield, belt packs designed to contain firearms have become ubiquitous, particularly in hot climates. Some in the world of the gun believe the fanny pack is the ultimate tip-off to an armed person. If so, they'll get awfully paranoid at the beach or Disney World, where every second person seems to be wearing one.

Good news: These are very convenient. When you have to leave your gun in the car to comply with the law, simply locking the fanny pack in the trunk draws no attention.

Bad news: Fanny packs offer a very slow draw. Weight can cause problems with lumbar spine for some wearers. The fanny pack is seen as the location of a wallet and folding money and may thus become the very focus of a criminal attack.

*Fanny packs aren't the fastest way to get to a gun, but are often the most convenient way to carry one. This one is home to a Kahr K9 compact 9mm.*

## Off-Body Carry

Since handguns have existed, people have carried them in saddlebags and purses, suitcases and briefcases,

mounted on saddles or in the glove boxes of automobiles. Today we have all manner of purses, attaché cases and day planners designed to contain hidden handguns. Particularly useful is the Guardian Leather "legal portfolio," which contains a panel of body armor along with the hidden sidearm.

Good news: These options are very convenient and are not fashion-dependent, meaning the gun might be along when it would otherwise have been left at home.

Bad news: When you've set it down, security has disappeared. People in other countries where loss of a firearm is considered presumptive evidence of criminal negligence have gone to jail for leaving their gun-bearing purse or case behind in a restaurant. Leave the room where you're visiting, and ask yourself if the host's child might wander in and pick through the purse you left beside your chair. Once again drawing from almost all these devices is painfully slow. Besides, the attack on you might revolve around a mugger or purse-snatcher grabbing the very object that contains your firearm.

## Common Questions

*"Should my holster be inside or outside the waistband?"* Inside the waistband is certainly more concealable. The drape of the pants breaks up the outline of the holster,

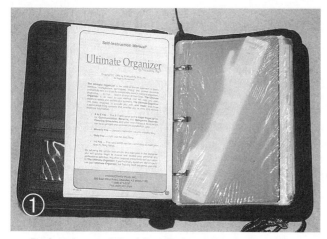

*Designed to work (and function) as a personal organizer, this handy little unit...*

*...helps organize survival by also concealing a Micro Kahr pistol.*

*Here is one of several variations of a briefcase...*

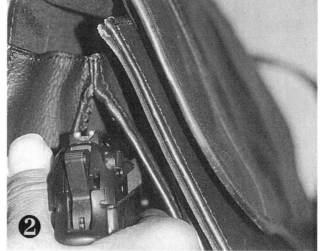

*...with hidden pockets that can easily carry this full-size Beretta service pistol.*

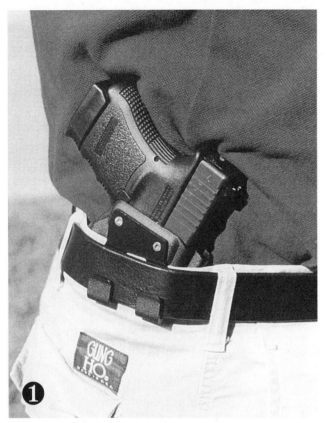

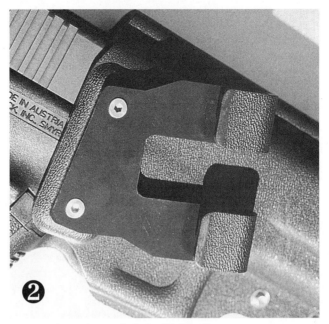
…and securing to the belt with J-hooks.

…protecting its finish against sweat thoroughly, thanks to the built-up inside surface…

This Kydex holster by Sidearmor holds a Glock 30 compact .45 comfortably inside the waistband…

A safety strap is always a good idea on a defensive holster. This scabbard with a thumb-break is by Galco and holds an HK USP.

and the concealing garment can come all the way up to the belt without revealing the holstered gun. For comfort, however, the pants should be about 2 inches larger in the waist than what one would normally wear. If you have tried inside the waistband (IWB) carry and found it uncomfortable, try it again for a week, but this time leave the top button of the lower garment undone. If it's now comfortable, you can buy new clothes with wider waistbands or let out the ones you have. (We could also lose weight, but hey, let's be realistic here.)

*"Should my concealment holster have a safety strap or other security device?"* It is a myth to believe that you'll never have anyone try to snatch your gun because it's concealed and they don't know you have it. The gun might momentarily become visible. The attacker might be a disgruntled employee you've fired, who not only knows that you carry a gun, but knows where you carry it. And any physical fight is likely to reach a point where the opponent grabs you around the waist to throw you, at which time he'll feel your gun and grab at it. Therefore, at least one "level" of retention, such as a simple

*The author has become particularly partial to these Toters™ jeans designed by Blackie Collins especially for gun carriers. All pockets are reinforced for small handguns, cuffs are cut for ankle rigs, and the "mature cut" waistband works well with belly bands and IWB holsters.*

---

thumb-break safety strap, is desirable. More snatch-resistant holsters than that are available in concealable styles, such as the Safariland 0701 or the Piece-Keeper from Strong Holsters.

*"Is quick access really important?"* Frankly, yes. When the general public sees a uniformed police officer with a gun in his hand, they're not afraid of him, they're afraid of the situation that made him draw his gun and they get out of the way. When the general public sees an ordinary person with a gun in his hand, panic often ensues and someone may try to be a hero and disarm him. There will be some situations where responding police officers might also mistake an unidentifed armed citizen for "the bad guy," setting the stage for a mistaken-identity shooting. Thus, the armed citizen is often wise to wait 'til the last possible moment to draw, meaning that speed of presentation is all the more important.

# Police Uniform Holsters

Through the late 19th century, most police officers bought their own handguns and their own means of carrying them. Many Eastern officers simply put their revolvers in a coat or trouser pocket. The Western lawman generally carried a heavier six-gun, normally in whatever scabbard was available at the gunsmith's shop or the saddle-maker's place of business.

The mid-1890s purchase of the Colt New Police .32 revolvers by the police departments of New York City and Boston began the trend of departments issuing guns and, inevitably, holsters in which to carry them. The earliest police holsters were simply gun pouches with something to hold the gun in place. Some departments opted for a simple safety strap to perform the latter function, while others preferred a military style flap. The rationale for the latter was three-fold. First, the flap holster had a military look that went well with the whole concept of uniformed police as a paramilitary structure during the early part of

the 20th century. Second, it gave the department-owned gun some protection from rain and snow when the cop was out there walking the beat. Third, some saw the flap as more impediment than the strap to a suspect gaining control of the officer's sidearm.

As the years rolled along, advocates of the "strap" won out over advocates of the "flap." S.D. Myres' holster company was one of the early pioneers in designing sparsely cut, fast-draw scabbards that need only have a strap over the hammer added to placate the security demands of police chiefs. Berns-Martin's radical break-front holster of the 1930s was the first effort in really

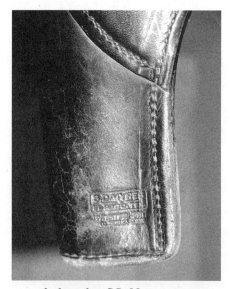

*...the legendary S.D. Myres company.*

*Dating to the first third of the 20 century, this duty holster was made for a 5-inch Colt service revolver by...*

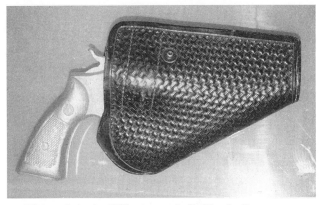

*High-tech, in the 1930s, was embodied by the Berns-Martin holster. Shown here with a K-frame Odin Press dummy gun...*

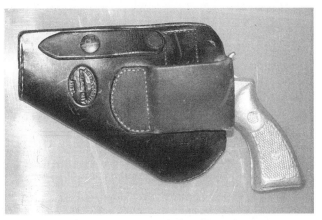

*...the Berns-Martin was generally carried with its frontal strap fastened thus out of the way for a quick draw.*

giving a cop a fast duty rig that was also secure. The gun came out the front, in keeping with the theory of the time that a draw should be a forward swing that ended with the revolver being fired from below line of sight.

Time went on. By the 1970s, three significant developments had taken shape. Bill Jordan's rigid steel reinforcement of the Myres type scabbard had become hugely popular. Jordan, the Border Patrol's most famous gunslinger, had redefined the paradigm. He had designed the holster to be worn unfastened, with the strap out of the way and fastened only when a cop was going into a bar fight or about to undertake a vigorous foot pursuit.

The thumb-break holster, pioneered at about the same time by the Bucheimer Company in Maryland and brilliant gunleather designer Chic Gaylord in New York, made so much sense that it took cops by storm. Don Hume, the sole licensed producer of the Jordan holster (though everyone seemed to make copies) offered the classic with a thumb-break attachment. This allowed the strap to be kept fastened with virtually no sacrifice in drawing speed.

The 1970s also saw the return of the Berns-Martin concept in John Bianchi's updated break-front holsters, the first of which was the Model 27. The first design had a

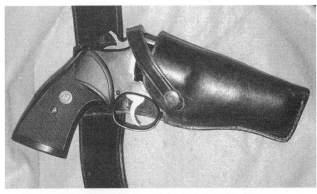

*By the 1970s, this was the paradigm: A S&W Model 10 (or Combat Magnum for the lucky ones) in a simple Jordan-style holster.*

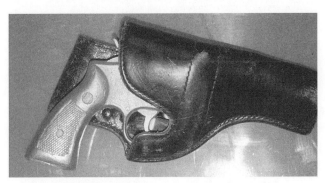

*The Audley duty holster never gained much popularity except on the East Coast.*

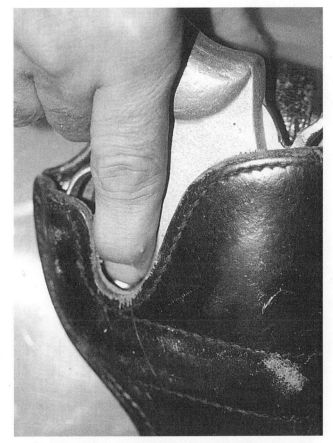

*The trigger finger had to be pressed into the trigger guard to release the revolver from the Audley holster.*

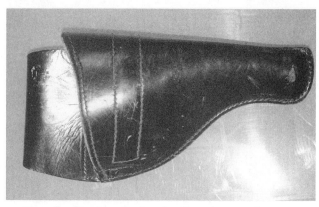

*Though ugly, cheap, and made of less than premium materials, the Jay-Pee NYPD holster was credited with saving multiple lives.*

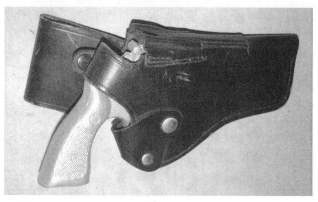

*Smith & Wesson's Security Plus holster was extremely popular during the last days of the police revolver era, and defined the "split-front" as opposed to "break-front" design.*

major in "fast" and a minor in "secure." The Bianchi break-front reversed the priorities. It had a major in "secure" and a minor in "fast." It quickly earned a reputation for saving lives, and the holster industry geared up for "security rigs" to attack Bianchi's dominance in the lucrative police gunleather market.

Along the way, several "gimmick" holsters came and went. Appearing primarily on the West Coast, especially popular with the LAPD, was the clamshell holster. A button was "hidden" in front of the trigger in the exposed trigger guard. When pressed, the spring-loaded holster flipped open like the shell of a clam. It was very fast, but since the trigger finger had to be working at the trigger area just to get the gun out of the holster, it lent itself to unintentional discharges under stress. Legend has it that smart-aleck kids learned to run up behind a cop, press the release button, and run away laughing when the service revolver clattered to the ground. Most episodes of the old TV cop series "Adam-12," still shown on some "oldies" channels, show the clamshell in use.

On the opposite coast, the Audley holster was regionally popular for decades. Like the clamshell, the trigger and guard were exposed, and the shooter had to reach past the trigger to release the gun. The Audley lock was a simple spring tongue that pressed against the inside front of the trigger guard. Like the clamshell, it was implicated in numerous accidental discharges.

If the Audley was an Eastern Seaboard phenomenon, the Jay-Pee holster developed for the NYPD had few fans beyond that city. Selling at one time for $12 per holster, it had an inner welt of leather that secured at the rear of the revolver's cylinder. A twist of the revolver in a certain direction released it for draw. At least, it had a covered trigger guard. All three of these holsters normally left the hammer spur unsecured, where it could be accidentally caught and drawn back, becoming cocked in the holster and setting the stage for unintentional discharges. This is one reason LAPD, and later NYPD, eventually ordered service revolvers altered department-wide so they could not operate in single action.

### Enter the Autos

As the competition rushed at the Bianchi break-front, new designs emerged such as the "split-front." Typified by the Security Plus from Smith & Wesson's then-popular leather division and also by Bianchi's own Hurricane, this was seen as a less radical alternative to the

break-front with similar security function. Instead of sweeping the whole gun out the front of the holster, the officer would release the thumb-break, rock the gun forward to clear the rear trigger guard shield, and then draw straight up and out. Truth to tell, this could also be done with the breakfront.

By the 1980s, more and more departments were going to auto pistols. Bianchi spent a then-unprecedented $100,000 in research to design the snatch-resistant Auto-Draw holster. It was difficult to draw from, but extremely retentive, against a disarming attempt. Meanwhile, an FBI veteran named Bill Rogers had designed a holster he called the SS-III. The officer had to break two safety straps and then rock the gun in a certain direction to release it for draw. The good news was it was so ergonomically designed that any committed officer could learn to make the draw quickly. The SS-III was to become the most successful security holster ever. By the year 2001, some 20 years after its inception, over a million had been sold. Early on, Safariland had bought out Rogers, kept him as a consultant, and renamed the SS-III holster the Model 070.

Rogers gilded the lily in 2001 when he came out with a higher-tech version called the Raptor. It effectively addressed what many police tacticians saw as the one weakness in the 070 design. While an officer could learn to quickly draw from the 070, it took a few seconds to re-fasten the two safety straps. This could be a problem when the officer had to holster and secure his weapon for

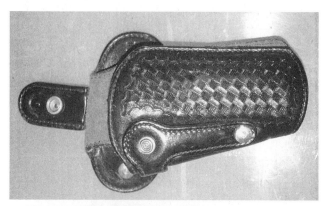

*This was the Bianchi Auto-Draw. The author carried one on duty with a Colt .45 for years.*

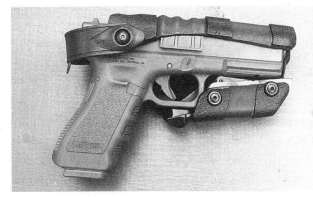

*A cutaway of the new Raptor security holster shows its state-of-the-art mix of modern features. The gun is a dummy Glock by Ring's.*

a foot chase or to handcuff a temporarily compliant suspect. With the Raptor, the securing device at the rear locked automatically as the gun was inserted into the holster, and the forward device locked back in place with a flick of the finger. This had been borrowed directly from a popular mid-1990s Rogers/Safariland development, the SLS (Self Locking System).

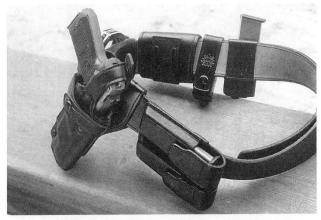

*The Safariland SS-III/070 is the "gold standard" in police security holsters. This one carries a Ruger P90 .45 auto.*

*The Safariland 070 is standard-issue for officers on the author's department. Old vets and newer officers appreciate its balance of high security with good speed of draw.*

## Duty Belts

The first police gunbelts were simple, soft strips of leather. After WWI, the military Sam Browne belt became almost universal issue among American police. More than 2 inches wide, it much better distributed the weight of the officer's equipment. The Sam Browne concept included an over-the-shoulder strap, which helped to bear the weight of the service revolver and other gear. To this day, some departments still use the diagonal Sam Browne shoulder strap. Officers also learned to wear belt keepers, simple loops of leather that snapped over both the "underbelt" – the officer's regular pants belt, usually a Garrison style – and the heavy belt that went over it. This held them together and prevented the duty belt from shifting during strenuous activity.

In the last 30 years of the 20th century, new refinements became popular. "Buckle-less" belts, using Velcro or sometimes hooks, were seen by some agencies as more streamlined and less evocative of Santa Claus (who also was usually depicted with a Sam Browne style belt, albeit without the shoulder strap). Some officers felt that removing the polished belt buckle also removed a "bull's-eye" that an opponent could aim at in a dark alley.

Safariland pioneered Velcro-lined belts that mated with under-belts with an outward Velcro surface. This did away with belt keepers. The result was a more streamlined belt, and several seconds taken off the time it took a cop to dress for work and remove the belt at the end of the shift.

Meanwhile, the police belt was beginning to resemble Batman's "utility belt." Photos of American police (and depictions of them in old movies) in the first half of the

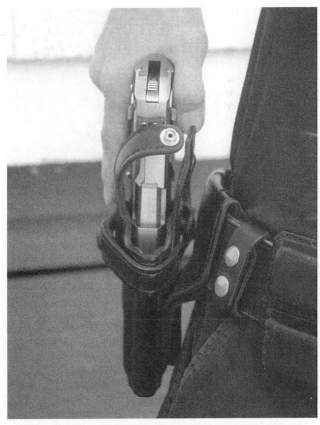

*Despite triple-level security, the draw is quick from the author's department-issue 070 holster. On-safe carry adds one more level of retention capability.*

20th century show them wearing a revolver, perhaps 12 spare cartridges, and a handcuff pouch. By the 1960s and 1970s, it came into vogue to wear a baton on the belt. Portable radios had become standard issue, and these, too, were belt-mounted for the most part. Streetwise officers learned to carry a second pair of handcuffs. In the 1980s and 1990s, awareness of the dangers of blood-borne pathogens made latex and nitrile gloves standard issue. While these didn't weigh much, their pouch took up more of the decreasing space on the duty belt. First Mace and then pepper spray became standard issue, and another pouch had to be added to the belt.

Police unionization was growing, and with it came more concern for occupational hazards. Studies finally quantified what had long been suspected: One of the occupational hazards of police work is lower back problems, much of it traceable to the massive equipment belt worn around the waist for eight to 10 hours a day. An officer with a heavy radio and a heavy police flashlight at his waist might have a belt that weighed 18 to 20 pounds.

There was a strong demand to lighten the load. With it came another concern, that blood-borne pathogen thing. Leather is organic and can absorb blood. It is very difficult to clean after it has been bloodstained. Enter the fabric duty rigs!

These were lighter. That was more comfortable. They were softer and more supple. That was more comfortable too. If they were splashed with blood, they could simply be machine-washed. But some departments didn't feel anything less than leather was professional-looking, so Uncle Mike's set the pace with their synthetic, leather-look "Mirage" line.

Female officers were particularly hard-hit by belt comfort and weight problems. The 1970s saw the development of an orthopedic curved belt that was instantly dubbed the "Sally Browne" style. It flared at the hip to better distribute the weight of the equipment load. Shortly after the turn of the century, Bill Rogers made another leap forward with his Levitation belt. As light as the lightest synthetic, it incorporated soft, rubbery tubes on the top and bottom edges to cushion the weight and pressure of the belt. It was determined that the belt shank of attached equipment pouches in general and of holsters in particular, tended to cause nerve damage after pressing into the body for a long period of time. Bill Rogers developed an ingenious new locking mechanism that secured the holster and accessories to the top and bottom edges of the belt. This left only a soft, smooth surface facing the officer's body. This writer has worn the Levitation belt system on uniformed duty and believes it may be the wave of the future in police duty equipment.

Another concept to emerge in the late 1990s was "duty suspenders." Pioneered by Magnum Software under their Orca brand and popularized by Uncle Mike's, these distributed the weight of the duty belt across the shoulders. They have become regionally popular, particularly in the Pacific Northwest. There is the possibility that they give a physical attacker something else to grab hold of to throw the cop around; that was always a concern with the Sam Browne shoulder strap as well. On the other hand, they make good "drag handles" for pulling a wounded brother officer out of the line of fire.

Some trends developed in combat shooting matches, proved themselves there, and were then gradually accepted into day-to-day police work. Revolver speedloaders and semiautomatic pistols are two cases in

*State-of-the-art today is the Levitation duty rig system from Safariland. Velcro lining mates with a Velcro underbelt…*

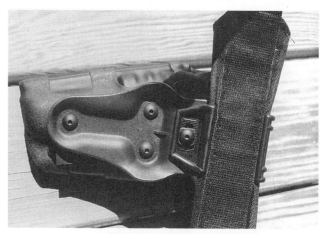

*…and a unique Bill Rogers attachment design prevents inner edges of the attachment loops from digging against wearer's body, yet…*

*…the system is strong enough that this NYPD officer can hang from his gun butt without pulling the holster loose from the Levitation belt.*

*Many consider the Rogers-designed Raptor holster to be the police duty rig of the future. The author tests this one on patrol with Glock 22.*

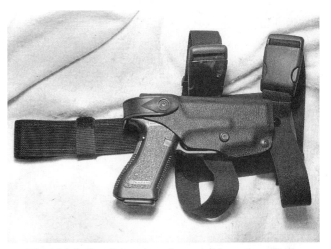

*The thigh holster is a concept borrowed from the military that has found favor with police tactical units. This one is a Safariland SLS style, shown with a Glock 17.*

point. However, some concepts that were successful in matches and even in real-world concealed carry just didn't make the jump into law enforcement. The Kydex holster is a case in point. Its anchoring on the belt has proven too weak to stand up to a determined gun snatch attempt, in most models. While certain plastics, like Safariland's "Safari-Laminate," have stood the test of time on patrol, most others have not.

If the first borrowing from the military was the flap holster and the second was the Sam Browne belt, the third – much later – was the tactical thigh holster. Popularized by the British SAS, it carried the holstered handgun down out of the way of heavy, hardshell body

armor and load-bearing vests worn by SWAT officers. Thigh holsters do not give the officer good leverage to defend against a gun-grab. However, a lunge for the holstered police pistol is not likely to happen when a SWAT cop and at least four of his colleagues blow open a door with explosive entry, throw in a "flash-bang" concussion grenade, and then charge in wielding MP5 sub-machineguns or M4 assault rifles.

Police duty "leather" has come a long way in the last century. Indeed, the term itself is becoming archaic. By many informed industry estimates, less than 50 percent of police duty belt gear is now actually made of leather.

# Ammo Carriers

A gun without spare ammunition is a temporary gun. This is why combat competition puts significant emphasis on the ability to quickly and efficiently reload. But you can't reload if you don't have ammo, and if you don't have a comfortable, convenient way of carrying it, you *won't* have it when you need it. Once you have it, you need to be able to access it quickly and get it into the gun. Because revolvers and semi-automatic pistols reload in completely different manners, they'll be treated separately.

### Revolvers

**Belt Loops.** Belt loops go back almost to the dawn of the self-contained cartridge. It their time, they were awesomely efficient. Even today they're not too shabby.

In cowboy days, the loops were sewn directly to the belt. Today, whether for concealed carry or for uniformed personnel equipped with revolvers, the loops are on a slide that attaches to the belt. The first thing a professional looks for is to see that the loops are at the very top edge. This will allow the rounds to be plucked out much more quickly. Only amateurs (or those issued the cheapest equipment bought on bid) use carry loops that are sewn to the middle of the belt slide. You practically need tweezers or forceps to get the cartridges out of the latter.

It is no trick to load two cartridges at a time. Use your dominant hand: This is a dexterity-intensive function, and

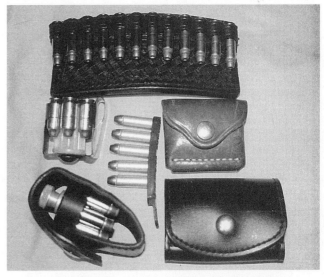

*There are half a dozen options for spare revolver ammo. Clockwise from noon: shell loop slide (Don Hume), dump pouch (Bianchi), 2X2X2 carrier (DeSantis), Rogers-style speedloader carrier w/HKS speedloader (Safariland), .45 full-moon clip in Shoot-the-Moon carrier. Center: Bianchi Speed Strip downloaded by one round as the author suggests.*

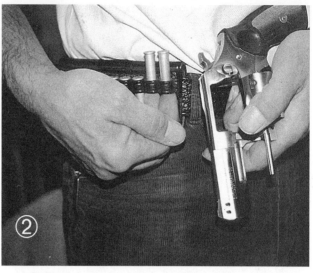

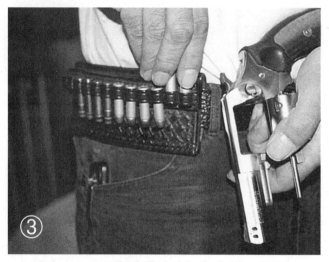

*Loading with belt loops. The revolver is a Ruger SP-101 with Bob Cogan recoil reduction venting. The belt slide is by Don Hume…*

*…the Hume loops sit out from the slide, making it easy for two fingers to pop up two rounds…*

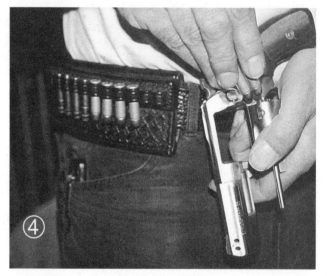

*…that are now easily plucked up by the first two fingers and the thumb…*

*…and, inserted on this slight angle for greater speed…*

Mother Nature demands that you use your dexterous hand if you want to accomplish it under stress. Carry the loops on your strong-hand side. As your hand comes down, palm toward you, use the tips of your index and middle fingers to push up the bullet noses of two rounds. This will bring the bases of the cartridges up clear from the loops. Now, grab them at the base with those two fingers and the thumb. Angle them slightly as you feed them into adjacent revolver chambers, and you can load two-by-two. I've seen very practiced people who could load three cartridges at a time this way.

**Cartridge Pouches.** Slim, flat, and streamlined, these looked good on police duty belts. Stamped with a single die and then sewn together, they were cheap to make and always won low bid. This is why they were almost standard by the 1960s. Pouches as a rule are the slowest method of reloading. Some "dump pouches" were designed to flip down and spill the rounds into the officer's palm; as a result, they were also known as "spill pouches." Trouble was, leather can shrink over time. Many of us can remember seeing officers claw desperately to get their

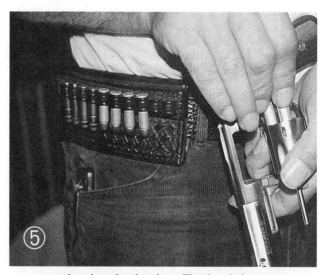

*…snap them into the chambers. The thumb then rotates the cylinder to receive the next "ammo delivery" while the dominant hand is returning to the belt loops.*

rounds out of these pouches, or jumping up and down trying to shake them loose. That wouldn't work if you were down on your knees behind cover. Some resourceful cops learned to take tin shears to a license plate and cut liner strips for the inside of their spill pouches so the cartridges would actually spill.

John Bianchi was a young policeman during the years when the cartridge pouch was the dominant spare ammo system for cops. He later became a master holster designer, and he also designed the brilliant Bianchi Speed Strip, a little rubber thing that would hold six .38 or .357 cartridges in line inside the pouch. Once you got your Speed Strip out of the pouch and learned how to use it, you could reload about as fast as with belt loops, which was reasonably fast.

The best of the stand-alone pouches were the "2X2X2" style. These became standard issue for FBI in their last years with revolvers. The pouch would tilt out to about a 45-degree angle when its flap was opened. The cartridges were held in three pouches of two each. This could be about as fast as using Speed Strips or loops, but the added leather required by the design made for a bulkier unit that was harder to conceal, though less obvious if it became exposed.

**Bianchi Speed Strip.** Developed to augment the belt pouch, the Speed Strip was also a stand-alone device. It was exactly the right size to fit in the watch pocket of a pair of jeans, or that little business card pocket you often find inside the right outside suitcoat pocket. This made spare ammo convenient to carry, especially for concealed revolvers.

This writer discovered over the years that the fastest way to use a Speed Strip was to load it one round down from capacity, leaving the sixth hole near the handling strip empty. Instead of six rounds flopping on the end of a soft tab, you had five rounds that you could quickly stabilize for a positive, fast reload. The middle finger would curl around the space left by the removed cartridge, and the index finger lined up along the spine of the Speed Strip. This is the way most surgeons hold their scalpels,

with the index finger along the back, and in both cases it gives tremendous accuracy. Feeding of the five remaining cartridges into the chambers is faster and more positive.

In the old days when auto pistols weren't as reliable as current ones are today, law enforcement justified its reliance on the revolver with the principle, "six for sure beats 14 maybe." This method with the Speed Strip gave you five for sure, positive and fast, instead of six with fumbling. Today, a huge number of revolvers carried for

*The Bianchi dump pouch is small and unobtrusive, but not the fastest of reloading devices…*

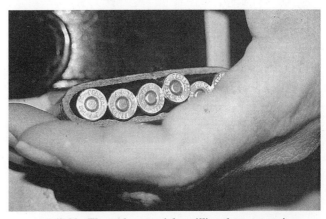

*…available. The author uses it by spilling the contents into the palm of the non-dominant hand …*

*Here is a DeSantis 2X2X2 pouch in action, loading two at a time. The revolver is a .38 Colt Detective Special with Pachmayr Compac grips.*

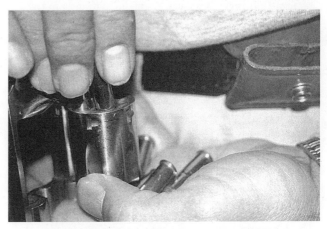

*…and using the palm as a "loading tray" as the dominant hand inserts the cartridges into the cylinder.*

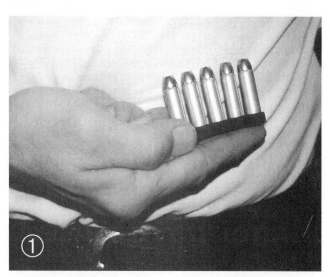

*The author developed this grasp of the Bianchi Speed Strip shortly after it came out. The round near tab is removed beforehand, allowing the middle finger to lock there securely while the index finger takes a scalpel position on the back of the strip...*

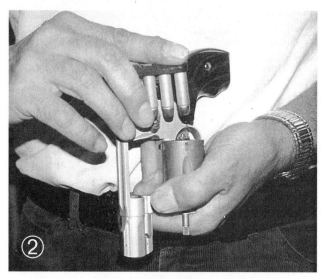

*...the top two rounds will enter the S&W AirLite's cylinder first...*

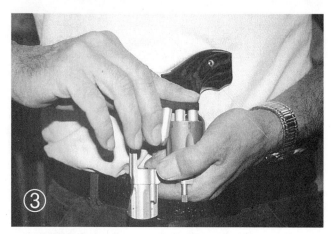

*...with the index finger snapping them into the chambers...*

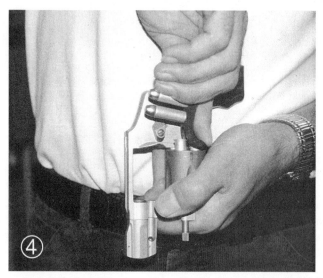

*...and the Strip is peeled off the cartridge rims as shown...*

self defense are small-frame five-shot guns anyway, so the concept comes together better than ever.

**Speedloaders.** There were six-shot charging units for the first Colt revolvers with swing-out cylinders in the 1890s. The concept did not catch on with combat shooters until the 1960s. Even then, because each loader was the width of a revolver's cylinder, the pouches in which they were carried bulged on the belt and were seen as "unsightly" and "unprofessional."

Then, in 1970, came the Newhall Massacre. Two heavily armed robbers in the course of a felony car-stop in Newhall, California, killed four young California Highway Patrolmen. The last survivor was down on his knees, wounded through the chest and both legs, desperately trying to reload his revolver. He had to take one cartridge at a time out of his pouches, access to which was partially impaired by his kneeling position. He had been taught to fire six, reload six, fire six more, and had reverted to training under enormous stress. He was just closing the cylinder on the fresh load when one of the killers completed his stealthy approach, screamed "Got you now,

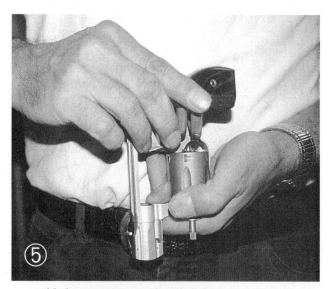

*...with the process repeated until all five rounds are in the gun.*

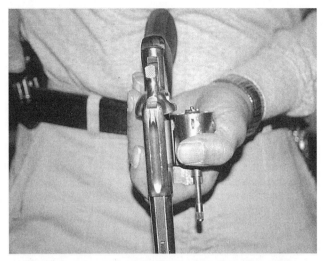

*Here is how to speed-reload the revolver. Once the empties have been punched out, the weak hand holds the gun thus as the dominant hand goes for speedloader pouch…*

*…the fingertips are extended past the bullet noses to help guide the loader into the cylinder of this Sile-gripped Ruger .357…*

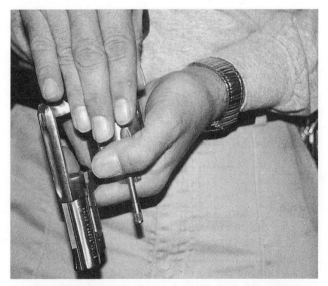

*…and insertion is accomplished thus. Release the payload, let the empty loader fall away, close the cylinder, and go back to business.*

(expletive deleted)," and shot him in the head. In the wake of this tragedy, the CHP became the first major department in the nation to authorize, and later issue as standard, speedloaders for duty wear. Not until 20 years later would CHP adopt a semiautomatic pistol, the .40 Smith & Wesson Model 4006, which carried 12 rounds and offered a fast reload.

Numerous speedloader designs have come and gone. Two have remained: the HKS and the Safariland. The latter is faster, being a one-stroke unit. It releases as the center hub of the unit hits the center of the revolver's ejector star. The HKS is a two-step device; after insertion, it requires the second step of turning a release knob.

Does a second step make it second rate? Not at all. The HKS is by far the most rugged speedloader ever put on the market. Years ago, this writer loaded some up with .357 Magnum hollow-points and put them in an empty paint can, and then put the can in a Red Devil paint mixer and flipped the switch. (And, admittedly, took cover.) When the cycle was over, the paint can had been torn apart, and all the bullets had expanded back to their case mouths. However, the HKS speedloaders still worked. Other brands turned into plastic dust under the tremendously powerful vibrations.

Safariland makes three variations of speedloaders. Their smallest and oldest, the old JFS design, is called the Comp I. It is very compact and very fast, but John Farnam has noted that after about 500 reloads, it will break. I also found it breakage prone. Since no one counts their reloads, and no one throws away equipment that still seems to be functioning, this unit is an accident waiting to happen. The Comp II is proportionally larger and proportionally sturdier, and just as fast. The Comp III is huge. Modeled after the old Austrian Jetloader, it is shaped like an old German "potato masher" hand grenade. Duty pouches for it are disproportionately large. However, it is extremely fast and does not seem to break. The trick is concealing it. This writer did find that the shape is such that when it is tucked into the right side of a right hip pocket, with a handkerchief in the same pocket to keep it in position, it tucks into the natural hollow of the gluteus maximus. Carried thus, the Comp III is reasonably concealable and comfortable, and very accessible.

Lining up six or so cartridges with as many same-size holes is a dexterity task, and once again Mother Nature demands that we use the dexterous hand to perform it. Keep the speedloaders on the dominant hand side. After ejecting the spent cartridges, I like to grab the revolver around the front of the frame with my left hand, using the left thumb to hold the cylinder out, and bring the gun butt in to touch the center of my abdomen. This creates a felt index that keeps the gun in the same spot all the time, and also orients the muzzle downward so I can take maximum advantage of gravity to help insure that the fresh cartridges fall all the way in and don't tie up the cylinder.

Years ago, a speedloader designer named Kubik came up with the most effective grasp of such a device. Hold it with the fingertips ahead of the bullet noses. This shapes the fingers to the shape of the cylinder. Even in the dark, as your fingertips feel the cylinder, all you have to do is give the loader a light jiggle and all the rounds should slide into place.

When the cartridges release, let the loader fall away. Close the cylinder before you bring the gun up, so centrifugal force doesn't throw a round backward as the cylinder is closing and jam things up. Once the cylinder is closed, return to firing position.

*A full-moon clip goes right into the gun with the ammo.*

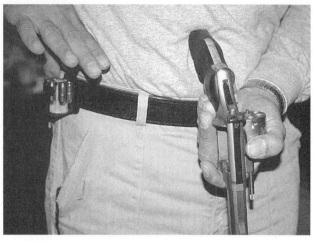

*Reloading with a moon clip. The spent "moon" has been ejected from this S&W Model 625, and the dominant hand goes for the loaded moon…*

**Moon Clips.** Half-moon clips were developed by Smith & Wesson to adapt rimless .45 auto cartridges to revolvers, for their 1917 Model, in WWI. It would be more than 50 years before someone would figure out that a single "full-moon clip" of six cartridges would be far more practical than two "half-moon clips" of three cartridges each.

The full-moon clip is, without question, the fastest way to reload a revolver. There is nothing to release, and no empty loader to cast aside. You simply shove the whole thing in and close the cylinder. With a .45 ACP sixgun and a moon clip of round nose jacketed ball, you can literally throw the loader into the cylinder!

How fast is fast? Jerry Miculek holds the record for firing six, reloading, and firing six more from a double-action revolver (and hitting the target with every shot). He used a Smith & Wesson Model 625 and full-moon clips. The time? 2.99 seconds!

The only down side of moon clips is that they can become bent, which renders them inoperable in the gun. This means that they must be carried in a rigid, protective pouch of some kind. On a duty belt, a pouch that will hold one N-frame .357 or .44 Magnum revolver speedloader will hold *two* short, efficiently sized moon clips of .45 ACP. A compact, protective unit suitable for concealment that holds the moon clip with the bullet noses toward the wearer's body is available from leathermaker Chris Cunningham at 1709 5th Ave., West Linn, OR 97068.

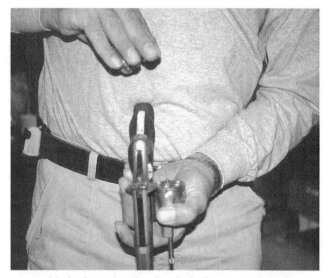

*…with the fingertips ahead of the bullet noses to interface with the cylinder, the fresh charge is on the way…*

## Autoloaders

Many see firepower as the auto's cardinal advantage over the revolver and this certainly holds true in reloading. You can easily get so fast with a speedloader that you'll refill your sixgun faster than a criminal can recharge his stolen autoloader. You can even get so fast that you can reload your revolver faster than the average trained cop can reload his service pistol. But you'll never get so fast with the revolver that you can reload it faster than *you* can reload a semi-automatic pistol with the same amount of practice.

Reloading the revolver is a fine motor skill that requires dexterous manipulation by the dominant hand. Shoving a large magazine into a large receptacle and thumbing a lever or jacking a slide are simple gross motor skills, much more easily learned and more easily applied under stress.

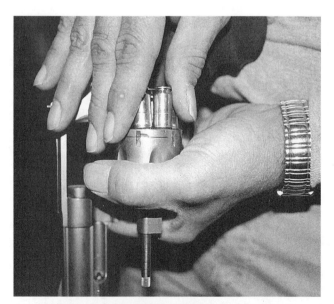

*…and the whole kit and kaboodle goes into the gun, making it the fastest of all revolver reloads.*

*A combination magazine pouch and flashlight carrier (Glock and SureFire, respectively) was first conceptualized by gunwriter Dean Spier. This one is produced by Blad-Tech.*

*Unlike a revolver, the auto doesn't need to be brought down to the ammo supply at the belt. It's faster to do as the author does with this Colt Government in this multiple exposure, and keep the auto in your line of sight as you reload.*

The spare magazines should be on the weak-hand side of the body. The frame of the pistol should be held in the dominant hand, using the support hand to perform most or all of the reloading function. Most fabric magazine pouches are floppy and slow, hard to conceal because they lean out from the belt, and require an action-slowing flap to hold them in place. Leather pouches can be too tight when they're new, and stretch to become too loose after extended wear. Kydex pouches, properly made, are "just right." They hold the magazines friction tight when you run or even somersault, yet give you maximum speed of access.

Police, soldiers, and outdoorsmen have traditionally used flapped pouches to protect the equipment, which is worn exposed, from rain and snow, and from mud when the wearer goes prone out there in the elements. The concealed pouch is protected by the garments over it, and is normally worn behind the hip for concealment, eliminating concerns of mucking it up if one dives to one's belly. Thus, most concealment pouches, like most competition magazine pouches, are open-top.

Worn vertically on the weak-hand side with bullet noses forward is the orientation that the overwhelming majority of experts and shooting champions prefer. This allows the support hand to drop down to the magazine, with the palm touching the floorplate. Thumb and middle finger, the two strongest digits on the hand, grasp the inside and outside surfaces of the magazine respectively, while the index finger takes a position outside the pouch and pointing down. Now, the hand pulls the magazine out and rotates to a palm up position. The magazine is correctly oriented toward the magazine well in the butt of the gun, and the tip of the index finger is under the nose of the topmost cartridge.

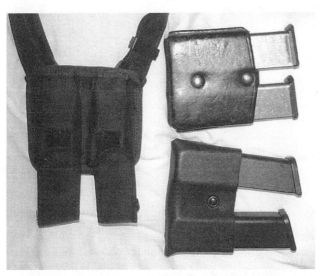

*Magazine pouches are available in leather (Bianchi, top right), "plastic" (Safariland, bottom right), and fabric (Bianchi, left).*

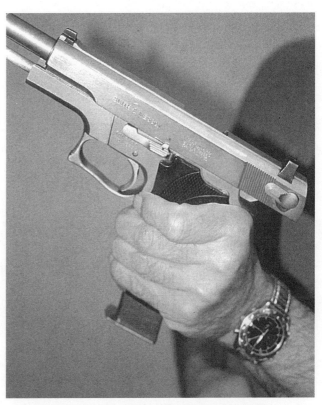

*Left hand magazine ejection: The trigger finger of a southpaw can probably reach the magazine release button faster than the thumb of most right-handed shooters.*

This allows the index finger to do its job and *index,* literally pointing the fresh magazine into the gun. The reason for the bullet noses being forward in the pouch now becomes apparent: At the moment of insertion, the entire line of the forearm's skeletal support structure is directly aligned with the magazine, virtually guaranteeing a positive, full insertion. A tip: With most pistols and magazines, it will be smoother and faster if you allow the flat back of the magazine to make contact with the flat back of magazine well as the insertion begins.

If the pistol has been shot completely dry, its slide will probably have locked back, and the speed reload or emergency reload must be completed by bringing it back into battery. Instructors seem to split down the middle on this. One camp holds that thumbing the slide lock release lever is the preferred method, since it is much faster and can be done as the support hand is returning to the two-hand firing grasp. This also guarantees that the support hand doesn't "ride" the slide, which could cause a failure of the first round to chamber. The other school of thought

*Here is a speed reload of an auto pistol. The support hand goes for the spare magazine as the thumb of firing hand moves to the magazine release button...*

*...as soon as the hand is on the fresh mag, the depleted one in the gun is ejected...*

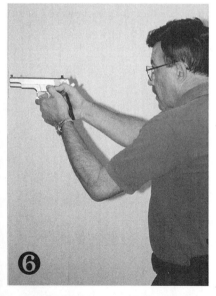

*...and the palm rotates upward as the fresh magazine approaches the butt...*

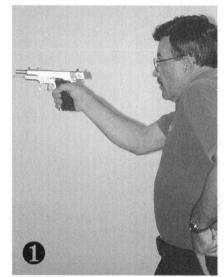

*...with the index finger guiding it in as the shooter watches the threat zone...*

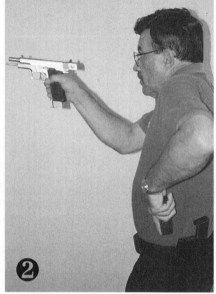

*...the palm drives the magazine firmly home, and the support hand prepares to return to its two-hand grasp position...*

*...thumbing down the slide stop and chambering a round on the way. The S&W .45 is now reloaded, cocked, and ready to continue firing.*

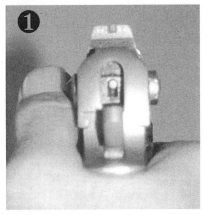

**❶** *Tactical reload, seen from shooter's eye view. There are some unfired rounds in the gun that you want to save; the double-action S&W is cocked and off safe…*

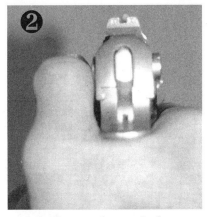

**❷** *…the first move is to get the finger out of the trigger guard and decock. Note that the lever is down and the hammer is forward. Immediately push the lever back up so you can fire if necessary…*

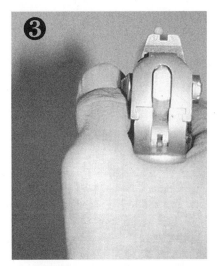

**❸** *…the spare magazine is brought up to the gun as if for the speed reload…*

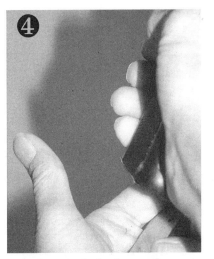

**❹** *…but now the fresh magazine goes between the index finger and the middle finger as the hand maneuvers into position…*

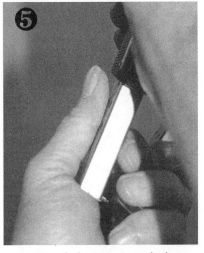

**❺** *…to catch the spent magazine's floorplate at the base of the thumb, with the thumb and index finger grasping it…*

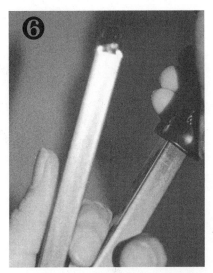

**❻** *…the spent mag is pulled free and the hand rotates slightly to insert the fresh magazine…*

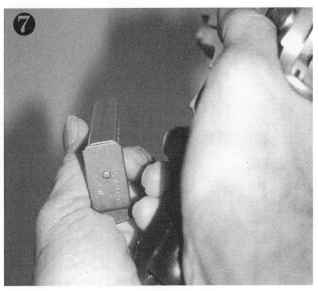

**❼** *…the palm slaps the fresh magazine home…*

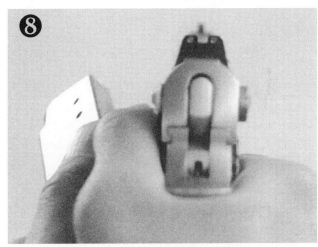

**❽** *…and, still holding the depleted magazine, the support hand takes a firing hold in case the sound of the reload has brought on a second attack. When all is secure, the free hand will put the spare magazine away.*

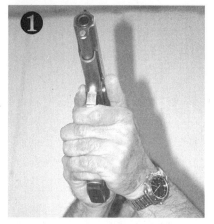

*Here's another tactical reload technique the author is fond of. As always, the index finger leaves the trigger guard before anything else. A single-action is put on safe and a double-action is decocked…*

*…the support hand drops to grab a fresh mag in the normal fashion…*

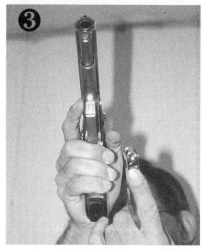

*…as the support hand comes up as if to do the speed reload, the hand rotates under the butt as shown…*

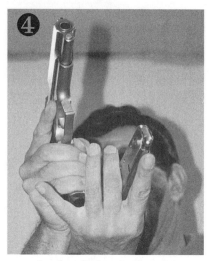

*…the ejected magazine is caught at the heel of the palm. The little finger splays out…*

*…and the little finger and ring finger are now in position to wrap around the ejecting magazine…*

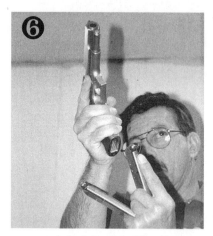

*…and pluck it out, holding it in place as the hand rotates the fresh magazine (with ball ammo) up to insert it the same way as in the speed reload…*

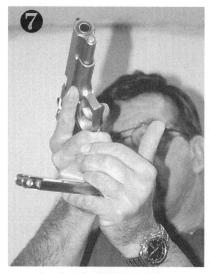

*…slapping the fresh mag into place…*

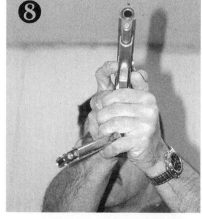

*…and the hands resume a very strong firing hold. The magazine held as shown is not in the way. Once it is determined that there is still no further need to fire…*

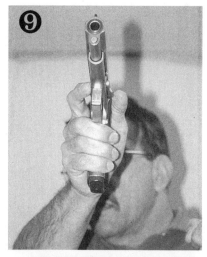

*…the S&W 4506 is held on target as the free hand puts the partial magazine away.*

holds that vigorously jerking the slide back and letting it slam forward is more positive and more "do-able" under pressure. Lethal Force Institute injected volunteers with enough epinephrine to equal a "fight or flight" state and then ran them through a double speed combat course in 1998. We saw that simply thumbing the slide release lever was much faster and less fumble prone in the shaking hands of the volunteers.

As noted, the above protocol was the "speed reload," sometimes called an "emergency reload." It is the logical technique to employ when the gun has emptied and there is still immediate shooting to be done. A useful but less necessary, technique is known as the "tactical reload." This maneuver is done when the practitioner believes the shooting is over, or that there is at least the proverbial "lull in the action." It makes sense to use this time to fully reload the pistol in case a need to fire resurfaces, but the shooter does not want to throw away the partial magazine of live ammo still in the pistol.

Every instructor seems to have his own signature method of the tactical reload. Some are dangerously overcomplicated. Let's look at just a couple of techniques that are easy to learn.

International Defensive Pistol Association encourages a technique it calls "reload with retention." This is the simplest to learn. The shooter pulls the partial magazine out of the pistol and places it in a pocket or some other location where it can be quickly recovered on demand. Then the shooter inserts a fresh magazine as outlined above. This is the simplest such technique, and the easiest to learn and teach. However, many tacticians feel the "down-time" is too great. That is, there is too much time in which the pistol can fire only one shot or, if it has a magazine disconnector safety, cannot fire at all.

A method attributed to Clint Smith is almost as easy to learn and results in a fully reloaded pistol much more quickly. Smith reportedly developed it while chief instructor at Gunsite before moving to his own school, Thunder Ranch, and it is still taught at both facilities. It goes like this.

First, remove your finger from the trigger guard. I suggest you also decock or on-safe the pistol, since a tactical reload can be a fumble-prone procedure. Draw the fresh magazine as if you were going to perform a speed reload. As the support hand comes up to the gun, move the full magazine over "one finger." That is, where the index finger was under the bullet nose, the magazine should now be between index and middle fingers. With the now-free index finger and the thumb, pull the partial magazine out of the gun and keep it between those two digits. Rotate the support hand and shove the fresh mag into the pistol, taking care to roll the fingers forward so

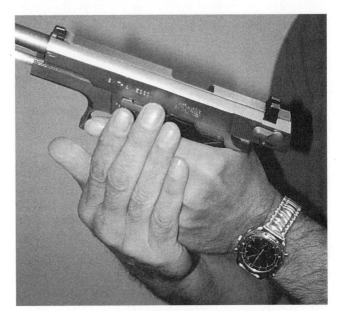

*Slide release for southpaws. After the supporting right hand has slapped in the magazine, it is positioned to "spear-hand" up with the fingertips and quickly release the slide stop before sliding back into firing position.*

they don't block insertion. You now finish in a good approximation of a two-hand hold, with the partial magazine between the thumb and forefinger of the support hand. Scan your area, put the partial magazine away, and carry on.

Let's discuss a few points on tactical reloads. 1. As noted above, they are difficult to accomplish. 2. In an actual fight, a tactical reload sounds like some poor SOB trying to reload an empty gun. You have just given a wounded rabbit call to the coyotes! This is a high-risk time for a secondary attack, which is why minimized downtime is so important. 3. Be sure the partial magazine is someplace where you'll reach for it under stress if you *do* need it later. If you put the partial in your pocket, spend some practice time retrieving it from the pocket and reloading. Conversely, if you carry only one spare magazine, you can simply put the depleted one in the now-empty pouch. It's where you're used to reaching, and with the one fresh magazine now in the gun, there's nothing for it to get mixed up with.

Fast reloading isn't always needed in actual defensive shootings, but it happens often enough that being able to quickly and positively reload is an important skill. Make sure you've practiced it sufficiently that you can do it in the dark.

# Tips For Faster, Smoother Draw

Defensive handgunning isn't all about quick-draw, but that's a definite component. We've all heard the bad joke about the guy who brought a knife to a gunfight. More than one good guy has died because he didn't get his gun to the knife fight in time. The person not readily identifiable to all in sight as a good guy (off duty cop, or armed citizen with carry permit) may not be able to draw his or her weapon in public as soon as a uniformed officer

when the danger is not yet clarified. Thus, drawing quickly is important.

A draw breaks down into two steps: access and presentation. *Access* is actually the hard part. This is where the hand makes its way to the sidearm, takes a firm firing grasp with everything but the trigger finger and, perhaps, the safety-manipulating thumb, and releases all security devices that keep the gun in the

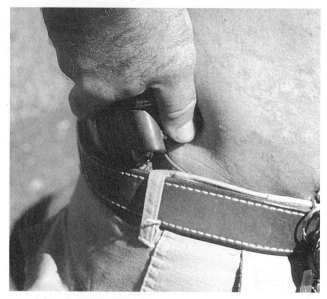

Dennis Luosey demonstrates the Hackathorn Rip, the most effective technique for drawing from a hip holster that is worn under a closed bottom garment. As better seen in close-up...

...the gun hand is executing a perfect thumb-break movement with the safety strap version of the classic Bianchi #3 Pistol Pocket inside-the-waistband holster designed by Richard Nichols. The revolver is a 3-inch S&W Model 65.

holster. *Presentation,* by contrast, is a simple gross motor skill. This is where the already-grasping hand pulls the gun from the holster and brings it into line with the target or the threat.

Ray Chapman, the first world champion of the combat pistol, was an engineer in his first career and a master small arms instructor in his second. He brought his engineering mindset to both careers, and his ability to analyze things was what made him such a great teacher. Chapman said, *"Smoothness is five-sixths of speed."* I first heard him say that in 1979, and nothing I've seen since has caused me to question the validity of his advice. Go for smoothness, and the speed will take care of itself. Go for speed, and all you're likely to get is a faster foul-up.

Let's go through each type of draw, step by step.

### Strong-side Hip

**Access.** You always want to be prepared to make the draw from concealment. Assuming that the concealing garment is an open-front jacket, begin by letting all four fingertips of the dominant hand touch your abdomen at midline. Now immediately sweep the hand back to the gun. The fingers will automatically brush the coat back without you having to think about a separate movement.

The hand immediately falls to the gun in a firing grasp with all but the trigger finger, which should be kept clear of the trigger guard area. The web of the hand should be pressing firmly into the grip tang of an auto pistol, or located high on the backstrap of the revolver's frame. The thumb now presses straight in toward the body to release the safety strap if one is present.

When the gun is under a closed-bottom garment, you may not have both hands to do a Hackathorn Rip. In that case, the author recommends...

...this one-handed draw. The author's thumb is pointed inward, tracking up the peroneal nerve and lifting the shirt hem to allow the left-handed draw of a baby Glock .40.

① *A straight draw from the hip with an open-front concealment garment…*

② *…begins as four fingertips of the drawing hand touch the centerline of the body. As the hand tracks to the gun, the coat will automatically clear. Meanwhile, with fingers pointed forward for better self-defense ability, the heel of support hand also touches the centerline of the body…*

③ *…the firing hand takes a high grip, with the thumb breaking the safety strap, and all fingers but the index taking a firm hold on the handgun…*

④ *…the pistol is cleared with this "rock and lock" motion…*

⑤ *…and the support hand comes in from the side and behind the muzzle to meet the firing hand. Note that the trigger finger has at no point entered the trigger guard…*

⑥ *…and the shooter flows into the preferred firing stance. If the need to fire is present, it is now that trigger the finger enters the guard, as shown.*

*Access is the tough part. Six-time national champ Bob Houzenga has achieved that and is halfway through presentation when he pauses at low ready, awaiting the signal of the author's PACT timer...*

*...and when it comes, completion of the presentation and the first shot with a Glock 23 are almost instantaneous.*

During this, the support hand has been brought in to the centerline of the body at about solar plexus level. If the inside of the wrist touches the body and the fingertips point straight ahead of you, you're in the strongest and safest possible position. 1.) That hand is poised to fight off a close-range physical assault or a felon's grab for the gun. 2.) That hand now will not be crossed by the gun as it is drawn. 3.) The support hand is in place to most efficiently join its mate in a two-hand hold as the draw continues.

**Presentation.** Lever back on the gun butt and bring the muzzle up level with the downrange target or threat as soon as it clears leather. This movement, called a "rock and lock," allows you to most quickly engage a fast-closing threat if necessary. Thrust the pistol straight forward to the target, letting it come up to line of sight naturally. *After the muzzle has safely passed the support hand,* it (the support hand) thrusts forward and takes its position to complete the two-hand hold.

As you draw, *be sure to keep your elbow straight back!* This creates the strongest alignment of the arm's skeleto-muscular support structure, giving you more leverage and thus more speed, strength, and efficiency. It is doubly essential with "directional draw" security holsters.

If the concealing garment has a closed bottom, like a sweatshirt or pullover sweater, an alteration is needed. Ken Hackathorn developed the most efficient draw for use with this garment. For what is called a "Hackathorn Rip," the right-handed shooter uses the left hand to grab the bottom edge of the garment at about appendix level, and jerk it upward to the shoulder. This pulls it clear and allows the gun hand to draw as above. The garment may not have enough stretch to reach the shoulder, but if you try for the shoulder you should at least get it up high enough to allow the gun to clear. It's kind of like, "If you aim for the stars, you at least hit the moon."

In case the support hand is needed to fend off a contact-distance assault, you also want to practice a one-handed version. Let the thumb of the gun hand point toward your body and track upward, on a line level with the trouser seam or the common peroneal nerve of the leg.

This will catch the hem of the waist-length closed-bottom garment and lift it enough to let the hand reach the gun. Throw your hips straight to the side away from the gun; that is, to the left if you are right-handed. This will give you more range of movement to complete the draw.

### Crossdraw

The across-the-body-draw is not efficient if done facing the threat squarely. Crossdraw holsters are banned from most ranges and many police departments because of their tendency to cause the muzzle of the loaded gun to cross a shooter standing beside the practitioner on the firing range. A crossdraw can also be very easily blocked

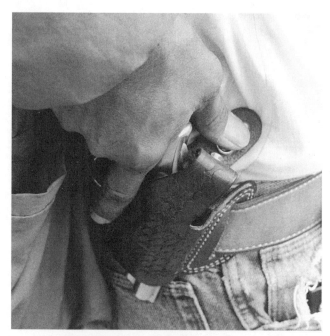

*A thumb break holster is useful for gun retention, and takes almost no additional time to release if done properly. Here the author draws a short-barrel Ruger .357 from a Bianchi Black Widow belt holster.*

at contact distance. Finally, with the butt forward, if you stand square to the opponent it is easier for him to reach and draw from your holster than it is for you.

So, before the draw begins, turn your body edgeways so the holstered gun is toward the threat. Make sure your arm on the holster side is up out of the way where the gun muzzle won't cross it.

**Access.** Point all fingers straight, like a martial artist's "spear hand," and keeping the palm close to your torso, knife the hand in to the gun. This will help you reach through partially closed coat fronts, a situation where a crossdraw can be advantageous to the wearer. Take a firm grip and release the safety strap as with the hip draw, above.

*...with a step-back of the gun side leg to blade the holster side of the body. Simultaneously, the free arm rises in a blocking position, for protection against close-range assault and to clear it from the path of the muzzle, as the firing hand knifes through the opening in the garment to grasp the holstered gun...*

*...the draw path is straight back instead of a crossways sweep, putting the muzzle on target almost immediately...*

*...as the pistol is thrust forward toward the threat (note that the finger is still away from the trigger) and the support hand moves in from above and behind muzzle...*

*...and the two-hand hold is achieved and the shot can be fired at this point, as indicated by the finger on the trigger of this S&W 4506. The classic Weaver stance shown lends itself to crossdraw work.*

**Presentation.** Again rock the butt back and the muzzle up as it clears the holster; if you are standing edgeways, the gun is now immediately pointed at the threat and can be fired from here if necessary. Now thrust the gun forward toward the target, letting the gun rise to eye level if possible. After the muzzle has passed it, the support hand takes its position for a two-hand hold. This gets the gun on target much faster than a swing across, which would have been necessary, had you not bladed your body.

### Shoulder Holster

Drawing from a shoulder holster is much like executing a crossdraw, but with a slight variation. Because the gun is higher in relation to the arm, and literally located under the armpit, it is important to take extra measures to make sure you don't cross your own support arm with the gun muzzle.

**Access:** As with the crossdraw, blade the body with the holster side toward the threat. *Raise the support arm sharply until the elbow is shoulder high and pointed toward the threat.* It also creates a simple and extremely effective block to a punch or bludgeon attack, developed decades ago by police martial artist Kerry Najiola. Let the drawing hand "knife" in to the gun's gripframe through the garments as with a crossdraw. Take a firm grasp and release the safety strap, as above.

**Presentation:** As with the crossdraw, bring the gun out and back across your chest so it is immediately pointed at the threat. Now thrust it forward toward the threat, bringing the gun to the line of sight if possible. The support hand comes to the firing hand from above and behind to safely take a two-hand hold. Note: With the crossdraw hip holster or the shoulder holster, it will generally be fastest to draw to a Weaver or Modified Weaver/Chapman stance, since the body is already pre-bladed for that position.

*Safety point:* When reholstering, you may have to turn your body with your back to the target to keep the gun downrange, particularly if the shoulder holster is the horizontal or upside-down type.

### Small of the Back Holster

In essence, this is same as strong-side hip. Be aware of the following, however.

Many SOB holsters rake so sharply that a draw crosses a practitioner standing next to you on your weak hand side at the firing line. It may also cross a range officer behind you. The same can happen upon reholstering. This, and reasons cited in the chapter discussing that holster, explains why so few professionals choose this mode of carry.

### Belly Band Holster

In the usual front crossdraw position, draw as if with a crossdraw holster at the same point on the belt. If the gun is carried on the strong hand side, use strong-side hip draw techniques as above, with Hackathorn Rip.

### Pocket Holster

Use a "spear hand" to get into the pocket. Since locking the thumb in a firm firing grasp creates a fist that can snag coming back out of the pocket, place your thumb on the back of the hammer or slide. This narrows the profile of the hand, and causes the thumb to act as a "human hammer shroud," thus minimizing snag potential in two ways. Otherwise, this is the same as strong side hip holster draw.

*You play like you practice. Bill Fish demonstrates his practiced draw of the Glock 19 he usually carries. Note the support hand coming in from behind the muzzle of the gun...*

*...and he does it the same way under pressure at an IDPA match with his Glock 34, showing the value of getting the core movements down!*

A shoulder holster lends itself to use with heavy winter clothing. The shoulder draw begins…

…with backward step of the strong-side leg to quarter properly. The free hand rises in a blocking position as the gun hand "spears" through the opening in the coat to the grip-frame of the holstered weapon…

…as the gun hand draws the pistol straight across the chest, the support arm has already risen to the "Najiola block" position. This not only protects the head from close-range assault, but clears the upper arm from the path of the muzzle during the draw…

…ote that the muzzle is pointed toward the threat even before the heavy coat is cleared…

…once cleared, the gun thrusts forward toward the threat as the support hand begins to drop down…

…and the firing hold is achieved. The classic Weaver stance as depicted works particularly well with a shoulder holster draw.

*The ankle holster is particularly easy to draw from when supine...in a relaxed position like this, or knocked down on your back in a fight.*

### Ankle Holster

There have been many techniques taught for this the most difficult to reach of holsters. Some look like the strange mating dances of demented storks. The following technique was developed at Lethal Force Institute and is the fastest we've seen.

**Access.** Plant the leg to which the handgun is strapped. Use the support hand to grab a fistful of trouser material above the knee, and pull it sharply upward. Step widely outward with the free leg, and perhaps also back. (The gun-side leg is stationary; you don't want to move the gun away from the reaching hand.)

Rather than bending at the waist, bend sharply at the knees so you can watch what is going on in front of you. With the dominant hand, grab the gun's grip-frame in a proper firing grasp as above and release the holding strap if necessary.

*The author demonstrates the high-speed/high-mobility ankle holster draw he developed at LFI. The first move is for the weak hand to grab the weak-side trouser leg and pull up. The non-holster leg takes a deep step back, and the pelvis drops as the gun hand begins the reach...*

*...which allows a fast draw as the S&W Model 442 clears the Alessi ankle rig. The support hand is now free to move to a two-hand hold...*

*...and the shooter can either fire from a low cover crouch as shown, or rise to a preferred firing stance if time allows.*

*The author begins the draw of a backup gun with his weak hand. Note that the index finger is straight and clear of the trigger guard, and the thumb is over the hammer area to lower the profile of the hand for a more snag-free draw...*

*...and the shooter can finish with a one-handed or two-handed firing posture.*

**Presentation.** Rock the muzzle forward as soon as it clears and thrust the gun toward the target. Support hand can come in for a two-hand hold at this point. You may fire immediately from this deep crouch, or if time permits, rise to your preferred stance.

*Option:* If you are down on your back, orient yourself so the sole of your holster-side foot is toward the target or opponent. Snap the ankle up toward the reaching gun hand and take firing hold, releasing the strap if necessary. As the gun is pulled, stomp the foot forward and *down* to clear it from your line of fire as you prepare to shoot from the supine position, one- or two-handed.

### Fanny Pack

If the fanny pack is worn toward the strong-side hip, use a strong-side draw. If the pack is worn at the front of the torso or toward the opposite hip, use a crossdraw. The support hand may be needed to open the fanny pack. If so, practice intensively ripping it open and then getting that hand immediately out of the way so you won't cross it with your own gun. Spend half your practice time with the support hand in a position to fend off the attack, using the gun hand to both open the pouch and make the draw.

### Off Body Carry

Carry the purse, briefcase or whatever in the non-dominant hand or slung from the weak-side shoulder. When the time comes, swing the whole thing to body center, blading your body so that your weak side is toward the threat. Now draw as if from a crossdraw holster, keeping the muzzle downrange. With some guns, this will allow you to fire through the container if necessary, and with all handguns should allow you to get one shot off. Hold the container with the hand high to minimize crossing that hand with the gun muzzle. You can now drop the container and go to your preferred two-hand hold. If the container includes a panel that can stop bullets, press it flat to your torso with the weak hand and pivot at the hips so that it is squarely between you and the incoming fire as you prepare to shoot back one-handed.

### Final Advice

A combat *match* shooter may spend 100 percent of drawing practice time on the draw to the shot, automatically finishing each presentation with a pull of the trigger. The real world defensive gun carrier can't do that. It conditions you to fire every time you draw, and history shows that "we play like we practice." Most of the time, police and armed citizens alike do not have to fire the guns they draw to ward off a criminal threat.

If it turns out that you do need to immediately fire as soon as you draw, you'll know it. There should be no perceptible loss of speed. As a general rule, those who carry guns "for real" probably should make at least 90 percent of their drawing practice a draw to "gunpoint," not a draw to the shot.

As in all dry fire practice, make sure the gun is always oriented toward something that can safely stop the most potent round the gun is capable of discharging. A "dummy gun" of similar weight to the real one is an excellent practice tool for this.

In regular dry fire, our watching of the sights will tell us if we had the trigger press down pat or not. A draw is more complicated. If you can't do it with a friend to critique each other, take a video camera to the practice session and set it up on a tripod, and critically review your performance on tape later. Finally, while practicing in front of a mirror is over-rated in terms of most types of firearms training, it is an excellent way to learn smoothness and economy of movement as you drill on access and presentation.

# Since The Last Edition...

Holsters have been around for a long time, and are largely mature technology. Thus, we don't see great leaps in five-year increments.

In the intervening half-decade since the last GUN DIGEST BOOK OF COMBAT HANDGUNNERY, holster makers were reminded that safety straps needed to be wider than trigger guards. Otherwise, the strap gets caught inside the guard during holstering and snags on the trigger. Trigger now stops, gun keeps going, and wearer shoots self. It happened several times, precipitating callbacks on two well-known brands.

In one highly publicized case that could have happened with *any* holster that had a covered trigger guard, a peace officer got the drawstring of his windbreaker lodged inside the trigger guard of his Glock 40 S&W as he holstered. When he went to take things off, the pistol discharged, wounding him. Nature may be telling us all to remove the drawstrings from windbreakers, sweatshirts and other such gun-concealing garments.

Kydex continues to rule, but it's not the only useful synthetic holster material out there. Using its own blend, Blackhawk products created their CQC holster line with a "carbon fiber" motif. These quickly proved popular among IDPA shooters and concealed carriers. The big hit was Blackhawk's revolutionary SERPA holster. Concealable, with every model sold with both belt slot attachments and a removable paddle device, these rigs have a low-profile paddle on the *outside* of the holster, which is hit by a straight trigger finger during the draw, and which – with a little practice – releases the pistol effortlessly. Without the paddle being depressed, the gun is locked in place by a hidden component that secures on the inside front edge of the trigger guard.

The SERPA became a huge success, particularly among plainclothes cops, though I've seen quite a few of them among armed citizens, too … proof that there are folks out there who realize it's not just uniformed cops in Sam

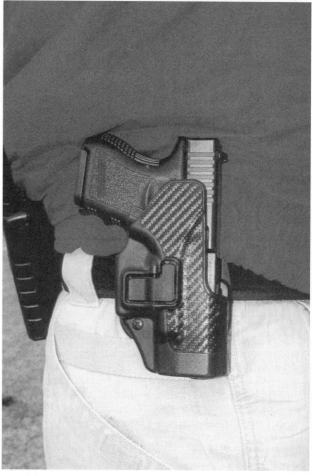

*SERPA holster is big news in last few years. This one holds a Glock 39 on the belt of a Georgia State Patrol sergeant in plainclothes.*

*This Kydex holster from Blade-Tech is concealable, and carries author's Glock with heavy duty InSight M3X tactical light already mounted.*

*Springfield Armory's plastic XD Gear holster has quick release rail attached for carrying tactical light unit, in this case a Streamlight TLR-2 combined white light and laser. It will attach to the rail on the frame, visible on this Springfield Armory XD45ACP Compact.*

*Bianchi Carry-Lok, shown here* **(with full-size Glock)** *in the variation that snaps onto belt, gives automatic locking upon holstering, has a hidden weapon retention feature that is easy for the user to manipulate — and is still made in traditional high-quality leather. Photo courtesy Bianchi.*

*Not a security holster, but very fast and adequately concealable, Blackhawk CQC is becoming quite popular in IDPA circles. Pistol is Springfield Armory XD45ACP Service model.*

Browne belts with guns hanging out who have to worry about weapon snatches. This is particularly important with renewed private citizen interest in open carry of handguns in public. Meanwhile, the SERPA has morphed into a popular thigh holster for military and tactical officers, and a new Level II police uniform scabbard.

Bianchi's Carry-Lok series is also proving popular as a fast-draw, concealable holster with a hidden retention device, for those who prefer leather. Another advantage in both the Bianchi and the Blackhawk approaches is that these holsters secure the gun automatically; self-locking when the handgun is inserted, without requiring a separate movement to fasten a safety strap.

Another trend has developed in the past five years: carrying pistols with flashlight units already attached. First the province of SWAT cops and K9 officers, this quickly spread to police patrol units, and even to concealable holsters for guns so equipped. Blade-Tech is one maker that produces concealed-carry holsters for flashlight-mounted guns in both outside and inside-the-waistband variations.

# Chapter Nine

# Close Quarters Battle

## Conventional CQB Techniques

Most gunfights don't occur in the middle of Main Street at high noon. Most gunfights take place with the participants within 7 yards of each other, and the majority of *those* are at more like 7 feet. The conventional response has always been to shoot from the hip or some other position below line of sight that hopefully keeps your weapon out of the close-range attacker's reach. There is good news and bad news with this. Good news: for a brief moment, at least, you've kept your firearm beyond the attacker's grasp. Bad news: if you can't see to aim, you probably won't hit what you want to hit.

*Close quarters combat shooting is often taught like this. However, there is a possibility that at this angle, the heavy winter coat could block the auto pistol's slide.*

Consider this real-world case in point, from the book "A Cold Case" in which author Philip Gourevitch shares the recollection of a New York City beat cop who had to kill a criminal named Sudia. For our purposes we'll call this brave lawman "Officer 1."

"Officer 1" told Gourevitch, "They were heroin addicts, and deserters from the Marine Corps, and they'd got in a shooting in the Hotel Whitehall on 100th Street and Broadway. I didn't know it. I was standing down on Riverside drive, a new cop, on what they call a fixer. That's a fixed post. You have to stand there. This was December, a cold December night, and for some reason they decided to run toward me. I could hear them running down the street. There was no one else around from West End Avenue to the Drive, just a lot of doctors' cars. I figured they'd broke into a car, no big deal. So when they got abreast of me, I stepped out and had my arms out with my nightstick. Sudia put a pistol to my head and said, 'You c---sucker, hand me your gun, or I'll kill you.' So – I'm not sure of this exchange, but I'm pretty sure – I said, 'OK, OK.' And I went into my coat. We had big heavy coats that you're too young to have seen. They wrapped around you. Terrible heavy coats. If you could stand up in them all night, you were lucky to walk home. Anyway, when I cleared the holster, I fired through my coat. I shot at him six times. You know how many times I hit him? Twice. Once in the heart – he had a tattoo of a heart on his heart – and once in the knee. The others passed through his clothing, and our noses were touching, so I guess I was frightened. He was dead by the time his head was by my knees."[1]

This account is worth some time to digest for all its learning points. First, we are dealing with one *very* lucky police officer. Even being so close to his attacker "our noses were touching," only two out of six shots actually took flesh, striking 3 feet apart on the offender's body. Only one of those hits was really dynamic, the heart shot, unless the knee hit came first and buckled the would-be cop-killer's body down into the path of the gun to allow for the cardiac shot.

Let's contrast that with a shooting some years later involving another NYPD officer. We'll call him "Officer 2." He was off duty in a subway car, also in the winter, with his 4-inch Model 10 .38 under his suit coat and overcoat and his 2-inch Colt Detective Special .38 in his right hand coat pocket. Suddenly, two men sat down on either side of

[1.]Gourevitch, Philip, "A Cold Case," New York: Farrar, Straus and Giroux, 2001, pp. 16-17.

**140 • Combat Handgunnery**

him. The one on the right pulled a knife, and the one on the left drew a Sterling semiautomatic pistol and placed the loaded gun to the officer's head, demanding his wallet.

Like Officer 1, Officer 2 feigned compliance, reaching with his right hand into the coat pocket as if for a billfold. Then, in a single fast move, he brought up his left hand and slapped the gun away from his head, his palm staying in contact with the attacker's wrist and the back of his gun hand to keep the weapon diverted. At the same time, he swung the snub-nose .38 up with his right hand until he could see it in peripheral vision and fired one shot into the gunman's brain, killing him instantly. He spun to engage the armed felon on his right, who leaped away. The pair had timed the robbery just before a stop to facilitate escape, and the second offender was able to run through the opening door and escape into the crowd. He was subsequently captured and sent to prison.

In both cases, the officers had loaded guns held to their heads. Both exhibited great valor and tenacity, and both prevailed and emerged unhurt. Clearly, though, if we are going to emulate one or the other, the second is the role model. The first officer fired six shots with one immediately stopping hit and one wounding hit, a 33 percent hit delivery and 16.7 percent delivery of "stopping hits." The second officer delivered 100 percent on both counts.

He did two things differently than the first officer. For one thing, *Officer 2 waited the tiniest fraction of an instant until he could see his gun in peripheral vision, to target*

*the shot, before he fired.* Investigators were impressed to note that the single .38 Special bullet had struck the gunman squarely between the eyes. Perhaps more importantly, *he diverted the suspect's weapon before he did anything else.*

We need to remember our priorities. Shooting the attacker is not the object of the exercise. Not getting shot is the object of the exercise. Shooting the attacker is certainly one legitimate way of accomplishing it, but if we get the goals confused, we do so at our peril. With the assailant's weapon unrestrained in the first case, the officer had to fire blindly and desperately, and was lucky to score the hit that saved his life. With the weapon at least momentarily diverted from him, the second officer was able to take the tiny extra fraction of a second to put the first shot where it would immediately end the deadly threat to him.

### Analyzing Conventional Techniques

We are taught that all we have to do to hit something with a gun is point it as we would point our finger. The problem is, the gun does not always point in the direction of your finger. When the gun is pulled back, away from the attacker, our gun naturally points low.

This is a critical problem with "hip-shooting," either Bill Jordan-style or with the technique called the "speed-rock." Bill Jordan was my friend and one of my mentors. I witnessed his awesome display of point shooting skill in which, from the hip, he shot aspirin tablets at a range of

*With the gun hand rotated out 45 degrees the slide will be clear of body and clothing, and Kimber .45's muzzle will be angled in more to the center of your opponent's body.*

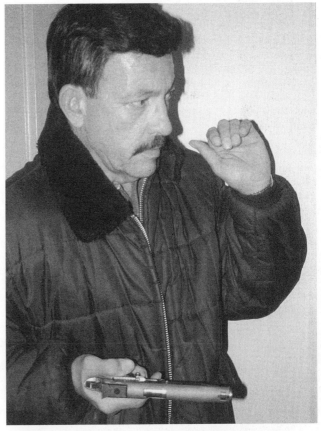

*This sometimes-taught technique angles shots inward to the opponent's center, but takes shooter's wrist to the end of its range of movement and leaves him vulnerable to being disarmed.*

10 feet with wax bullets! Interestingly, the targets were mounted somewhat low.

Look at pictures of Bill shooting. You'll find them in his classic, must-read 1966 book "No Second Place Winner," now published by Police Bookshelf, PO Box 122, Concord, NH 03302. You'll see that his revolver barrel appears to be angling downward. In the book, he also makes reference to the effectiveness of "a bullet judiciously applied to the region of the belt buckle." He later confirmed to me that this was his point of aim for gunfighting. "Seems to hit a man like a solar plexus punch," he drawled. Now, you have to remember that Bill Jordan was a long drink of water who stood about 6 feet, 7 inches tall.

Put that all together. Bill is taller than his opponent. His gun arm is pointing downward enough to strike the shorter opponent at waist level. You and I are the same height as our assailant, or perhaps our attacker is taller. Our gun is angling in the same downward direction. We're likely to deliver a leg shot, not a fight-stopping hit.

The fast draw artists of the 1950s, who learned to compensate for it by rocking their upper bodies backward at the hips to bring the gun more level, noted this tendency to shoot low. The problem is, rocking back hyper-extends the back and takes the shooter completely off balance. If there is still aggressive forward movement by the opponent – even if he falls into us – he's going to plow right into our off-balance bodies and take us to the ground with him. And he'll be on top, pinning us under his weight. Not good.

Does this mean you shouldn't get some practice shooting from the hip or using the speed rock technique? No. If the attacker has you backed up against a wall with his forearm across your throat, hip-shooting may be the only option you have left. If he has you bent back over the hood of an automobile, he has already put you into a speed rock. Either of these techniques will work well for a cop making a traffic stop on a typical passenger sedan, because the seated driver is now right in line with the cop's duty gun belt and the hip shot or the speed rock will be most effective.

When practicing either technique, get up close and personal with a cardboard silhouette target in a soft wooden frame. Don't use a steel target frame. Until you have it down pat, you can wind up like that first New York cop and put some of the shots wide even at the closest range. If the lead bullet strikes the steel frame it's going to send some vicious particles your way, enough to cause penetrating gunshot-like injury.

Here's a tip for handgunners in general and auto pistol shooters in particular: you might want to rotate your gun hand about 45 degrees to the outside when doing this. We tend to practice on sunny days in T-shirts, but may have to fire on a cold, rainy night when we're wearing a billowing raincoat. If the auto pistol is oriented straight up, the slide may foul on the garment and jam the pistol. A very overweight male or large-busted female can stop the slide's mechanism against his or her own body. The outward rotation of the pistol prevents these mishaps, because the slide now clears both body and loose garments.

The outward rotation has another advantage. If you are face-to-face, squared off with one another, and you're right-handed, a shot from the hip with the gun straight up will strike the far left side of your opponent's torso. You don't want to hit the love handles; you want to put the

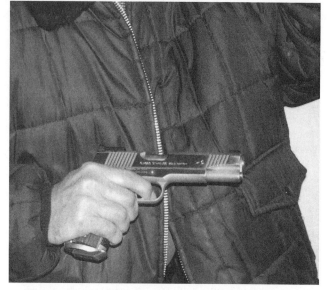

*The gun is angled the wrong way here, and highly likely to jam when the slide is fouled in a coat or blocked by the body after first shot.*

bullet in the boiler room. The outboard rotation angles the muzzle proportionally inward, and within arm's length is more likely to put your shot in the middle of his torso, at least in terms of windage if not elevation.

Don't go overboard with the angle. I have to disagree with those who teach rotating the gun all the way over on its side, i.e., so the right side of the slide is toward the ground in a right-handed man's grasp. This brings the gun hand's wrist to the very end of its range of movement, and weakens the joint against upward pressure. If the opponent tries to shove your gun up away from him, it will point right up into your face. With the wrist at a 45-degree angle, you'll have a much stronger lock and a better chance of resisting that ploy.

### The Step-Back

It is widely taught that you should step back, possibly striking your opponent first, then draw your gun and come up to an extended-arms stance and shoot. This works much better on still targets than on moving attackers. Another school of thought holds that you should back-pedal, firing as you go.

The problem here is that in the real world, dealing with a living, thinking, reacting, and homicidal human aggressor, *you can't back up faster than the aggressor can move forward.* The human body isn't built to move rearward as effectively as it moves forward.

Excellent videotape exists graphically proving this point. Offered by Paladin Press, it was put together by a friend and graduate of mine who is an accomplished police trainer, named Ralph Mroz. In live action sequences using non-lethal guns, Ralph vividly shows how quickly you can be overrun by an aggressive man with knife or club when you try hip-shots, speed-rocks, step-backs, and shooting while backing up.

Ralph found only one technique that worked, the same CQB principle that we've taught for years at Lethal Force Institute. It's a parrying movement off mid-line that "changes the structure of the game." We'll look at that principle next.

# Advanced Techniques

In the early 1990s, I met Reynaldo Jaylo at an American Society of Law Enforcement Trainers seminar. Rey has been involved in more than two dozen shootings. The Manila newspaper at the time credited him with killing some 23 criminals in gunfights, most of them at point-blank range. Working in the Philippines for their equivalent of FBI, he was a very senior commander who "led from the front." Many of his

*The LFI circling parry is demonstrated. Snow falls as the officer, at 6 o'clock, confronts a suspect at 12 o'clock, who suddenly produces a weapon. With the gun side hip back, the suspect is out of reach of a smothering disarm…*

*…and the officer's right hand goes to rear of shoulder joint on the non-gun side. The suspect is simultaneously spun toward the gun side as the officer takes a deep step behind him. The object of the combined movements is to get the good guy behind bad guy so the bad guy, at least for a moment, will have to shoot through his own body to hit the good guy…*

*…The officer's left hand now takes control of the shoulder, "monitoring" movement and helping to keep himself behind bad guy, as the officer's right hand draws the service pistol…*

*…and parity has now been restored. If the suspect does not immediately drop the gun, officer is justifiable in firing because in a fraction of a second, suspect's gun can again be pointed at the officer.*

*Note how the bladed hand strikes exactly at the point where the arm meets body, from the rear. This seems to be a high-leverage "pivot point" for moving a resistive adult's torso.*

shootings had occurred at arm's length distances during drug buys.

I asked him what technique he used. "Point shooting," he replied. I asked him to demonstrate. I used a Spyderco Police knife as Rey demonstrated with my carefully unloaded Colt .45 auto. As I moved toward him, he parried to my weak hand side, brought his weapon to eye level at arm's length, and instantly "fired" directly into my chest. I observed that he lowered his head in line with the gunsights as if to verify a sight picture.

Rey Jaylo confirmed that this was exactly what he was doing, and this was what he meant by point shooting. He explained that this close, if you didn't get the other man

dead center immediately and shut him off, he was certain to kill you.

This is unarguable logic, and Reynaldo Jaylo is living proof that it works. It was absolute validation of what many others and I had been teaching along that line.

At close range, it's not a shooting contest; it's a fight. Specifically, it is a gunfight at knife-fighting range. This means it's not so much a shooting thing as a martial arts thing, and the martial arts are where you have to look to find the answer.

No practitioner of any martial art will tell you to lean back off balance to escape your attacker, nor to try to back-pedal from him. As the opponent is seen to commit to a line of force – whether he's projecting it with his fist or the muzzle of a gun – the only proven counter is *lateral movement away from the midline of the attack.* If you are on the antagonist's weapon-hand side, as with Officer 2 in the previous chapter, logic says that you should strike the weapon hand aside. If his weapon hand is out of reach, as mine was when Rey Jaylo demonstrated, then you should move in a circular pattern around his non-weapon side, toward his rear. In a fistfight, this would put you beyond the range of that fist. In a knife fight, it would put you for a moment beyond the blade's effective field of action, a knife fighter's term for what a boxer calls reach. If the opponent has a gun, you have for this instant made him unable to shoot into the center of your body without hitting the edge of his own. This is what buys you time to draw, index your weapon, and make the hit that stops the fight.

### Action/Reaction Paradigms

Keys to understanding the reality of such encounters are the action/reaction principles. Principle I: **Action**

*When you and your opponent have opposite hand dominance, the circling parry is done thus. Mark Maynard (right, in attacker role) uses his left hand to draw first on defender Mike Briggs…*

*Briggs uses his left hand at the rear joint of Maynard's non-gun-side shoulder to turn him as he simultaneously steps to the "safe side" and draws…*

*…and is able to perform a head shot barely ahead of opponent's ability to stay on target. Rationale of the shot to the head is the instant cessation of action, and best guarantee that the defender doesn't shoot his hand in the real-world swirl of violent movement. Note that the control hand remains at shoulder.*

**beats reaction**. If the two of you are very close together and he moves first, he will complete his move before you can react to evade what he's sending your way. This works even if he is less skilled than you, less swift than you, and armed with a less suitable weapon. This is why master combat firearms instructor Clint Smith makes the point we'll call, for the moment, Principle II: **Proximity negates skill.**

If proximity negates our superior skill, we need to negate the proximity to restore dominance. We need to create **reactionary gap**. Space buys time, and time allows us to react and stop the threat. Thus, Principle III: **Time and distance favor the trained defender.**

Plan A for applying this, of course, is never allowing the belly-to-belly confrontation in the first place. A police officer has to get close to a suspect; how else can he handcuff and search him? The alert citizen can more easily see danger signs and evade such close-quarters traps, in most cases.

That alertness is the key. The mightiest air armada is useless if it has no radar to alert it to the approach of enemy bombers that can destroy it on the ground. The radar is useless if no one monitors it for warning signals. The warning signals are useless if no one on the ground responds to the alert of impending danger. So it is in individual conflict. This is why most training programs in this discipline follow Jeff Cooper's "color code" principles. Cooper used four different color codes; some of us use five.

*Condition White* is unprepared. If you are caught off guard, you are likely to be too far behind the power curve to ever catch up in time.

*Condition Yellow* means relaxed alertness. You're not checking around corners with a periscope, but you make a point of knowing where you are and who's around you. At any given time, you could close your eyes and point out lanes of access or egress, and objects nearby that could be used for cover. You don't have to be armed to be in "yellow," but if you are armed that should certainly be your mental status.

*Condition Orange* means an unspecified alert. Something is wrong, but all the details aren't confirmed

yet. You now focus acutely on sensory input and other intelligence that will help you determine what is going on.

*Condition Red* is, in essence, an armed encounter. The threat is identified, and dangerous enough for you to draw your weapon and take the suspect(s) at gunpoint.

*Condition Black* means the presence of maximum danger, as on the pigment color scale black is the presence of all colors. This means that you are under lethal assault. At this point, your response is to unleash the deadly force you held at bay in the gunpoint situation, and return fire.

Alas, not every human being can maintain a perfect and continuous alertness scan. If the Plan A of seeing the danger in time to avoid or outflank it doesn't work, and we're trapped in that unforgiving arm's length range of deadly danger that instructors have come to call "the hole," we need a Plan B. The studies of Ralph Mroz mentioned in the previous chapter, centuries of martial arts experience, and simple common sense tell us that Plan B is to move quickly off the line of attack, if possible parrying or controlling the opponent's weapon, as we counterattack with an encircling motion.

### Training Problems

Why are these principles not taught more? They take some time, they don't lend themselves to mass practice like square range shooting drills, and they are not particularly fun.

Shooting is fun. Even shooting while moving backward can be fun, if it is done safely under careful supervision. The circling parry movement and similar drills require you and a practice partner to be grabbing arms and slapping shoulders, and that starts to hurt. If you're not into martial arts, this action soon ceases to be fun.

Shooting from the hip or while moving backward or whatever can be done en masse. A circling parry, which can be as much as 180 degrees of movement, is all but impossible to arrange on a firing line with more than one shooter and one coach. It is not time and cost effective for large training groups. It should only be done with people who already have a very strong grounding in firearms safety, quick presentation of the firearm, and decisive confidence in their shooting skills. At our school, we don't get into circling parries and similar CQB drills until the second level of training.

This training should be done primarily with dummy guns and live partners, in a gym or dojo environment. It can be done that way 100 percent. On the range, some of these techniques will end up with muzzle contact shots, which quickly tear apart paper or cardboard targets, and muzzle contact shooting will swiftly ruin expensive three-dimensional targets.

Nonetheless, these techniques are your most certain route to survival of an aggressive, real-world lethal force assault that begins at arm's length.

We must heed the warning of Abraham Maslow: when the only tool we have is a hammer, every problem begins to look like a nail. We are conditioned that if the opponent has a deadly weapon, we must respond with a deadly weapon. That is often the case. It is the case more often than not when some significant distance separates the parties at the moment of truth. But there are times at very close range when, even if you are armed with the best fighting handgun and are extremely skilled with it, there might be a better option for you than to draw and fire. We'll examine that option in the next chapter.

**Always use dummy guns in this type of training!** *Left, an actual Smith & Wesson .40 caliber Sigma SW40F. Right, an identical copy rendered in "dead metal" by Odin Press.*

# Close Quarters Battle

## Disarming

One more time, is the object to shoot the other guy, or is it to not get shot? Correct, it is the latter! With that in mind, continuing at the distance my friend Cliff Stewart, the master bodyguard and martial artist calls WAR (Within Arm's Reach), let's look at a non-shooting option.

You are facing the other person a yard away. He goes for his gun. You go for yours. You are good at this: you can react, draw from concealment, and get off a shot in 1.5 seconds. Hell, let's say you're *extremely* good at this and can do it in a second, flat.

You're still behind the curve. The best you can hope to do, realistically, is shoot him just before he shoots you, or shoot each other simultaneously. Only if your bullet has hit upper spinal cord or brain will you be certain of interdicting the message his brain has already sent to his trigger finger, and then only if you fired first.

He is already past the apex of the power curve by the time you can react. His hand is already on his gun, completing the tough part of the draw, the access. Now all he has left to do is the simple gross motor skill part, the ripping the gun up, shoving it toward you, and jerking the trigger. Even if he's a bozo with a stolen gun he has never fired before, he can do this in half to three-quarters of a second. You are so close you have to assume you'll take a hit. Remember what Clint Smith said in the last section: "proximity negates skill."

Even with your one-second draw and lightning reflexes, there is an excellent chance that his shot will go off a quarter-second ahead of yours. Have there been men who could "beat the drop," and outdraw even a drawn gun? It has happened in the field. Post-fight analysis usually indicates that the man who started with the drawn gun didn't think his opponent would be crazy enough to resist, and when he did, was so surprised that

he had a long reactionary gap. The person who outdrew that drawn gun got inside that gap.

However, this is not an overconfident schmuck holding you at gunpoint and making demands. He's an angry homicidal criminal, trying to draw a gun and shoot you as fast as he can, and his attempt to do so is already underway. That's why you're behind the curve.

A handful of human beings have been fast enough to react and shoot first even in this situation. The late Bill Jordan is on film reacting to a visual start signal and

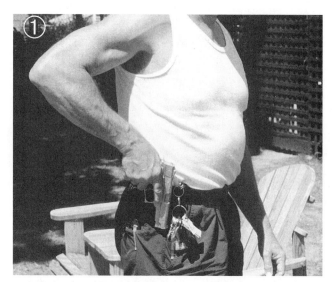

*Bad guy at left begins his draw. Good guy at right is behind the curve. However, human instinct is for the hands to attempt to smother the threat...*

*...and the good guy's forward-thrusting hands block the gun as it is coming up. The lower hand seizes the barrel/slide of the pistol as the upper hand seizes the opponent's wrist...*

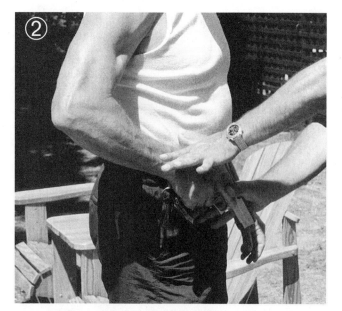

*...and as the wrist is pulled out to the side, the gun muzzle is levered toward opponent's body and almost effortlessly stripped from his hand. In this close, disarming works faster than a reactive draw, if you know how to do it. Note: such techniques should always be practiced with dummy guns. This is an Odin Press model of S&W 5946.*

accomplishing a draw/fire/hit sequence with a K-frame Smith & Wesson double-action revolver in 0.27 of one second, including the reaction time. My friend and holster-designing colleague Ted Blocker established the world fast draw speed record with a single-action revolver out of a speed rig of his own making at 0.25 of one second.

But I know I'm not nearly that fast, and you may not be either, and that's why in this situation the best we can hope for, realistically, is that we shoot the bad guy an instant after he shoots us.

Dying together in the same ambulance is not victory. This won't work.

Why couldn't you catch up? Remember what we discussed earlier: the drawing and firing of a pistol is a complex psychomotor skill, a chain of events in which each link must be accomplished with something close to perfection if we're going to make that 1.0 to 1.5 second time. Our reaction time to an anticipated stimulus, based on Lethal Force Institute's extensive research, will be about a quarter second, on the average. Perhaps as little as 0.17 second in the athletic young adult, maybe even faster than that in people like Bill Jordan with uncanny reaction speed. A quarter second into things, we begin a chain of dexterity-intensive events against a man who only has to perform the easier, faster, gross motor skill of "present and fire."

Suppose we had the option of responding with a simple gross motor skill ourselves. Suppose further that ours was easier to accomplish than the opponent's. Would we now have a fighting chance to beat the draw he has already begun? Yes, absolutely.

And, oddly enough, that option exists.

If you are an arm's length apart and facing one another, as he goes for his gun, *you go for **his** gun too!* It is instinctive for humans to use their hands to ward off danger coming toward them at close range. Let your hands do what is instinctive. Depending on how fast your opponent is your hands should interdict his gun and gun hand as the weapon is coming out of the holster or just after it has cleared leather.

This movement will "stall the draw" or "smother the draw." It will keep his gun muzzle pointed down away from you for an instant. You have just bought yourself time. You have just created reactionary gap. You have just kept him from shooting you, at least for the moment.

Now, finish what you began. With your lower hand, firmly seize his gun and with your higher hand, grab his wrist. Ideally, against a right-handed opponent, you'll have more leverage if your left hand is topmost to grab the wrist, and your right hand is just below it to grab the gun, but this hand placement is not absolutely essential.

There is a principle of human body movement that comes into play here. "If he's moving north and south, he has no resistance east or west." That is, once an opponent has committed himself to move in a certain direction, he cannot immediately resist lateral force delivered from a 90-degree angle.

The "north and south" line of force here is his bringing the gun up toward you. The "east and west" movement is what you need to do now. Your left hand, holding his wrist, pulls to your left as your right hand, holding his gun, pulls to your right. You will feel an almost effortless release as his hand separates from his gun.

Where you go from here is up to you. Run away with his gun. Shift his gun to your other hand as you create distance between the two of you and draw your own gun. Options are wonderful. But the point is, you have stalled his draw and disarmed him faster than you could have drawn your own gun and shot him...*and you haven't been shot!*

# Controversial New Techniques

The search for a better mousetrap never stops. Sometimes the quest is for a hardware fix that will make a dangerous task less so. Sometimes a software fix is a better approach to reducing long-recognized dangers, or new dangers that have emerged with changing patterns of encounter.

Some new approaches work. Some just plain don't. Some are so new that field testing and training analysis are still underway, and the jury simply isn't in yet.

Let's review some current "hot-button topics."

### Finger On Or Off The Trigger?

All the way through the early 1990s, FBI agents were taught to place their fingers on the trigger as a part of the draw process. Countless TV programs and movies showed everyone from cowboys to cops with their fingers on their triggers as they went into danger.

In the last few years, properly trained police and the best-trained armed citizens have learned to keep their fingers off the trigger until the actual moment to fire has arrived. The reason is, we know a lot more than we used to about sudden, convulsive movements as they relate to unintended discharges of firearms with potentially fatal results. In the 1990s, the work of a brilliant physiologist named Roger Enoka was widely circulated through the professional firearms training community. Dr. Enoka's study of accidental shootings had shown that the startle response, postural disturbance, and interlimb response were the primary culprits. When we are startled, our muscles react, and at least in the human hand (if not in the anti-gravity muscles of the legs), flexor muscles are stronger than extensor muscles. This is why if you're startled with a gun in your hand, you are far less likely to drop the weapon than you are to fire it unintentionally. When we lose balance or fall (postural disturbance) similar reactions can occur, triggering an unwanted shot. When the support hand closes (as when grabbing a suspect or applying handcuffs) the primary hand sympathetically wants to close with it. BANG! Another accidental discharge tragedy.

A strange and atavistic article appeared a few years ago in a privately published newsletter that sometimes resembles a medical journal and sometimes resembles a parody of one. A leader of the organization in question co-authored an article on a "study" that purported to show significant difference in lag time if the officer did not already have his finger on the trigger if a suspect held at gunpoint chose to attack. Ironically, though this organization attacks others for not performing studies to sufficiently scientific standards, this "study" they did

*Sometimes derided as the "Sabrina Position," named after the character on the old "Charlie's Angels" TV show, the tactical high ready position seen here can actually be the best choice in some scenarios. The operator can easily scan a dangerous scene looking past the pistol, but with the muzzle in line with the eye, and can come on target faster. If the gun is grabbed, this is the most defensible start position for such a struggle. The pistol is an STI.*

themselves did not quantify the experience or training of the officers involved, the types of handguns used, nor the technique of holding the finger off that was used in the testing. The writer in question issued a strong editorial urging police to have their fingers on their triggers when making gunpoint arrests or performing dangerous searches.

The professional community reacted with predictable anger and strong criticism. The people who published the deeply flawed "study" backpedaled quickly, but their credibility with professionals had taken a severe hit.

Real professionals, such as Manny Kapelsohn, had done more scientific studies that showed you would probably lose no more than a tenth of a second of reaction time by having your finger outside the trigger guard instead of on the trigger. There is an undeniable history of

*Different takes on how to keep the finger off trigger in a "ready" grasp. The finger at the ejection port, recommended by some, is awkward for many hands and can weaken primary grasp of pistol...*

*...the finger straight along the frame is most commonly taught, and is acceptable...*

*...the finger straight at the front of the trigger guard is dangerous. The author believes the finger can be held taut and can snap back to the trigger and fire an unintentional shot...*

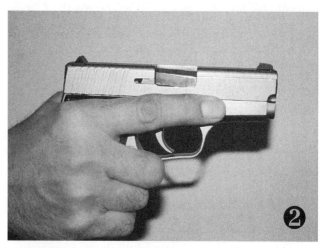

*...for reasons described in the text, Ayoob prefers this technique, with finger flexed and indexed on the frame. The demo pistol is a Kahr K40.*

many cases of tragic accidental discharges in which a finger prematurely on the trigger was a culpable factor. There is also the unassailable logic of Dr. Enoka's research. This is why any credible instructor today will tell you to keep your finger off the trigger until you have actually decided to fire.

That old bugbear, combat semantics, enters the scene again. It became common to teach "on target, on trigger; off target, off trigger." This was good enough for the range but not sufficient for the dynamic realities of the street. When the suspect was taken at gunpoint, the good guy subconsciously considered himself "on target," and therefore went "on trigger," bringing us back to square one and re-setting the stage for tragedy.

The principle needs to be, "keep the finger outside the trigger guard *until the intent to fire immediately has been formulated.*"

### Where To Place The Finger

Any good concept can be carried too far. Some have advocated keeping the fingertip so high that it touches the flat of the slide or even the barrel of the auto pistol. The problem with this is that in many if not most combinations of hand and gun, this can bring the finger up so high that it breaks or at least weakens the grasp, and lowers the muzzle to an extreme degree. This may be going too far.

The finger on the front edge of the trigger guard *is not safe!* The problem is that with a long guard and a short finger, the fingertip may not be in firm contact. The extended finger is "held taut" in this position, and when there is a startle response, a postural disturbance, or an interlimb reaction, the finger can snap back toward the trigger with so much force that there is a high likelihood of unintended discharge.

The most commonly taught technique is to keep the index finger straight along the frame above the trigger guard. This is better, but still not perfect. There are four problems identified with this grasp. 1) If there is a lateral strike to the gun, the most common opening gambit of an expert disarming attempt, the extended index finger is now hyperextended. It has to let go or break, and the other three fingers sympathetically release as well. 2) If the hand-to-gun interface involves a long finger and a short trigger guard (i.e., a big hand on a 1911 pistol), the frontal portion of the trigger guard may get in the way and slow the finger's access when it does become necessary to fire immediately. 3) If the finger does somehow get into the guard, it has again been held taut, and therefore is again likely to strike the trigger with rearward impact. 4) With some guns (1911, P-35, some S&W autos, and many other guns) a right-handed shooter will inadvertently be applying leftward pressure to the exposed stud of the slide stop, which might also be called the takedown button. If this part is moved to the side by this pressure, the gun can lock up after the first shot has been fired.

All four of these problems are remedied by the StressFire (TM) technique that goes back to the 1970s. Here, the trigger finger is flexed, and the tip of that finger is placed at an index point on the side of the frame. On a revolver, the index point would be the sideplate screw. On a P7 pistol, it would be the forward edge of the grip panel. On a Glock, it would be the niche of the takedown lever, which due to the Glock's design cannot inadvertently begin takedown. On a 1911, Browning, or

Smith, the fingernail is placed behind the slide stop stud, where it can now exert pressure in any direction without doing harm.

### Fingerpoint Technique

One fellow on the Internet and some of his friends are responsible for a rather aggressive campaign pushing a radical technique. The shooter points the usual trigger finger, the index finger, at the target, and uses the middle finger to actuate the trigger. The primary advocate of this technique admits that he has little handgun experience, and that when he shot better than he thought he would firing this way he had the epiphany that he had discovered the ultimate shooting technique. He recommends and all but requires a finger shelf attachment that affixes to the pistol's frame to facilitate this technique.

This group is not the first to suggest this shooting style. The famous photos of Jack Ruby murdering Lee Harvey Oswald in Dallas in 1963 show Ruby using his middle finger to trigger the single fatal shot from his hammer-shrouded Colt Cobra .38 Special revolver. Some assassination buffs decided that this was a secret technique of master gunfighters that showed that Ruby must have been a professionally trained hit man. Actually, the reason Ruby fired his gun this way probably had more to do with the fact that the distal portion of his index finger had been bitten off in a fight years before.

The theory is that the handgun will automatically point at the target and enhance "instinctive" hit potential. Unfortunately, the theory does not translate well to reality. Ace law enforcement weapons trainer Tom Aveni published a calm, reasoned analysis of this technique in *The Firearms Instructor*, the respected journal of the International Association of Law Enforcement Firearms Instructors. He pointed out that when firing right handed, the index finger can bind the slide or block the ejection port of many auto pistols, and that the officer now has a very feeble two-fingered hold on the gun when the middle finger leaves the trigger. Since modern handguns are designed to point naturally with the index finger at the trigger, using the middle finger drops the muzzle so far

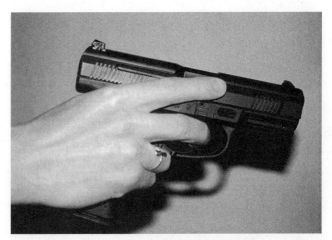

*Problems with the radical "fingerpoint" shooting technique include: only two fingers around grip-frame to secure the gun in case of snatch attempt; the index finger can block ejection port; and the muzzle of gun is radically lowered, impairing "pointing" characteristics. This pistol is an SW99, cal. .40.*

*Fingerpoint shooting technique can be dangerous with small pocket pistols like this Seecamp LWS-32. The tip of the finger is exposed to muzzle blast at the very least.*

that a shot "pointed" at the opponent's torso is more likely to hit at the opponent's feet. The technique is obviously too weak to allow effective weapon retention, and the "finger flange" device that is all but required would cause serious holstering problems.

All things considered, it's safe to say that the "point with the index finger, shoot with the middle finger" is impractical for the serious combat handgunner.

### Position Sul

As the use of special tactical teams grew in domestic American law enforcement, it became increasingly apparent that when personnel were "stacked" one behind the other while making entry through narrow areas like doorways or preparing to do so, Officer A's gun muzzle could end up pointing at Officer B. Accidental discharges occurred with tragic results.

Respected tactician Max Joseph's answer was a technique he called "Position Sul." In Portuguese, "sul" means "south," and the technique draws its name from the fact that the handgun's muzzle was pointed south, that is, straight down. This entailed drawing the gun in close to the front of the torso and bending the wrist of the shooting hand, while releasing the two-hand grasp.

*Tactical high ready comes into its own when the searcher is moving upward, as shown. The pistol is a Ruger P90 .45.*

This technique is also one answer to the question, "How do you do a 360-degree danger scan after firing without pointing your loaded gun at victims, innocent bystanders, and brother officers who might be present?"

I know of tactical teams that have adopted this technique. Though it has some obvious good points, it also brings some concerns with it. The gun is now low enough that it is out of the field of peripheral vision, particularly if tunnel vision has kicked in. This means that if the gun muzzle points at one's own lower extremities, the operator may not notice. The bent wrist also forces the gun arm

*In lieu of this more commonly taught tactical ready position, some instructors and operators prefer...*

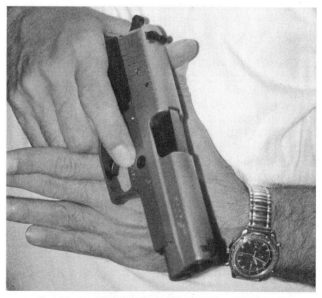

*..."position sul," demonstrated here with a SIG P220 all-stainless .45.*

*Respected defensive shooting instructor Andy Stanford demonstrates Position Sul, a concept he likes.*

into something approximating a "chicken wing" arm-lock that could severely impair the operator's ability to protect the gun from a snatch attempt.

"Position Sul" is still a fairly new concept. The jury of real-world users has not yet come in with a definitive verdict on its usefulness. Time in the field will tell us how well it works.

## The Scan

The wise shooting survivor, recognizing the internal danger of tunnel vision and the external danger of vicious criminals who travel in packs, wants to immediately scan his or her environment for additional danger once the first identified threat has been neutralized. This has led the more advanced instructors to teach lowering the gun after firing and scanning the area.

All good, so far. Unfortunately, there are smart ways to do it and stupid ways to do it. Sometimes, the easiest way to make a good thing into a bad thing is to overdo the good thing.

DO NOT SWING THE GUN ALONG WITH THE HEAD AS YOU SCAN! The statistics are sketchy on this, but the best information we have is that about 40 percent of gunfights involve multiple bad guys. Conversely, this means that *60 percent of gunfights involve only a single opponent.* Just because he's down doesn't mean he's out. He could be playing possum and waiting for an opportune moment in which your attention is diverted so he can pick up his gun and attempt to murder you a second time. An opportune moment like, oh, your swinging your gun off him to look for someone who isn't there.

Suppose you have turned to look 90 degrees to one side to scan for criminal accomplices when, out of the corner of your eye, you see the first downed felon reach for his fallen weapon. You must now swing the gun back toward him. You'll have to slow down as it comes onto him or you'll swing past. Or, you'll have to pull the gun into your chest, pivot, and then punch your gun out at him. Either of these things will take time…perhaps enough time for him to shoot you.

But suppose instead that you have been smart enough to *keep the gun trained on the downed suspect while you turned only your head to scan for accomplices.* Now all you have to do is get your finger back into the trigger guard and fire immediately. Try it on a safe, 180-degree firing range with an electronic timer and see for yourself. By keeping the gun trained on the identified threat, de-cocked if double action or on-safe if single-action, and of course with your finger removed from the trigger guard, you will be *much* faster if you have to engage the identified threat a second time.

But what if as you scan, you *do* see a second lethal threat? How much will it slow you down if the gun is pointed at the first bad guy 90 degrees away instead of at the new one you just spotted? The answer is, not much. You need to identify the threat, determine that deadly force is justifiable, and make the decision to shoot. While you're doing that, there will be time to bring the gun around 90 degrees and get it indexed.

DO NOT SCAN 180 DEGREES AND ASSUME THAT THE AREA HAS BEEN CLEARED. Nintey degrees left and 90 degrees right only clears half the circle. You still have to clear the most potentially lethal area, that which is 180 degrees behind you at 6 o'clock. Remember, the smartest predators will ambush you from behind.

Bring it all together and you get the following recommendation for performing the scan. When the initial threat goes down, analyze it for a moment and determine if it seems neutralized. Remove your trigger finger from the trigger guard, and de-cock or on-safe the gun, depending on its design. Take a quick look to your most exposed side. Now look back to the threat and make sure it's still neutral. Now you can check to 6 o'clock on the same side or to 3 or 9 o'clock on the side you haven't scanned yet. Now back to the initial threat to check it again. Finally, check whatever the last quadrant is that you have not visually scanned. During this procedure, it would be wise to be moving toward cover. You'll also find that as you scan toward your 6 o'clock in the last portions of the scan, the gun will stray less if you pull it closer to your body, as illustrated in the accompanying photos.

There is another reason not to perform the scan with the gun tracking along with the head and eyes. What you have trained yourself to do is what you most certainly WILL do when deadly danger has you in its grip. There is an excellent chance that the shooting scene will contain, or even be filled with, innocent bystanders. If you have performed the scan with your gun held on the downed, identified threat, those witnesses will perceive that "the person with the gun shot the suspect and then looked around to make sure we were all OK." However, if your gun has tracked with your eyes, they will perceive that "the person with the gun shot the suspect and then pointed the gun at all the rest of us, too!"

The scan is a life-saving technique. Armed conflict expert John Farnam reported the case of a South African police officer that shot and killed a terrorist. He was seen to scan left and right, and then lower his gun, apparently thinking himself safe at last. He was then shot in the back of the head and killed instantly by a second terrorist with an AK-47, who had been directly behind him and had gone unseen in the "half a circle scan" the brave officer had performed.

Yes, the scan is a good thing and you should practice it. But you should practice it *correctly,* because there is very definitely a right and a wrong way to do it.

*Ayoob demonstrates the post-shooting tactical scan. With the shooting over, gun de-cocked and finger removed from trigger guard, the gun stays on the identified threat, presumably downed in the snow, ...*

*...as the officer quickly checks to his right, with gun still on the identified threat...*

*...and glances back to make sure the downed suspect is not playing possum...*

*...followed by a quick check to officer's left...*

*...and back. The pistol is drawn slightly more into the shooter's body to make it less likely to turn off target as...*

*...the officer re-scans to the right, this time looking behind him to his 6 o'clock...*

*...and back...*

*...the scan is completed with final sweep to the left to six o'clock...*

*...and in a very short time, a 360-degree scan is completed and focus returns to downed identified threat, who has been monitored throughout the scan.*

# CHAPTER TEN

# Better Technique = Better Performance

## Enhancing Grasp

Ethicists say that their discipline exists on two levels. There is simply "ethics," which can be a sterile and philosophical debate that often takes place in the proverbial ivory towers. Then there is "applied ethics." The latter, says Professor Preston Covey, head of the Center for Advancement of Applied Ethics at Carnegie-Mellon University, "is where the rubber meets the road."

In handgun shooting, particularly the kind that is done rapidly under stress, we have to do something similar. We need to make the transition from "shooting" to "applied shooting." Many long-standing rules of marksmanship go out the window when the adrenaline dump hits and the "fight or flight" response sends dexterity down the toilet and strength up through the roof.

As noted elsewhere in this book, the grasp of the firearm is where operator meets machine, and a key point where "the rubber meets the road." Let's review necessities for *combat* handgunning that might not be required for sport or recreational shooting.

The grasp **needs to work with one hand only,** in case the other hand is performing a critical survival task and "can't make it to the appointment" for the two-hand hold that might have been the original plan.

The grasp also **needs to work two-handed,** for maximum life-saving efficiency, in case the circumstances evolving from the surprise that has called the combat handgun into play allow this to happen.

The grasp **needs to be strong enough to maintain control of the firearm even if the gun or hand are grasped or struck,** both predictable occurrences in the sort of situation that is the combat handgun's *raison d'etre.*

### Master Grip Concept

Called the "master grip" by many instructors, a grasp of the gun that fulfills the above parameters is essential. Ideally, if the gun fits the user's hand, the following coordinates will all be achieved.

The trigger finger will have good leverage on the trigger. The web of the hand will be high up into the grip tang of the auto, or at the highest possible point on the backstrap of the revolver's grip-frame. The barrel of the gun will be in line with the long bones of the forearm.

*With most handguns the author prefers the "wedge hold." The index finger of the support hand is wedged under the front of the trigger guard, camming the muzzle up and driving the grip tang more forcibly into the web of the hand. The V-shaped wedge of flesh and bone under the front of the guard also helps prevent lateral deviation of the gun muzzle due to a frisky trigger finger. Here, he demonstrates with a Glock 22.*

*The rear of the butt of a baby Glock is ideally shaped to pull into the hollow of the palm. With the little finger tucked under the butt, if you don't use a Pearce grip extender, this grasp gives a surprisingly strong hold. Note the white fingernails, indicating desirable crush grip.*

*Thumb-lock grip. The thumb of the support hand presses down on the median joint of the bent thumb of the firing hand, bonding both hands together. This grasp works particularly well with handguns producing jackhammer recoil, like this S&W J-frame Bodyguard in .357 Magnum.*

*Note "ripple of flesh" effect at the web of the hand with a high hold, reinforced by the wedge grasp of the support hand's index finger under the front of trigger guard. With a crush grip applied with both hands and the trigger finger at the distal joint contact, the shooter has maximum control of this GlockWorks custom Glock 17.*

The hand should have firm enough a contact that the gun does not slip or move in the hand during recoil. No part of the hand(s) should be blocking essential functions of the handgun. No part of the hand(s) should be blocking the function of other parts of the hand(s).

While most of the last paragraph is self-explanatory, some of the last points need explanation for newer shooters. With a small gun and a large hand, if the grasping hand takes a natural "fist grasp" with the thumb curled down, the thumb may block the trigger finger's completion of the trigger pull. In larger hands, this can occur with the small J-frame revolvers or with the small Kahr pistols. The solution on the revolver is custom grips that extend backward from the grip-frame, which move the web of the shooter's hand back, lengthening the reach to the trigger and preventing "overtravel" of the trigger finger through the trigger guard. With the Kahr, the easiest solution is to go to a "high thumbs" grasp.

Obviously, we don't want to use the old-fashioned two-hand hold still seen on TV in which the thumb of the support hand crosses over the back of the firing hand. The hyperextension of the thumb in this direction weakens the grasp of the support hand, but this is the least of our concerns. With most auto pistols, this grasp puts the weak hand thumb directly behind the slide. This tends to result in a nasty laceration, could cause even worse physical damage than that, and also is likely to jam the gun at the worst possible moment. Even with a conventional revolver, this grip when taken hastily, or by someone with big thumbs and a smaller revolver than they are accustomed to, can block the hammer's rearward travel and prevent the gun from firing.

As we shall see momentarily, sometimes compromises must be made. Let's say that you are a right-handed shooter who uses a Beretta 92F, a Smith & Wesson Model 4006, or a Ruger P90 or something similar. Each of these guns has a slide-mounted de-cocking lever that also serves as a safety catch. The lever will need to be in its "up" position, the length of the lever parallel with the length of the bore, for the pistol to fire when you need it to. Carrying the gun off-safe is not enough to guarantee that this will happen. We have documented cases where such a safety "went on" without the user's knowledge. This is not something the gun does by itself. It usually occurs if there is some sort of struggle for the gun, or the user accidentally hits the de-cocking lever while operating the slide, or the user has left the lever down while chambering a round and forgotten to raise it.

There are also those of us who intentionally carry such guns "lever down," on-safe, for handgun retention reasons. In either case, whether you carry off-safe or on, you want to either get that lever up as you draw or *verify* that it's up even if that's where you left it. This means a grasp in which the thumb of the firing hand is about 45 degrees upward, pointed straight toward the ejection port. The support hand thumb goes directly underneath it in a two-hand grasp. However, this hold often causes one thumb to ride on the slide stop and may prevent the pistol from locking its slide open when the magazine runs empty. This will vary from shooter to shooter and from gun to gun, depending on the size and shape of pistol and of the hand. The author, for example, does not have this problem when shooting the S&W or Ruger, but invariably deactivates his own slide stop when taking this grasp on the Beretta pistol. Sometimes, the balance of competing harms and needs requires us to violate a lesser rule to more strictly enforce a more important one. In this case, it is less important to me to have the fastest of all possible reloads after I've fired 16 rounds of 9mm from my Beretta 92F, than it is for me to be certain that the first shot from that gun will be delivered as expeditiously as possible if needed in self-defense. The first shot is usually the most important, and the 17th is rarely the deciding factor.

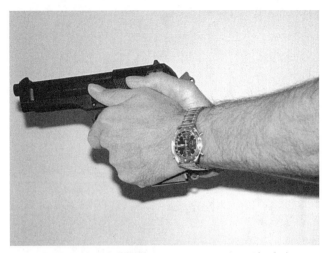

*A "Straight thumbs" hold guarantees proper manipulation of the slide-mounted safety on this Beretta 92F, but one thumb will ride the slide stop and keep gun from locking open when empty.*

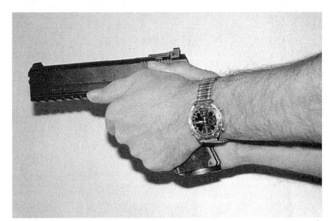

*The Leatham-Enos hold is demonstrated on a Springfield Tactical Operator .45 auto. The support hand cants downward from the wrist, creating a strong lock. The thumb of the gun hand rides the safety as that of the support hand points downrange, aligning the hand with the radius bone of the forearm.*

This is one of three chapters in this book in which grasp is discussed, the others being "lost secrets of combat shooting" and "handgun fit." In those we explain in greater detail the importance of the barrel being in line with the forearm and the web of the hand high, and in the former we explain in detail the rationale of "crush grip" versus other concepts of strength of grasp.

A key element to finding a comfortable, effective hold for the individual combination of handgun and shooter is the placement of the thumbs. This is a good point at which to examine that issue in detail.

### Thumb Position

Handgun coaches and marksmanship manuals often simply say or demonstrate, "hold your thumb(s) like this." It is disturbing that they often don't explain why. For the shooter to determine if a technique is right for the gun, the job, and the moment, he or she needs to understand the reasons for use of the technique: what its purpose is, whom it was developed for, and why it was developed. Let's apply this to thumb positions. We'll be focusing here on the "master grip," that is, on the primary hand's interface with the combat handgun.

**Thumb Down.** This is the way most people instinctively hold a gun, and there is much to be said for it. We're talking about a grasp in which the thumb is bent at the median joint and the tip of the thumb is pointed toward the ground. It resembles a tightly curled fist. Most top revolver shooters use this grasp on their double-action wheelguns.

There is no stronger hold. The human hand evolved to work off its unique opposing thumb, and hyper-flexion of the thumb strengthens the hold. You can perform this simple test with one hand, without even putting this book down: Take your free hand, raise the thumb, and close the four fingers as tightly as you can. Mentally measure the

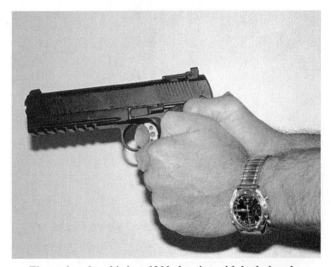

*The author does his best 1911 shooting with both thumbs curled down in this "thumbprint over thumbnail" grasp that engenders maximum hand strength. The 1911 trigger guard is too short for him to take the wedge hold he prefers.*

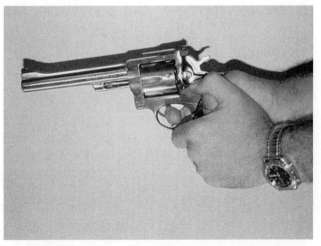

*A thumb-lock grasp works perfectly with powerful sixguns like this Ruger .357 Magnum. If the thumb of the support hand crossed over the back of firing hand it would weaken the grasp, possibly block the revolver's hammer, and be in the way of an auto pistol's slide.*

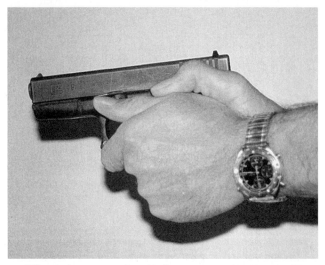

*What feels most comfortable is not necessarily what you'll shoot best with. The author's hands are more comfortable with this Leatham-Enos type grasp, augmented with wedge hold on his 9mm Glock 19...*

*...but he shoots faster and straighter with his thumbs curled down, as shown here. The wedge hold works regardless of thumb position.*

strength you are applying. Now, still exerting maximum gripping force and still mentally measuring, *slowly close the thumb until its tip is pointed down.* You just felt a significant increase in strength as the hand closed.

An advantage to the thumb-down grip is that it puts a bar of flesh and bone, the thumb, in position to close what is otherwise an open channel on the side opposite the palm of the hand. If an opponent, one who knows what he's doing, attempts to disarm you, he will begin with a lateral strike to the gun to move it off his midline. If that strike is directed toward the open side of the hand, your gun could be knocked or torn loose from your grasp before you could react. With the thumb locked down, you have at least a fighting chance of keeping the gun in your grasp

long enough to react and perform a handgun retention technique.

When the support hand comes in to assist, that hand's thumb has three options. It can simply hang out in space, a technique used by some to ensure that it doesn't block a part of their gun like the slide stop. While it's true that a thumb held in this fashion isn't getting in the way of anything, it is also true that it isn't doing anything positive to help you shoot faster and straighter. A second option is to lock the support hand's thumb at or behind the flexed joint of the primary hand's thumb. This works particularly well with revolvers, and frankly, it also works with most auto pistols. It is probably the single best "universal grasp" that is "friendly" to all manner of

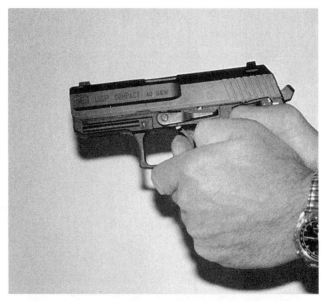

*The thumbs are curled down with this Variant One HK USP pistol. If the thumb rides the USP's frame-mounted de-cocking lever, it can accidentally drive the lever down into de-cock position during a string of fire.*

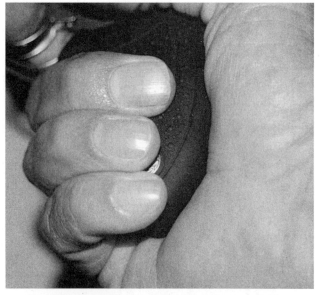

*The pinky finger curls under the grip of a concealable, short-butt Taurus CIA. Though it can't help hold the gun directly, this finger's hyper-flexion adds strength to the other fingers that are wrapped around the stocks.*

handguns. I call it the "thumb-lock grip" because when the support hand's thumb presses down on the median joint of the flexed thumb on the shooting hand, it bonds the support hand to the firing hand. This prevents the hands from separating when there is really powerful recoil, as with a super-light .38 or with a .44 Magnum. Finally, the thumb of the support hand can come in with its thumbprint placed on the thumbnail of the firing hand. Now both hands are flexed and exerting maximum gripping strength.

Note that with some hands on some guns, the downward-pointing thumb can hit the magazine release button inadvertently. We have seen this on occasion with really huge hands on the 1911 pistol, and with average size male hands on the scaled down Colt .380 Government-style pistols.

**Thumb Straight.** This is the preferred technique of the target shooter. With the thumb pointing parallel to the barrel, the trigger finger will have its straightest and smoothest track to the rear. The difference is very subtle and very small, but master competitors take every edge they can get. It is also a fairly strong position, as it aligns the extended thumb with the long bones of the forearm. Japanese archers learned centuries ago to hold their bows with a similar grasp.

With a two-hand hold, the support hand's thumb is also straight. It tends to be forward of the firing hand's thumb, and parallel to it, perhaps a little below it. In the version of this grasp popularized years ago by combat match champions Rob Leatham and Brian Enos, the thumb of the firing hand thumb has little, if any contact, with the gun and rides atop the base joint of the support hand's thumb. Many shooters using 1911 pistols will leave the thumb of the shooting hand placed atop the manual safety lever.

Though not as strong a primary hold against a disarming attempt as the thumb downward master grip, this hold is much stronger in that regard than any of the high thumb positions. It is also very conducive to a grasp

that evolved in IPSC shooting in which the support hand is canted slightly down from the wrist, so that the thumb is directly in line with the radius, the upper bone of the forearm. Some physiologists who have applied their skills to analysis of combat handgun technique insist that this gives the forward arm more strength with which to work.

**Thumb 45 Degrees Upward.** This is the grasp explained earlier in the chapter, and recommended for pistols with slide-mounted manual safety levers.

**High Thumb.** Characterized by a thumb that is in a high position with the median joint flexed and pointed upward, this hold is widely taught with the 1911 and similar pistols with frame-mounted safeties. While it does

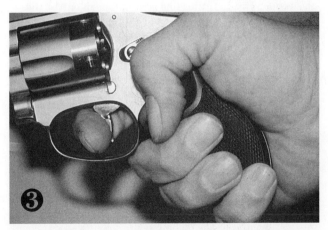

*The master grip is important on small-frame revolvers like this S&W Centennial with Uncle Mike's Boot Grips...*

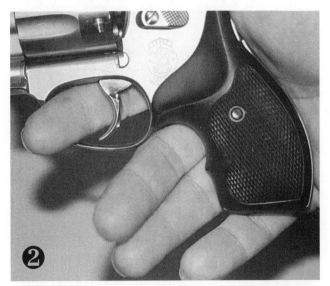

*...as the web of hand goes all the way up to the top edge of the rear gripframe the curve of the backstrap will be pulled tight into the hollow of hand. Note that only two fingers will be able to grasp the stocks, and that there is "too much trigger finger" for the short trigger reach. So...*

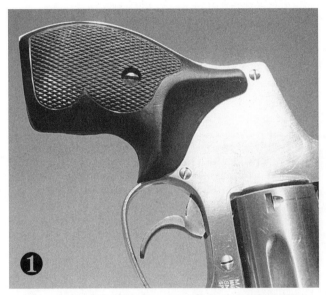

*...the little finger is locked under and the index finger is cocked out slightly to the right so distal joint makes contact with the trigger. The thumb is curled down for strength, and is barely clear of the tip of the trigger finger in the rearward position. If the hand was any bigger, the thumb might have to be moved upward out of the way. Note that on "hammerless" style guns, the web of hand can ride higher than with conventional revolvers, proportionally lowering bore axis and giving the shooter more control.*

indeed depress the thumb safety, it tends to pull the web of the hand away from the 1911 pistol's grip safety. This can render the gun unable to fire at the worst possible time. Those who have taught this grasp have traditionally, for obvious reasons, also recommended that the grip safety be deactivated. However, as explained elsewhere in the book, it is a Herculean task to try to convince a jury that someone who would intentionally deactivate a safety mechanism on a deadly weapon is anything but reckless. This grasp also tends to apply thumb pressure to the slide, particularly when gloves are worn or when strength goes out of control in a fight-or-flight state, jamming the pistol. The prevalence of this grasp caused Pachmayr and others to develop a device called a slide shield that keeps the high thumb from binding the slide. Common sense tells us that any technique that requires a mechanical fix to shield your gun is probably a technique that could present problems in a life-threatening emergency. This writer cannot in good conscience, recommend this grasp.

**Vertical Thumbs.** This is a stylized technique that is a signature of certain schools. The thumbs are pointed straight up. We have seen slides retarded in this fashion, causing jams. As the earlier experiment with your open hand showed, this thumb position minimizes your hand's overall grasping strength. Try as we might, we have not been able to elicit a logical, bio-mechanical explanation of any advantage offered by this technique. All we hear is "high thumbs equal high scores." That's a slogan, not an explanation, and frankly it's a slogan not borne out in major competitions where speed and accuracy of fire are directly and fairly tested.

### Summary

Fingerprints and palm prints are unique to the individual. Hand sizes and shapes as they interface with gun sizes and shapes are almost as much so. The shooter wants to spend lots of time experimenting with different grasps to see what works for *that* combination of user and hardware.

# Two-Handed Stances

Virtually all credible experts agree that when it is possible, a two-handed grasp of the handgun will give the combat shooter more control, and thus more speed and accuracy. If one accepts that defensive shooting is a martial art, it is similar to other such arts in that practitioners love to argue over subtleties of style. In Korean martial arts, the debate might revolve around the circular blocks of *Tang Soo Do* versus the more linear blocks of *Tae Kwon Do.* Among combat handgunners, when the topic of stance comes up after the guns are locked away, it's more than a two-beer argument. Lay in at least a case before the discussion even opens.

Countless hours have been whiled away discussing the Isosceles stance versus the Weaver, with modified forms of each (usually the latter) often thrown in to spice up the discussion. This is rather like boxing fans debating the merits of the left jab versus the right cross versus the uppercut. The difference is, no knowledgeable boxing fan would recommend his favorite punch to the exclusion of all others, but an amazing number of shooters insist that their preferred shooting stance is so superior to every other stance in every respect, it is the *only* way to shoot.

The fact is, each stance became popular among knowledgeable people because it had significant strengths. By the same token, each stance has become less than first choice for some other knowledgeable people because it may have had significant weaknesses. A more sensible approach might be the one taken by boxers: an understanding that while every fighter will have a best punch, a one-punch fighter will not last long in the ring. There is a time and a place where each stance may come into its own and be the technique of choice, even if it is not the given shooter's particular favorite.

Is the shooter long-limbed or not? Does the shooter have limited range of movement? Does he or she wear body armor, or perhaps clothing that could restrict body mobility? Is the shooter muscular or slim? Are the shooter's dominant eye and dominant hand on the same side, or does "cross-dominance" exist? Any of these factors and more could determine the best stance for each individual shooter at a certain time in their lives.

*The proper Isosceles stance: With the chest squared to the target, both arms are locked straight out, the upper body is very aggressively forward with the feet still farther apart, front-to-back as well as left-to-right.*

*Grandmaster Mark Mazzotta has won countless matches with the Isosceles stance.*

*Firearms instructor Simon Golub shows students how to begin in a ready position favored by competitive shooters and special forces operators...*

Let's examine the three primary stances, warts and all, listing strengths and weaknesses.

### Isosceles

This is perhaps the oldest two-handed pistol stance; this one involves thrusting both arms all the way forward until they are straight, forming an Isosceles triangle with the chest, which faces the target. Capt. William Fairbairn depicted it in the early 20th Century in his classic gunfight survival text "Shoot To Live," and Jeff Cooper at one time referred to the stance as the Fairbairn Isosceles.

Over the decades, this stance has gone through all manner of permutations. Done correctly, it is extremely powerful and has been used to win many championships shooting at high speed with powerful handguns. Done improperly, it may be the weakest of all shooting stances.

In the old days, when cops qualified with mild .38 Special wadcutters with insignificant recoil, they were taught to face the target squarely, standing straight up. If one Isosceles triangle (the arms) was good, coaches of the time seemed to be thinking, then two must be better: the officer was taught to spread the legs wide apart and often

*...and quickly extend...*

*The Isosceles stance is the near unanimous choice of today's top professional shooters, such as Doug Koenig, shown here at the Mid-Winter National IDPA championships at S&W in 2001.*

*...to the Modern Isosceles stance, firing the whole way, if needed, with good accuracy.*

*Better Technique = Better Performance* • 159

to lock them as well. Since there was now only precarious front-to-back balance, the legs being parallel, the outboard weight of the gun at the end of two fully extended arms tended to pull the shooter forward. To correct, shooters were taught to lean their shoulders back.

Balance was now completely gone. Even the .38 wadcutter would cause the gun's muzzle to rise significantly upon recoil. A more powerful gun could rock the shooter back on his heels with a single shot, and by the second or third round from a rapidly fired .44 Magnum, the officer might be tottering backwards. This sort of stance was to a proper Isosceles stance as Frankenstein's Monster was to humanity: a grotesque parody of the real thing.

A proper Isosceles stance, as taught in the StressFire (TM) shooting system, will see the chest squared to the target (as Dr. Walter Cannon, the first in-depth researcher of the fight or flight response, said the human body would do naturally in such a state), and the arms locked straight out to the target. However, the feet will be wide apart, not only side-to-side *but front to back,* and the head will come aggressively forward. Knees will be flexed; with the front leg's more so than the rear, but not to the exaggerated extent of the old, obsolete "FBI

*Various upper body shooting postures may be needed to adapt to certain positions when shooting from behind cover. Here, author finds the Isosceles works well from kneeling barricade position.*

*The Isosceles stance, in squaring torso with an identified threat, maximizes the portions of the body protected by armor...*

*...while the more bladed Classic Weaver stance opens the armpit and some of the side to incoming fire. The Weaver stance predated the development of soft, wearable body armor.*

crouch." The head will be forward of the shoulders, and the shoulders forward of the hips.

**Isosceles Advantages:** 1) This is a very simple posture. We take the fight or flight stance defined by Dr. Cannon and simply put a handgun at the end of two arms that extend fully toward the target. Physiologists who have looked at Isosceles shooting describe it as a simple gross motor skill, the kind easily accomplished under stress. 2) From Col. Rex Applegate to today's Bruce Siddle, trainers who look at these things scientifically find the Isosceles the most natural and logical two-hand hold for use under stress. 3) If the shooter is wearing body armor, this stance maximizes the armor's protective value as it squares the torso with the identified threat. 4) With the gun the maximum distance from head, the Isosceles minimizes ear damage if hearing protection cannot be worn. 5) It is ideal for night shooting. The Isosceles lines up the gun with the center of the shooter's head and body, and the head and body will align themselves instinctively in the direction of a suddenly perceived threat. 6) The Isosceles is ideally suited to pivoting toward the body's dominant hand side when feet are trapped in position and stepping is not possible.

**Isosceles Disadvantages:** 1) It works poorly if the shooter is off balance. 2) The stance may be impossible for those with elbow injuries, and difficult or impossible for those with inflamed elbow joints. 3) The gun bounces more than in a Weaver stance if the shooter fires when moving. 4) It is not compatible with tight, restrictive upper body garments such as tailored business suits, fastened motorcycle jackets, or some types of cold weather gear. 5) It provides a limited range of pivot toward the non-dominant side of the body when the feet are trapped in position.

**Cross-Dominant Correction:** None. Since this stance brings the gun to the centerline of both the head and body, the left eye and the right eye align themselves naturally with equal ease no matter which is dominant. This is the easiest technique, by far, for the cross-dominant shooter.

*Master shooter and instructor, and gunfight survivor, John Berletich prefers the Isosceles stance for all two-fisted handgunning. The pistol is Para-Ordnance LDA .45 auto.*

### Weaver Stance

In the 1950s in California, Col. Jeff Cooper began gunfight simulation contests originally called "Leatherslaps" as a research tool to determine the fastest, most accurate ways to return fire with handguns. It was thought originally that unsighted fire and one-handed

*Look what's on Phil Goddard's gun arm. Tendonitis or other arm problems can make Classic Weaver the technique of choice...*

*...as it is for Phil.*

shooting, being fastest, would rule. In the late 1950s a figure emerged to change that assumption forever. Jack Weaver was a deputy with the Los Angeles County Sheriff's Office. He brought his duty gun, a 6-inch Smith & Wesson K-38 revolver, to eye level for aiming and fired from a two-handed stance. He did both no matter what the distance...and he almost invariably got the center hits faster than the competition. Soon, his competitors realized that it wasn't just talent but superior technique that was at work.

The late John Plahn, an associate of Col. Cooper, was the one who really quantified Weaver's technique as more than just two-handed, eye-level shooting. He noticed that Weaver stood in a somewhat bladed stance, the strong side leg back to about 45 degrees, and that Jack bent both his arms sharply at the elbows. Weaver pulled back with his forward hand and pushed forward with his firing hand, with equal and opposite pressure.

*The classic Weaver Stance: Forward elbow down, both elbows bent, gun hand pushing, support hand pulling back.*

Decades earlier, J.H. "Fitz" FitzGerald of Colt's had written a book on combat handgun shooting in which, as an alternate technique for use when one had time, he demonstrated the exact same technique, nuance for nuance. There is no reason to believe that Weaver copied him. Rather, Weaver appears to have re-invented the stance independently, and used it to great advantage. It was Col. Cooper who named the stance after Weaver and was almost single-handedly responsible for promulgating it. During the 1980s, it was probably taught as the technique of choice by more police departments than any other, though by the 90s departments were tending to return to the Isosceles stance for a number of reasons.

Like the Isosceles, the Weaver is often interpreted incorrectly. If the body is too bladed, i.e., completely edgeways to the target, balance is lost. Great emphasis must be placed on a firm forward push of the gun hand and an equal and opposite rearward pull with the support hand. Without this dynamic, the bent arms lose force and not only is the gun's recoil exaggerated, but the frame can move so much that the slide "runs out of steam" and a cycling failure occurs, jamming the autoloader.

To avoid confusion with the many variations of "modified Weaver" stance, we'll refer here to the stance of Weaver and Cooper as the "Classic Weaver."

**Classic Weaver Advantages:** 1)Because the bent arms are foreshortened and do not extend as far, this Classic Weaver stance offers the shortest and therefore fastest path from holster to line of sight. 2) Because the gun is closer to the shooter's main body mass, it has less distance to move when the shooter must track multiple targets or moving targets, and is thus slightly faster in that regard. This is simple geometry based on the ARC principle (Axis, Radius, Circumference). 3) Because recoil is absorbed by the taut, bent arms acting as shock absorbers, this is the only two-handed stance that will survive an off-balance position in which the shooter's shoulders are leaning backward over the hips. 4) Because the gun is closer to the body and the elbows are tautly bent, that same shock absorption effect works from the ground up as well, making the Classic Weaver the most stable upper body position to use when firing while moving. 5) The Weaver's bent arms posture is much more comfortable for those with elbow injuries or ailments. 6) It is ideal for engaging to non-dominant side flank if the feet are not where they can quickly move. 7) Bringing the gun sights closer to the eyes, the Classic Weaver stance may work better for myopic shooters or with guns with small sights.

**Classic Weaver Disadvantages:** 1) The Classic Weaver is not at its best with shooters who are light on muscle mass and tone in the arms. 2) With body armor, the somewhat bladed torso posture of the typical Weaver practitioner turns the vulnerable open portions of the vest toward the threat. 3) This stance is poorly suited for engaging to dominant-side flank if the feet cannot quickly step to a new position. 4) The gun is held closer to head than with other two-hand stances, increasing potential for ear damage from gunshot report when used in the field without hearing protection. 5) It is generally considered a complex psycho-motor skill by physiologists, and is more difficult to learn than the Isosceles.

**Cross-Dominant Correction:** Drop the head toward strong side, i.e., right cheek to right shoulder to align left eye with gun in the right master hand. The original Weaver stance usually proves to be the most difficult two-handed technique for the cross-dominant shooter.

*Seasoned competitor and daily gun carrier Bill Fish finds Chapman's stance works best for him. The pistol is a Glock.*

## *"Modified Weaver": The Chapman Stance*

Ray Chapman, a contemporary of Jeff Cooper, understood the advantages of the Weaver stance over the old-fashioned version of the Isosceles. A fan of strong shooting platforms, he did not like what he perceived to be the weakened firing mount that occurred when the elbow of the firing arm was bent, sometimes bent to the point where the wrist also unlocked. Chapman shot his way to the top of the heap with his own technique. The gun arm was locked at every joint, rigid behind the gun, and the forward arm was bent at the elbow and pulling the whole locked gun arm into the shoulder, as if pulling in tightly on a rifle stock.

Because the gun arm is locked, it can become a lever that jerks upward with accentuated recoil if the shoulders are at body center or tilting backward, the same dynamic that made the old-fashioned Isosceles a poor choice. Unfortunately, some who teach this stance did not get it direct from its developer and teach a rearward lean, which limits the level of speed their students can achieve with it. Chapman himself always emphasized that the body should be in a forward lean, with the shoulders forward of the hips at least slightly, to get maximum benefit from his shooting stance.

Chapman called his technique simply a modified Weaver stance. In the last quarter of the 20th Century, it had come into vogue to call almost every two-handed stance a "modified Weaver," and this became imprecise and confusing. Those who knew Chapman and saw and copied specifically what he was doing, called the posture "the Chapman stance." Some schools, ranging from Lethal Force Institute to Firearms Academy of Seattle, still use this term to distinguish the stance developed by Chapman from the myriad other "modified Weavers" that abound in the shooting field.

The Chapman stance can be seen in many ways as a bridge between the two more famous-name stances, the Classic Weaver and the Isosceles. On the dominant hand side we have the locked skeleto-muscular support structure of the Isosceles stance, and on the support hand

*The Chapman stance, AKA Modified Weaver. The gun arm is locked with the shoulder forward; the bent forward arm pulls back tightly against gun arm. Note that feet are slightly farther apart and stance is slightly more aggressive.*

*Veteran street cop, combat shooting champion, and LFI instructor Denny Reichard uses the Chapman stance by choice with his preferred weapon, the Smith & Wesson .44 Magnum loaded with full-power ammo.*

side, we have dynamic tension, if not the truly isometric tension of the push/pull Classic Weaver. Thus, for many shooters this stance combines the best of both worlds without accepting the worst of either.

**Chapman Stance Advantages:** 1) This stance provides excellent commonality with long guns, as the gun arm functions like a rifle stock. 2) This posture is not particularly dependent on body shape or muscle tone/mass. 3.) It is better than the Weaver for those who wear body armor, since as the gun arm locks and the shoulder comes forward, the chest squares somewhat with the target.

**Chapman Stance Disadvantages:** 1) It does not give so much range of movement in pivot to the weak side as Weaver, nor to strong side as Isosceles. 2) The stance requires that shoulders be forward to work effectively, like Isosceles. 3) Not so effective for body armor wearers as

*SWAT cop and LFI instructor Larry Hickman demonstrates the correction for cross-dominance with a Classic Weaver stance...*

*...and with the Chapman stance...*

*...and with the Isosceles. The pistol is Beretta 92FS 9mm.*

Isosceles. Chapman himself taught police officers to shoot from Isosceles for this reason.

**Cross-Dominant Correction:** Keep the head erect, bringing the jaw or chin to the shoulder or bicep. While the tilted-head position necessary to make this correction with the Classic Weaver is awkward and "buries" most of the weak eye's viewing scan, the Chapman correction keeps the full danger scan and merely moves it a few degrees to one side. Though easier than with Weaver, the cross-dominant correction with Chapman is still not so easy as with the Isosceles stance.

*The author feels a competent defensive shooter should be conversant with all three of the primary two-hand stances. Here, at right, Ayoob leads a class through an empty-hand refresher on the Chapman stance just before they fire for qualification.*

## Notes On Terminology

Terminology in the world of the gun can be confusing, and once again "combat semantics" rears its ugly head.

Shooting champion and master pistolsmith D.R. Middlebrooks has developed a stance in which the

*As Ayoob fires a "double tap" from an aggressive StressFire Isosceles stance on the way to winning an IDPA match, Penny Maurer's high-speed camera clicks. Look carefully at the area around the STI Trojan 9mm pistol...*

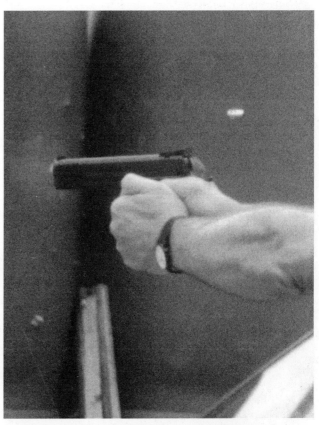

*...and you can see the blur of the hammer falling and the bloom of flame at the muzzle from the second shot while the spent casing from the first shot is still only inches from the ejection port. The Isosceles stance gives many people the best control. Photos by Penny Maurer.*

support arm is locked but the firing arm is bent, pushing against the locked gun arm. Some have called this a "reverse Chapman stance." The semantic correctness of this is debatable; it may appear that arms have swapped posture, but the dynamics are completely different.

A stance variously called "modern Isosceles" and "strong Isosceles" has become popular in IPSC circles. Both elbows are bent and a relaxed 40/60 percent pressure grasp is applied to the pistol. With elbows bent, the Isoscles triangle is broken into an uneven pentagonal shape. While this dexterity-intensive stance works in competition, and can certainly work in combat for someone who has practiced with it sufficiently to make it second nature, it may not be appropriate to call it any kind of an Isosceles stance.

Perhaps the most important point is this. Champions and gunfight survivors have used each of these stances alike. Each comes with a strong pedigree. Like the jab and the cross and the uppercut, there is a time and a place for each, and the competent fighter wants to know how to execute each of these techniques to perfection.

In the end, all those arguments over shooting stance may have been meaningless. For serious fighting, the ability to traverse from far weak side (favoring Weaver) to far strong side (favoring Isosceles) when you are caught on stairs or in tight spaces where you can't step into your favorite position has to be addressed. It really never should have been "Weaver versus Isosceles (versus Chapman stance)" at all. For the thinking practitioner of the combat handgun, it should be seen as knowing and being able to perform the true Weaver stance *and* the Isosceles stance *and* the Chapman stance.

*The author demonstrates an aggressive StressFire version of the Isosceles with a Kimber .45 auto while doing a Bill Drill (6 shots, 2 seconds, 7 yards, from the holster) at the IDPA New England Regional Championships, 2000.*

# One-Handed Stances

We all know that two-handed shooting is the most effective way to deliver fire with a combat handgun. Unfortunately, we also know that we won't always be able to use that method to return fire, so we have to have a Plan B in place. Plan B is a strong one-handed stance that gives you maximum delivery of accurate, rapid handgun fire under pressure.

Why can't we always do it from our strongest stance? It's one of those places where the rules of the range collide with the realities of the street. On the range, we normally

*Firearms instructor Sam Young shows one reason one-handed shooting skills are important: you may have to use one hand to communicate while the other covers the danger zone. His home defense pistol...*

*...is this .40 caliber Glock 22, mounted with an M3 Illuminator. Note that with the trigger finger manipulating the flashlight switch, it is kept safely off the trigger.*

know when we're going to fire and (we hope!) in what direction. Thus, we "address the target." That is, we get ourselves set to fire in a certain direction from a certain preferred stance, sometimes without even realizing we are doing it.

Unfortunately, attacks often come from unpredicted directions. A smart opponent will attack from the rear or the flank. As you spin to engage, one arm may reflexively go outward for balance as the other raises the gun. The subconscious, knowing that the support hand isn't going to reach its intended destination, sends its message to the trigger finger: "Open fire, *now!*"

Problems might arise because other situations besides the angle of attack. One hand could be pushing a victim out of the line of fire, or dragging a wounded partner, or clutching a communication device or a flashlight that's your only source of illumination in the darkness. There is also the possibility that the opponent has seized you by one arm, or has already wounded you there. Even those trained and practiced with two-handed shooting to the point where it constitutes 95 percent of their experience firing a handgun, may have to shoot one-handed when trouble strikes in the real world.

How often does that happen? Back in the 70s, I spent some time in New York City with the legendary Lt. Francis McGee, then head of NYPD's Firearms and Tactics Unit. I studied under him at the outdoor range facility at Rodman's Neck during the day, and picked his brains far into the night at his home, where I was staying. The SOP-9 study had by then been in place for several years. Standard Operating Procedure Number Nine, the intensive debriefing of every member of the service who fired his or her weapon anywhere but on the range, included the question, "Did you fire with one hand or with two?" The results thus far indicated that approximately half the shootings had caught the officers in such a position that they'd had to return fire one-handed.

### Strong Stances

With half as many hands as we had to control the gun before, we have to get every ounce of hand strength out of the one we have left to fight with. If you don't care to shoot with the thumb curled down in two-handed

*A locked-down thumb and a strong Shotokan Punch stance let the author easily control this powerful .357 SIG, Model P229.*

postures, you might want to consider going to it now for added strength. Years ago, I hosted then-world champion Rob Leatham to teach an advanced combat competition course. Though Rob was a pioneer in shooting with the thumbs pointing toward the target in his own version of an Isosceles hold, he made a point of telling the advanced shooters to curl their thumbs down for added strength when they had to fire one-handed.

What to do with the other arm? It needs to be out of the way where its mass, roughly 9 percent of body mass, won't pull the body to one side and take the gun off target. We teach that it be curled up tight to the side, palm up in a fist, the way the non-striking hand would be for a karate practitioner executing a reverse punch. This puts the hand about where it would be if it was holding a cell phone or police radio, or dragging a wounded partner. Turning the palm upwards and clenching the fist tightly creates a sympathetic tightening throughout the entire upper body's voluntary muscle structure, helping to tighten the firing hand still

*The locked down thumb is important for one-handed shooting, and the author will sacrifice it only for something more important – in this case, disengaging the safety of this Ruger P90 .45...*

*...or making sure the thumb doesn't block the trigger finger with this small-handled Kahr K40 Covert pistol.*

In the StressFire (TM) shooting system, if the opposite leg is forward you're in a reverse punch position...

...with feet parallel, you flex your knees and drop your butt back in a mild version of a karate "horse stance"...

...the single strongest stance is probably a forward punch posture, shown here...

...and all three can be combined with the McMillan/Chapman rotation of the pistol, which is especially suitable for cross dominant shooting. Note that in all cases the fist is drawn up to the pectoral muscle for added strength. A dummy Glock 19 is being used for photographer's safety.

*A lightweight, polymer-framed Ruger P97 is at the height of its recoil as Ayoob fires from 4 yards with .45 ball ammo.*

*LFI assistant instructor Cliff Ziegler demonstrates for students, keeping all hits in a tight chest group rapid-fire with his HK USP40 Compact.*

more. In fact, because human hands can manifest a phenomenon called interlimb response, the one hand won't reach full strength in grasp until the fingers of the opposite hand are sympathetically contracting.

It is interesting to look through a few decades of gun magazines and shooting manuals to see how the one-handed stance has evolved. In the old days, the shooter would stand erect, gun arm straight out, and free hand either hooked on the waist, tucked into a pocket, or on the

*Note that the rear leg is digging into ground, driving the upper body forward into the Colt 10mm during one-hand rapid fire. The recoil compensator on this Mark Morris gun helps, too!*

hip or behind the back. Some would just let the arm hang free. And, if the camera captured the moment of the shot, the gun muzzle could be seen to be kicking skyward.

The institutionalization of IPSC in the mid-1970s brought some conformity to technique as the top shooters, known as the "super squad," generously shared their shooting tips with others. A hand flat on the belly got it out of the way and eliminated the "pendulum effect" of the loose arm swinging, but did nothing to actually enhance the firing hand's ability to do its job. The simultaneous development of the StressFire (TM) martial arts-based "punch" techniques, with the free hand now a fist, palm up, under the pectoral muscle, also emerged. These were widely copied.

With the upper body aggressively forward, and the head also forward (because "where the head goes, the body follows") shooters achieved much more powerful one-handed stances than those of the past. With one hand recoil was now controllable to the degree of the early version two-handed Weaver stance, and actually stronger than the old-fashioned version of the Isosceles. It was not, however, possible to make the one-handed posture stronger than the strongest, most efficient two-handed stances, and in all probability that will never prove possible.

### Foot Position

The International Shooting Union (ISU) and practitioners of America's "Conventional Pistol" (i.e., bull's-eye) are taught to stand with their right foot forward if the pistol is in their right hand. This is because it applies no torque to the spine, it balances the shooter well, and it extends the outboard weight of the upper limb directly over the weight-bearing lower limb.

Unfortunately, we can't always jump into our favorite position when attacked. The shooter needs to know how to fire effectively whether his strong foot is forward, or his weak-side foot is forward, or his feet are parallel. In the latter case, flexing at the knees and dropping the hips back will give a stable posture if the head and shoulders are forward. If the weak side foot is forward, one can shoot from a well-balanced stance as if throwing what a karate stylist would call a reverse punch and a boxer, a right cross. The single strongest one-handed posture,

*In one-handed shooting, it is all the more important that the gun fits the hand. A Pearce grip extender for the little finger to grasp, and a locked down thumb help this shooter control the baby Glock.*

*Phil Goddard uses slight McMillan rotation when firing with the non-dominant hand only. The big .45 slugs from his Colt Combat Commander are staying in the "A" zone of the target.*

however, will still be dominant hand forward/same side leg forward. This is the position a boxer would call a jab and a karate practitioner, a forward punch.

### Turning the Gun

It has come into vogue in recent years to tilt the gun over to one side. Does this come under cinematic BS, or true secrets of the handgun ninja? Well, the answer is yes to both, depending how it's performed...

The technique goes back to the late 1950s. A young Marine pistol ace named Bill McMillan was shooting for the gold, but had one small problem: He was cross-dominant. He figured out that by adjusting the sights of his pistol, a cant of about 45 degrees inward aligned the sights dead on with the eye opposite his gun hand and still put the shots dead center. Soon he had moved to the head of the pack, winning the Gold Medal for the United States in the Pan-American Games circa 1960.

Ray Chapman picked up on this trick and made it his technique of choice for one-handed work in practical handgun competition. With less precise accuracy

required, the sights didn't need to be adjusted for the typical close range work. Chapman discovered that whichever side the shooter's dominant eye happened to be on, that slight turning of the wrist created a more propitious alignment of the skeleto-muscular support structure of the arm, resulting in a stronger hold. Chapman, it should be noted, always taught accuracy ahead of speed and always emphasized very strong shooting positions. Clint Smith, who later became head of the famous shooting school Thunder Ranch, has also taught the "McMillan rotation" for several years as the preferred one-handed technique.

Some find it works better for one hand than the other. At our school, we tell the students to feel free to "mix and match." Many end up preferring to shoot with the gun straight up on their dominant eye side, and in the McMillan/Chapman rotation when firing with their other hand. (Some shooters find that the rotation works in two-hand shooting as well. Larry Nichols, the nationally famous rangemaster and master police trainer from the Burbank (Cal.) PD, teaches this as technique of choice.

*Tilting of the gun may happen naturally when emergencies require you to fire at awkward angles like this...*

*...or like this, as one California StressFire graduate had to when he came under fire from an ambusher with a rifle. The graduate won, killing his assailant.*

*LFI student Joyce Fowler keeps them all in the A-zone with her .45 auto, while firing weak-hand-only using McMillan Tilt and StressFire Punch techniques. She went on to become multiple-time IDPA National Champion in the women's division.*

Gila Hayes, another nationally known instructor, teaches it as a two-handed option for the cross-dominant shooter.)

The proper rotation is between 15 and 45 degrees. Less than that doesn't do much; more than that, and the arm is past the point of maximum strength. However, several years ago films exploiting urban violence began showing gang-bangers shooting with a strange hold in which the pistol was turned over 90 degrees. "Life imitates art," and soon this technique was being observed on the street, generally in the hands of the bad guys.

Where did it come from? We may never know for sure. One theory is that a director or a technical advisor saw a security camera film of a felonious shooting in which the armed robber held his gun this way to reach over a counter and shoot a clerk who was trying to hide from him, and apparently decided that this was the new signature technique of the "gangstas." Another theory is that directors figured out that turning the pistol over

*Despite an injured elbow, Phil Goddard keeps every shot in a heart-size group with a straight-up hold and StressFire Punch technique, strong-hand-only.*

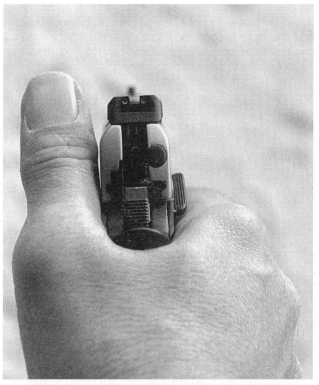

*A shooter's eye view as the thumb prepares to "wipe" a 1911's safety catch. One should always use the gun hand thumb to manipulate the safety, since often that's the only thumb that will be available to perform the task.*

*Firing from this awkward downed position, a shooter can't get body weight into the gun; the triceps muscle of the arm should be practiced in pulling this Glock 22 down from recoil.*

allowed the menacing gun, and all of the actor's facial features, to be seen in the same frame by the camera. Who knows?

In any case, it is demonstrably a stupid way to shoot. The wrist has by this point run out of range of movement, and a person holding a handgun in this fashion can be disarmed with minimal effort. The recoil tracks the gun violently toward the weak hand side. This limits the ability to put multiple shots into the same stubborn aggressor, and it also probably accounts for some of the innocent bystanders hit by gang members who fire at one another this way.

The only time we've seen anything like this prove useful is for the person who is ducking to one side as they fire. As the body goes forward to the side, it will prove awkward to keep the sights upright, and it will be almost impossible to align them. In one California shooting, an officer trained in StressFire (TM) shooting came under fire from a suspect with an autoloading rifle as he bailed out the door of his patrol car. Raising his SIG P220, he saw the service pistol was turned over 90 degrees, but also that the sights were on the suspect. Remembering his instructor's admonition that if the sights were on target the shot would go true, he fired...and center-punched his attacker through the chest with a 230-grain .45 hollow-point, saving his own life.

Numerous "downed officer" positions, such as down laterally on the weak hand side, may make this position natural. However, vis-a-vis the body position, it *is* natural from here, since the shooter's arm is in its usual alignment with the torso.

### Bottom Line

You want to practice with the one-handed techniques just as with the two-handed, to see which work best for you. Your brother may be a straight-up shooter and you may do your best with the McMillan tilt, or vice-versa. You won't know until you try them all and analyze your performance.

Be sure to spend lots of time practicing *weak-hand-only* shooting. This is a good reason to have an ambidextrous safety and/or decocking lever. History shows that because humans look at what threatens them, and what threatens the armed criminal is the gun in the good person's hand, the good person's gun arm is disproportionately likely to draw fire and take a bullet. While a wound to the gun arm or hand may not leave you incapable of firing with that hand, there are no guarantees.

We also need to think ahead. We may not be disabled in a fight. We might simply break our dominant arm or wrist in a routine accident. This will be a lousy time to start learning how to defend ourselves and our families with a weak-hand-only option. It makes sense to start thinking right now about having an ambidextrous gun in a weak side holster from which we are familiar with drawing and firing using the non-dominant hand.

None of us seems to practice enough on one-handed shooting. When street results indicate that a good half of the time, that's exactly what we'll have to do, logic may be telling us to restructure our training priorities and schedule a whole lot more one-handed combat pistolcraft drills.

*Using techniques recommended in this chapter, Ayoob is on his way to winning the revolver class at an IDPA match, sweeping an array of targets weak-hand-only with a Bob Lloyd-tuned S&W 4-inch Model 686.*

# CHAPTER ELEVEN

# Avoiding Mistakes

## Gun Accidents

In the term "defensive weapon," the emphasis is normally on the first word. But as far as safety, the emphasis has to shift to the second. A weapon, by definition, can become a vehicle of unintended harm if handled or stored carelessly. We do not leave a can of lye open on the floor where the baby can reach it. We do not leave our car parked on a hill with the transmission set in Neutral. The firearm demands similar rules of common sense.

In the early 1990s, I was teaching a class being filmed by a crew doing a documentary on private ownership of firearms in the U.S. The topic had come around to home safety, and when I was done speaking, we opened it up for questions and answers. The person in charge of the documentary had noticed that my 9-year-old daughter was in the room, and he asked pointedly if I had taught her the safety rules I was propounding. I just said, "Why don't you ask her?"

They stuck the camera a few inches from my little girl's face and asked her about gun safety. With a perfect poise that approached nonchalance, Justine sweetly replied, "Treat every gun as if it is loaded. Never let it point at anything you aren't prepared to destroy. Never touch the trigger until you are going to fire, and always be sure of your target and what is behind it."

The film crew was dumbstruck. The father, on the other hand, had an ear-to-ear grin of pride. Justine had

just recited the four primary rules of firearms safety as promulgated by one of the great leaders in the field, Col. Jeff Cooper.

Justine, like her older sister Cat, had grown up among firearms. Both her parents were licensed to carry, and one was required to at work. When they were tiny, guns were stored in such a way that they could not reach or activate them. Each began helping me clean guns at the age of 5. This de-mystified an object that the entertainment media had glorified as an instrument of power, and also de-glamorized it. They understood quickly how guns worked. An important benefit of this was that if they were ever in a playmate's house and the other child took his parents' gun out of the closet or nightstand, I wanted my kids to know how to "de-fang the snake" – how to unload the gun and/or lock up its firing mechanism.

Both began shooting at the age of 6 with .22s. Both had progressed to more powerful weapons by the age of 10 or 11. Neither ever gave their mother or me a minute's worry about firearms safety.

Loaded guns should not be left unsecured. They are vulnerable to burglars (who might turn them on innocent people sooner than you think, perhaps even on you or a family member who comes home unexpectedly and interrupts the burglary). They are vulnerable to certain members of the family, friends, and acquaintances who drop by unexpectedly and rummage about in other people's homes without permission. We always think of securing guns from children, but irresponsibility knows no age limit: the guns should be kept from *all* unauthorized hands. As the responsible owner, you are the one who determines who is authorized to touch the firearm.

### Routine Handling

Every now and then you get something like a cartridge stuck in the chamber of an auto pistol. It will require you to forcibly manipulate the slide, maybe whack it with something, and you suddenly realize there's a live round that is stuck in there that can be fired from the gun. At such a moment, you'll want a safe direction in which to point the pistol. Accidental discharges have occurred during loading and particularly unloading. For all these reasons, think about something like a big bucket of sand in a corner of a kitchen. If a curious guest asks what it's doing there, you can honestly answer, "Fire safety."

All expert shooters can tell you that dry fire – going through the motions pulling the trigger of an unloaded gun – is an important route to shooting mastery. But we can all tell you stories of the day a live round somehow migrated

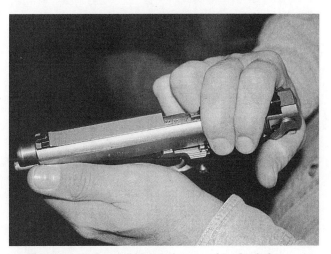

*This "armorer's grip" is sometimes used to check the chamber of double-action autos. It gives more control when pulling slide back against a hammer that is being held down by a powerful mainspring.*

into an empty firing chamber. This is why you should rigidly discipline yourself to dry fire only at something that could safely stop the most powerful bullet that might possibly emerge from that particular gun's muzzle.

This is one reason why basements have become favorite locations for shooting hobbyists' "gun rooms." I think it's a good idea for any armed citizen to own a bullet-resistant vest. I keep mine stored under the bed so I can throw it on any time the alarm goes off. Remember, the first definition of "alarm" is "a call to arms." Any situation for which I need a defensive firearm is a situation where a quickly donned vest would be comforting. And, more to the point at the moment, the bullet-resistant vest can always be set against a wall and used as the backstop for dry fire practice. It can always be set against the wall or on the floor when dealing with that pistol that had a round stuck in the chamber. It is simply one more safety net. How many things do we have in our homes that are designed to stop bullets? This is one.

### Safe Manipulation

When you check the chamber of an auto pistol, don't do it from the front. If the hands slip, the strong recoil spring will slam forward hard enough to leave the muzzle of the loaded gun pointing at one or more of your fingers.

It's not just "on target, on trigger; off target, off trigger." That creates a subconscious mindset of putting the finger on the trigger as soon as you're taking a suspect at gunpoint, since the subconscious may believe that you are indeed on target. The rule is, *do not let the finger enter the trigger guard until the immediate intention to fire has been formulated and confirmed.*

Safety devices can fool you. They're just one more net in a layer of safety nets, and you never rely on just one. In the Midwest, a police officer wanted to show someone how the round in the chamber of his S&W 9mm would not fire if the magazine was removed. However, he maintained pressure on the trigger as he removed the magazine. This action bypassed the disconnector safety. He then put the palm of his hand in front of what he knew to be a still-loaded gun, and pulled the trigger. He shot the hell out of his own hand. Oddly enough, his response was to sue Smith & Wesson…sigh.

Do not lower the slide of a 1911 pistol while holding the trigger back. It is an archaic practice that will eventually lead to a slip and an accidental discharge. In the immortal words of John Dean, who was admittedly talking about something else at the time, "That information is no longer operative."

Do not carry the 1911 pistol with the hammer down, or at half cock, with a live round in the chamber. No matter what generation or style of manufacture, there is likely to be an unintended discharge if the hammer is struck, and there is a high likelihood of an accidental firing when cocking or lowering the hammer because of the awkwardness of the procedure. If you are not comfortable carrying it cocked and locked as it was designed to be, go to a double-action pistol or leave the 1911's chamber empty.

It is always safer to retract an auto pistol's slide with the "slingshot" rather than the "overhand" technique (see photos). With an overhand grasp, the arm wants to align itself in the direction in which it is applying force and, if your concentration slips for an instant, you can find the muzzle pointing at the elbow or at someone next to you. Similarly, avoid pulling the gun into your body for leverage as you work the slide. If it is too hard to pull

back, use the heel of the free hand to cock the hammer. This will relieve mainspring pressure that is being exerted against the slide through the hammer, and allow the slide to be more easily retracted.

If the gun goes "poof" instead of "bang," *stop shooting!* An underloaded round has probably lodged a bullet in the barrel. Another shot behind it will lead to catastrophic pressures that can blow up the gun and cause serious injury.

Never assume that someone else has cleared a gun of ammunition, even if he appears to do so. If I or any other professional hands you a gun we have just cleared, we

*This old method of chamber-checking a 1911 is dangerous since, at various points in the procedure, finger gets too close to loaded gun's muzzle and thumb gets too close to trigger…*

*…this method is better, but still brings hand uncomfortably close to business end…*

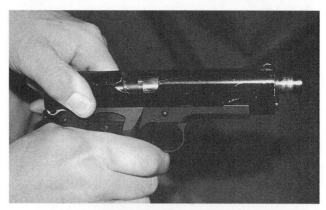

*…and this, the slingshot technique, is the safest way of all.*

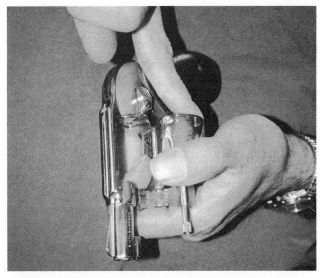

*When checking to make sure the handgun is empty, get into the habit of checking by feel as well as sight. With a revolver, like this S&W Model 38 Bodyguard, press the index finger of the dominant hand into every empty chamber...*

*...with an auto pistol, use the little finger of the non-dominant hand to probe the magazine well...*

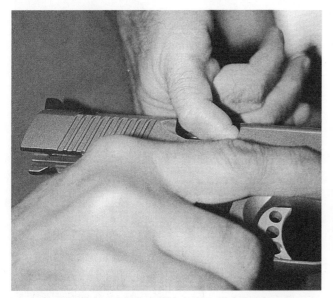

*...and the firing chamber. This habit will fail-safe you when checking handguns in the dark or when there are distractions.*

*expect* you to double check it to confirm that it is unloaded. We may even be testing you. If you check what we just checked, no professional will be insulted; if you *don't,* we'll think you're an amateur.

When determining that a gun is unloaded, check by sight and feel. With the revolver, get into the habit of probing each empty chamber with the tip of your dominant hand index finger (usually the most sensitive of the 10 digits) until you feel the sharp-edged recess. With an auto pistol, lock it open and probe the magazine well and the firing chamber with the little finger of your non-dominant hand (usually the narrowest of the 10 digits). You may feel stupid doing this in clear light where you can plainly see that it is unloaded, but you are programming yourself for some high-stress dark and stormy night when you have to check a gun and can't see what's in it.

When you have set down an unloaded gun and left the room, or even turned your back on it, *check it again.* When an unloaded gun has left your line of sight, consider it contaminated.

When you remove a live cartridge from a semiautomatic pistol's firing chamber, don't eject it into your palm. This practice is a holdover from the old days of early military pistol designs with short ejectors. A long ejector, as found on today's 1911 pistols, most double action autos, and the Glock, can every now and then get into alignment with the primer, and if the primer is driven against it hard, it can fire the cartridge. This "open chamber detonation" will turn the shell casing into a hand grenade that spews brass fragments at high pressure into the palm of your hand, lacerating vulnerable nerves. We have seen cases of this that resulted in a reported 70 percent nerve damage to the afflicted area. Let the cartridge fall clear, keeping your face away from it. Always be wearing some sort of eye protection.

When dry firing, make sure there is no live ammunition anywhere in the same room. Never practice speed reloading and trigger-pulling on the same night. When practicing reloading, use dummy ammunition or, better yet with an auto, weighted dummy magazines available from Dillon.

When cleaning the gun, make sure you're in a well-ventilated space, preferably outdoors. The carbon tetrachloride in some gun cleaning compounds can be toxic in cumulative doses. It is a good idea to wear latex or

*A thickly packed stand-up pile of books or magazines makes a safe backstop for dry fire. Mark Maynard demonstrates with an S&W Model 686 revolver.*

nitrile gloves while cleaning guns. This keeps lead and other toxins from getting into microscopic cuts on the hand. Wear an inexpensive gauze mask when cleaning. Remember, each time you pull that brush out of the barrel, you're putting tiny bits of lead into the same cubic yard of air you're about to inhale. Finally, always wear eye protection. In my experience, Gun Scrubber in the eyes is worse than pepper spray, and we know of one pistol champion who lost partial sight in one eye when the recoil spring cap of his pistol snapped free and hit his unprotected eye when he was taking the gun apart.

### Gun Abuse/Substance Abuse

Common sense tells us that if we're going to get smashed at the New Year's Eve party, we should leave the gun at home. We also need to be certain about prescription medication. Any prescription with a warning label that says, "Do not operate dangerous equipment" can also be read as "don't go shooting while taking this medication." It is telling us that our concentration will be sufficiently impaired that we won't be at our best in maintaining our usual rigid care in firearms handling.

Similarly, if you are fatigued or distracted or angry, it is not a good time to be handling potentially lethal weapons. Anything that gets in the way of your concentration will get in the way of safe gun handling.

### Things People Don't Think About

One reason shooting is such a great hobby is that it's a tremendously good stress-reliever. A lot of people don't understand how this works. They think that we go to the range, imagine our boss's face on the picture downrange, and act out some homicidal rage by shooting it again and again. That's not how it works at all.

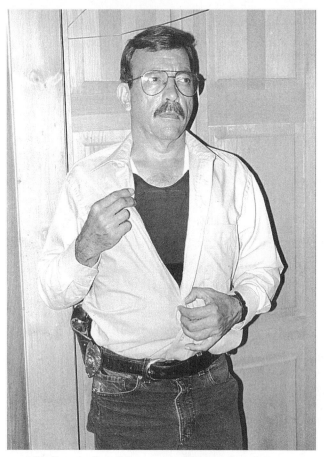

*A "bullet-proof vest" has more safety uses than the obvious, as pointed out in this chapter.*

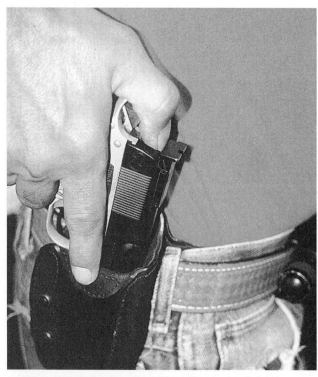

*When holstering, keep the trigger finger extended so it can't foul the trigger, and the thumb on hammer. The thumb can catch a hammer that starts to move forward before a shot is fired, as with this Colt 10mm auto...*

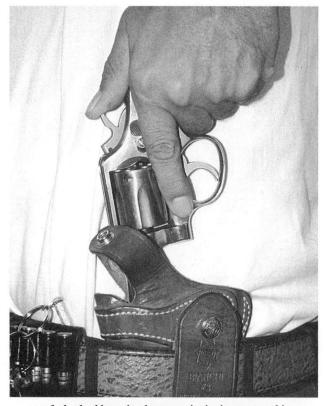

*...or feel a double-action hammer rise in time to stop things before that hammer can fall and cause a discharge.*

The reason shooting is such a good stress reliever is that, like sky-diving or rock climbing or SCUBA diving, *you have to concentrate on what you're doing to the point where all other BS is excluded from your mind. You must concentrate or you can get killed!* Our focus on safe shooting banishes our thoughts of job stress, family problems, or whether our team won the Super Bowl. If at

*The home defense gun should be only one of several layers of protection. Consider getting a good, properly trained dog...*

*...a good alarm system...*

*...and some kind of safe. Even the better hotel rooms, as shown here, have safes available for guests.*

any time we find ourselves on the line preoccupied with other, more compelling thoughts, it's time to pack up and stop shooting for awhile, perhaps for the rest of the day. Not because we're going to have a psychotic break, but because we can't concentrate sufficiently on something that demands our complete attention. We do it this way for the same reason that we tell our teenage children not to drive when they're upset.

In defensive shooting, as in martial arts, the practitioner seeks to become so skillful that the techniques may be employed automatically without thinking about them when the proper stimulus comes. This is all to the good. However, we must walk a fine line when it comes to firearms safety. Automatic pilot is a fine thing, but it cannot be trusted exclusively. We must always strive for a "conscious competence" level when we're performing firearms safety tasks. We must think about what we are doing. If we have achieved the ideal Zen state of unconscious competence in firearms handling and do everything correctly without thinking about it, that's wonderful, but we need to double check once more at the conscious competence level to confirm the good job that we hope our unconscious competence carried out.

We need to be ruthlessly and honestly critical of ourselves. If we have what are currently called "anger management problems," we won't be ready to have immediate access to loaded firearms until those things are under control. If we sleepwalk, it may not be a good idea having guns available in the bedroom.

A good friend of mine is a world-class competitive shooter with a strong background in law enforcement. He is one of the most well adjusted human beings and family men I know. He also happens to be a very deep sleeper, and tends to be a bit groggy and disoriented for several seconds when suddenly awakened. Recognizing that, he has made a point of keeping his home defense pistol, a Browning 9mm semiautomatic, in a secured drawer across the bedroom. It is stored with the chamber empty. He knows that by the time he has gotten up, crossed the room, retrieved the gun, and chambered a round, he will be awake and clear-headed. This is the kind of self-analysis we all need to go through.

### Layered Defense

The police officer on the street has layers of physical defenses. He is taught Verbal Judo (™), a crisis intervention skill. He is taught "soft" come-along holds and "hard" strikes with fist and forearm, with knee and foot. He carries pepper spray, and can resort, next, to his baton. He will have a handgun on the duty belt, and hopefully a shotgun and/or rifle in the patrol car if things get worse yet.

The citizen should have layered defenses in the home. Good locks in solid doors, secure windows, alarms, perhaps an intercom or even a closed-circuit TV at the door, perhaps professionally-trained protection dogs and, of course, firearms.

Gun safety also demands a layered series of defenses. We secure the guns from unauthorized hands. We are constantly aware of where any lethal weapon is and what its condition is. We check by sight and feel. Redundancy is the key. We want to create net after net after carefully deployed net to keep accidents from happening.

Let's close with a very insightful statement by an NRA Director and firearms instructor named Mike Baker. Says Mike, "Seemingly obsessive concern with firearms safety is the mark of the firearms professional."

# The Concealed Carry Faux Pas

*"Sex and Violence: You can't enjoy the one if you don't survive the other."*

> Richard C. Davis, inventor of soft body armor, armed citizen, and gunfight survivor.

*"I don't mind where people make love, so long as they don't do it in the street and frighten the horses."*

> Beatrice Tanner Campbell, arbiter of etiquette in days past.

Richard Davis and Beatrice Tanner Campbell aren't usually discussed in the same paragraph, but it's appropriate here. We lawfully carry guns because we want to stay alive to enjoy the good things in life. Because we are licensed to wear them in public, we do indeed "do it in the street," and therefore we must take all the more care not to "frighten the horses."

In most jurisdictions, concealment is not only authorized by the license, but also tacitly required. Rookie cops are known for the need to "flash," to just show someone that for the first time in their life, "they've got the power." Armed citizens are well advised to avoid that temptation. The mark of the professional is that few people know that they go about armed. Discretion is critical.

A spiritual descendant of Mrs. Campbell is Judith Martin, who writes the popular "Miss Manners" etiquette column for the newspapers. Some years ago she had a column that read something like this:

"Dear Miss Manners:

"My job requires me to carry a gun. Recently at a party, I sat down awkwardly on a couch and my gun fell to the floor in plain sight. Everyone stared and I was quite shaken. It was most embarrassing. What does one do in such a situation?"

(signed) "Armed and Confused"

The columnist's reply was similar to this:

"Dear Armed and Confused:

"You should have immediately picked up your firearm and secured it. You should have then self-effacingly stated, 'I'm terribly sorry. My job requires me to carry a gun. Don't worry, no one is in danger.' Then you should have made a graceful exit. And *then* you should have gone out immediately and purchased a holster that would not let your gun fall out. – Miss Manners"

Clearly, Judith Martin is one of us!

You want to avoid "flashing" the gun or allowing it to "print," that is, to become visible in outline under the concealing garments. If you carry in a pocket, use a pocket holster designed to break up the gun's distinctive outline. Another option is to fold up a road map or pamphlet lengthwise, and put it in the pocket between the outer fabric and the gun. If you have a shallow pocket, this will

*WRONG! A high reach with the hand on the holster side pulls up the jacket and flashes the gun, in this case an S&W .45 auto.*

*RIGHT! Discreetly holding down the hem of the jacket on the gun side, the pistol-packer makes the high reach with the opposite hand.*

The jacket covers the pistol, but let's say it's just too warm…

…however, leaving the gun exposed like this could "frighten the horses"…

…so instead you shrug off the jacket while seated, like this…

…and sort of puff it out around the holstered gun. You're comfortable. The gun is accessible but out of sight. Remember, however, to put your arms back into your sleeves before you stand up again!

also prevent someone standing in a waiting line behind you from glancing down and seeing the backstrap of the pistol peeking out of the opening of the pocket.

If you wear a shoulder holster, make sure the concealing garment is made of substantial fabric that the lines of the harness do not print. When you bend forward, use one hand or forearm to hold the garment closed on the holster side. Otherwise, a shoulder holster that is not secured to the belt may swing forward and become visible to someone on the side opposite the gun.

If you bend down to pick something up, do it like a back patient. Keep the spine and torso vertical, and bend at the knees. Bending at the waist causes a gun in a hip holster to print starkly.

Avoid middle of the back holsters. Anywhere else on your waistband, if the gun catches the hem of the garment and pulls it up revealingly, you'll quickly either feel it or notice it in peripheral vision. Neither will be true if the gun is in the small of your back. It may be completely exposed, and you'll be the only person within 300 yards who *doesn't* know that your gun is hanging out.

It will be apparent in this book that the author is a believer in safety straps. That's partly so the gun won't be lost in a fall or foot pursuit or other strenuous activity. It's partly because if you're grappling with someone and his hands go around your waist, feel the gun, and begin tugging, you want to buy some "reactionary gap" time. It is also partly to avoid something as simple as sitting in a lattice-back chair and having your gun suddenly leave the holster.

I was once vacationing in Florida, legal to carry a gun, with a 1911 .45 auto, in an open-top, inside-the-waistband holster, under a loose sport shirt. I sat down in a beach chair next to a pool, adjusted the back of the chair up and settled myself. I heard a "clunk." I thought, *Clunk? Vas ist das Clunk?* I glanced down and saw a remarkably familiar combat custom .45 auto lying at poolside. So did a couple of other rather wide-eyed people. I scooped up the pistol and tucked it away, remarking to one concerned onlooker, "Sorry, I'm a cop, they make me carry this damn thing." Then, like the poor soul who wrote to Miss Manners, I beat a hasty retreat.

What had happened was that as I shifted my weight upward to settle in the chair, the butt of the pistol had become caught in the open latticework at the back of the

chair. When I lowered myself, the movement in essence pulled the holster down and out from around the gun, which then toppled to the pavement.

This is also a good reason to carry a pistol that is "drop safe." It isn't enough to smugly say, "I don't intend to drop my gun." I didn't intend to, either. But if things we didn't intend to do never happened, we wouldn't have to carry guns in the first place. Out West, a lady with a cute little derringer in her purse dropped the bag accidentally. The pistol inside received the impact as the purse hit the floor and discharged, sending a bullet up out of the handbag and into the chest of a man standing nearby.

When you are reaching upward, particularly with a short jacket on, take care that the garment does not lift so much that it exposes the gun or even part of the holster. If the pistol is on your right hip, you might want to discreetly hold the hem of the jacket in place with your right hand as you reach with your left. If that will flash my spare magazine pouch, which some might find just as unsettling, this writer is of such an age that he can commandeer some passing youngster and say, "Excuse me, son, could you reach an item on that top shelf for an old man?"

If you have an ankle holster on, before you leave the house, sit down and see how much the pant's cuff rides up when you're seated. If the bottom of the holster becomes exposed, nature is telling you to pull your sock up on the *outside* of the holster, taking care that it does not come up over the edge of the holster mouth where it could snag a draw. Now, if the cuff lifts while you're sitting in a restaurant, it just looks like you have a baggy sock. You may get a summons from the Fashion Police, but the Gun Police will leave you alone.

When in restaurants, try to sit with your gun/holster side toward the wall. This will minimize chances of the gun being spotted as you get up.

*A good insurance policy against the gun coming out of the holster is a safety strap design. Here, an S&W Model 10 rides in a Strong Piece-Keeper…*

*…which uses a unique two-stage thumb-break that won't release by accident and is also likely to thwart an intentional gun-grab by unauthorized hands.*

If you are wearing a jacket and find yourself seated someplace unbearably hot, you can take off the jacket without flashing the gun. Simply sit down with the garment on, then shrug out of the sleeves and let the jacket sort of fluff up around your waist. Done with care, this will hide the gun. Now you'll be comfortable, and you won't become conspicuous by being the only person in the place wearing a jacket.

If you carry your firearm off-body in a purse or fake Daytimer (™) or whatever, *for Heaven's sake, don't get in the habit of setting it where you might get up and leave it unattended.* There are other countries where people have gone to jail for that, convicted of criminal negligence, if the abandoned weapon is stolen or found by a child. If the container is small enough, put it in your lap. If it's too big for your lap, put it on the seat *against* your hip. If you must, put it on the floor *against* your leg. Have it on the exiting side or between your feet. Yes, the exiting side is more accessible to the purse-snatcher, but ask yourself one question. How many times in your life has a thug snatched your purse or briefcase, compared to how many times in your life have you had to go back into a house or restaurant for a carry bag you inadvertently left behind? Between the feet is better, but on the exit side is acceptable too, because it's always where you can feel it and you can't slide out or get up without noticing it and reminding yourself to keep it with you.

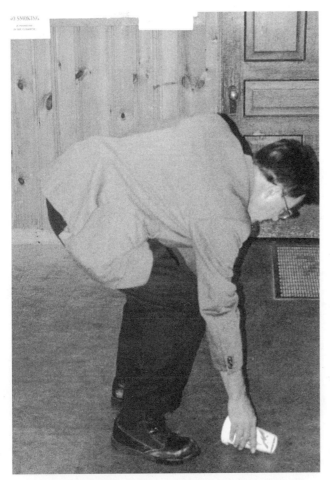

*Bending at the waist causes a hip-holstered gun to "print." Keeping the torso vertical and squatting, "like a back patient," would be much less revealing.*

## Securing Guns In Vehicles

Do the neighbors and passers-by need to see you carrying guns out to your car for a day at the range? Dedicated gun bags, like the excellent Waller unit, look more like high quality gym bags or travel bags, and don't attract attention. The new generation fully enclosed golf club cases designed for air travel are ideal for transporting rifles and shotguns. If the case of ammo you put in the trunk looks like a plain cardboard box, no one is going to look twice.

We have a generation of "gun-free workplaces" where an armed citizen can be arrested for trespass after warning if they enter the office armed. Federal buildings such as post offices are normally considered to be off limits for gun carrying, even if you have a license to do so in public, and in many jurisdictions the same is true for courthouses, schools, and even places that sell alcohol. This means that if you're an armed citizen on a day off doing errands that include mailing a package, picking up a copy of a deed at the courthouse, and purchasing wine for a dinner party, you'll have to take your gun on and off at least three times during the trip.

You don't want to do it conspicuously. A frightened citizen who sees someone "doing something with a gun in a parked car" violates Mrs. Campbell's edict, "Don't frighten the horses." A thug who sees you put a pistol in the console knows that he can smash out a window with a rock and steal a pistol as soon as you're out of sight.

If you regularly carry a gun, it makes sense to get a small lock-box that easily opens by feel with combination push buttons, and bolt it to the floor or the transmission hump of your car, within reach of the driver's seat. This allows you to secure the gun as you approach your parking space, and carefully slip it back out and put it back on as you drive away. Why do this while you're in motion? Because most people won't be able to see you. (Take care about being observed by people in high-seated trucks, however.) You're much more likely to be noticed by a pedestrian who is walking by your parked car, since his natural visual angle is downward into your vehicle.

You might also want to slip the gun into a sturdy cloth shopper's bag (a fanny pack might become a target for a thief because it looks like it might contain a wallet) and lock it in your trunk when you go into the post office, then retrieve it into the passenger compartment when you return to your car.

While we're talking about guns and cars, it's not sound tactics to have gun-related decals or bumper stickers on your vehicle. Did you ever make a political decision and change your vote because you saw something on someone's bumper sticker? Probably not, and no one will vote for your gun rights because they saw your bumper sticker, either. However, those things put some cops on hyper-alert when they pull you over for having a taillight out. Your NRA bumper sticker may give some road-raging bozo the idea to call the police and say you threatened him with a gun. When the cops pull you over and find out you do indeed have a gun, you "fit the profile."

You also have to consider that the criminal element isn't entirely stupid. When they see a gun-related sign on your car, it tells them that you feel strongly about guns. That tells them you probably own several guns. They love to steal guns because firearms and prescription drugs are the only things they can steal from you that they can fence on the black market for more than their intrinsic value, instead of maybe a nickel on the dollar. Now they know that if they follow this car to its home, they can watch the house until people are gone, and then break in and steal guns. This is why the bumper sticker thing is just not wise. Show where your heart is on your rights to own firearms by working and contributing to gun owners' rights groups, instead. It'll do everyone, and the cause, and particularly you, a lot more good.

### The Routine Traffic Stop

It can happen to any of us. We're driving along and suddenly the red, or blue, or red and blue lights start flashing in the rearview mirror. We're being pulled over! *And we're carrying a concealed gun!* What do we do?

Well, since we are law-abiding citizens and carrying legally, we pull over. Smoothly, steadily, turning on the signal as soon as we see those lights. At roadside, we park and turn off the ignition and engage the emergency flashers. At night, turn on the interior lights. Stay behind the wheel. If you get out and approach the officer unbidden, you not only indicate to him that there might be something inside the car that you don't want him to see, but your actions mimic the single most common pattern of ambush murder of police during traffic stops. Just stay in the car. Leave your hands relaxed in a high position on the steering wheel. Do not reach for license and registration in glove box or console or under the seat, either now or before coming to a stop. From a vehicle behind you, these movements mimic going for a weapon.

Remember Mrs. Campbell's advice. No cop gets through a police academy without horror stories of brother and sister officers murdered in traffic stops. The officer is carrying a gun and this is the *last* of Mrs. Campbell's horses that you want to frighten.

The officer will ask for license and registration. Make sure that when you open the glove box for the latter, there isn't a gun sitting there. If you have indeed left *la pistola* in the glove box, tell the officer, "I'm licensed to carry, and I have one in the glove box with my registration. How should we handle this?" It would be much better for the gun not to be in that location at all.

In some jurisdictions, when a permit is issued, there is a requirement that you identify yourself as armed any time you make contact with a police officer and are carrying. The easiest thing to do is carry the concealed handgun license next to the driver's license, and hand both to the officer together. Don't blurt something like, "I've got a gun!" It sounds like a threatening statement.

If you try to explain about the pistol and passing traffic obscures some of your words and the only thing the officer hears is "gun," your traffic stop can go downhill. Just hand over the CCW permit with the DL.

You'll want to do the same in jurisdictions where such identification may not be required by law, but where the Department of Motor Vehicles cross-references with issuing authorities on carry permits. In those jurisdictions – Washington state, for example, and many, if not most, parts of California at this writing – the officer will have been told by dispatch or will have seen on his mobile data terminal that you're someone who carries a gun. If you don't bring it up first, such action can seem to the officer as if you're hiding something from him. Again, hand over the CCW with the DL.

In jurisdictions where neither is the case, it's up to you. If I pull you over for a traffic stop in my community, and you are a law-abiding citizen who has been investigated, vetted, and licensed to carry a gun, it's none of my business. If I'm worried about it, I'll ask you if you have one, and will expect an honest answer at that time.

If at any point the officer asks you to please step out of the vehicle, things have changed. Either someone with a description similar to yours did a bad thing (which means you're going to be field interviewed and patted down until it's clear that "you ain't him"), or your operation was careless enough to give the officer probable cause to believe you're driving under the influence. This means there will be a roadside field sobriety test. In the typical Rohmberg test, arms will be going straight out to your sides, coats will be coming open, and this would be a very bad time to "flash."

So, if the officer asks you to step out, I would suggest you reply with exactly these words, if you haven't already handed over the CCW: "Certainly, Officer. However, I'm licensed to carry. I do have it on. Tell me what you want me to do." The cop will take it from there.

Now you're seeing why those of us who've been carrying for a long time understand a principle the courts call the "higher standard of care." It holds that we, of all people, should be smart enough not to make stupid mistakes with guns. This is why, among many other things, those of us who carry guns tend to rely more on the cruise control than the radar detector, and actually make an effort to drive at the speed limit, so we won't get pulled over in the first place.

# Securing The Combat Handgun

Shooter A is a professional instructor in combat arms. He's on the road about half the time, usually alone. He keeps a pair of handcuffs in his suitcase and travels with a primary handgun and a backup weapon. When he goes to bed at night in a hotel room, one loaded pistol is in one of the shoes he plans to wear the next day, at bedside. The other is in the other shoe on the opposite side of the bed. He untucks the sheets and blankets at the bottom of the bed before turning in.

Rationale? He can reach the gun immediately if there's an intrusion. If he has to roll to the other side of the bed, he can reach a gun there too. If, like some of the victims he has met over the years, he wakes up with

the attacker on top of him in bed, there will be no tucked-in bedclothes to bind him like a straitjacket and he can roll the attacker off. If he has to leave the guns behind for any reason, he can lock them in the hard-shell case he keeps inside his regular suitcase, then use the handcuffs to secure the case to pipes under the bathroom sink.

The latter tactic is because research has taught him that many hotel burglars have suborned hotel staff and use their keys to enter rooms while guests are out. It's unlikely that these punks will have handcuff keys with them. If they break the pipes to get at the case, it will call immediate attention to their activities. Hotel

*The latest S&W revolvers come with both external (shown) and internal trigger locks. On this one, the case is lockable to boot.*

management will alert to what's going on, change locks and keys, and kill the golden goose.

Shooter B is a police officer with young children not yet at the age of responsibility. He is subject to call-out from off-duty status at any time. He has arrested and sent to jail some people who aren't too happy about it, and he feels that nothing less than an instantly accessible loaded handgun will keep him and his young family safe enough for his peace of mind.

The solution is a lock-box secured in his closet. When he comes home from work he is carrying his duty sidearm, a .45 auto, as an off-duty weapon. He simply leaves it on his person until he goes to bed. When that time comes, he goes to the lock box. The .45 goes in, and out of the box comes another gun that has reposed safely there all day. It is a Smith & Wesson .357 Combat Magnum revolver, loaded with 125-grain hollow-points and customized with a device called MagnaTrigger, which is not externally visible. When he turns in, he slips this gun under the bed where it's out of sight but he can reach it immediately.

From his night-table drawer come two simple looking stainless steel rings. He puts one on the middle finger of each hand, and goes to sleep.

The rings have magnets attached to the palm side. There's one for each hand because he learned in police training that the dominant hand could become disabled in a fight and he might have to resort to his support hand. He is now the only one who can fire the MagnaTrigger gun, whose retrofitted mechanism blocks the internal rebound slide. At the bottom of the block is a piece of powerful cobalt samarium magnet. Only when a hand wearing a magnetic ring closes over the gun in a firing grasp will reverse polarity move the block out of the way and make the gun instantly "live." This device has been available and working well since 1975, and is currently available from Tarnhelm Supply, 431 High St., Boscawen, NH 03303. On the Web at www.tarnhelm.com. It can be applied only to a Smith & Wesson double-action revolver, K-frame or larger at this time.

Two very different people, and two very different approaches. Neither is likely to have a gun stolen. Neither is likely to have an unauthorized person handling their guns without their knowledge. Yet each is ready to instantaneously access a defensive handgun if there is a sudden, swift invasion of their domicile.

This writer has been a big fan of the MagnaTrigger concept since it came out in 1980. I no longer need it much, as my children are grown and have guns of their own. But with one child married already, I suspect it won't be long before the pitter-patter of grandchildren's feet calls the old Magna-Trigger gun out of mothballs. It is also useful for any time I want to have a gun in off-body carry instead of on my person. The gun is in the bag, but the rings are on me, and if anyone grabs the bag and runs, there's nothing they can do with the gun inside.

Why have you not heard about the MagnaTrigger from the mass media, in all their articles about gun control advocates calling for "smart guns"? Well, simply because those gun control advocates don't really want smart guns. They want no guns at all. Their strategy is to pass legislation requiring something that does not yet exist on

*Here's how to use handcuffs to lock up a 1911 single-action auto. The hammer cannot come forward even if the trigger is pulled and the sear is tripped.*

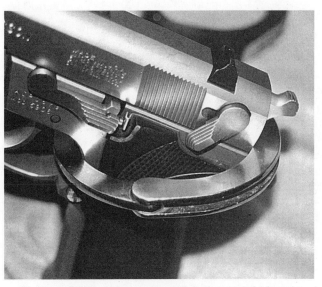

*The latest S&W revolvers come with both external (shown) and internal trigger locks. On this one, the case is lockable to boot.*

the market: electronically controlled pistols. This will give them an avenue to ban "stupid guns" as dangerous, and then leave gun owners with nothing because the "smart guns" promised to replace them don't come through. If the public found out there actually was a smart gun that worked, the anti-gunners fear that people who don't buy guns now would buy these, and that would thwart their plans. The smart gun that works now is indeed the MagnaTrigger, hampered only by the fact that the technology has not yet been successfully translated to semiautomatic pistols.

### Lock Boxes

The lock box, a small, rapid-access gun safe, has been a boon to armed citizens and off-duty police and security personnel. It leaves the gun as secure as if it was in a gun safe if the lock box is bolted to a floor or otherwise made so that it can't be just picked up and walked away with. I've personally had good luck with the Gun Vault brand, but there are several good units out there.

More lock boxes come out every year. Do yourself a favor and visit a gun shop with a wide selection, and try several demonstrator models. A combination dial will be difficult in dim light with shaking hands. You want push buttons, set well apart in ergonomic fashion, and one reason to try it in the shop is to make sure the unit you like fits your particular hands. Be sure to practice with it frequently. Remember that anything battery operated needs to have its batteries changed regularly. Get into the habit of changing the batteries in such a lock box when you change the batteries in your emergency flashlights and your smoke alarms: twice a year, when you change the clocks for Daylight Savings Time.

*An ergonomic push button pattern and keyed over-ride are good features of the Gun Vault unit. This one is bolted to the transmission hump of an automobile. It is an ideal set-up for people who cannot bring their carry guns into certain buildings.*

*This old S&W Model 39 9mm auto is kept in a cut-out book. Note the warnings the owner has surrounded it with.*

### One Safe Place

No matter where your gun is stored, it is possible that a violent intrusion will happen so rapidly that you can't get to it in time. The one way to always be certain you can reach your gun is to always wear it. This doesn't mean you have to walk around the house with a Sam Browne belt, a high-capacity 9mm, and 45 rounds of ammo in pre-ban magazines. A snub-nose .38 in a side pocket will do nicely.

With the gun on your person, it is at once readily accessible to you and inaccessible to unauthorized hands. I wrote that more than 30 years ago in one of my first magazine articles. It was true then, and it is just as true now. Perhaps more so: armed home invasions seem to have become more frequent in certain areas.

There's another advantage to simply always being armed. You don't forget and leave your gun at home. I'll never forget one cop, the hero of one fatal gunfight a few years before, who told me, "I was on my own time, downtown, shopping. I heard the first gunshot go off, and my hand went to my hip, and there was nothing there because I had forgotten to put my gun on…" That particular event turned out all right, but I doubt that he ever made that mistake again. Educators call it "a reinforcement of the learning experience."

### Gun Locks and Trigger Locks

For decades in police work, it has been common practice to keep gun lockers at the entryways to each booking area or fingerprinting setup. We learned to slip our service weapon into the small locker, secure it, and pocket the key. Law enforcement quickly learned to put the guns in loaded, leave them loaded, take them out loaded, and re-holster them loaded.

Each time you load and unload, you're handling a live weapon, and that always creates an opening for an accidental discharge. There was always the possibility of an officer forgetting to reload and going back on patrol with an empty gun. This collective experience has proven that a loaded handgun in a lock box is as safe as safe can be.

I do not like the idea of trigger locks. If someone puts one on a loaded gun, the lock can jiggle against the trigger and cause an unintended discharge. There is no trigger lock that will keep the gun itself from being loaded. I simply don't trust that technology, and a lot of other long-time firearms professionals share that opinion.

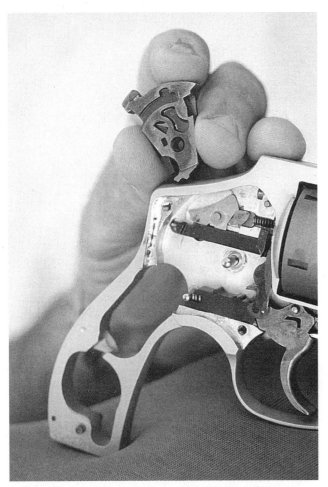

*These are the operating parts of Smith & Wesson's internal gun lock, introduced in 2001.*

If I have to lock up the gun without putting it in a container in which the firearm cannot be touched, I prefer something that locks the firing mechanism. First Taurus, and now Smith & Wesson, have begun producing their revolvers with integral locks. While some people oppose this concept on principle, I've so far seen nothing wrong with it mechanically. Neither the hammer-mounted lock of the Taurus nor the side plate-mounted integral flush lock on the S&W seem capable of "locking up" by themselves when you need them to fire, and I've hammered the heck out of these guns with hard-kicking ammo. We're talking full-power .454 Casull in the Taurus Raging Bull revolver and full-power .357 Magnum in the Smith & Wesson 340 PD, which weighs only 12 ounces. Similar technology exists now in some auto pistols.

One of my colleagues has speculated that if some of these guns are dropped into sand, the keyways will be blocked and the owners won't be able to make the lock work to "turn the gun on." Unless one is camping out of doors, I don't see too much problem with that. There's no reason for a locked gun to be exposed anyway; it should be in a container if you're someplace where the gun must be secured.

### The Handcuff Trick

Since long before this old guy pinned on a badge, cops have been securing their guns at home with their handcuffs. With the conventional double-action revolver, the bracelet goes between the rear of the trigger and the back of the trigger guard, and over the hammer. This at once blocks the rearward travel of the trigger and the rearward travel of the hammer, positively preventing firing. On a "hammerless" style revolver, the trigger is still blocked.

On a single-action such as the 1911 or the Hi-Power, the handcuff's bracelet is applied differently. On the 1911, which has a sliding trigger, it goes under the outside of the trigger guard at the juncture of the grip-frame, and over the back of the slide in a way that holds the hammer down if the chamber is empty, or back if the gun is cocked and locked and loaded. With the Browning, which has a freestanding trigger, it can be done just as on a revolver or

*An easily manipulated key operates the hammer lock on standard model Taurus revolvers. Note the keyway between hammer spur and frame.*

*This is a double-action revolver secured with handcuffs. The hammer can't rise (and therefore can't fall), and the trigger can't be pulled far enough for discharge, because a handcuff bracelet blocks those parts on the S&W 686.*

*Avoiding Mistakes* • **185**

*A wise police instructor, Peter Tarley, came up with the concept of unloading the Glock and then field stripping it. A practiced shooter familiar with the gun can quickly reassemble and then load it.*

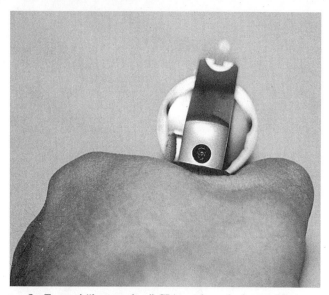

*On Taurus' "hammerless" CIA revolver, the integral key lock is high on the backstrap of the grip-frame, just above the web of this shooter's hand.*

if the gun is cocked and locked, the bracelet can be between the hammer and the slide while also blocking the trigger's travel toward the rear of the guard. A double-action auto would be secured the same way, holding the hammer in the down position.

I don't see any way to effectively lock up the Glock pistol with handcuffs. What the Glock does lend itself to better than most other guns, is a home safety concept I first heard suggested by Peter Tarley, the world-class instructor who used to work for Glock. Simply unload the pistol, and field strip it. The Glock's barrel/slide assembly comes off *en bloc* as with many other guns, but unlike most others, there is no takedown lever that has to be manipulated a certain way during reassembly. When danger threatens, grab the barrel/slide assembly with your non-dominant hand, your frame assembly with your dominant hand, and put the two back together. Then holding the gun in the dominant hand, seize the loaded magazine, insert it, rack the slide, and you're holding a loaded Glock pistol. It's surprising how quickly this can be done. The old HK P9S, no longer produced, was one of the few other guns with which this trick works as well.

Remember, it's our gun. Power and responsibility must always be commensurate. When we need the power, we must accept – and live up to – the responsibility. In the end, most of the time, you never needed the power, but you feel good about having fulfilled the responsibility.

# CHAPTER TWELVE

# Accessorizing

## Responsible Customizing

Man has enhanced his weapons since he first stood erect and picked them up. Perhaps one caveman realized that a club with a wider end would have more momentum and hit harder then the untapered club used by the leader of tribe in the next valley. Sometimes the personalizing was just in the form of decoration to mark the weapon as this warrior's own and helped prevent theft. It also gave him more ego investment in the tool that might one day save his life.

A couple of men I respect enormously, who've both "been there and done it", are known to possess what they call "barbecue guns." These are fancy, nay, *ornate* pistols that certainly work just fine, but most of the attention lavished upon them has been cosmetic rather than utilitarian. For one shooter it's an engraved and gold inlaid Colt .45 automatic with ivory grips. For the other, it's an engraved Smith & Wesson .44 Magnum with stag handles. My friends wear these guns to commemorate special occasions.

Pride of ownership is a good thing. Having your name or initials engraved on your gun makes it less desirable to a thief and easier to recover if stolen, though it impairs resale value. Today, most custom work done on handguns is more utilitarian than cosmetic.

That includes refinishing. While a gun with a new hard-chrome finish may look better than before, it's also more impervious to the elements. Some finishes, like Robar's NP3, add an element of lubricity that make the gun work better.

### Action Jobs

In many cases, the most useful modification will be an "action job" that allows the trigger to be pulled more smoothly and cleanly. Remember, you don't need "light" so much as you need "smooth." That said, some guns that come with very heavy triggers – Colt DAO autos, the Kel-Tech P-11, and some others – can afford to lose a few pounds of pull weight.

What you don't want on any handgun that might actually be used to hold a human being at gunpoint is what a layman might call a "hair trigger." Most gunsmiths and forensic evidence technicians would define 4 pounds as an absolute minimum pull weight. Some go a little higher.

It never hurts to have the trigger's surface smoothed off, at the front and on the edges. Some may need the back edge of the trigger and the rear edge of the trigger guard smoothed as well. Certain shooters may benefit from having the inside bottom surface of a Glock's trigger guard

*The author's Glock 17 has all "working mods," most from GlockWorks. Sights are Heinie Straight Eight with tritium. Pre-ban +2 magazine brings the fully loaded capacity to 20 rounds of 9mm Parabellum. InSights M3 light installs quickly on the frame and comes off almost as fast.*

*A "Barbecue Gun." This engraved, gold-inlaid S&W Model 629 also sports an action job by its owner, Detective Denny Reichard, and MeproLight night sights. Yes, he can control .44 Magnum recoil with those slim bone grips. You have to know Denny. The hand-tooled holster, with a miniature of the owner's shield, completes the ensemble.*

*White spots on an anodized blue S&W Model 3944 show where Rick Devoid has taken the sharp edges off. Such a job is cheap and the "user-friendliness" is huge. Devoid usually blends finish back as it was...*

*Garrey Hindman at Ace Custom did the superb trigger work on this S&W 4506. The rear of the trigger guard and the trigger have been polished glass-smooth to match the internal action hone. The jewelling on the trigger and barrel are cosmetic, but nice touches.*

taken down a little as well, if the size and shape of their fingers are such that the trigger finger drags on the inside of the guard. Smooth triggers are also an important amenity for those who train seriously. We've found that after two or three days of intensive shooting on the range, a serrated trigger will often have produced a weeping blister.

It is always a good idea for any revolver that is going to be kept or carried for self-defense to be rendered double-action-only. This eliminates the danger of both a hair trigger discharge if the gun is cocked, and the false allegation that such a thing happened when in fact it didn't. Grinding off the hammer spur isn't enough. The

*You want smooth, not light. This Gunsite Custom S&W Airweight by Ted Yost is just as slick, and even more reliable, with a long mainspring (top) instead of the shorter, slightly lighter aftermarket replacement spring, below.*

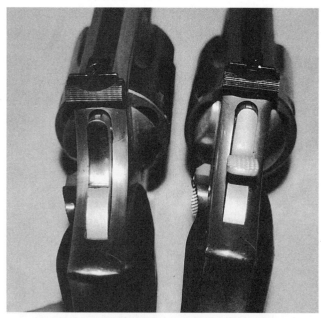

*Right, a stock S&W Model 686; left, the same gun rendered double-action-only with the hammer spur removed. Reshaped and lighter, the hammer falls faster — better reliability in double-action shooting and slightly faster "lock time," i.e., a shorter interval between when the hammer begins to fall and when the shot goes off.*

*In addition to double-action-only action slick and spurless hammer, Al Greco has installed a permanent trigger stop on the author's S&W Model 625 to reduce backlash.*

single-action cocking notch on the hammer (internal) needs to be removed by a competent and qualified gunsmith or armorer, or a new DAO hammer needs to be fitted.

This seems less necessary on semiautomatic pistols. The more rearward placement of the hammer spur on an auto makes it more awkward to thumb-cock and, thus, less believable that someone would do so. A cocked auto pistol will also usually have a heavier trigger pull than a cocked double-action revolver. That said, fear of both accidents and false accusations of accidents have led a great many police departments, and more than a few citizens, to go with the double-action-only trigger concept on semiautomatic pistols as well as revolvers.

### Safety Devices

A 1911 grip safety can dig and even lacerate the hand if it is not wide, edge-free, and smoothly polished. The thumb safeties of 1911 and P-35 type pistols are often too small, and rarely ambidextrous. An enlarged thumb safety lever makes that part more positive in use for many shooters, while the ambidextrous safety is desirable for any serious potential combatant and is of course a necessity for southpaws using such guns.

Excellent aftermarket parts of this type are available from Cylinder & Slide Shop, 800-448-1713; Ed Brown Products, 573-565-3261; and Wilson Custom, 870-545-3618, among many others. These three sources can usually retrofit the parts to your gun for you.

A thumb safety can be added to some guns that don't normally come that way. Joe Cominolli, at www.cominollio.com, can install one for your Glock, though at this writing he makes the unit for right-handed use only. Do you have a DAO S&W auto with a "slickslide" design? Rick Devoid, at www.tarnhelm.com, can install a dedicated, ambidextrous thumb safety on its slide for you. He's also the source for the one functional "smart gun" available at this writing, the MagnaTrigger-modified S&W revolver, and finally, he can install a Murabito safety on any frame size S&W wheelgun to make the cylinder latch perform double duty as a thumb safety that works with a downward stroke like a 1911.

Removing or deactivating a safety device can get you into a world of trouble if you're ever accused of

*Most oversize magazine releases cause problems, but this useful one from GlockWorks is the exception. Author's Glock 17 also sports a Cominolli thumb safety.*

wrongdoing with a gun. A good lawyer won't have much trouble convincing a dozen laypersons that anyone who would deactivate the safety device on a lethal weapon had to be reckless. However, when you pay out of your pocket to enhance the safety devices on a firearm – to literally make it safer than it was when it left the factory – you can easily be shown to possess an unusually high degree of responsibility.

As a rule, any after-market "safety" that makes the gun go to the "fire" position faster and more positively when needed, will also make it go to the "on-safe" position faster and more positively, and it's hard to argue with that.

### Reliability Packages

Some guns need an internal work-over before they achieve optimum function. For many years, this was true of the 1911 and the Browning P-35. For most of their history, they were military-specification pistols designed to work with mil-spec ammo. That is, full-metal-jacket round nose. Out of the box, they would feed hardball ammo, or Remington hollow-points that were jacketed up and over the tip to the same ogive as hardball, and that

*A thumb safety the size of a gas pedal is too big for carry, but some like it for competition. Adjustable sights can be argued either way. Springfield Armory, however, has already replaced the too narrow grip safety with a beavertail on current versions of this gun, their Trophy Match .45.*

*You want your defense gun work done by a master. Bill Laughridge, shown in the middle of his busy Cylinder & Slide Shop, fills the bill.*

*Shown are two of the author's favorite "combat custom" Colt .45 autos. Top, is the LFI Special by Dave Lauck; below, is a "Workhorse" by D.R. Middlebrooks.*

was about it. If you wanted them to run with more efficient, wider-mouth JHP bullets, you had to pay a gunsmith to "throat them out."

Both types of guns are now produced by a number of sources. Some companies still make "mil-spec" versions of

*The author is partial to this Glock 23 for certain competitions. Modifications include…*

the Colt and the Browning, of which the above remains true. But there are many versions that now come from the box "factory throated" and ready to feed most anything you stuff in it. These include currently produced Colt and Browning brands, and also the Kimber, the Para-Ordnance, and the upper lines of Springfield Armory production.

Your Beretta, Glock, HK, Kahr, Kel-Tec, Ruger, SIG, S&W, or Taurus auto as currently produced should not need a "reliability package." However, like some of the other models mentioned, they might benefit to a greater or lesser degree from having some of the sharp edges beveled at hand contact points. This is particularly true of the standard-line Smith & Wesson pistols. Any of them might also benefit from a good action hone, too.

### Recoil Reduction Devices

The general consensus among defense-oriented combat shooters is that most recoil reduction devices pass the point of diminishing returns because they vent hot gases upward in a way that could strike the shooter in the face or eyes when shooting from a "speed rock" or "protected gun" position. That said, they also tame muzzle jump very effectively. Some people who carry guns simply don't have those close-to-the-body shooting positions in their repertoires and don't feel a loss in carrying a "compensated" gun.

For concealed carry, you don't want one of those humongous comps that hangs off the end of the gun and looks like a cross between a TV spy's "silencer" and Buck Rogers' ray gun. A good "Carry-Comp", as executed by Mark Morris in Washington State (www.morriscustom.com), will end up the same size as a Colt Government Model, but will feel almost recoil free. I have one in 10mm on which the comp works so efficiently, the gun all but recoils downward. When they're properly installed, you won't lose accuracy; my Morris 10mm CarryComp has won first place open-sight, big-bore awards for me at 100-yard NRA Hunter Pistol matches, shooting against Thompson/Center single shots and long-barreled Magnum hunting revolvers. It will just let you

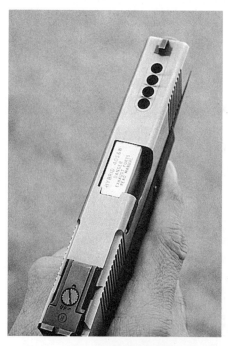

*…Schuemann Hybrid-Porting, which radically reduces recoil, and BoMar sights, which enhance the capability of precision hits. Note the warning stamped on the chamber area of barrel, however.*

shoot a whole lot faster. This is the gun I was shooting when my daughter, Justine, and I won the speed-oriented match that made us National Champion Parent/Child team in sub-junior (child age 13 and down) class at the first National Junior Handgun Championships. The ammunition was Triton's powerful Hi-Vel, spitting a 155-grain bullet at an honest 1,300 feet per second. With the CarryComp, the gun just sort of quivered as it went off.

With the exception of the brilliant Mag-na-Port concept pioneered by my old friend Larry Kelly, most recoil reduction jobs will magnify the blast of each shot, often to unpleasant levels. Mag-na-Port, I've found, works best on revolvers and long guns, and on autos with open-top slides like the Beretta, Glock Tactical/Practical, and Taurus. The factory-compensated Glocks work on a similar principle.

*Seen in profile, Hybrid-Ported Glocks look like ordinary full-size (top) and compact .40s. The stainless Caspian slide on the bottom gun is easier to mill for adjustable sight installation than the super-hard Glock slide.*

Hybrid-porting, developed by the brilliant Will Schuemann, gives dramatic recoil reduction with a series of big ports that go down the top of the barrel. The upside is great recoil reduction; downside is bright flash in front of the eyes in night shooting and significant velocity loss. This system seems to be at its best on the revolver and the Glock pistol, though the best gunsmiths can carefully balance a 1911's action to make it work with the reduced recoil that comes with the concept.

### Beveled and Funneled Magazine Wells

When the 1911 single-stack pistol was *the* gun for serious combat shooters, a popular modification was beveling out the magazine well so a magazine would slip in more easily during loading or reloading. This worked, and has become a standard feature, on top-line 1911's by Colt, Kimber, Springfield Armory, etc. The guns with wider, double-stack magazines benefit less from this feature, since the tapered top of the magazine combines with the already large magazine well to create a funnel effect.

The cottage industry developed the concept into magazine chutes, which could either bolt onto the gun (requiring padded-bottom magazines, since the edges of the chutes extended below the pistol frames) or be swaged or welded into the gun butt by a good pistolsmith without lengthening the grip frame. For a single-stack magazine pistol in particular, this is an excellent idea. There is a distinct improvement in reloading speed even for experts, and those new to the gun will benefit even more.

Magazine chutes are now even made for the Glock, which probably doesn't need it. The bottom line of any

*Combat pistol champ Marty Hayes has won awards with this Hybrid-ported Glock 22 in .40 S&W. He prefers...*

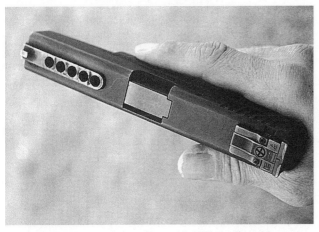

*...this full-length sight radius, with Millett adjustable sights.*

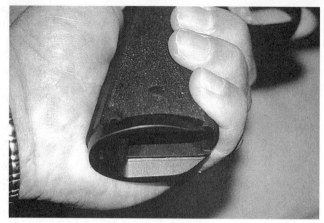

*Variations on a theme. The extended, oversize magazine well on this Springfield TRP enhances reloading speed, but makes gun slightly less concealable and demands padded-bottom magazines for positive seating.*

*Merely beveling the frame without add-ons works quite well, as on this Springfield Trophy Match.*

modification is, if it doesn't hurt anything and it helps something, it's probably a good idea. Properly installed magazine chutes and beveled magazines fit that description. If they don't extend the length of the grip-frame, they have no disadvantages except cost. They definitely do make magazine changes easier all the way around.

### Extended Slide Releases

As a rule, these are not a great idea. The slide releases of most standard pistols are adequate in size. Enlarging them can cause holster fit problems. There are also reliability issues. Oversize slide lock levers put extended weight on the part that levers it out of position and either keeps it from doing its job when the magazine runs dry, or more commonly, causes it to bounce up and lock the slide open prematurely while the pistol is cycling.

The single exception is probably the Glock pistol. Glock intentionally made the slide release a low-profile part, assuming that most shooters would jack the slide to reload the gun instead of the faster method of thumbing the lever. A slightly extended slide stop lever is available

from Glock, originally developed for the target model guns, that will fit the concealed carry and duty models. The FBI has reportedly ordered it on all its duty Glocks. If you have trouble operating the standard lever, definitely retrofit with this one. It is a Glock part, so it doesn't void the warranty, and it works fine and has no disadvantages.

### Checkered/Squared Trigger Guards

Some of the earlier practical shooting masters, such as Ray Chapman and Ross Seyfried, shot with the index fingers of their support hands wrapped around the front of the trigger guards of their Colt .45 autos. They had large hands and short guards and could get away with it. To make it work better, they checkered the front of the trigger guard and sometimes changed the guard to a more square shape.

For the overwhelming majority of shooters, having the support hand's index finger under the trigger guard will work better. If, however, the shooter insists on securing the weak hand finger on the guard, checkering will help reduce its natural tendency to slip off.

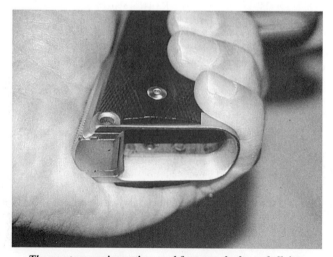

*The most expensive option, and for some the best of all, is a swaged out magazine well, this one by Dave Lauck on a Colt.*

*You shouldn't need an oversize slide release lever or magazine release button on most pistols; standard 1911 size parts do fine, as seen on this top-grade Springfield Armory pistol.*

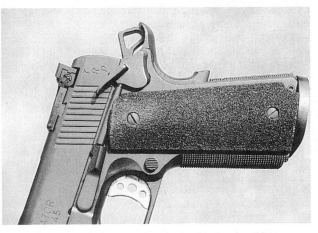

*Well thought out "factory customizing" is seen on this Springfield Armory top-grade TRP (Tactical Response Pistol). Rugged adjustable night sights, easily manipulated ambidextrous thumb safety, "just right" street trigger, Barnhart Burner grips, checkered front-strap for a non-slip hold, and ergonomic beavertail grip safety with "speed bump" to allow activation in any reasonable firing grasp.*

### Flashlight Attachments

The HK USP began the trend of a dust cover (the front portion of the frame) molded or milled to accept a quickly attaching and detaching flashlight. HK had its own, called the UTL (Universal Tactical Light). Other companies quickly followed suit.

Glock, Springfield Armory, and a broad array of other brands have this option. The M-3 Illuminator by Insights Technologies works particularly well in this function.

*Looks spacey, works great. The author's bedside Beretta, a 92FS tuned by Bill Jarvis. A 6-inch Bar-Sto barrel gives pupil-of-the-eye accuracy at home defense distances, and added velocity that brings hot 9mm ammo up to otherwise unattainable ballistics. The extended barrel is Mag-na-Ported to reduce muzzle jump. Trijicon night sights allow precise shooting if the user chooses not to activate the powerful SureFire flashlight. The extended magazine creates a 21-shot pistol. The result is a high-capacity handgun with surgical accuracy that combines the recoil of a .380 with the power of a .357 Magnum and gives the user command of various light situations.*

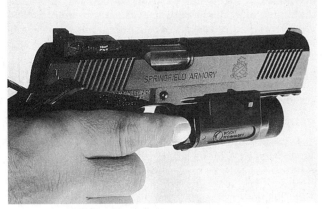

*The trigger finger can operate the M3 light one-handed on this Springfield TRP Tactical Operator pistol. Adjustable night sights give a back-up option in dim light.*

If your pistol does not have an integral attachment rail, do not despair. SureFire makes a pistol-mounted flashlight that attaches to a standard 1911, Beretta, or other auto, with a part that replaces the slide stop. This is my personal favorite "gun flashlight"; it is naturally ergonomic, extremely bright, and ruggedly durable. I keep one on the pistol that I usually have at my bedside when at home. It is intended to be a dedicated unit, not a quickly attaching and detaching accessory.

The flashlight can be a lifesaver in more ways than one. We'll never know how many people who were shot when they reached in the dark for "something that looked like a gun" would be alive today if the person who shot them had been able to see that they were holding a harmless object. It wasn't the shooter's fault, but this technology would have saved those shooters much suffering, internal self-doubt, and lawsuits.

The powerful flashlight can also blind and intimidate an opponent. I've seen it happen in the field. However, remember that using your flashlight to search is like using the telescopic sight of your rifle to scan for game: you're pointing a loaded gun at anything you look at. I want a heavy trigger pull and/or an engaged safety on the

*There's nothing wrong with personalizing. This Seecamp .32 was special ordered with the author's initials as the serial number.*

weapon to which my light is attached. This will minimize the chance of a "startle response" causing an unintended discharge when the user sees something that startles him but doesn't warrant a deadly force response. Obviously, the finger should be clear of the trigger guard when searching with such a unit, but the heavy trigger and/or manual safety is one more redundant safety net to prevent tragedy.

### Liability points

Few creatures can be more desperate than an attorney who has no case. Many people involved in law enforcement have seen attorneys try to find negligence in after-market grips, colored or glow-in-the-dark gun sights, even the name of the gun. "Persuader" sounds more sinister than "Model 500," and "Cobra" sounds more violent and deadly than "Agent," even though in both cases it is essentially the same shotgun and revolver, respectively, under discussion.

Does this mean you shouldn't modify your gun, as some have suggested? This writer personally thinks that is going too far. Certainly, it would be a good idea to avoid a gun with a controversial name like "Pit Bull" or "Bonnie and Clyde," both of which have actually been used by American gunmakers. More important, however, is to avoid a "hair trigger" (lighter than 4 pounds) or a deactivated safety. Either can create the impression of a reckless gun owner.

We've covered the innards and what might be called the superstructure of the handgun, but have not yet touched upon two critical points, the sights and the type and fit of the grips or stocks. That's because each is so important that they're worth their own chapters. We'll get to that immediately.

# Combat Handgun Sights

The sights are your weapon's primary aiming tools. When a defense gun has to be employed, the sequence is something like this: Enemy fighter sighted, need to shoot confirmed…missiles locked on target…missiles launched…track target, prepare to launch more missiles if necessary.

The "missiles locked on target" part is accomplished by indexing the handgun, and that is best accomplished with the sights. But we must be able to see the sight under adverse conditions such as dim light, tunnel vision, and animal instinct screaming at us to focus on the threat when knowledge tells us to focus on the sights.

Sights on a combat handgun should be big, blocky, and easy to see under assorted light conditions. They should be rugged enough that they won't fall off the gun or be knocked out of alignment if the wearer falls on the holstered gun in a fight, or the gun bangs against a wall as the user ducks for cover, or if the gun is dropped on a hard surface in the course of a struggle.

The general rule of thumb is that fixed sights are more durable than adjustable sights. There are exceptions to that rule, however. We've seen fixed rear sights held in place in their dovetail by an Allen screw come loose and drift sideways or even fall off a pistol. The plastic fixed sights that come on some modern guns may be more likely to break than the most rugged steel adjustable sights. The latter include such time-proven units as the BoMar or the MMC adjustable night sight, which has large, shielding "ears" on either side, similar to the current S&W service auto adjustable sight design.

### Night Sights

Tritium night sights go back to the Bar-Dot developed by Julio Santiago back in the 1970s. They have come a long way. Available in a multitude of shapes and colors, they not only aid in sighting on an identified target in the dark, but can help an officer find a gun that was dropped in the dark after he has won the struggle with the offender trying to take it. For those of us who travel a lot, waking up in the middle of the night in a dark, strange room is not conducive to finding your pistol. The glowing dots of the night sights, if the gun has been positioned

*Master revolversmith Andy Cannon built up the front sight of this Model 940 S&W 9mm revolver for the author, and widened the rear sight proportionally. The improvement in "shootability" is dramatic.*

*Because of the precise adjustments many consider these BoMar adjustable sights target equipment; but, they are extremely rugged and suitable for heavy duty.*

*The big rear notch of standard Beretta fixed sights…*

*…coupled with its proportionally large front sight, makes an easy combination for old or myopic eyes to see.*

with the sights toward the sleeping owner, are like airstrip landing lights that guide the legitimate user's eye and hand to the defensive weapon.

You can get three dots all the same color that line up horizontally, the type that works best for this writer. You can get one dot on top of the other; the configuration master pistolsmith and designer Dick Heinie dubbed the "Straight Eight" because it resembles a figure-8 in the dark. IWI pioneered an option now available from most other makers: one color front dot, a different color for the rear dots. If the front dot is the brighter color, the eye goes to it instinctively, and this concept also keeps the new shooter, or the one whose gun doesn't fit, from aligning the dots incorrectly and shooting way off to one side. Some, like officer survival expert Jim Horan, prefer just

the single tritium dot on the front sight with no corresponding rear reference.

Eyesight varies hugely between different people. Any of these concepts can work. The best bet is to try them all and see which works best for you. This writer has found the three-dot system to be most visible to his particular eyes. It also works with the StressPoint Index concept mentioned in the point-shooting chapter. When the shooter sees an equilateral triangle of dots, the top one will be on the front sight, and the StressPoint Index is in place.

There are many brands. At one time, it was a choice of Trijicon and a few also-rans. Today, the quality has gone up across the night sight industry, though I don't think anyone has yet exceeded Trijicon. I've been happy with the IWI night sights on my department-issue Ruger .45, with green up front and amber at the rear. I have no problem with the Meprolight sights on a pet Glock 22 that I carry often. Trijicons adorn my bedside Beretta, and a couple of my Glocks and SIGs. I have Heinie Straight Eight sights on a Morris Custom Colt .45 and a Glock 17. They all work fine.

It has been said that you shouldn't need night sights, because if it's too dark to see your sights it's too dark to see your target. That's untrue for two reasons. First, the vagaries of artificial illumination and natural light and shadow are such that you might indeed be able to identify your opponent but not get a clear sight picture. Moreover,

*The big rear notch of standard Beretta fixed sights…*

*…and which is seen here in its multiple variations on Ring's brand dummy guns.*

if the shape in the dark yells at you, "Die, infidel American!" and you see a muzzle flash, I think your target is identified and I for one would like for you to have the option of night sights.

### Express Sights

Pioneered by my friend and student Ashley Emerson, whose company Ashley Outdoors is now in other hands and making these excellent sights under the title AO, the express sight with Ashley's copyrighted Big Dot makes a lot of sense for a lot of situations. The far-sighted person who can see to identify the threat just fine but can't see anything but a fuzzball at gun-sight distance is an ideal candidate for these. The rear is a shallow "v" with a white line down the middle, and the front sight is a humongous white (or glowing Tritium) circle. Put together, it looks like a big lollipop. Easy to see, fast to hit with in close. The express sight got its name because it has been used for well over a century on the powerful Express rifles hunters used for the biggest, most dangerous game at close range.

As noted earlier, it's subjective. This writer can't shoot worth a damn with express sights on a pistol at 25 yards. At very close range, though, they are slightly faster for me and tremendously faster and more accurate for those who can't see a regular sight picture. Definitely worth looking at, no pun intended.

### Full- And Half-Ghost Rings

"Ghost ring" was Jeff Cooper's term for the 19<sup>th</sup> century deer hunter's trick of removing the sight disk from an aperture ("peep") sight and just looking through the big circle that held it to get a faster, coarser sight picture with his rifle. On a rifle or shotgun it turns out to be remarkably accurate, and Jeff did us all a favor in revitalizing the concept.

It has been tried on pistols with less success. Because the aperture is so much farther from the eye than it would be on a long gun, you don't get the same effect. It can be fast in close, and does give a big sight picture for those who can't focus on conventional sights, but there don't seem to be a lot of people who are terribly accurate with them. Some are, mind you, but not many. There are various brands available; for current options, check the advertising pages of *American Handgunner* magazine.

More useful to more people is a concept developed by gun expert Gary Paul Johnston and made a reality by Wayne Novak, master combat pistolsmith and designer of the famous, streamlined Novak fixed rear sight. The ghost ring is simply cut in half. A big, rectangular post front sight is now seen through a huge rear "u" notch. It is easy to line up even for myopic people with their corrective lenses off. I shot the one on Gary Paul's Novak Custom Browning when we were at a Winchester ammunition seminar together at Gunsite Ranch in Arizona, and was very favorably impressed with the combination of speed and accuracy it delivered. *Definitely* better than full ghost ring sights in this writer's opinion, but an apparently well-kept secret and, to my knowledge, available only through Novak's .45 Shop, 304-485-9525.

I once told William McMoore, designer of a fascinating work in progress called the Sceptre pistol that blends elements of the Glock and the 1911, that I thought the best "geezer sights" would be simply a square notch rear and a post front, but both absolutely huge. He tells me he has Ashley Emerson working on that very concept. Stay tuned.

*Police gun expert Gary Paul Johnston displays the "half ghost ring" sight he designed for Wayne Novak. The author feels this brilliant concept has not achieved the popularity it deserves.*

### Optical Sights

Conventional telescopic sights for handguns are too big for all-day-carry holstering, and because of their long eye relief generally too slow to aim with under combat conditions at combat distances. World champion Jerry Barnhart proved in the 1980s that the internal red dot sight was faster than any conventional iron sight. He proceeded to kick butt with it in matches until, in open class, red dot sights were all you saw.

They are so fast and accurate because the unit's big screen gives a "head's up display" that is much more easily seen than the image in any telescopic sight when you're moving and shooting fast. The aiming dot and the target appear to be on the same visual plane, so the old problem of good focus on opponent or good focus on sights but not good focus on both is eliminated. U.S. military elite teams have gone to these in a big way. In Somalia in 1993, and much more so in the Afghanistan reprisal of 2001 and beyond, international news cameras caught countless images of these high-tech sights on American M-4 assault rifles.

*"Geezer sights" Gunsmith/cop Denny Reichard "hogged out" the rear sight of this N-frame S&W for an aging shooter, and created a sight picture even fuzzy eyes can see.*

The author's friend John Pride, gunfight survivor and many times National Police Handgun champion and Bianchi Cup winner, has a Tasco Pro-Point on the match gun he's wearing on his hip. But in his hand is a compact S&W auto with what may be the only practical concealed carry red dot optical sight at this writing…

…the extremely compact Tasco Optima…

…which fits on a pistol thus.

The state of the art has improved enormously since the early days, but there are two problems. One is that they run on batteries, and anything that is battery-dependant can fail you at the worst possible time. The other is that most of them are too bulky to carry in a holster, particularly concealed.

There have been numerous attempts to make a small, practical, concealed carry internal dot sight. Only one, in my opinion, is worth looking at: the Optima 2000 from Tasco. Resembling a high, circular rear sight, it sits behind the ejection port on the slide of a semi-auto pistol, clear of the holster. It may not hide under a T-shirt well, but it can conceal under a sport jacket. To conserve battery life, it turns itself off in the dark and turns itself on when exposed to light. (Hmmm…could this be a problem in a very dark room?)

The concept isn't perfect, but Tasco sets it up so you can use the pistol's regular sights right through the lens of the Optima 2000, whether you can see the red dot or not. This protects against battery failure. If you have vision problems and are ready to try a high-tech solution, this is worth looking at. Unfortunately, Tasco has recently closed its doors. While Tasco products will remain available on the secondary market, there won't be anything new rolling off the production line. At this time no one can tell what this will do to prices.

## Laser Sights

Because I didn't embrace the laser sight as the wave of the future I've been described in letters to gun magazine editors as an old Luddite who can't understand new technology. *Au contraire.* I merely pointed out that while the laser sometimes has intimidation effect, it sometimes doesn't, and may even provoke a homicidal response. I speak from experience.

This doesn't mean the laser has no tactical place in the defensive handgun world, it just means it has to be seen and used rationally. Says famous police combat instructor Marty Hayes, "Maybe the laser will intimidate the bad guy, and maybe it won't. But if there's even a chance it will, I want the laser on my side and my officers' side."

Personally, I don't think "intimidation factor" is anywhere near the top of the list of the laser sight's attributes. In a tactical setting, I think a laser-sighted pistol is the tool of choice for anyone working with a "body bunker," the bullet-resistant barrier that is carried like a shield. To aim through its Lexan viewing port with conventional sights, you have to bend your arm to an angle so weak that you risk gun malfunctions, and accentuated recoil slows down your rate of accurate fire. Keeping the wrist locked (and most of the arm behind the shield, another advantage), aiming with the projected laser dot, simply makes more sense and is safer for the officer. (Or the civilian: I also think the ballistic raid shield would be an extremely useful thing for an armed citizen to have in the bedroom closet in case of a home invasion.)

If both your arms are injured and you can't raise the gun, the laser dot gives you options. If you insist on using point-shooting techniques, the laser sight may indeed be the only thing that saves you. Marty Hayes' tests with students indicate that they handle night shooting problems distinctly better with laser sights than with regular night sights.

Certainly, there are downsides. The laser beam can track right back to you visually, giving your position away

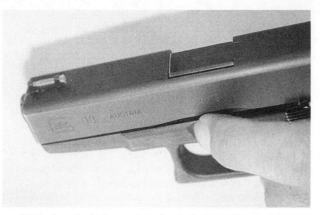

*While they don't do much in the dark, these fiber-optic sights…*

*…can be a Godsend for aging or myopic eyes when there is any reasonable amount of ambient light for them to gather.*

in the dark. This is made worse in fog or smoke, including gun smoke. A laser beam aimed through a window can be refracted, and the dot is no longer truly indicating where the gun is really pointed. If more than one of the good guys have lasers, it can be hard to tell whose dot is whose. If the bad guy is holding a hostage, you and your partner raise your guns, and one dot appears on the hostage's head and another on the criminal's, which one of you pulls the trigger?

In the end, all these problems can be solved by simply turning off the laser in dim light and fog, and trusting your regular gun sights when multiple dots are on multiple people or you have to shoot through glass. However, many instructors worry about shooters becoming "laser-dependent" and losing core skills. That, really, will depend on the students more than the instructors.

I feel the laser sight absolutely comes into its own as a firearms instructional aid. I use mine often to show students how easily a shot can be jerked off target by bad trigger control, or how accurately the students can shoot with their hands shaking violently. The demonstration can be done dry-fire in a classroom with a neutralized gun. In the students' own hands, the laser gives proof when they're jerking the trigger, and gives them instant positive feedback when they make a smooth stroke. In live fire in the dark, students can follow the laser dot's track and see graphically which techniques are working better for them in terms of recoil control.

Of the many laser sight options available, the most practical seem to be the modular ones that don't change the profile of the gun. At this writing, you're talking about two companies: Lasermax and Crimson Trace. Crimson Trace LaserGrips work particularly well in this regard. If you don't like them or don't need them, you can take them off. They are easily adjustable. On some models, the "finger in register on the frame" position can block the laser dot if you are shooting right-handed. The firm offers

a pair on a dummy gun that is practical and economical for classroom training purposes.

The Lasermax unit replaces the recoil spring guide rod on Glock, SIG, Beretta, S&W, and 1911 pistols of that design, among others. This puts the light directly under the bore, an advantage. However, being at the "working end" of the pistol, the unit is also subjected to more heat and battering during firing than grip-mounted units. The Lasermax projects a pulsing dot, the Crimson Trace a solid one. The Crimson Trace best serves my own needs, but the Lasermax has also earned staunch supporters.

### Fiber Optic

A fiber optic cylinder that gathers and focuses light and replaces your front sight can be a great aid in a fast, close pistol match done outdoors or in fading light. In the dark, it's useless – you want night sights for that – but for something like a bowling pin match, these things are ideal. There are also a number of people whose guns are likely to be used in lit conditions – shopkeepers, for example, given the fact that most store robberies take place during business hours or just before or after closing, when the lights are still on – for whom such sights might be ideal. Accuracy is not so precise as the conventional post-in-notch sight picture, but speed can be awesome.

### See the Proof

To determine what sights will be best for you for self-defense work, there is no substitute for getting out there and shooting under different conditions. You have to find out for yourself what works best. Eyes are too individual for another person's suggestions to necessarily be the best for any one shooter. Once you've found something that works for you, check the other systems every few years. As we age, our eyes change, and a sighting system that just didn't work for you five years ago might be absolutely perfect for you now, and vice versa.

# Making The Handgun Fit

Suppose you had to run a marathon, but they issued you the wrong running shoes. Three sizes too small, or three sizes too large. It's safe to say you won't perform

your best, and if the mismatch in size is too grotesque, you may not be able to run at all. You might even get an injury trying.

*A K-frame S&W is a perfect fit in the average adult male hand with (Hogue) grips that expose the backstrap. Note that the trigger finger is perfectly centered at the distal joint.*

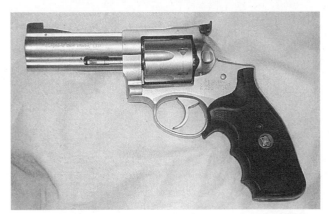

*The author won this Ruger Security Six more than a score of years ago at a regional championship. It has a Douglas barrel and action by Lou Ciamillo. Pachmayr Professional grips, cut only to the backstrap, give a perfect fit.*

Different race: the stock car championships. You've got the most powerful, most maneuverable car on the track. Unfortunately, the driver's seat has been locked into position for someone a foot different from you in height. If you're too close to the wheel, you're hunched over it with a profoundly slowed ability to steer, and you can't reach the pedals without banging your knees on the steering column. If you're too far back, you have poor leverage for steering and cannot operate the accelerator, clutch, or brake pedals efficiently.

It's safe to say you're not going to win the race. In fact, the driver behind you in a less capable machine, but one that fits him perfectly, will soon leave you behind. And, if

things get hairy and you can't manipulate the controls quickly and positively enough, you might go into the wall and be hurt or killed.

The police department doesn't issue every officer size 14 uniform shoes, nor does it lock the seat of every patrol car into position for a 6-foot, 7-inch lawman like Bill Jordan. Yet an amazing number of police departments issue the same size gun, often one that fits only larger hands, to all officers including the smallest. Then they seem surprised when many officers don't perform up to their potential.

As my teenager would say, "Well, *duh...*"

Fit of the equipment is critical to performance with the equipment. One advantage the private citizen has is that he or she doesn't have to trust his or her life to an issue firearm that's the wrong size. The "civilian" can go to the gun shop and buy something that fits properly. Now he or she is on the way to a maximum personal performance level.

As noted elsewhere in this book, the key dimension to fit is trigger reach. The index finger of the firing hand should be able to contact the trigger at the proper point

*Show and Go can go together. Hogue stocks on the author's Langdon Custom Beretta 92 fill the palm and feel great, while also looking great.*

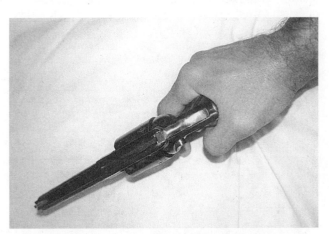

*A Ruger Service Six .357 Magnum gives perfect fit for an average male hand with these Craig Spegel grips cut only to the backstrap of the grip-frame. Note that the barrel is in line with forearm, and the distal joint of the index finger is centered on the trigger.*

*Here is a Beretta double-action 9mm in the hand of a 5-foot, 10-inch man…*

*…and 5-foot woman. Note that she can barely reach the trigger.*

while the barrel of the gun is in line with the long bones of the forearm. This will give the strongest combination of firm grip to control recoil in rapid fire, and maximum finger leverage for good trigger control at high speed.

Let's look at some examples of adapting guns to fit hands. The hands of the aforementioned Bill Jordan were huge, at least a digit longer in the fingers than those of the average man. Bill had to have his gloves custom made. Accordingly, the famous Jordan grips he designed for Steve Herrett had a big portion of wood added to the backstrap area, to push the web of his hand backward and give him "reaching room" to get his finger right to the joint on the trigger. The first time I picked up one of Bill's personal service revolvers, I felt like a little kid holding Daddy's gun. Bill, in turn, would have felt cramped using the smaller grips of my revolver.

The design factors are such that the revolver is much easier to adapt to different size hands than is the auto. This is particularly true of larger hands. Note how many big-handed men have put custom grips on tiny J-frame revolvers, grips that come rearward from the backstrap to increase their trigger reach. A petite female, conversely, will find that the J-frame fits her exactly when the web of her hand meets the backstrap. A female 5 feet 5 inches or shorter, with proportional hands, will usually lack about one digit's worth of finger length compared to the average adult male.

The more research-oriented gun manufacturers have recognized this. Beretta figured out early on that their full-size Models 92 and 96 were big guns with long trigger reaches. They have offered their customers at least four hardware fixes for this. First came a shorter-reach trigger, which could be retrofitted at the factory or by a factory-trained police armorer. Next came a special frame done for the Los Angeles County Sheriff's Department, which issues the Beretta 92 to deputies of all sizes. It had some material taken out of the frame at the upper backstrap area to get the web of the hand more "into" the gun and give the trigger finger greater reach.

Next came their Cougar series. Engineer types were most taken with the gun's rotary breech, but shooters and firearms instructors had far more appreciation for the altered frame dimension. The upper backstrap area was "niched out" to bring the hand more forward. Available in 9mm, .40 S&W, .357 SIG, and even .45 ACP, the Cougar was and is a much better fit for the small hand. Most recently, a redesigned 92/96 series pistol called the VerTek was introduced by Beretta. Essentially, it's the same gun with a light attachment rail up front and, much more importantly, a grip frame distinctly thinner in

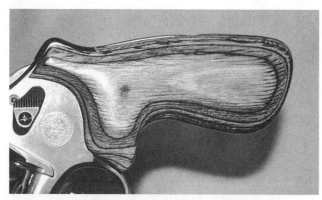

*These slim N-frame revolver grips were designed by world record holder Jerry Miculek to give maximum reach to the trigger. They come standard on this S&W Performance Center Model 625 in .45 ACP.*

*Today's manufacturers pay more attention to "human engineering." This 9mm Ruger P95 is an extremely good fit in the average male hand.*

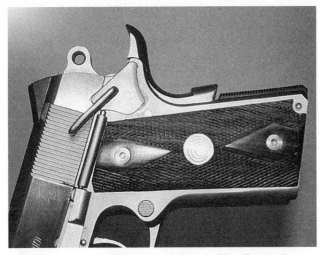

*This compact .45 caliber ParaOrdnance LDA Companion comes from the factory…*

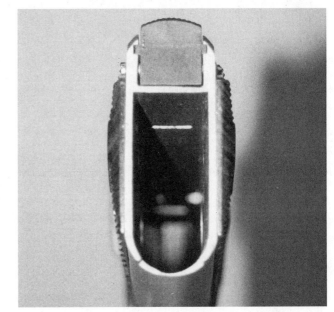

*…with these slim-line grips. A slight enhancement for concealment, they can deliver huge enhancement of feel and control.*

circumference. The shooter can not only get the trigger finger more forward, but can also get a stronger shooting hold with proportionally more of the grasping fingers in contact with the more svelte "handle."

Certain guns have had the almost mystical ability to feel good in hands of all sizes. The D-frame Colt revolver, typified by the Detective Special, is big enough for big hands yet small enough for small hands. In auto pistols, the classic examples are the Browning Hi-Power and the slim-grip M8 version of the HK P7.

Walther pioneered the concept of an auto pistol with grip inserts that could adjust the size and circumference of the grasping circle. It was kept in the SW99 pistol, the collaboration between Smith & Wesson and Walther. This is a step forward.

### Case In Point

The gun fit issue can be seen in microcosm by studying the history of the famous pistol that Colt introduced in 1911. In the early 20s, a study of how small arms had performed in the Great War determined that many

soldiers felt the trigger of this pistol was too long to reach well. By the end of the decade, the military had created specifications for the 1911-A1. Among other changes, it had a much shorter trigger and a frame that was niched out just behind the trigger on each side. The intent was to enhance trigger reach, and that intent was dramatically fulfilled.

Before long, target shooters (who preferred to use the pad of their trigger finger, instead of the joint, for precise shooting) were having their personal guns retrofitted with longer triggers. Time went on. By the 1960s, the manufacturers' standard in place was that the "carry" Colt .45 auto, the Government Model or one of the Commander series, would have the short 1911-A1 trigger. In contrast, the Gold Cup target model would have a long, broad-surfaced trigger in what is known as the National

*With the short 1911-A1 trigger on this Springfield Micro .45, the average adult male hand has perfect leverage with distal joint trigger finger placement…*

*…while a petite woman has a proper grasp with the pad of the trigger finger in contact on the same gun.*

*The Browning Hi-Power, this one tuned by Novak, has the "magical" ability to fit well in the hand of the average man…*

*…or a petite woman.*

Match configuration. This actually worked out pretty well for all concerned. Tastes changed as time wore on, and by the turn of the 21st century, most guns sold for carry had long triggers again. Progress is sometimes circular.

Let's say you have someone with truly huge hands. One of the regular competitors at the old Second Chance shoots was about 6 feet, 9 inches tall with proportional hands. He had a custom gunsmith build him a 1911 .45 auto with an incredibly long trigger, almost out to where the trigger guard is on a factory gun. The 'smith welded up a new trigger guard farther forward on the frame. This in turn, of course, demanded custom holsters, but the good-natured (and good-shooting) giant handgunner now had a 1911 that was literally made for his hand.

On the other end of the spectrum, the smartest female shooters and their coaches analyzed the situation too. In WWI, nutrition and prenatal care not being what they are today, the average adult male stood about 5 feet, 6 inches. The 1911-A1 trigger had in essence been engineered for hands proportional to that height, or smaller. The average adult female of today in this country stands about 5 feet, 5 inches. This means that the 1911-A1 pistol is *exactly the right size to fit most petite female hands* in terms of trigger reach. If the grip-frame is too long, the shorter Officer's size is readily available from Colt and other manufacturers. Thus, incongruous as it may sound, the big .45 auto – the gun of Mike Hammer and Sergeant Rock – is actually an excellent choice for the petite female hand. Privy to the 1920s study and 1911/1911-A1 metamorphosis and the reasons behind it, John Browning and Didionne Souave kept essentially the same trigger reach dimension as the 1911-A1 when they carefully crafted the Browning Hi-Power of 1935.

This is why the Hi-Power fits so well in so many different hands, and why it is particularly appreciated by those with shorter fingers. Now, fast-forward again, to a modern pistol first produced in the 1990s, the Kahr. This gun is also particularly well configured for the small hand. It also points well. If you lay a Kahr over a Browning Hi-Power, you will see a remarkable similarity in shape. One of two things is clearly proven here: either Kahr designer Justin Moon did his homework and adapted the best of the Browning/Souave design to his own brainchild, or it is indeed true that great minds work in similar directions.

## After-market Revolver Grips

In the occasional moment when there's nothing else to argue about, bored gun experts are known to debate whether those "handle thingies" are properly called "grips" or "stocks." For our purposes here, let's use the terms interchangeably.

Wooden grips, or synthetic grips that duplicate wood, tend to be smooth and unlikely to snag clothing. They conceal well. They also look good; there's a definite "pride of ownership" thing there. Custom grips with finger grooves and palm swells put you in mind of that hoary saying, "It feels like the handshake of an old friend." However, wooden grips do relatively little to absorb recoil. Smooth ones, especially without finger grooves, tend to shift in the hand when the gun kicks. The old, tiny grips that used to come with small revolvers, known to shooters as "splinter grips," made controlled shooting notoriously difficult. Checkering to secure the stocks to the palm helped some, but not much.

Composition stocks, known colloquially as "rubber grips," have long been a favorite of serious revolver shooters. The ones that cover the backstrap cushion recoil into the web of the hand like a recoil pad soaking up kick

*These big Trausch grips give maximum recoil control with the author's hard-kicking S&W lightweight Mountain Gun in .44 Magnum, but note that they also restrict trigger reach for double-action work.*

*Standard J-frame S&W grips give adequate trigger reach to the very short fingers of 5-foot-tall woman...*

*...but allow too much finger to get in the guard when the average adult male hand is applied...*

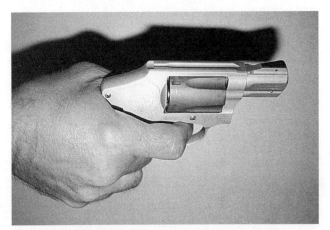

*...requiring that male shooter to "cock" the median knuckle of the trigger finger slightly outward to adjust.*

on a shotgun. Pachmayr led the market with their Decelerator brand by actually using, in the backstraps of the grip, the same shock-absorbing materials found in state-of-the-art recoil pads. Hogue offers a similar model.

This sort of stock tends to give the most comfortable shooting. Especially in the Hogue finger-grooved version, they allow much less slippage even when firing Magnum

loads. The main revolver-makers have picked up on this, and so accoutered many of their double-action models at the factory. Smith & Wesson has used mostly Uncle Mike's and lately Hogue; Colt has used Hogue and Pachmayr; and Ruger has come up with its own in-house version made of what they call "live-feel" composite for their SP-101 hideout gun, their GP-100 service revolver, and some of their larger double-action Magnums. Taurus also uses in-house grips; particularly useful are the Ribber ™ style found on the .454 and .480 big boomers, and some of their "baby Magnums."

From a practical standpoint, the only downside is that the tacky surface of some "rubber" grips adheres to jacket or shirt linings and causes the fabric to lift, revealing the guns. This doesn't happen with all such grips nor with all clothing.

Try before you buy, if possible. Finger-grooved grips don't fit all fingers. Women's police combat champion Sally Van Valzah of Georgia came up with a neat idea that was rediscovered a few years later by Lyn Bates, long time president of Armed Women Against Rape and Endangerment (AWARE). This is to simply remove the top flange, the one between the top two finger grooves. In that "average adult male hand" the industry always talks about, this leaves the middle finger and the ring finger with nothing in between, which is really no big deal. However, for a typical woman with slender fingers, all three of the grasping digits now wrap securely and fit well in the space of two male fingers. Most women who've tried this report improved feel and control.

### Auto Pistol Grips

The auto pistol shooter seems less likely to need aftermarket grips than the revolver stalwart. Most semiautomatic designs, being more recent, have taken more account of human engineering factors. This makes them more likely to fit the shooter's hand as they come from the factory.

That's the good news. The bad news is if the gun doesn't fit to start, there's less you can do with it. A revolver's grip frame needs only hold the mainspring, and it lends itself to being reshaped, sometimes radically. The auto pistol's grip frame has to house the magazine *and* the mainspring, and the dimensions required for this limit your options as to reshaping.

If a gun feels a little thin in your hand, Pachmayr or Hogue auto grips will fill the palm, and also give you a non-skid surface. However, a lot of us have found that the "rubber" grips slow the draw ever so slightly, because they're a little less forgiving of last-instant hand adjustment as the gun hand slides into position.

Sharply checkered wood or Micarta ™ grip panels are more commonly seen. These come in a variety of styles. Many years ago, ace shooter and pistolsmith Mike Plaxco created the first slimline 1911 (for combat shooter John Sayle's lovely wife, Sally). Part of the job was taking metal off the front and back of the grip frame and tang, and part of it was creating the thinnest possible grip panels. This gives a dramatically improved reach to the trigger. Jeff Cooper pronounced it desirable not only for women but for most male shooters. Having that "average adult male hand," I can attest that a "slimline" job seems to give me a greater sense of control, and certainly more trigger reach. The last I heard, Plaxco is no longer doing gunsmithing, but the Gunsite custom shop does grip-slimming of the 1911 as a regular procedure. So does pistolsmith Dane

*The very short trigger reach of this SIG P239 is one reason such a small gun seems so controllable in so many hands, even when chambered for the powerful .357 SIG cartridge like this specimen.*

*Slim-line grips are factory standard on the STI Trojan pistol, and allow the average length adult male finger to reach relatively long trigger with the distal joint.*

Burns. For many shooters, just the slimmer grip panels will be enough, and these are advertised in the gun magazines from a variety of sources. Some makers offer slim-line .45 autos right off the gun factory production line. These include the Springfield Armory Micro .45 in a small hideout gun, the Para-Ordnance LDA Companion

*Jerry Barnhart's "Burner" grips, seen here on the Beretta Elite of multiple IDPA national champion Ernie Langdon.*

in a carry-size piece, and the STI Trojan in a full size Government Model.

On the other hand, some like a more substantial grip on a 1911, but may want something a little less tacky (in surface, and sometimes in looks) than neoprene. Makers such as Kim Ahrends (Custom Firearms, Box 203, Clarion, IA 50525) offers thicker 1911 panels that fill the palm with an exquisite feel, and pride of ownership is enhanced by finely finished exotic wood and superbly executed checkering.

Custom checkering has historically been part and parcel of handgun grip customizing. On a revolver, it's usually on the backstrap. Make sure, however, that you're comfortable with the grips you have now. If you go later to a grip design that covers the backstrap, hiding that fine workmanship you paid for will be like putting a drape over a Vermeer painting.

Auto pistols are more commonly checkered, usually on the front strap of the grip-frame and often on the back. We've found in training that the finer checkering gives all the slippage reduction you need, and doesn't chew your hands up during day after day of rapid-fire training with full power ammunition. Note that if you have checkering on both the frame and the grip panels, there can be so much traction that you wind up in the same situation as with wraparound neoprene grips and have difficulty making last-instant adjustments. For this writer, the combination that has always worked best on an auto has been either checkered stocks and smooth front and backstraps, or checkered frame front and back and smooth grip panels. Remember, though, our hands are not all the same.

Another option is the Burner grip sold by Jerry Barnhart. The world champ crafted grip panels for 1911s, Berettas, and a few other guns with surfaces that feel like sandpaper. They give a rock-solid hold in the hand. I've worn them on a carry gun briefly and experienced no problems, but a friend who competes with the Beretta he carries says the Barnhart grips tend to eventually chew up coat linings. The surface is, after all, abrasive.

### Reshaping The Glock

The Glock pistol exhibits excellent human engineering and fits many hands perfectly as it comes out of its box.

*If a factory produced "Glock sock" seems too expensive, you can make one like this out of bicycle inner tube.*

Some, however, want something bigger in their hand. They are customers for what have become known as "Glock Socks," rubber sleeves that fit on the grip rather like a piece of inner tube but with checkering, sometimes finger grooves, and always more class. Hogue, Pachmayr, and Uncle Mike's all offer suitable units. Some with smaller hands agree with the great architect Mies van der Rohe that "less is more." For them, Robbie Barrkman pioneered the concept of filling the hollow back of the Glock grip frame with epoxy, then grinding the whole thing down. The Robar frame trim brings the web of the hand and the trigger finger forward. If you are among the one in 100 or fewer with hands so large the slide of the Glock contacts your hand as the pistol fires, he can also craft on an extended grip tang that will solve the problem. Dane Burns is another who has mastered the grip slimming and reshaping on the Glock. The addresses for Burns and Barrkman appear elsewhere in these pages.

The grip area of the handgun is the interface between the operator and the machine. A gun that fits is critical to good performance. You can get to where you can shoot very well with a gun that doesn't fit your hand. Hit with it, qualify with it, even win matches with it. But you will never achieve the personal best that you are capable of with a gun that does not fit you. The pinnacle of your ability to shoot fast and straight with a combat handgun will not be reached until you and that firearm fit together at the interface point as if you were made for one another.

# CHAPTER THIRTEEN

# Beyond the Stereotypes

## Women And Combat Handguns

The public stereotype is that the gun is an icon of violence, that men are inherently violent, and that therefore women should be anti-gun. Like most stereotypes, this is flat-out wrong.

Why did a cluster of left-of-center political activists call that joke they started "the Million Mom March"? Probably because they knew from the start that they couldn't get a million *dads* to march in favor of banning guns. Guess what? It turned out they couldn't find a million moms, either. It wasn't even close. The Million Mom thing petered out as soon as it stopped being trendy. Perhaps the fact that at the end, the Misguided Moms were outnumbered at rallies by their opposite number, the Second Amendment Sisters, had something to do with it.

A society that expects women to be anti-gun is a society still mired in sexist stereotypes. It is a cruel irony that some of the strongest opponents of gun owners' rights consider themselves part of the women's liberation movement. It is as if these speakers were saying, "You can have your own career, you can support yourself, you can become politically active. You can be financially and politically and emotionally independent…but you must always have a man around for protection, because you can't protect yourself to the extent a man could." What kind of enfranchisement is that? One book written by a noted feminist said that women should not own guns because the gun was the very icon of male violence, and each time a woman acquired one marked a symbolic triumph of male domination.

What a crock.

*Terri Strayer, left, and Lieschen Gunter lecture an LFI class on concealed carry options for females.*

*How many men do you know who can do this? LFI instructor Debbie Morris fires five 12-gauge Magnum rounds into a target in one second, flat, with her Benelli Super-90 shotgun. Those flying cigar-shaped objects are a trio of 3-inch Magnum spent shells simultaneously airborne.*

*This is a Second Amendment Sisters Mothers' Day rally. It outdrew "Million Mom March" in same state in terms of attendance.*

*Dexterity in action. Shooting southpaw, right-handed Gila May-Hayes pumps out a perfect qualification score with her 9mm Glock.*

*Natural flexibility gives women better balance when firing from awkward cover positions. Jana-Pilar Gabarro demonstrates with her carry gun, a 9mm S&W Model 3913, during an IDPA match.*

If you look at it, the history of women's successful entry into male-dominated job markets was a history of using mechanical devices to make up for lack of upper body strength. Women didn't start off in construction as hod carriers, but at the hydraulically operated controls of tractors and backhoes. Similarly, women were able to function very well on police patrol because their batons and guns served as mechanical equalizers of strength…"force multipliers," as the current military terminology goes.

*Attorney Rebecca Rutter shows masterful control of full-power Colt .45 automatic*

### Women's Strengths

It is true that most handguns and holsters were designed by men, for men. It is true that the average woman has less upper body strength than the average man. Yet it is the almost universal observation of handgun instructors that females learn the handgun faster than males.

We can postulate several reasons for this. It is certainly true that firearms are dexterity intensive tools, and women tend to have greater fine motor dexterity than men. This is why women perform almost all the hand-assembly of the finest watches in Switzerland, and most of the precise hand checkering on expensive gunstocks like those of Ruger's top-line rifles and shotguns. Activities like knitting are considered so exclusively the domain of the delicate female hand that when a football player like Roosevelt Grier takes up knitting, it becomes national news.

There is also evidence that, given the same training and understanding of the situation, women can handle crisis better than men. In the past we have hooked up LFI students to sophisticated telemetry, and sometimes just

*Gila Hayes at instructor school with a perfect target fired during the revolver phase with a J-frame S&W .38. She outshot all the male instructors on the firing line.*

taken their blood pressure and pulse, then sent them into a high-stress role-playing scenario. At the end of the exercises, we found that the women's vital signs did not increase so rapidly as the men's with what some would call "anxiety factors," and they would plateau sooner and at a lower level.

If a woman hasn't been brought up with the cultural predispositioning that tells her to faint when spoken to sharply or to jump onto a chair and scream when she sees a mouse, she has the internal wherewithal to handle stress and quite possibly, to do so better than her brothers.

Being more flexible (on the order of 30 percent more flexibility in the

*Female shooters tend to learn the handgun quicker than males; this student has already exhibited perfect stance on first day of training.*

pelvic girdle alone), women can adapt better to awkward, expedient shooting positions or cramped zones of protective cover. The same factors that allow so many women to bend at the waist with their legs straight and put their palms to the floor, when so few of their brothers can do the same thing, allow this adaptation. Even standing the same height and weighing exactly the same, the female will have a lower center of gravity and, pound for pound, proportionally stronger legs.

Many experts believe that women have greater powers of concentration than men, and longer attention spans. They are able to stay focused on a task longer. In a discipline that requires concentration, such as shooting, this is a distinct advantage.

*The author congratulates Sally Bartoo, who led her LFI-I class with a perfect 300 qualification score, beating all the males including the SWAT cops.*

Perhaps the most important factor is that women do not have a gender-based ego investment in gun handling. The motorcycle instructor, the karate sensei, and the firearms coach can all tell you the same thing: many males instinctively resist being taught something with macho overtones by another man. The psychological process seems to be, "The teacher is the parent and the student is the child. But this thing is a manly thing. For me to accept that the teacher knows more than me about this is for me to accept that he is more of a man than I am. This I cannot do, so I must resist what I am being taught."

Female students are not burdened with this testosterone-filled baggage. Their attitude is generally more like, "I paid good money to learn how to do this, and it better work. What did he say to do? OK, I'll do it. Hey, it worked. OK, what's next?" There seems to be a much faster learning curve.

As the great female instructors have noted, women learn things differently than men. When women are asked to do something, they want to know why. Let's say that on two different sides of the city, a man and a woman, total strangers, are each about to buy their first firearm. I can about give you odds that when they go to the gun shop, the woman will spend more time asking the gun dealer how each specimen works. She will spend more time looking at lock-boxes and other safety devices. She will ask more questions in general, and she is more likely to seek formal training with her new gun. She tends to build at the foundation.

These are all good things.

### Resources

In this book, we've taken care to address female needs in each chapter, including holster and gun selection, and gun fit. The stereotype that women should have cute, tiny little guns has been behind us for a long time. When I re-read the chapter on female shooters in one of my own early books, I am reminded of how far we have come.

*The gun and other force multipliers were what allowed women to function effectively as police officers.*

SECOND AMENDMENT SISTERS
Guardians
Of the RIGHT to Defend
Ourselves ★ Our Families

*Penni Bachelor of the Pennsylvania chapter of Second Amendment Sisters addresses a rally for gun owners' civil rights.*

Because of the pervasive cultural predispositioning that says guns are for boys and not for girls, a female often requires more soul-searching than a male before she arms herself. It is helpful for her to have access to positive female role models. Back in the 1980s, Lethal Force Institute was the first of the major training academies to offer special all-women's classes. We recognized that some of the students would likely be survivors of male violence, and that the presence of alpha males could detract from their learning experience. We tried as much as possible to have all-female training staffs.

In our regular "co-ed" classes for private citizens, which tend to average around 15 percent female enrollment, we find the women often outshoot most of the men. The big difference I noted in the all-women's classes was that the students were more enthusiastic, as if they felt free to be themselves and discuss their personal concerns.

It is always good to start with reading. Two books I recommend so strongly that I keep them in stock are Paxton Quigley's *Armed and Female*, and *Effective Defense: the Woman, the Plan, and the Gun* by Gila Hayes. Each of the authors is a woman who at one time had little use for firearms; indeed, Quigley began as an anti-gun activist. But, in each of their lives, they lost loved ones to hideous criminal violence that could only have been prevented by armed force. Each came on her own to the logical conclusion: when you are the smaller type of the species, when society itself calls you "the weaker sex," some sort of an equalizer is needed. Against the sort of force that produces death or great bodily harm, the only effective such equalizer is the firearm. Gila and Paxton make that more clear than I ever could.

The books do not duplicate themselves. *Armed and Female* is a manifesto for the empowered woman. It is a major in why a woman should be armed, and a strong minor in how to go about doing it responsibly. *Effective Defense* is better on the details of how to shoot, what hardware to select, and where to get training, and a strong minor in the philosophy and rationale of the armed woman. The two books thoroughly complement one another. They are available from Police Bookshelf at 800-624-9049.

Paxton is a moving and powerful speaker. Gila is one of the finest combat small arms instructors of either gender that I've had the pleasure to work with. Lyn Bates, former president of AWARE, is another powerful and inspirational spokesperson for the concept of the armed woman.

Consider treating a lady you care about to an excellent magazine called *Women and Guns*. Produced by the publishers of *Gun Week*, *W&G* has always been edited by women who carry guns. Gila, Lyn, and many other knowledgeable authors appear in every edition. Like the aforementioned books, this magazine reminds the public in general and women in particular that men have no hegemony over strength, and that no woman need sacrifice her femininity in any way when she seeks to not only own, but master, the defensive firearm. To order a subscription to *Women and Guns* call Second Amendment Foundation at their *Gun Week* publishing headquarters, 716-885-6408.

The Second Amendment Sisters, mentioned above, has state and local chapters. A visit to one of their meetings or rallies will do wonders to inform a woman who is thinking about picking up a gun. This group has also been extremely effective in neutralizing the bogus statistics that the now almost defunct "Million Mom March" group has been able to over-publicize and promulgate, and they've been extremely effective testifying at state legislatures against poorly conceived anti-gun and anti-self-protection legislation. For more information, including a referral to your nearest state chapter, contact Second Amendment Sisters, Inc., 900 RR 620 S., Suite C101, PMB 228, Lakeway, TX 78734, toll free phone 877-271 6216.

### Empowerment

It's not about "I can do your 'guy thing.' " It's about empowerment. Responsibility and power are commensurate. Responsibility without power is doomed to become helplessness, and power without responsibility can easily become tyranny. One responsibility of every adult is the ability to manage life-threatening crisis at a first responder level. That crisis might take the form of a fire, a car crash, someone choking on a piece of meat, or a violent assault. If we are going to be responsible for holding the line against these threats to life until the designated professionals get there to deal with it, we need wherewithal. This is why we have smoke alarms and fire extinguishers in our homes. This is why we learn first-aid. This is also why defensive firearms exist.

The arming of America's women is slowly breaking down the last bastion of the "Susie Housewife" mentality. It is nothing less than empowerment. It is the fulfillment of a final step to achieving full enfranchisement.

# Minorities And Combat Handguns

The defensive handgun is a tool possessed primarily to protect oneself and others lawfully from violent criminal assault. Violent criminal assault is more likely to occur in high-crime neighborhoods. High-crime neighborhoods also tend to be low-income neighborhoods. Low-income neighborhoods tend to be peopled largely by minorities. Most crime victims share ethnicity with their assailants.

Therefore, one doesn't need a Masters Degree in socio-economics or criminology to figure out that the decent people who constitute the overwhelming majority of residents of minority neighborhoods are more likely than anyone else to be victimized by violent criminals. This means that these are the people who most need firearms to protect themselves and their loved ones.

The stereotypes fed to the public by the media strike again. While a great many people from the rainbow of ethnic backgrounds in high-risk areas do indeed acquire a firearm for self-defense, and are more likely than the average Joe Sixpack to need it for its intended purpose, they are less likely to seek training and skill with the gun.

Society has painted the gun as a symbol of the "white right," and the "gun culture" as a "whites-only" club. It has been a long time since any of us have seen a mainstream newspaper publish a political cartoon that caricatured an African-American as Sambo or Stepin Fetchit, or a Jew as a hook-nosed Shylock, though there are many alive in this country who can remember when both images were commonly seen in such places. Even in the emotional turmoil that followed the atrocities of Sept. 11, 2001, we don't see cartoons that depict Arabs as snaggle-toothed vultures anymore. Yet, constantly,

*An African-American officer tests his combat handgun skills at the Smith & Wesson Championships of 2002. Pistol is SIG P229 in 9mm.*

*Attempts to ban inexpensive small-caliber pistols such as this perfectly functional Raven .25 auto have had a strong negative impact on law-abiding citizens in lower income communities and disparate impact on minority citizens.*

*Ken Blanchard, ex-lawman and author of* **Black Man With a Gun,** *is one of our most persuasive voices for the black community's need to preserve their civil rights as gun owners. Here he addresses the annual Gun Rights Policy Conference hosted by Second Amendment Foundation and the Citizen's Committee for Right to Keep and Bear Arms.*

and female competing in the same arena. You'll see millionaires hanging out with laborers.

Perhaps a small part of it is the gun's history as an equalizer. A far more significant reason is that the combat handgun range is a meeting place of people with similar values...people who have looked at life, seen the same responsibilities, and come to the same conclusions. This is why the world of the combat handgun is perhaps the most egalitarian sphere in the galaxy of sports-related activities.

Kenneth V. Blanchard has written an excellent book titled *Black Man With A Gun*, available from the Second Amendment Foundation (425-454-7012). In it he

mainstream newspapers caricature American gun owners and NRA members as drooling troglodytes with Cro-Magnon foreheads. The depiction is invariably that of a white male.

This sort of prejudice has left a lot of the public believing that the gun world is racist. Ironically, the exact opposite is true, particularly in defensive handgun shooting sports such as IDPA and others. You don't see a lot of poor people or blue-collar workers at the golf club or at tennis matches. But if you go to a combat shoot (or a Second Amendment rally) you'll see a rainbow of ethnic backgrounds and religious backgrounds. You'll see male

details the single best philosophical argument I've seen for why every responsible, law-abiding member of the African-American community should not only own a gun, but join the NRA. He points out how members of the National Rifle Association welcomed him and other black people of his acquaintance with open arms, while a number of supposedly more liberal organizations were neither so forthcoming nor so honest.

Ken makes the point as well that the Dred Scott decision had to do with firearms. In the most shameful chapter in the history of the United States Supreme Court, that body ruled that the slave Dred Scott had no

*The Klan won't be riding in any time soon on this African-American citizen, testing his skills with his Colt .45 auto at an IDPA match in New Hampshire. Many laws restricting firearms ownership have been proven to be based in postbellum racism.*

rights as a citizen, in part because if such a precedent were established, people of his race would be able to go armed.

The Dred Scott decision was not the last evidence that "gun control" in this country has been aimed largely at the black population. Prior to the Civil War, no citizen needed a permit to carry a loaded and concealed weapon in public. It was done as a matter of course, absolutely legal, and left to the citizen's discretion. The law merely forbade the practice to convicted felons and the mentally incapable. But in the post-bellum years of Reconstruction, fearing the wrath of freed slaves no longer forbidden to own

*Minority citizens, often at the greatest risk of becoming victims of violent crime, have a proportionally great need to own, and become skillful with, defensive firearms.*

history of gun control, beginning in the early part of the 20th century and escalating until, before the millennium, auto-loading rifles and all handguns had been confiscated by the British government.

Flash back to the present in the U.S.A. The same "divide and conquer" strategy is in play when anti-Second Amendment forces prey on the fears of minorities by painting gun owners as white racist. The gun club or pistol match as a "Caucasian only entity" has suffered from a self-fulfilling prophecy effect. We will never know how many people of color who wanted to get into organized combat pistol shooting decided not to, because they had been falsely led to believe that they would not be welcome.

Other sociological factors were at work as well. Poverty not only breeds crime, it leads to broken families. The matriarchal family is a strong tradition in lower income African-American communities. Mothers there know that criminal violence is the greatest danger their sons face. Strongly influential in their sons' lives, they aggressively warn their male progeny against drugs, gangs, and guns. Thus, the gun itself becomes psychologically demonized along with the true causes of crime and danger. It is a big obstacle to hurdle when a law-abiding young black man comes to realize that he needs more than phrases like "just say no" to keep his loved ones safe in a dangerous place.

A number of African-American police recruits have had to overcome this deeply-instilled prejudice against firearms to qualify with their service guns when they became law enforcement officers.

### Improving The Situation

Because there was an image in the black community that police were hostile to African-Americans, that group rarely applied to become law enforcement officers. The police community was able to improve that situation by aggressively recruiting for officers in the black community. It is time for the "gun culture" to do the same.

Ditto the Asian community, ditto the Latin community, ditto every "hyphenated-American" community. The egalitarianism of the "gun culture" is a well-kept secret that needs to be told. Gun clubs, shooting associations, and gun owners' civil rights groups need to be more active in recruiting minority members. We need to be arranging firearms safety training programs, affordably or at no charge, in the inner city and in other ethnic enclaves.

It is here that decent citizens are most at risk. It is here we find the people who need to exercise this freedom the most…and a huge, untapped resource to help us defend that freedom, for the sake of us all. Not only our generation, but also those to come…a topic we'll go to next.

weapons, an ethnocentric white majority passed laws that would require a license to carry a gun in public. The plan was to make the sheriffs the issuing authority, and then be sure to elect only white males who would be sure to issue the permits only to other white males.

The strategy worked, with such frightening efficiency that it remains in force in many jurisdictions today. While more than 30 states have "shall-issue" laws that give equal rights in this respect to rich and poor, white and black, and male and female alike, there remain several states where the issue of the permits is discretionary. There are jurisdictions where "discretionary" is a code word that means, "We'll give you the permit if you're white, male, rich, and politically connected."

The motivation lay in economics as well as race. Industry and management had the clout to elect politicians, and they didn't want to empower labor to be able to shoot back at strikebreakers. The wish to "declaw" the working public is more clearly seen in Great Britain's

# Young People And Combat Handguns

In February of 2002 in South Bend, Indiana, a man held a box-cutter to a widow's throat and demanded her valuables, including her late husband's weapons collection. A convicted armed robber and self-confessed drug dealer, the 27-year-old intruder meant business. The woman, Mrs. Sue Gay, thought she was going to be killed.

But Mrs. Gay's grandson ran upstairs and obtained a loaded .45 caliber pistol. He rushed back down and confronted the man, who tried to use the grandmother as a human shield. However, the petite hostage proved to be too small to hide behind. Seeing an opening and fearing for his grandmother's life, the grandson fired one shot.

The criminal turned and ran out the door. Mrs. Gay rushed forward and slammed it shut behind him and called 911. When police arrived, they found the career criminal outside, bleeding from a .45 caliber gunshot wound of the chest. He died in the emergency room.

Mrs. Gay told South Bend Tribune reporter Owen O'Brien of her rescue by her grandson. "He hit the bottom of the stairs with the .45 and stood (in a) ready stance with the gun…one shot and he got him. He's my little hero."

The boy who fired the rescue shot was 11 years old.

The youngster had lost his father to a heart attack three years before. Prior to his death, however, the conscientious father had taught the boy shooting skills and gun safety. "Before his dad died, they'd go target shooting. He knows they're not toys and not something to mess with," the grandmother confirmed.

St. Joseph County prosecutor Chris Toth almost immediately ruled the shooting justifiable. "The young man reasonably believed his mother and himself to be in danger of dying. It was clear to us this was a justifiable homicide," the prosecutor told reporters.

The killing of a human being was "an unfortunate burden for an 11-year-old to have on him," the prosecutor said, and surely all of us can agree with that. At the same time, there is no question that having his grandmother murdered before his eyes as he stood helpless would have been much more traumatic.

As we look over the lists of righteous armed citizen shootings that have been compiled for decades by the National Rifle Association, we see things like this cropping up, albeit infrequently. We mention elsewhere in this book the case of a much younger boy who saved his mother, who was being beaten to death by an adult male psycho. A .25 caliber bullet fired by the child from an inexpensive Raven pistol into the attacker's brain preserved his mom's life. In another incident, a boy only slightly older than the one in South Bend was home in bed when a stalker broke into the family home. Obsessed with the woman the boy's father had brought into the home, the stalker had come to commit murder, and did. He killed the woman and the boy's older brother, and shot and gravely wounded the father, leaving him for dead. As the mass murderer entered the young man's room to complete what he thought was the extermination of the family, there was one thing he didn't know.

The dad had trusted the youngster to have a handgun of his own in his room. By the time the stalker entered, the kid had been able to arm himself with his Ruger Single-Six .22 sporting revolver. A moment later the rampage ended as the murderer fell to the floor with one of the boy's small caliber bullets in his brain. The youth and his father survived.

We don't like to think of it, but any of our children could be caught alone in a terrible situation. We tell

*This little one is learning that parents Heidi and Jeff Williams will reward her for her responsible behavior in adult-oriented theaters.*

*This little guy is still in elementary school, but he turned in a strong performance with a Smith & Wesson K-22 at the National Junior Handgun Championships.*

**Beyond the Stereotypes • 213**

them what to do (drop and roll) if their clothing catches fire. We put them through "drown-proofing" programs when they're little. This is simply another emergency that could befall a child for whom we are responsible when we aren't there to physically protect them.

It doesn't always involve an adult human predator. Some years ago, a pack of vicious dogs attacked a little girl playing in her yard. Her older brother, an early adolescent, grabbed a .22 rifle and used it to excellent effect, saving his sister's life.

A few years ago in California, a girl in her early teens was in charge of her younger siblings when an adult male, who could be described as a homicidal maniac, burst into the home, armed with a pitchfork. She ran for her father's guns, which she knew how to use, but they were locked up and inaccessible to her. She managed to escape to a neighbor's house, begging for a gun; the adult neighbor refused the weapon and kept her with him, but called the police. When officers arrived the maniac attacked them, and they shot him dead. They entered the home to discover that he had already murdered the other children. Their grandmother has since publicly stated her conviction that, had the older child been able to access a gun, she could have saved the lives of the little ones.

*The parents of this little boy don't know that his shooting coach is a psychologist and an accomplished combat handgunner; as they watch from beyond camera range, they only know that their son is in safe hands.*

the Congressional Medal of Honor. Each was preserved, thanks to his shooting skills, to return home to his family.

This book is not suggesting that young children be taught "gunfighting." What is suggested is that children be taught firearms safety, and safety protocols for every other potentially dangerous "adults-only" object in the adult-oriented world that surrounds them.

We know that the Eddie Eagle firearms safety program for younger children has been a huge success.

### Perspectives

When the U.S. was more rural than urban, children were taught firearms safety and marksmanship as a matter of course. When they were little boys, Alvin York and Audie Murphy were sent into the woods, alone, with a .22 rifle and a few cartridges, and expected to bring home meat for the family table. They lived up to these responsibilities, and the skills they learned served them well when they had to defend their country, in WWI and WWII respectively. Each earned

*The author watches as Samantha Kemp coolly and precisely perforates a target with her dad's Glock 19.*

Few people realize that it evolved from a program developed by Florida firefighters to prevent injury to children who came upon blasting caps or other explosives that had been left unattended. A Spokane firefighter who was also a firearms instructor, Robert Smith, learned of the program and suggested to the NRA that they develop something similar for children who find themselves in the presence of a firearm not supervised by an adult.

The program teaches children to memorize a four-step protocol. "Stop! Don't touch! Leave the area! Tell an adult!"

The entertainment media has made the gun in general and the handgun in particular an emblem of heroism and power. Child psychologists tell us that because children are little and weak and dependent, they crave strength and freedom. They seek responsibility and power, the cornerstones of adulthood, and the gun becomes an embodiment of both. Bill Watterson for many years wrote a fabulously successful comic strip called "Calvin and Hobbes," about a 6-year-old boy with an active fantasy life that revolved around his stuffed tiger. Watterson's work, like Mark Twain's, was multi-dimensional, simple humor on one level but biting social satire on another. In one telling cartoon, Calvin describes to Hobbes what adulthood should be: "Women should all wear tight clothing," he tells his toy tiger, "and men should all carry powerful handguns."

Satire is a reflection of social values, and here, Bill Watterson had it nailed. Calvin constantly imagined himself a private eye with a .38 or a .45, or "Spaceman Spiff," armed with a deadly ray gun. This is precisely the effect that TV and movie depictions have on our nation's youth. It makes a real gun almost irresistible to touch.

What is a parent or guardian to do? The father of the little boy in South Bend had it right. Outdoor sportsmen say, "When you take your child hunting, you won't have to go hunting for your child." When a parent or other trusted adult takes a child to the range and teaches her or him to shoot, the curiosity about guns aroused by the media is satisfied, and channeled safely and appropriately.

Your state's department of Fish and Game or Wildlife has responsibility for Hunter Safety Programs. You can phone them for a list of courses and instructors near you. This in turn will lead you to a list of gun clubs in your area. Your local gun shop (though probably not the clerk at the firearms counter of the Big Box discount store) can also guide you to gun clubs and firearms learning opportunities near you.

At this writing, the Boy Scouts of America still endorse optional firearms safety programs and offer merit badges for riflery, though there is no provision within the current BSA for handgun shooting. Your local 4-H Club may also have youth shooting opportunities available.

The National Rifle Association has Junior Rifle training and competition programs available nationwide. Contact them to learn about local programs at 11350 Waples Mills Road, Fairfax, VA 22030. Some of the hosting clubs also have junior shooter programs available that involve handguns.

The National Junior Handgun Championship was created at the famous Second Chance Shoot in 1997. John Maxwell, already coaching his son Cody successfully toward a spot in Olympic shooting, led the study team. Tom Sheppardson of Michigan, a middle school administrator, and this writer joined him. Sheppardson, with access to extensive research in physical education for young people, determined that the best breaking point between child and young adult would be age 13. Because

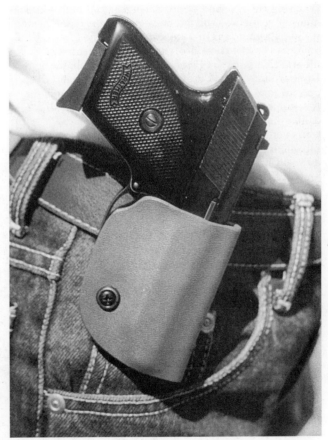

*Gun expert Andy Kemp bought this combination – a Walther TP-22 pistol and Ky-Tac holster – to teach his little girls safe gun handling. Gun and holster were proportional. His oldest was winning IDPA awards with a Glock 19 in 9mm by age 11.*

*An LFI-III graduate supervises a youngster with an adult-size Beretta 92 9mm. Note that the coach's folded hands show body language of confidence, but this responsible adult is in position to reach instantly and correct things should there be a lapse of safety.*

the Second Chance format of bowling pin shooting requires powerful guns, we wanted to make sure that youngsters with growing and forming bones didn't damage themselves by absorbing too much recoil from powerful sidearms. Age 14-17 was set for Junior class, and age 13 and down for Sub-Junior. The kids in the Junior class shot the same target array with the same type of handguns as the adults, while the younger ones had a "five-pin tipover" event with the pins set at the back of the tables so they could shoot lighter-kicking .38s, 9mms, and even .22s.

*Firearms instructor Jeff Williams coaches a youngster with a full-size SIG P226 9mm. In a few minutes, the boy will "fly solo" under watchful guidance.*

The first National Junior Handgun Championships, sponsored by Richard Davis at Second Chance in 1998, was resoundingly successful. Unfortunately, after that year the Second Chance Shoot went on hiatus and another venue was sought. Steve and Clare Dixon hosted it the following year in Iowa, using the same format. That venue was suspended also, and the event went into hibernation until the Pioneer Sportsmen Club, Inc. in Dunbarton, NH, took it over and, with the support of the Second Amendment Foundation, scheduled a match for the summer of 2002. The format was changed to all .22 caliber handguns, and the course of fire was made a mix of bull's-eye shooting, a Steel Challenge event, and an NRA Hunter Pistol stage of fire. Sub-Juniors could shoot two-handed throughout, while Juniors would have to shoot the bull's-eye stage in the traditional one-handed fashion. Information is available through Pioneer Sportsmen, Inc., P.O. Box 403, Concord, NH 03302.

### Tool Of Parenting

This writer can honestly say that he has found the gun to be nothing less than a tool of parenting. My kids started shooting at 6. My older daughter won her first pistol match against adult males at 11, and she was 19 when she won High Woman at the National Tactical Invitational at Gunsite. She beat not only a very strong field of highly accomplished adult female *pistoleras,* but most of the male SWAT cops, etc., as well. My younger daughter was 11 when she shot her first match, a side event at a national tournament, and at 13 carried her dad to National Champion Parent/Child Handgun Team in Sub-Junior class in 1998.

The awards were the least of it. Throughout the years of their growing up, their handgun owning and shooting

*Taking your kids shooting exposes them to wonderful people. Justine Ayoob was 13 in this photo when she listened carefully to the advice of famed grandmaster shooter Ken Tapp.*

privileges gave their mother and I one more way to show them the path to adulthood. As young women in a world dominated by adult men, they learned that if they developed their skills and understood the rules, they could beat grown-up men at their own game on a level playing field. They learned that when they were given power, commensurate responsibility would be expected of them, and when they lived up to that responsibility, they would be given more power, and so on…a microcosm of adult life path.

Each grew up comfortable in adult company, not intimidated by those who for the moment had more power than they, and learning how to give respect without obeisance. Each earned academic honors that both parents were proud of, but more importantly, each grew up to be a natural protector, someone to whom their peers would come when in trouble.

Understanding of when to use force was something else they absorbed. When the younger was about 10, she switched from karate to aikido because she had learned that in the latter art, she could spar against adults instead of children. When she had been a *karate-ka,* her father had watched from the back of the dojo with heart in mouth as she sparred against young men three years older than she and head and shoulders taller. She never lost. In one such encounter, she evaded a vicious punch to the head and countered with a roundhouse kick delivered so hard that it emptied the air from the boy's lungs temporarily and dropped him, heavy protective gear notwithstanding. A few years later, attacked for real by a mentally ill young man much stronger than she, who was trying to smash her in the head with a bottle, she coolly performed the exact same maneuver, saving herself and dropping her attacker in a gasping heap.

The older daughter had taken comfortably to the gun, and was issued a concealed carry permit at the unusually early age of 18. A little over a year later, she was targeted by two adult males as she came from the sidewalk up the steps of her house. Realizing that she could not get her key in the door before the first fast-running attacker would be upon her, she spun to face them and went for the Smith & Wesson Model 3913 9mm she carried in her waistband. The would-be rapists turned and fled. I suspect they were less intimidated by the small, silver-colored pistol than by the body language and facial expression of the resolute young woman who so swiftly and expertly drew it.

### Parent As Teacher

Just as the teacher is a surrogate parent for much of a child's day, the parent is also a teacher for much of the rest of the time. Before the baby bird leaves the nest, it must be taught to take care of itself.

Whether or not a given parent wants their child to possess firearms even when they grow up, the fact remains that some 40 percent to 50 percent of American homes contain guns. Unless we keep our children from ever visiting a friend's home, we cannot guarantee that they won't be exposed to guns. But knowledge is power, and there is no safety in ignorance.

A child who knows how to make a firearm safe is a child who is not endangered by the mere presence of one. There is no set age at which to introduce a child to firearms; only the parent can gauge the development of the necessary responsibility. I have been hunting in the field with little kids whom I trusted behind me holding loaded guns, and I have been in the presence of adults who are still not ready for the responsibility. One good barometer is watching how the child handles pets. If they keep feeding and brushing the puppy even when the newness has worn off, it's a positive sign.

The "gun culture" is an aging one. Opponents of the civil right of firearms ownership have used the same techniques of "manufactured social undesirability" that worked to reduce cigarette smoking, to demonize interest in legitimate firearms ownership among the young. It is working. We of this generation need to remain tirelessly politically active if we are to pass on to our successors the right to own weapons to protect oneself and one's family. Concomitantly, we must work to educate the young to appreciate this right, and to protect and cherish it as we do, or it will be lost forever.

John Maxwell said it best, simply and starkly: "The children are the future."

# CHAPTER FOURTEEN

# The Latest And Best Combat Handguns

In the five years since I wrote the Fifth Edition of the GUN DIGEST BOOK OF COMBAT HANDGUNNERY, there have been some interesting and useful advances in combat handgun design. During this period I was writing for several gun magazines and law enforcement publications. One was *On Target*, edited by Ben Battles. My title on that particular masthead is "Defensive Handgun Editor," and my job each issue is to wring out one of the "latest and greatest." Ben has given me permission to reprint and/or adapt and update those reviews for the Sixth Edition of COMBAT HANDGUNNERY. Some of what follows appeared there first, and it has been updated and edited by yours truly to allow for things we've learned about each particular handgun since, in the field. We'll run them in alphabetical order.

### Beretta Px4 And Cougar

Beretta has done a number of good things since the last edition of COMBAT HANDGUNNERY. They've invested a huge amount of money in their US production facility in Accokeek, Maryland, which I recently toured. The result has been an even better level of accuracy for the already famously accurate Model 92 pistol.

Beretta appears to have finally dumped its first excursion into polymer pistol production, the egregious Model 9000. Sleek external styling by the House of Giugiaro was, in this case, a classic example of trying to make a silk purse from a sow's ear. As I wrote in the GUN DIGEST BOOK OF BERETTA in 2005, I suppose they'll have to put an example of the 9000 in the Beretta museum in Italy to keep the collection complete, but they should drape that particular exhibit in black crepe. It would be appropriate to mourn the poor human engineering, mediocre accuracy and substandard reliability – all grotesquely uncharacteristic of Beretta – that were embodied in this fortunately short-lived gun.

Better were the upgrades to the superb 92 series, well-proven by time and battle. The M9 pistol saw heavy use in Iraq and Afghanistan, and the only problems reported by the troops were poor stopping power with the 9mm NATO ball *(predictable, and certainly not the gun's fault)*, and malfunctions with cheap Checkmate magazines bought on bid. Beretta and MecGar magazines *(the same thing, really)* became *the* gifts to send to American soldiers and Marines fighting in those hotspots, and with those, the M9 service pistols became reliable again.

In 2002, at about the time the Fifth Edition of GUN DIGEST BOOK OF COMBAT HANDGUNNERY was coming out, Beretta introduced the Vertec. This was the 9mm Model 92 and/or .40 S&W Model 96 with a straighter grip angle, and a slimmer one that brought the hand deeper into the gun and the finger deeper into the trigger, significantly improving handling for many shooters. National Champion Ernest Langdon, who shot his way to fame with the Beretta 92, switched to the Vertec and told me he considered it the best pistol Beretta had ever made. High praise indeed from the master of that particular gun, who abandoned it when he went to work for Smith & Wesson.

*The Beretta Px4. This is the slickslide "C" model, with revolver-like DA pull.*

*Ninety-two is latest incarnation of the Beretta 92.*

*New grip shape is a cornerstone of the Beretta Ninety-Two redesign.*

The latest iteration of this modern classic is the Ninety-Two. Jack up the barrel/slide assembly of an original Model 92, run a polymer chassis under it, and you have Beretta's answer to trendy plastic frames with, of course, the obligatory flashlight rail. I haven't put one through its accuracy paces yet, but those who have tell me they see no difference in that regard between it and the original, which is a good thing. Trigger reach is good. Feel is decent. Hopefully, the Ninety-Two update will keep this good gun in the running among those for whom modernity is the watchword. *(But, I have to ask, why that name? How does one, with the spoken instead of written word, distinguish between Model 92 and Model Ninety-Two? In my circles, folks describe it as the "Ninety-dash-Two." Some more thought should have gone into that moniker…)*

I think the big design news from Beretta in the last five years, as far as combat handguns anyway, is the Px4.

I was one of several gun writers flown to Maryland by Beretta USA for the gun's debut in the summer of 2005, and we all liked what we saw, for the most part. The interchangeable grip panels were well thought out, and very easy to install or change out. Takedown was simple, and designed to thwart the mythical "they'll field-strip the gun in your hand" disarm. *(Talk about ingenious solutions to non-existent problems. My feelers have been out for a long time, and the best I can determine, a "rip the slide off your Beretta disarm" has never occurred in the field.)*

I liked the grip angle and the pointability of the Px4. Accuracy was good, and recoil was soft. We were all shooting CCI's 180-grain Gold Dot .40 S&W ammo, perhaps the hottest of the subsonic hollowpoints in that caliber, and the kick was no problem at all even in rapid-fire hosing. None of us could make it jam even with intentional limp-wristing, and we were shooting the Gold Dot by the case. Accuracy was decent, too. I would have liked a grip that was a little rougher on the surface for a bit more traction, but that's subjective.

The Px4 designation stands for "pistol times four," since four calibers were planned: 9mm, .40 S&W, .357 SIG and .45 ACP. I've seen only the first two thus far. Of particular interest was the police-only option called the Type C fire control mechanism, a new take on double-action-only. The "C" stands for "constant action." It's a true DAO, and one of the few which, in an auto pistol, really feels revolver-like. The first ones in the U.S.A. went to the Chicago Police Academy, since Chicago requires DAO pistols and the Beretta is one of the most popular brands on their approved list. I tried the Type C in Chicago, and discovered why the coppers who test-drove it said they liked it so much. Some dealers are telling me today that the Px4 is their best-selling Beretta, though it's certainly not their best-selling *pistol*. My one big gripe about it was that the safety and/or decock levers on the F and G series were unpleasantly sharp, and did not operate as smoothly and naturally for the thumb as the Models 92 and 96, or even the Cougar.

Now, the Cougar is a particularly interesting story. Utilizing a rotary breech design that does indeed suck up recoil, this gun proved itself adequately reliable over the years but never developed the *cachet* of its older brother. My personal favorites were the big blasters. These were

*Ayoob testfires the Beretta Px4 in .40 in Maryland. He was impressed with the new gun's features.*

*Px4 F works well for southpaws. Safety lever was intended to be improved in shape over that of the 92 series.*

the Cougar 8357, made especially for the North Carolina Highway Patrol, which adopted it as standard in the F style and in the .357 SIG. Carried on safe, like the Beretta 92 and Beretta 96 pistols the Patrol had carried since the early '80s, it continued to save lives when bad guys got the guns away from troopers. The 8045, at least one run of which in a special barrel length was produced exclusively for the LAPD, was an excellent service .45 auto. Unfortunately, Beretta Cougars stopped coming into the United States in 2005. Only a few Beretta .45s remain in service in L.A.; the popular approved .45s there (*always bought out of the officer's own funds unless they're on SWAT or the Special Investigations Section*) are the S&W stainless and the Glock 21.

There's an interesting story behind that sudden disappearance of the Cougar. Beretta had moved its Cougar production line to Turkey, in part hoping to take advantage of cheap labor, and in part because they had supposedly gathered up a huge contract for service pistols in that country. All seemed well, rumor has it, until

someone in Turkey cited a law there that forbade shipping weapons to countries that were at war. The United States, of course, was actively engaged in the War on Terror.

In late 2006, the Cougar resurfaced stateside. My old friend Dick Metcalf got the scoop and broke the story in the pages of *Guns & Ammo* in its January, 2007 edition. He reported that Stoeger had been acquired by the Beretta Holdings Group in 2002, and was in charge of the Beretta effort in Turkey…and that the guns would be coming into the U.S.A. after all.

The most important element of his scoop, Dick reported, was that the plan to make the guns more economically had worked. He wrote, "Best part? The recommended retail price for a new Stoeger Cougar is a mere $349. Ten, count 'em, 10 years ago, the recommended retail price for an identical Beretta-label Cougar was $697."

Now known as the Stoeger Cougar but otherwise identical to its predecessor, this gun at that price is *big* combat handgun news. It will literally undersell the Ruger P95, now perhaps the "best buy" economy 9mm on the U.S. market. Good news, indeed. Quality self-defense should not be limited to those who can spend four figures per gun.

### COLT

Still struggling to stay alive, and keeping its doors open mainly through large military contracts for its splendidly-produced M-16 and M-4 series, the firm can still make a fine 1911 pistol when it gets around to it. After all, this is the company that created the 1911. The .45 and .38 Super autos they're producing today are, in my opinion, distinctly better guns than the Series '70 pistols that have engendered such cultish lust among shooting enthusiasts.

Indeed, Colt has brought back the "pre-Series '80" guns due to popular demand. The best of these by far is the GSP, Colt's iteration of the Gunsite Service Pistol as envisioned by Jeff Cooper. It feeds superbly, has a good trigger and it delivers surprisingly good accuracy – all commensurate with its price. Less successful were the "retro" 1911 and 1911A1, which as a friend of mine says, "coupled a premium price with all the worst features that we all worked so hard for decades to get past." Apparently, most of the rest of the gun-buying public felt the same.

*The 1911 .45 has never been more popular than today.* **Top to bottom:** *Kimber Custom II, Colt 1991A1 (modified by Mark Morris), SW1911, Springfield Armory TRP Operator, and ParaOrdnance single-stack.*

*Colt still produces a fine .45 auto. Here, author wins an IDPA match with an out-of-the-box Commander-length Colt and .45 hardball.*

Colt's double-action revolvers appear to be gone for good now, more's the pity, though rumors persist of modernized versions that wait on the drawing boards in the bowels of the Connecticut plant. In the meantime, the many of us who have learned to appreciate the subtle advantages of double-action Colt revolvers continue to haunt the gun shops and gun shows looking for good samples, and wincing at the constantly rising prices of used Colt six-guns.

## CZ75 Tactical Sports

The CZ75! Discovered at its ComBloc roots some three decades ago by Jeff Cooper and pronounced by him a superb design, this Czech 9mm service pistol soon became an iconic gun the world over. One of the most avidly copied of modern handgun designs, renditions of the Czech 75 have been produced in England, Italy, Switzerland, Turkey and the U.S.A., and I may have missed some. Of course, the one firm with the most experience making it continues apace, Ceska Zbrojovka in the city of Brod in what is now the Czech Republic. Their latest offering is a sophisticated match target variation of the CZ75, called the Tactical Sports model. Our test sample bears serial number A121834, and was shipped to us by CZ-USA in Kansas City, Kansas.

The barrel is a full five inches in length, with slide and frame lengthened correspondingly. (Standard length is 4.72 inches.) Like the SIG P210 and other European pistols before it, this gun uses the Petter principle of the slide running *inside* the frame rails instead of outside them.

Workmanship was impressive. I've seen sweet CZs over the years and rough ones, and this one is *nice*. The silvery matte finish of the frame has almost a "crackle" look, and the slide and barrel are nicely polished and blued.

The Patridge front sight is big, square and blocky, just as it should be to give a fast and clear sight picture in an action-shooting match. The rear sight is *huge,* and serrated horizontally to break up glare. The rear notch is wide enough and deep enough for fast "flash sight pictures" without compromising precision accuracy potential.

One thing I've never liked about the CZ75 design is that the slide is buried so deep inside the frame rails, there's little for the hand to grasp. That big sight is actually the easiest grasping point for working the slide!

*Test sample CZ75 gave occasional extraction failures with Winchester ammo.*

This variation of the 75 has forward cut grasping grooves in the slide, but they are well back from the front, almost at midpoint of the slide. This solves my pet peeve with front grasping grooves, which is that they bring the support hand too close to the "business end" of a pistol. Not on this one.

No serious competitor much cares how a match gun *looks*. We care about how it *feels*.

Looks and feel are both subjective, but all of our several testers liked the feel of this one. Coarse machine checkering on the front and back straps of the grip frame combined with the checkered hardwood grip panels and the natural "shape" of the CZ frame to allow a secure and hand-filling grasp. Fit is perfect in the average adult male hand, if you want the barrel in line with the long bones of the forearm and the pad or tip of the index finger in contact with the trigger.

While the standard CZ75 is DA/SA optional, meaning it can be fired double action or single action for the first shot, the Tactical Sports is single action only and must be carried cocked and locked. The thumb safety is ambidextrous and, in the CZ75 tradition, is mounted fairly high on the frame. One good thing about that is that even with a big hand, the knuckle of the trigger finger won't accidentally knock the ambi-lever up into the "safe" position in the middle of a string of fire, as can happen with some iterations of the ambidextrous safety on 1911 pistols. The only sharp edges on the test gun that irritated shooters were on the bottom edges of the safety levers, which dug into the thumb when pushing the lever up to *safe* the pistol.

Trigger reach is long, again a traditional element of CZ75 design. Colonel Cooper always taught high thumb placement and the use of the far end of the finger on the trigger; the CZ75's dimensions virtually require this, which may be one reason the good Colonel liked it so much. These same dimensions, however, can require a bit of a stretch for those with shorter digits.

The magazine release button extends almost 1/2-inch from the forward part of the frame, making it easy to reach for quick mag changes without breaking your primary grasp. Reloads won't be that frequent, though, since this pistol comes with three *20-round* magazines. We found 19 rounds went in easy; getting the 20th into the mag just wasn't worth the effort. Empty mags dropped out cleanly at a touch of the release button, and a flower

*CZ75 Tactical Sports is an impressive handful of target pistol.*

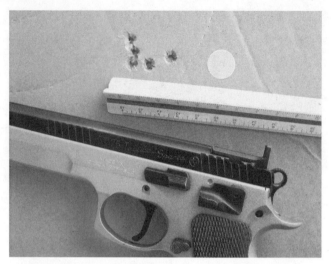

*Tactical Sports CZ put five shots in a little over an inch at 25 yards.*

pot-size mag well (1.3 inches wide side-to-side, 1.8 inches wide front to back!) allowed super-fast reloads. The mags fit a standard Glock-size magazine pouch.

The trigger pull immediately gets attention. Adjustable, this one came from the factory with a feathery let-off. Pull-weight averaged 2 pounds, 10 ounces at the center, and 1 pound, 14 ounces when the pressure was applied at the toe, or tip, of the pivoting trigger.

The Tactical Sports was taken to the 25-yard bench with five high-quality 9x19 loads, encompassing three manufacturers, three bullet weights and velocities from subsonic up through standard, +P and +P+. The clear, crisp sight picture and the light, sweet trigger pull made good groups come easy.

Winchester brand comprised three of those loads, and the two most accurate. Amazingly, the cheapest ammo shot the tightest. Winchester USA white box, generic 115-grain ball with full copper jacket, plunked five shots into a group that measured 1.20 inches center-to-center. The best three of those were exactly a half-inch apart. Often available for around thirteen dollars per hundred, the "WWB" (Winchester white box) gave champagne accuracy at a beer price.

The same company's 147-grain 9mm subsonic jacketed hollowpoint, originally developed as the OSM (Olin Super Match) load to give SEAL Team Six brain-hitting

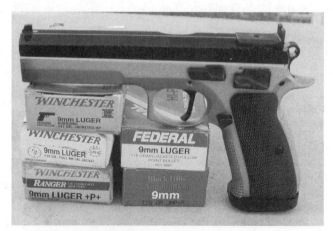

*Current CZ75 is built to take the hottest 9mm.*

accuracy at 50 yards with their sound-suppressed HK MP5 9mm sub-machineguns set on semiautomatic, has proven to be one of our most accurate pistol loads in this caliber. It lived up to that reputation with the long-nosed CZ pistol. The Winchester subsonic punched a quintet of holes that measured 1.25 inches center-to-center. The best three shots in the group constituted a cluster of merely 0.65-inch.

Another famously accurate 9mm jacketed hollowpoint is the Federal Classic 115-grain, factory code 9BP. Often the most accurate cartridge in 9mm handgun tests, the 9BP didn't take those honors this time, but still produced a satisfying group of 2.30 inches, with the best three hits in 1 inch even.

Coming up out of standard-pressure 9mm Luger ammo into hotter loads, the test gun wasn't quite as accurate. It wasn't a handling thing. This is a big, heavy, all-steel pistol and even with the hottest loads, its recoil is remarkably mild. It just didn't spin the faster bullets into such tight groups. Black Hills 115-grain +P JHP was only a little more open in grouping than the Federal standard pressure, delivering a 2.80-inch group for five shots and 1.5 inches for the best three. Velocity out of the five-inch barrel would have been a bit over 1300 fps. Winchester's 127-grain +P+ Ranger, factory-rated at 1250 fps, produced a 3.65-inch group, though the best three were in 1.45 inches.

Let's put that in perspective. CZ's website, www.czub.cz, says the Tactical Sports model was developed for IPSC, the International Practical Shooting Confederation. IPSC has large targets, for which any load we tested in this gun would deliver ample accuracy. NRA Action Pistol, which reaches its apotheosis at the Bianchi Cup, is built around a target whose 10-ring is eight inches in diameter and whose tie-breaking center X-ring measures four inches. Keep in mind that the "best three" measurement is intended to factor out unnoticed human error and give a prediction of the gun's inherent mechanical accuracy, and you realize that the CZ75 Tactical Sports is a pistol that could win the Bianchi Cup's stock gun iron sight class.

All groups were slightly left of the aiming point. If I were going to keep this gun, it would be the work of moments to drift the big "fixed" rear sight a tad right and tighten it down with the set-screw. No problem there.

In the hands of a half-dozen or more shooters, the CZ75 digested assorted reloads and several brands of factory ammo – hundreds and hundreds of rounds – without cleaning. There were three malfunctions; all extraction failures leading to "double feeds," and all with Winchester white box ball. That's one of the most reliable 9mm rounds in existence, and I'm at a loss to explain it. The CZ75 has a robust outside-mounted extractor, and this gun worked fine with everything else.

If I still shot Bianchi Cup every year, I would strongly consider the CZ75 Tactical Sports for the next stock gun event there. At $1152 suggested retail, the price is not at all bad for the accuracy, capacity, and features this 9mm target pistol delivers.

### Glock 37: Promise Fulfilled

By the late 1990s, Gaston Glock's G22, a 16-shot pistol chambered for the .40 S&W cartridge, was the single most popular law enforcement handgun in the United States. But Gaston hadn't gotten to where he was by sitting back smugly and resting on his laurels. He knew that there were still a lot of police departments – and individual purchasers – who preferred a .45 caliber. The problem was, in his guns, the .45 ACP cartridge required a frame large enough to be awkward for those with small hands.

We're talking about a guy who made it big by looking at problems and sitting down to solve them on a fresh sheet of paper instead of looking to old solutions. Big-frame performance in a medium-frame gun required a proprietary cartridge. The result is the .45 GAP: **G**lock **A**uto **P**istol.

At CCI Speer, Ernest Durham led the team that designed the new round. It was, essentially, a shortened .45 ACP, though in the technical details it's much more than that. Speer thought at first that to keep pressures safe within the short overall length, a bullet no heavier than 200 grains would be the ticket, and their first loads offered 200 and 185-grain heads. However, Winchester had learned a few things about putting heavy bullets in short cartridges without exceeding safe pressures while developing their successful WSM (Winchester Short Magnum) line of high-power rifle cartridges, and they were able to make the GAP work with a traditional 230-grain bullet. Glock was now ready to introduce their medium-frame .45 automatic.

They said the frame would be identical in dimension to the standard size service pistols: the Glock 17 in 9mm, the G22 in .40 S&W, and the G31 in .357 SIG. They succeeded.

They said it would take the same size magazine, fitting the magazine pouches you might already have for your standard size Glock. They succeeded.

They said their new short cartridge, the .45 GAP, would equal the power of the tried and true .45 ACP. With a little help from their friends in the ammo industry, they succeeded there, too.

They said the gun would fit your regular-size Glock holster. Well, they *almost* succeeded…

The Glock folks discovered that modern metallurgy notwithstanding, a slide originally dimensioned for the 9mm Luger cartridge simply wasn't right for the powerful buffeting it would receive from the equivalent of a .45 ACP. The slide had to be widened, to approximate the .45 ACP slide of the big-frame Glock 21. However, all other dimensions of the slide appear the same.

This means that the gun is too thick to fit a Glock 17 holster, unless the holster in question was a pretty sloppy fit to begin with. However, we found that holsters made for the Glock 21 .45 or the dimensionally identical Glock 20 10mm seemed to fit the Glock 37 very well. There may be some very specifically fitted holsters out there that were made for the big Glock and might be a little loose around the trigger guard with this smaller one, but we haven't seen one. I've been wearing the test gun in a Glock 21 rig by Aker and have tried it in several others, and it works just fine therein.

All other promises were kept to the letter. The Glock 37 magazine fits a Glock 17 magazine pouch. If you stuff it all the way full, it holds ten rounds, the maximum allowed under the old Crime Law before the sunset clause mercifully killed it. The last two or three cartridges, particularly the very last, are a bear to force into the magazine. We found that people with weak hands, injured hands, or just very cold hands couldn't always get that last round in without help. When the magazine is finally full, it needs a sharp rap to get it into the pistol frame if the slide is forward. This is because there is literally no flexion left in the magazine spring, and it's a very tight fit. If you don't slap it in firmly, you run the risk of failing to seat it. We see the same thing in many other magazines where capacity has been maxed out. A lot of the ten-rounders for guns originally designed to be high-caps, for instance, and eight-round magazines for 1911 .45s. Once the magazine is inserted, the compacted spring is pushing cartridges upward, which means the magazine is being pushed downward against the internal latch. This in turn requires a very firm press on the magazine release button to dump a full magazine when you're unloading.

My solution was simple. I load my G37 all the way up, since it's always calm when you do "administrative loading," and make sure the magazine with ten rounds is fully seated, giving me eleven rounds to start, counting the cartridge in the chamber. I then carry the spare magazine(s) downloaded to nine rounds to better guarantee full insertion in a fast, stressed-out speed reload or tactical reload.

The .45 GAP cartridge was originally introduced by CCI Speer in 185 and 200-grain bullet weights. In the latter, we found that it exceeded the standard-pressure .45 ACP in velocity. The 200-grain Gold Dot .45 ACP from a Glock 21 averaged 956 fps, while the same weight Gold Dot .45 GAP from the Glock 37 ran an average of 971 fps. Some said, "It won't be a *real* .45 until it shoots a 230-grain bullet!" Winchester has answered that, introducing a half-dozen loads for the .45 GAP, of which at least four feature 230-grain bullets. Ranger SXT 230-grain .45 GAP spat its high-tech hollowpoints at an average 862 fps, with the 230-grain ball rounds averaging 805 fps (conventional full metal jacket) and 803 fps (brass enclosed base). The new round is necessarily short in length to fit a "9mm pistol envelope," but it is by no means short of power.

There were few unexpected surprises shooting the Glock in .45 GAP. The slide of a standard Glock is slightly thinner than its frame; that of the Glock 37 is not. So that shooters could reach the slide lock lever, Glock installed the slightly extended one they make for the G34 and G35 Tactical/Practical models. This makes the lever easier to manipulate. It also means that if you shoot right-handed with your thumbs pointed straight to the target, one or the other thumb may override the slide stop and interfere with its functioning.

In the hand, the G37 feels like a heavier G17 due to the slightly more massive slide. It's a little like switching from a Browning Hi-Power in 9mm to the same gun in .40 S&W, since the Browning's manufacturers also had to increase slide mass when they went to a more powerful cartridge.

*Big news from Glock is their .45 GAP series. This is the smallest, the 7-shot Glock 39.*

As is true any time you go to a .45 from a 9mm, the G37 kicks more than the G17. It's a little snappier than the .40-caliber G22, and not much different from a .357 G31. We shot it for comparison with a .45 ACP Glock 21, and reviewers were mixed as to which kicked more, with some saying they couldn't tell the difference. Personally, I thought the smaller gun had a tiny bit more recoil, but not enough to worry about.

Accuracy was typical "standard-size Glock service pistol," not quite up to the spectacular standard set by the .45 ACP G21 and G30. We shot 200-grain Speer Gold Dot and flat-nose Lawman, Winchester 230-grain SXT and hardball, and Federal's new 185-grain Personal Defense series Hydra-Shok. All delivered about the same accuracy, in the 2-1/2 to 4-inch group range for five shots at 25 yards, hand-held from a benchrest.

Reliability was top-notch, which is also up to expectation with the Glock service pistols. We experienced no extraction failures, ejection failures, feed failures or cycling failures. Our test pistol was one of the first G37s, and had the early magazines with followers that extended a little too high. The slide would occasionally catch on the rear edge of the follower instead of locking open on the slide stop. This required the shooter to pull the empty mag out manually, at which time the slide would snap closed on an empty chamber. Glock took a few thousandths off the follower while retaining the same shape, and with the new magazines, the pistols work perfectly.

The big question seems to be, "Why a new .45 auto cartridge?" The answer is so the legendary ballistics of the .45 ACP, which historically required a large-frame pistol, can be transferred into a smaller-frame gun. The reach to the trigger is certainly easier with the smaller-frame G37 than with its big brother, and the shooter can wrap proportionally more stabilizing flesh and bone around the grip-frame, resulting in the perception – and perhaps the reality – of a more solid hold. We found the trigger reach about identical to that of a 14-shot Glock 21 .45 ACP whose frame had been "slimmed" by Robar, Inc. Purchasing the G37 means you're sacrificing three rounds to save the money it would cost to customize a G21 to better fit your hand. The only additional "cost" is having to buy .45 GAP ammo instead of using stores of .45 ACP you might already have on hand.

Some Glock fans will stay with their big-frame .45 ACPs, grips slimmed or not. Some will opt for the seven-shot Glock 36 subcompact .45 ACP, to get the advantage of its even slimmer grip profile and shorter trigger reach. But, for many, the Glock 37 in .45 GAP will prove to be the ideal compromise of size, power and cartridge capacity.

Glock predictably followed the "service size" G37 with the compact Glock 38 (analogous to the Glocks 19, 23, and 32 in 9mm, .40, and .357 SIG respectively), and with the subcompact Glock 39, a "baby Glock" comparable to the G26 9mm, G27 .40, and G33 .357. I tested them for *Tactical Response,* a controlled circulation professional journal for SWAT personnel. Both turned out to be remarkably controllable for their size and power. The G38 carries eight rounds in the magazine and a ninth in the chamber, exceeding the firepower of a single-stack GI-issue 1911 by one round, and equaling what you'd get in a modern commercial 1911 with today's eight-round magazines, or in a full size double-action .45 "service automatic" by Smith & Wesson or SIG. The G39 baby Glock carries six-plus-one rounds of .45 GAP.

Both proved accurate. The G38 put five rounds of Federal American Eagle 185-grain full metal jacket training ammo into 2.15 inches, with the best three clustered in a group exactly an inch smaller than that. Speer Gold Dot 200-grain hollowpoint put five shots into 1-3/4 inches, the best three under an inch. All this was at 25 yards.

The G39 did the "4+1" thing, with the first hand-chambered round going to a slightly different point of aim/point of impact than the next four automatically cycled cartridges. Thus, the Gold Dot had a measurement of just over 4 inches for all five rounds, but four of them were in 1.65 inches and the best three measured 1.05 inches. Winchester 230-grain .45 GAP hardball from the baby Glock delivered a 5-shot group that went 3.90 inches counting the first shot, with the last four in 1.90 inches and the best three in 0.95-inch.

Reliability? In all three sizes, the Glocks in .45 GAP live up to the company motto: "Glock Perfection."

### HK 2000SK 9mm Compact

It was a dark and stormy night.

Well, it *was,* dammit!

The dark and stormy night in question was December 23, 2004. It was stormy enough to shut down the Philadelphia airport, stranding thousands of people including me. Frigid rain swept Philly in torrents, a blizzard was smothering the Midwest, and planes weren't coming in *or* getting out. It became national news: thousands of us stranded there, and tens of thousands of suitcases lost. People were sleeping in the airport because hotels were full and there was "no room at the inn."

Fortunately, a buddy of mine lives in Philadelphia, and when I called him, Dr. Tony Semone was there for me. In my circle of friends, certain protocols are observed, and when you pick up a stranded friend at the airport, you have more in the car for him than a cool CD on the Boze. Tony knows I'm legal to carry in Pennsylvania, and knew that my weapons were locked in my lost checked baggage, so when I got into the car a couple of things were already waiting for me. One was a neat little Elishowitz folding knife.

The other was Heckler and Koch's new subcompact pistol, loaded with hot 9mm hollowpoints: the Model 2000SK.

That, I'm here to tell you, is a comforting thing to have on a dark and stormy night. I liberated it from its fanny

*Approved in the ICE tests for Homeland Security, the HK pistols of today are robust and reliable.*

pack, slipped the spare 10-round magazine into a side pocket of my Royal Robbins 5.11 BDUs, and tucked the loaded pistol inside my waistband at the spot where I'm used to reaching for it.

So, you might say, I was predisposed to feeling a bit warm and fuzzy toward the HK 2000SK when editor Ben Battles told me it was my next assignment for *On Target* magazine.

Heckler and Koch has earned the reputation as one of the most respected armsmakers over the latter half of the 20th century and thus far into the 21st, and it's no surprise that the 2000SK carries an impressive pedigree. HK introduced the very first of the polymer-framed semiautomatic pistols, the P9 and P9S series, going back to 1977. It was a gun ahead of its time, and production ceased in 1984. Next came the excellent USP (Universal Service Pistol) of 1993. This was the first successful marriage of the polymer frame with traditional double-action, outside-hammer design, and it remains popular among law enforcement and armed citizens alike. Third came the P2000, introduced in 2003, initially for the European market but quickly winning fans in the U.S. Similar in size to the USP Compact, it was more streamlined. It also came with molded frame rails of the Picatinny style for the InSight and SureFire attachable flashlights, a concept that had superseded the UTL (universal tactical light) and its roll-on side grooves which, in the original USP, had gotten that whole "light attached to service pistol for quick on and off" thing going a decade before. The P2000 was the first successful service pistol to be designed with an ambidextrous slide lock lever, making it truly southpaw-friendly. It also featured the interchangeable backstrap pioneered by Walther in their P99 series.

Now comes the 2000SK, an even more compact version of the P2000. With a magazine capacity of 10 rounds in 9mm Luger and nine in .40 S&W, plus one more in the firing chamber of each, this pistol has a shorter barrel that brings overall length down to 6.4 inches. It is comparable in size and weight to a baby Glock, such as the G26 or G27, or an all-steel, small-frame snub-nose 38 revolver.

At the heart of our test gun is the LEM concept, the Law Enforcement Module. I was present at the introduction of the USP at the SHOT Show in the early 1990s, and a double-action-only trigger was one of the seven fire control options HK offered for it. Let's just say that it was not the best option. Long, heavy, and a little bit gritty, the original DAO pull on the USP lacked the controllability of a traditional double action such as the Variant One, which proved by far to be the most popular HK USP format, and the one in which I chose to buy every one of my own USPs.

However, the law enforcement market was calling for double-action-only trigger systems in the name of simplicity of training and civil liability insulation against accidental discharges. HK responded with the LEM trigger, first seen in the U.S.A. by the Border Patrol. The trigger pull was much lighter. Moreover, if the shooter had the subtlety of technique, and the presence of mind under stress, to maintain finger contact with the trigger as he fired, the trigger would reset itself with only a partial forward return after the first shot, making subsequent rounds still easier to squeeze off. There had been complaints about DAO trigger systems by companies like Glock, Kahr, Para-Ordnance and Smith & Wesson which did not allow a second pull of the trigger if the first did not cause the shot to go off and the slide to cycle. The LEM system had built in a fallback mechanism, which would allow another crack at the recalcitrant cartridge in the chamber, albeit at the price of a heavier trigger pull.

Thus, the search for a good double-action-only pull had ended with, not a single uniform pull for every shot, but two different kinds of trigger pull depending on how the trigger was manipulated, and a third kind of trigger pull as insurance against misfires. The good news is that the first-shot pull is very nice indeed, even if your finger doesn't "ride the link" and get the even nicer pull for follow-up shots. It's similar to the sweet and easy pull you get with the Para-Ordnance LDA: one of the lightest, easiest and most controllable DAO trigger pulls that the industry offers. This LEM trigger group was part and parcel of our test HK 2000SK.

The test gun arrived the day I was leaving for the SHOT Show, so I left it with my crew at home base and they put several hundred rounds through it before I got home and took my turn. They had no malfunctions. Neither did I. We all found the recoil mild.

Accuracy testing was done off an MTM rest on a concrete bench at 25 yards. Each 5-shot group was measured once overall for "practical accuracy," and once again for the best 3 shots to factor out human error and get a better idea of potential "inherent accuracy." Three good brands of JHP carry ammo, in as many bullet weights, went downrange.

The 147-grain 9mm subsonic JHP was developed for accuracy, and the Winchester Silvertip in this formula continued that tradition, putting all 5 into 1-3/8 inches, the best 3 in 1 inch even. If they had centered on a 50-cent piece, all 5 bullets would have nicked the coin. Federal's famously accurate 9BP Classic, a 115-grain conventional JHP, went 2 inches even for all 5 and snugged its best 3 hits into 1-1/4 inches. Black Hills +P, with the street-proven combination of a 124-grain +P Gold Dot loaded to 1250 fps, delivered 2-1/8 inches for 5 shots, and the best of the "best 3" measurements, with a trio of bullet holes only 15/16ths of an inch apart, center-to-center. This is outstanding accuracy for a pocket-size 9mm pistol.

The big, blocky sights helped. They were easy to see quickly. The gun shot a little bit left, but the rear sight is movable in its dovetail and that would be easily corrected.

The only sharp spot is at the toe of the trigger. Carried inside the waistband without a holster in PA, I found nothing that dug into me or caught the clothing. At home, this light, small pistol was exquisitely comfortable in its high-ride hip holster and mag pouch from Galco's well-made Concealable series, this set bearing HK logos.

My only complaints were about that sharp toe on the trigger, and the fact that the accessory grooves on the frame were too short to lock in the InSight M3 and M6X, and SureFire X200 flashlights I tried to attach. I would have liked to try it with one of the mini-lights Springfield Armory offers for its similarly-sized XD subcompact, but didn't have one available. Overall, the HK 2000SK 9mm is a handy, ergonomic, remarkably accurate and utterly reliable concealed-carry gun, true to its HK pedigree.

And I can tell you from personal experience that it is a comforting thing to have with you on a dark and stormy night.

### HK USP Tactical .45

As noted above, many years ago I was at the SHOT Show writers' seminar where Heckler and Koch introduced their USP. The designation stands for "Universal Service Pistol," and that about sums it up. HK had priced itself out of the service pistol market with its P7 squeeze-cocker, a BMW of pistols; the unpretentious, conventionally styled polymer-frame USP was more of a Ford 150 pickup truck. It wasn't pretty, but it got the job done with reliability, precision and user-friendliness. As the line expanded, there would even be an F-350 version, as it were, the giant Mark 23 SOCOM pistol.

The USP has earned its good reputation. Only it and the SIG-Sauer passed the demanding tests for the Homeland Security contract. It has been adopted by police literally coast-to-coast, with the Washington State Patrol carrying USP.40 pistols and the Maine State Police issuing the USP.45.

The latest variation is the USP Tactical with high-profile adjustable sights and an extended barrel threaded for a sound suppressor. (I didn't test it with a "silencer" because I couldn't find one that would fit the HK's unusual threads. It's set up for the $1000 Reed Knight suppressor, and I understand GemTech now has one out to fit it.) Amenities include an adjustable trigger stop, and a frame in the currently trendy desert tan.

All small arms will shoot a little better with some types of ammo than others. On occasion, you find a gun that just seems to shoot well with everything. The HK Tactical fits the latter category. Three of the 6 loads tested grouped within 0.05-inch of each other.

The high-profile adjustable sights were spot on, right out of the box. This shows excellent attention to detail and bottom line performance at the factory. I can't say I've seen this on every Heckler and Koch pistol I've ever tested, but I've seen it so often I've come to think of it as something of an HK hallmark.

Despite its relatively light weight, this is a big, robust pistol that was built to handle heavy loads. It's in the family of HK's big SOCOM gun, for which the Special Operations Command acquired a large lot of 185-grain, 11.40 fps +P hollowpoints on a special contract from Olin. Olin does not offer that load to the public, but Remington, which pioneered it, still does. From the USP Tactical, the Remington 185-grain JHP +P delivered 2.85 inches for a five-shot group, with the best three of those hits 1.20 inches apart. All accuracy shooting was done hand-held from an impromptu benchrest at 25 yards, with "all five"

*HK USP Tactical .45 is a handful, but has many good features.*

**Uber-tacti-cool** *protruding muzzle threaded for silencer is a distinguishing feature of the USP Tactical .45.*

and "best three" measurements done to the nearest 0.05-inch. Hornady's famously accurate, deep-penetrating XTP 230-grain +P left the muzzle at 950 fps and punched five holes through the target in a 2.30-inch group, with the best three in a cluster measuring 0.70-inch.

That 230-grain bullet weight is the one most associated with the .45 ACP, and a good plan is to load "for the street" with a high-tech hollowpoint in that weight and then practice with inexpensive 230-grain FMJ hardball, both at standard velocity (830-880 fps). This gives you identical recoil and trajectory, carry round to training round. The representative pair in this test was CCI Gold Dot for the HP, and remanufactured "blue box" Black Hills for the FMJ. The Gold Dot gave the best 5-shot group of the test. This group measured 1.60 inches, with the best three shots in 0.70-inch, tying the Hornady round.

Testing also included that famous old "manstopper," the copper-jacketed Speer 200-grain JHP with a mouth so wide that the late, great Dean Grennell dubbed it "the flying ashtray." This particular load was from the economy Blazer line, with the aluminum Berdan-primed casing. The 5-shot group measured 2.25 inches, with the best three nestled into 1.40 inches. Finally, this sweet-shooting pistol would be suitable for some types of competition that don't require the full .45 ACP power levels, such as Steel Challenge shooting, PPC, the Bianchi Cup stock gun division, IDPA Enhanced Service Pistol, etc. A good light load for that kind of work is Winchester's 185-grain mid-range Match, with a 185-grain full jacketed semiwadcutter bullet. In the USP Tactical, this load gave us 3.0 inches exactly for all five shots, with the best three in 0.65-inch, the best 3-shot group of the test.

Let's take a moment to analyze that. The six loads tested pretty much covered the range of available .45 ACP power levels. The 5-shot groups measured 1.60, 2.25 (2x), 2.30, 2.85 and 3.00 inches. The average was 2.375 inches. This shows user-friendliness, a gun amenable to letting the shooter "keep 'em all in the X-ring."

Perhaps the most significant figure comes from the "best three" groups, which are measured in hopes of factoring out human error sufficiently to serve as a "poor man's test of inherent accuracy" when you don't have a machine rest available. With this pistol, those measurements were 0.65, 0.70 (2x), 0.80, 1.20 and 1..40

*USP Tactical, upper right, compared to author's 9mm HK P9S Sport Target, below. The P9 series inaugurated plastic-frame pistols, before even Glock.*

*The unit that started the detachable gun-light craze, HK's UTL (Universal Tactical Light) is geared to HK's proprietary rail system.*

inches. *All* were under 1-1/2 inches at 75 feet, for an average of 0.908-inch.

That, my friends, is remarkably good accuracy potential. It also demonstrates extraordinary consistency, which tells you that we're shooting a finely made machine here.

Accuracy is almost meaningless without reliability, but reliability is another HK hallmark. In the entire test, I experienced only a single malfunction. This was a failure to go into battery with the 200-grain Blazer. That flying ashtray bullet is a notorious gun jammer, partly because of its very wide mouth and partly because of its short overall length. That single stoppage was cleared by a quick rack of the slide that ejected the round from the large ejection port, and swiftly chambered another. The Gold Dot 230-grain has a similarly aggressive wide mouth, but it is longer overall with a more "hardball-like" ogive, and it never presented any sort of feeding or cycling problem with the test pistol. There were no other malfunctions of any kind.

This is a big pistol, and won't feel at home in a very small hand. In single action mode, it feels about like a full-size Glock in .45 ACP or 10mm, and with the trigger forward in double-action mode, the reach for the index finger is even longer.

The double-action pull was fairly smooth, but nothing to write home about. If you want a truly sweet DA pull in an HK service pistol, you want the LEM (law enforcement module) trigger group, which was not installed on the test gun. The DA stroke averaged right at 11 pounds even, measured on a Lyman digital trigger scale.

The single-action pull *was* something to write home about. It averaged 4 pounds, 7 ounces on the Lyman device, and it felt lighter. This comes from the pivoting trigger design: get your finger down low on the trigger, and you have more leverage. When the trigger is pressed, the hammer falls with a soft "tick" in dry fire. In live fire, you feel only a gentle bump as the pistol recoils. I think the polymer frame is definitely absorbing some of the recoil shock, and a lot of the rearward momentum is also dissipated in cycling the big slide against its recoil spring. Thus, while the gun has a high bore axis, it doesn't jump all over the place. It's very controllable and very comfortable to shoot, even with the potent +P loads it digests so enthusiastically.

The adjustable sights not only give a sight picture above an attached "can," but a sight picture that's easy to see. For true "tactical" work, though, we'd favor night sights over the plain black target shooter's image these afford the user. The flashlight rail molded into the frame is for HK's proprietary UTL (Universal Tactical Light). This is a good unit, but I'd rather see a generic rail that allowed the shooter to attach a more powerful, more modern InSight or SureFire white light unit.

I wish the combination safety/decock lever were ambidextrous. It can be reversed for left-hand use, but HK recommends armorers for that, and there's no time for an armorer when you're searching dangerous premises and need to change hands as you approach a weak-side corner. The options of off-safe double action, on-safe double action, and cocked and locked carry are good for the shooter in my opinion. Because of trigger reach considerations, I found myself using it single action, on-safe.

All in all, though, the USP Tactical .45 was a very pleasing package. The tan color option will appeal to many. Everyone who handled it during the test period liked it. Costlier than a regular HK USP, the Tactical is worth the higher sticker price for features that some end-users genuinely need. Overall, it's an excellent service/target pistol.

*Head shots at 25 yards proved easy with the USP Tactical .45.*

### Kahr PM9

With a bumper crop of wild and exotic new handguns these days, why did I put a plain-looking subcompact 9mm up for an Editor's Choice award in the pages of *On Target* magazine? Because for every shooter who buys a huge, thousand dollar 500 Magnum for stalking the elusive wooly mammoth, there will be hundreds who have need for a small, reliable, accurate handgun powerful enough to protect them from human predators. The PM9 fills the bill.

The latest evolution of the Kahr pistol, which has become remarkably popular in the relatively short time it has been with us, has a polymer frame that brings weight down to under a pound unloaded. Slimmer than a Glock, it hides easily in pocket or waistband – or even ankle holster. It is one of the few small autos that can withstand the grit that accrues with ankle carry and still work.

We've achieved surprising accuracy with Kahr pistols in the past. When you're hosting an accurate pistol, you want to serve accurate ammo, so we put four of the most

straight-shooting 9mm rounds on the PM9's table. Accuracy testing was done from the 25-yard benchrest with a two-hand hold.

Most ammo exhibited the common auto pistol phenomenon called "4+1," with the first hand-cycled round printing its bullet a little away from the cluster formed by subsequent, automatically cycled rounds. Winchester's once-trendy 147-grain subsonic put five shots in 3-1/8 inches, with the best three measuring 1-5/8 inches. Federal's 9BP 115-grain at standard velocity stretched to 3-3/4 inches, its best three in 2-1/4 inches, while Pro-Load's hotter Tactical 115-grain at +P velocity went 4-7/8 inches for everything including the errant 4+1 shot, with its best three in 2-1/4 inches. Best accuracy came with the cheapest ammo: Black Hills blue box 115-grain remanufactured. The 5-shot group measured a pleasing 2-1/4 inches for five shots, the best three in 1-5/16 inches.

All the above loads were hollowpoints. They fed fine. The only malfunction of the test was one failure of a spent casing to clear the ejection port when firing the low-momentum Winchester subsonic. Kahr guns thrive on hot loads. Feeding was excellent.

Recoil was surprisingly soft for such a light gun. All testers commented on the mild kick, even with the Pro-Load +P ammo.

These little guns compete with the Airweight 5-shot 38s. They are slimmer and flatter, shorter overall and hold two more shots. The "carry" magazine holds six rounds, not counting the seventh in the chamber, and leaves the grip-frame so short you have to tuck your pinky finger under it to fire. Each comes with a second, longer magazine that holds one more round and, when inserted, allows you wrap the last finger of the firing hand around something solid.

The trigger mechanism, double-action-only, is butter-smooth and surprisingly light. Kahr has one of the best actions of this type in the industry… quite possibly *the* best. Sights are generous and easy to see. Workmanship is good, and fit is snug, as you'll be reminded every time you take one apart for cleaning.

If the accuracy of the tiny PM9 doesn't sound up to Kahr's usual standards, consider that some precision is generally lost when you make a gun smaller. For perspective, the center zone on an IDPA silhouette target is 8 inches in diameter, and this .380-size pistol would never have missed it. Buy a larger all-steel Kahr 9mm as a companion gun for training, recreational shooting and

*Available Kahr sizes. From top, target-size T9; standard-size P-.40; Covert model with standard barrel/slide and shortened butt; and subcompact, PM9 shown.*

*Tiny polymer-framed Kahr will take today's hottest (and most desirable) 9mm self-defense and police duty loads.*

*Hiding in the hand, small size and low price of the Kel-Tec .380 have made it extremely popular.*

home defense; they function identically. The PM9 is an excellent deep concealment protection sidearm, and well worth its price of $625 suggested retail, $719 with Tritium night sights.

I'm not the only one who thinks highly of the PM9. In late 2005, Andy Stanford at Options for Personal Security (OPS) inaugurated his annual series of training summits with the Snubby Summit. I had the honor of doing the kick-off talk on the history and role of the snub-nose defense revolver, and a hands-on bloc on shooting it through concealment: through a coat pocket, etc. Andy had assembled an all-star cast of instructors that my colleagues and I immensely enjoyed training with. One was Tom Givens, who took the role of the loyal opposition in explaining why he felt a powerful subcompact auto

pistol made the small-frame short-barrel revolver obsolete. He made a compelling argument; his recommended gun? The Kahr PM9.

Over the years this neat little pistol has been available, I've known a great many people who owned and carried them. Only two had any problem. Both found malfunctions, and in both cases the pistols were made good with a single trip back to the factory. My one problem with this pistol is that when I carry it in a pocket, because I wear my backup guns on my weak side, it's in the *left* trouser pocket. The magazine release button on all Kahrs is on the left hand side of the frame behind the trigger, and it is not reversible. This caused the button to be depressed enough if I bumped my left side into something that it would release the magazine in the pocket. I experienced no such problems carrying the little Kahr in a right-side pocket, or in any belt holster.

Finally, I have to address the PM40, the same little gun chambered for the .40 S&W and with one round less capacity than the 9mm PM9. To make a long story short, I don't like it. While recoil isn't bad at all in the ultra-light 9mm, it's downright nasty and right at the edge of controllability with the .40 round, especially with the hotter loads. I've also seen the magazine release break, and the recoil spring lose its tension and stop working properly, on too many PM40s to trust it. I believe a gun this small and light just isn't going to stand up to the high slide velocity and nasty buffeting to internal parts that

*Ruger SP101 .357 Magnum, top, was designed for concealment but appears huge in comparison to Kel-Tec .380.*

*Size comparison: Top, Ruger SP101 5-shot ..357 Magnum; center, 7-shot Kahr PM9 9mm; below, 6-shot Colt SFVI .38 Special.*

*P3AT was tested with three brands of ammo.*

the relatively high-intensity .40 S&W cartridge delivers. George Kehlgren found the same thing with the little Kel-Tec polymer-frame pocket autos he has manufactured in the same weight range in .40, and he discontinued that caliber but kept the 9mm in the series. There is, I humbly submit, something to be learned from that.

### Kimber

Until recently, Kimber was selling more 1911 pistols than any of the many other manufacturers. Dealer feedback tells me that Springfield Armory is now neck-and-neck with Kimber and may even be surpassing them. This is due to two good reasons. One is that Springfield came out with a very good, very reasonably priced, bare-bones 1911A1 pistol that caught the fancy of the market. Another is that Kimber made the ill-advised decision to go with an external extractor on most of their models, and reliability suffered greatly and notoriously. When the U.S. Marine Recon troops sought a 1911 with conventional *internal* extractor, Kimber built them one the old-fashioned way and won the contract. This told them something. LAPD SWAT, by the way, ordered two Kimber .45s apiece for their famed SWAT team – one with and one without dedicated flashlight, per officer – and I'm told they also specified internal extractors.

The market voted with its wallet, and Kimber now seems to be in the process of phasing out the external extractors. I applaud their decision. The history of external extractors in 1911 pistols goes back a long way, and has never been a distinguished one. Even the excellent SIG GSR conceptualized by Matt McLearn has had the occasional problem with its external extractor, traced to a single production run as near as I can figure. Only Smith & Wesson seems to have made it work, and their SW1911 is indeed one of the best available today. But Smith & Wesson has been making service-caliber auto pistols with external extractors for more than half a century, and has the arcane subtleties of the process nailed down.

Kimber still makes a great pistol. Just get it with the internal extractor. And always remember: it's not nice to fool Mother Nature *or* John Browning.

### Ruger's New P345 .45 Auto

Sturm, Ruger & Co. has of late put most of its emphasis on sporting as opposed to defensive handguns, but its products in the latter vein all seem to be well thought out. Consider their latest .45 auto, the P345. All "lawyered up" with safety devices, this best-buy big-bore

is also "gunned up" with accuracy, reliability and controllability.

Right after the P345 was announced, *On Target* editor Ben Battles called me on my cell phone and asked me how soon I could get my hands on the new .45 ACP from Ruger. "Oh," I answered, "as soon as I can find a spot to pull over and get it out of the trunk." I had one in the car because I

*Author has traveled thousands of miles around the country with this Kimber Custom II .45…*

*…and been to many a barbecue with this stainless Kimber Classic, dressed with engraved pewter grips from Colt Collectors' Association. He likes his Kimbers…*

*…but insists they have original internal extractors, to which Kimber is returning after ill-fated flirtation with external extractor design.*

was testing it for my police department, having already written it up for one of the other gun magazines.

Ruger's first .45 auto, the P90, came out in the early '90s. This gun has earned a reputation for reliability that would do Mikhail Kalashnikov proud if he had designed it, instead of his friend William B. Ruger, Sr. The P90 was as accurate as a target pistol. However, it had a blocky frame and looked and felt clunky to some shooters, even though it had a good trigger pull in both double and single action. Fed up with complaints about the "clunkiness factor," Ruger followed with their next .45 autoloader. The P97 had a polymer frame instead of aluminum, the same sweet trigger pull, and much better fit in the hand. However, in my experience it didn't have quite the Camp Perry-like accuracy of its predecessor.

Enter the third Ruger semiautomatic in this caliber, which is probably why the company designated it the P345. The reach to the trigger is the shortest yet. The grip shape of its polymer frame fills the palm nicely, and pointing characteristics are excellent. The P97 was made in only decocker or double-action-only styles, and was never commercially available with a manual safety option like its budget-priced polymer stablemate, the 9mm P95, or its predecessor, the P90. The manual safety was important from my perspective because about half of the cops in my department carried their issue P90s on-safe, in case the bad guy got the .45 out of their duty holster.

Under strict new "safety legislation" in California and some other states, new pistols have to be sold with loaded chamber indicators, integral gun locks, and even magazine disconnector safeties. The P345 has all of that, and is the first Ruger to have the latter.

When I first put the P345 on the bench at 25 yards, it stunned me with a group measuring less than an inch. Five rounds of 230-grain Federal Hydra-Shok plunked into a cluster measuring 0.95-inch. Rather than repeat a test with the same ammo as in another publication, I pulled into the range with the half-dozen different .45 ACP ammo types I had in the car. They encompassed a couple of match loads, two brands of inexpensive generic "hardball" training ammo, and a couple of jacketed

*Author considers the P345 to be the epitome of Ruger service autos.*

hollowpoint duty loads. Each 5-shot group was fired two-handed from a benchrest at 25 yards, and measured once for the whole group and once again for the best three hits.

Nothing equaled that magnificent group with the Hydra-Shok, but the accuracy was certainly adequate with virtually everything we shot. The three-best-shot measurements were especially promising, particularly with the match loads by Triton and Winchester. Each printed 3-shot clusters in under an inch.

The good human engineering, the slight flex inherent in the polymer frame, and a cam block design that intercepts the slide before it smashes into the frame, all help to make this a particularly soft-shooting .45. Testers ranged from cops to kids, from slender-wristed people to hairy-armed weightlifters, and all the men and women who shot it commented on how comfortable it was in recoil. That combined with its excellent pointing characteristics to bring it back on target very quickly in rapid fire. It was no trick to keep every shot in a ragged hole at 7 yards.

The most important thing about its feel is that when you pull the trigger on a live round, you get a "bang." The P345 will not blacken the Ruger .45 autos' hard-won reputation for total reliability. In almost a thousand rounds fired, the test pistol did not malfunction in any way. It was not cleaned or lubricated during this period. We want to see how long that sort of abuse will take to make it malfunction. It hasn't happened yet.

I didn't have a uniform duty rig for this gun at that time, but I wore it in plainclothes quite a bit. It fit a concealment holster I had for an HK USP. Concealment is better than with the square-edged old P90. There are no sharp edges to bite the hand. Even the crisply knurled thumb safety lever does not chew flesh. The officers of my department who test-fired it found the P345's safety very easy to release during the draw, easier than the safety on their familiar P90 pistols.

Those with short fingers were delighted with the easy reach to the P345's trigger. In fact, those with longer fingers actually found it awkward: their fingertip was sometimes bumping on the frame before the sear released. A light touch of the Dremel tool should fix this problem. A senior Ruger executive I discussed that with said he saw no problem in taking a little bit of material off the frame behind the trigger guard.

| Brand | Bullet Type | 5-Shot Group | Best 3 Shots |
|---|---|---|---|
| Black Hills | 230-grain JHP | 3 1/8" | 1 3/4" |
| Hornady +P XTP | 230-grain JHP | 2 5/8" | 1 3/8" |
| MagTech | 230-grain FMJ | 3 7/8" | 3.00" |
| Triton Competitor | 165-grain FP | 1 5/8" | 5/8" |
| Winchester Match | 185-grain JSCW | 2 1/4" | 7/8" |
| Wolf | 230-grain FMJ | 4 1/2" | 1 13/16" |

**JHP**: Jacketed Hollow Point.
**FMJ**: Full Metal Jacket.
**FP**: Flat Point.
**JSCW**: Jacketed Semi-Wadcutter.

The P345 will accept 7- and 8-round magazines furnished by the factory for the P90 and P97, and the 8-round Millett aftermarket magazine for the P90. The magazine release button, though not reversible, is easy to reach and magazines dropped cleanly. The slide always locked back when the gun was empty, even if shooters were slightly riding the slide stop with a forward thumbs hold.

The test pistol shot distinctly high with 230-grain ammo, and more to point of aim with lighter bullets. I think it needs a higher front sight. Ruger was all over that when the initial complaints came in, and I no longer run across that problem with P345 pistols.

Since the brand's inception, Ruger has been synonymous with quality firearms at a bargain price. That has been true of the P90 and the P97 and is now true of the P345. The gun has it all: promising accuracy, carrying comfort and excellent "shootability."

And it has more. There are some who act as if new safety devices on firearms are somehow un-American, but the fact is, a lot of consumers will find good use for them. This is the first Ruger pistol to come with a magazine disconnector safety. The gun will not fire a live round in the chamber if the magazine has been removed. This is useful as a weapon retention tactic. If you believe the man who is trying to disarm you is gaining the upper hand, you can punch the mag release button and "kill the gun." It's also one less tragedy that can occur if someone less familiar with it than you gains control of it when you are not present. The pistol's manual safety is a proven lifesaver in gun snatch attempts, too.

The integral lock works off the right side of the ambidextrous safety/decocking lever. Thumb the lever down into the "on-safe" position. Now, insert one of the two keys provided by Ruger into the hole in the manual safety and into the slide. You've now entered the keyway. Turn the key, and the firing mechanism is all locked up. The pistol also comes with something resembling a bicycle lock, which is designed to be run down through an open magazine well through the slide's ejection port, locking the unloaded pistol securely.

Some appreciate these features. Some see them as creeping big-brotherism. If we like them, we can use them. If we don't, we can simply not activate them.

In 2005, my department's P90s were twelve years old. They had given noble service, but the night sights had died out from age and we didn't want to wait for wear-out

and breakage to replace the guns. After testing several .45 autos, including some that weren't in production when we did the exhaustive testing that had resulted in the 1993 adoption of the P90, we adopted the P345. To a man (and woman) the troops like these guns better than the P90, because of their ergonomics. More are carrying them on-safe and thus gaining a weapon retention advantage than did so with the P90, because on the P345 they can reach the safety lever more quickly and easily.

The new pistols have proven totally trouble-free. We consider ourselves well-armed with the Ruger P345.

### RUGER P95: The Best Economy 9mm?

In 20 years of building 9mms, Ruger has brought all it has learned into the currently-produced P95.

Well over twenty years ago, I sat with Bill Ruger, Sr. in the executive office at his Newport, N.H. plant as he swore me to secrecy and showed me the blueprints for the new pistol he planned. It was a high-capacity 9mm semiautomatic, engineered to give high quality at a low price. A hi-cap 9mm for Everyman. It would debut as the P85, and over the years was to go through several upgrades. After a score of years, during which a huge number of Ruger 9mm autoloaders have been sold to police departments, military units and particularly the ordinary armed citizens Bill Ruger loved, we have the latest refinement of the concept: the P95 pistol as currently produced.

Announced a decade ago as Ruger's bid to catch up with Glock, the market leader in this type of handgun, the P95 has the cost-effective, lightweight polymer frame the market has come to love. Its grip frame is more ergonomic than the earlier, all-metal P85 and P89.

Recent tweaks have made it even more desirable. The grip area has been stippled for a more secure hold. An attachment rail has been added, with flashlight mounting working very well on this gun. With a SureFire X200 snapped on, it was no trick to hit the steel silhouette in the dark at 50 yards with the test pistol. Law enforcement is definitely going in this direction – for rank-and-file patrol in many departments, as well as the traditional light-mounted gun bastions of K9 and SWAT – and an attached light can make enormous sense for home defense pistols.

Best of all, the current P95 is the high value, economy-priced pistol Bill originally envisioned. Suggested retail price is $425. By comparison, a Glock 17 in the same caliber lists at $624. The Ruger will often be found discounted to well under $400.

This pistol comes out of the box comfortably light in weight, though a bit large for most people's idea of a concealed carry gun. Ours was finished blue on the slide; the stainless version is slightly more expensive.

The P95 is available with three fire control options. One is DAO, or double action only. This has not caught on well with the private gun buying public, but has an enormous following among institutional purchasers. In Chicago's police department, where officers purchase their own DAO autoloaders from an approved list, the Ruger is hugely popular because of its great value. TACOM, the U.S. Army's tank command, recently purchased several thousand Ruger P95 DAO 9mm pistols.

The P95 is available in two versions of what is called TDA, or traditional double action. This means that only the first shot requires a long, heavy double-action pull, and thereafter the pistol cocks itself to single action

*Ayoob finds the safety easy to manipulate on his department-issue Ruger P345, and likes the loaded chamber indicator feature. PD guns have these Trijicon fixed night sights.*

during the firing cycle, necessitating decocking if the string of fire is interrupted before the gun runs dry. One option is the P95 DC, which stands for DeCock (only). If you want the easy pull on shots after the first, but don't want to mess about with a manual safety catch, this is the P95 you want.

Finally, there is the standard model, which is what I got to test. It's TDA, and the decocking lever doubles as a safety catch. On this gun, it's an ambidextrous lever, larger on the left than on the right on the assumption that it will be a right-hander's thumb doing the manipulation. This variation would have been my choice. I like a pistol I can carry on safe in case the wrong hands get on it in a struggle. But each of us decides based on our needs, and the point is, Ruger gives us the choice.

This pistol sits well in the hand. Trigger reach was good for average size adult male hands. In the right hand, the safety was perfectly easy to manipulate. The flatter lever on the southpaw's side was a bit more difficult to operate.

There were some sharp edges. For a $425 MSRP, there isn't much in the manufacturer's budget to allow a "melt job" that rounds all the surfaces. The front edge of the pistol is smoothly rounded, though, and the slide tapers slightly, which speeds holstering significantly and, some think, accelerates the draw slightly as well. The sharp edges that proved irritating were on the front of the safety decock levers, and became palpable when working the slide.

The double-action trigger is on the heavy side and stacks slightly; that is, when you draw the trigger back slowly, the resistance seems to increase. That sensation disappears in rapid double-action work, however.

The single-action pull is roughly five pounds, with a clean release. As with the long pull, the short one feels different in slow fire than in rapid. With a leisurely squeeze, you can feel a tiny bit of movement in the sear. This makes it feel almost like a two-stage pull. In rapid fire, however, all you feel is a clean release that doesn't have objectionable backlash.

But the proof is in the shooting. It was time to take the P95 to the range.

On the 25-yard line, we shot NRA timed- and rapid-fire bullseye centers with the P95, using a two-hand hold from the bench. It shot a bit high, so a six o'clock hold made sense. Black Hills +P with the 115-grain Gold Dot bullet punched five holes in 3.30 inches center-to-center, the best three measuring exactly 1.00 inch. Federal 9BP standard pressure 115-grain JHP plunked five 9mm holes in 3.25 inches, with the best three in a 1.80-inch cluster. Winchester 147-grain subsonic JHP did a five-shot group measuring 3.40 inches, its best three shots 0.95-inch apart. Groups in the three-inch range were about what I'd expected from a Ruger 9mm, though the consistency – 3.25, 3.30 and 3.40 inches – clearly showed this pistol wasn't finicky about its ammo.

But then, Jon Strayer loaded the Ruger with one of the very best 9mm carry loads out there, the 127-grain +P+ Ranger police round from Winchester, and put five of those high tech hollowpoints into a group that measured only 2.40 inches, exactly an inch tighter than the Winchester 9mm loading most famous for its accuracy, the 147-grain subsonic. Go figure.

The "best three" cluster with the 127-grain Winchester measured 1.45 inches. If one accepts the hypothesis that the best three hits of a hand-held five-shot group that had no called flyers will closely predict a five-shot group from the same gun and ammo with a machine rest, this means the test P95 could be a one-inch pistol at 25 yards. All were under two inches in this measurement; three out of four were under an inch and a half; and two were an inch or better.

The tightest three shots give you an idea how accurate a certain handgun can be. The total of five shots give you an idea of how accurate *you* can be. To find out how accurate you can be with the same gun and ammo under pressure, you have to test the gun with some pressure on. I shot one of my state's approved off-duty gun courses with this pistol. The course of fire entailed one-hand-only shooting with each hand, assorted standing and low cover positions, and several speed reloads, all under time.

The pistol pointed well, the sights going directly to the center of the target without last-instant adjustment of hand or wrist. The second shot fired, from a weak hand only stance, went a little low right because I had forgotten just how sweet this gun's single-action pull is once you're past the double action, but the bullet stayed in the center zone. The trigger was predictable after that, nicer than the trigger of a gun this inexpensive has a right to be in this day and age. Reloads were smooth and uncomplicated, using a mix of new magazines and old ones, going all the way back to the original P85. All full-length Ruger 9mm mags seem to work in this latest model.

When it was over, 50 shots had resulted in as many center zone hits and a perfect score of 250 out of 250 possible on the challenging IPSC target. Forty-nine of those bullet holes were in a group that measured just under four and a half inches, but that darned second shot had opened the total to over six inches. That was my fault, not the Ruger's, and I was very happy with the pistol's performance.

In keeping with the economy theme, I used an Uncle Mike's duty holster for the qualification and a Bianchi Cobra for when the flashlight was attached. I used a SureFire X200, which fit perfectly, went on and came off easily and smoothly, and absolutely centered the sight picture in its brilliant LED beam.

My only real complaint was that this particular P95 shot high. A taller front sight, not hard to install since the front post is securely but removably pinned, would fix that. Throughout the test, in the hands of several shooters, the P95 never malfunctioned despite hundreds and hundreds of assorted rounds.

Reliable. Remarkably shootable. Surprisingly accurate. Low in price. The Ruger P95 may well be the best value in an economy-grade 9mm auto today. Bill Ruger, Sr. would be proud.

### Smith & Wesson Model 327TRR8

Herb Belin, the head of revolver production at S&W, first showed me the new TRR8 at the 2006 SHOT Show. My first reaction was, "You've GOT to be kidding." He wasn't.

At first, it looks almost like a parody of *uber*-cool tactical ninja automatics. Picture a revolver with a Picatinny rail under its barrel, mounting a white light and laser unit, and with a red dot optical sight atop its frame on another Pic rail. My first reaction was to laugh.

I shot one for several weeks. And I'm not laughing anymore.

But I'm still smiling.

The Model 327 TRR8 (**T**actical **R**evolver with **R**ail, **eight**-shot) is the latest descendant of the original .357 Magnum. The timeline goes like this. **1935:** After consulting with period experts Phil Sharpe and Elmer Keith, Smith & Wesson and Winchester create the first .357 Magnum revolver/cartridge combo. The cartridge is based on a .38 Special, lengthened so it can take more gunpowder and so it won't fit an older .38 and blow it up, and it's capable of running a 158-grain bullet in the 1500 fps velocity range. The very first goes to J. Edgar Hoover, head of the FBI. **1948:** When production resumes after WWII, the design is updated with more efficient adjustable sight, and short action. **1954:** An economy version, the Highway Patrolman, is introduced. **1957:** When S&W goes to numeric model designations, this one becomes the Model 27 and the Highway Patrolman, Model 28. Subsequent dash-suffix designations will indicate changes such as doing away with pinned barrels and recessed chambers. **1989:** A short-lived stainless version is introduced with unfluted six-shot cylinder and heavy, underlugged barrel, called the Model 627. **1994:** The Model 27 is discontinued. **1997:** The 627 designation is resurrected for a series of special-run Performance Center N-frame .357s with eight-shot cylinders. **2005:** The Model 327 with lightweight scandium frame and eight-shot cylinder makes its appearance. **2006:** The TRR8 is introduced at the SHOT Show in Las Vegas.

The more experience you gain with the TRR8, the less funny-looking it becomes. The barrel is 5 inches, the length Skeeter Skelton and some other experts always felt gave the best balance – in both the visual sense, and the tactile sense – with these large-frame revolvers. Milled flat on the side and using S&W's recently developed two-piece barrel construction, it consists of a rifled steel tube within an outer sleeve. This keeps it from being muzzle-heavy, and gives it a "lively" feel, yet still allows it to hang steady on target.

An interchangeable front sight offers numerous options: Ours came with the gold bead that master wheelgunners from Ed McGivern to Jerry Miculek have

*Joe Bergeron, head of auto pistol production for S&W, gives a briefing on the company's products. Joe was the lead designer of the M&P auto pistol.*

favored for speed shooting. The tactical light rail was perfectly formed, and an InSight M6X heavy-duty combination white light and laser unit fit perfectly, and slid on and off easily. The rear sight is the same one that's been on the 27 series for 58 years, and still works just fine. The topmost Pic rail of the test sample carries a Tru-Glo red dot sight.

The eight-shot cylinder is made of stainless steel, machined on the breechface side to allow the use of moon clips with standard rimmed .38 Special and .357 Magnum cartridges. Three clips are included with the revolver. Each chamber has been laboriously chambered to allow faster insertion of cartridges.

The frame is scandium. This brings the weight down from the typical mid-forty-ounce range to 35.3 ounces…slightly less than a Model 19 Combat Magnum, the classic "carry weight" .357. This definitely contributes to the "lively" feel of the gun when tracking quickly between multiple targets such as steel plates or bowling pins.

Grips are soft Hogues, shaped with finger grooves and cut to expose the backstrap of the grip frame. The trigger is semi-narrow, smooth in front and rounded at the edges, clearly designed with double-action work in mind, and comes with a trigger stop perfectly fitted. The hammer spur is a triangular spade shape, easier to thumb-cock quickly than the conventional service style, but not likely to get in the way like the old beaver-tailed Target hammer.

More than half a century ago, gun expert Bob Nichols wrote that the heavy all-steel S&W .357 had more recoil with magnum ammo than most men could handle. What's it like with ten or so ounces of recoil-absorbing weight taken off?

The answer is: *sweet*. This gun has no recoil reduction devices *per se*, but the Hogue grips soften the bite to the web of the hand. The barrel configuration, including the forward-mounted accessory rail, holds the muzzle down. The test shooters included a couple of petite females, and none experienced discomfort even with full-power magnum loads.

From the first, the Model 27 series has been accurate, and this revolver certainly lives up to the tradition. We tried it off the bench with target .38 wadcutters, an all-around .357 load, and a hollow-point magnum round suitable for hunting. All grouped well, hand-held from the 25-yard bench on an MTM pistol rest and fired single action.

Federal's Gold Medal Match 148-grain mid-range wadcutter .38 Special is famous for accuracy. It delivered a five-shot group that measured 1.65 inches center-to-center and, allowing for human error by measuring the best three shots, we got 1.20 inches.

Winchester's 145-grain Silvertip .357 hollowpoint out-shot the target load. It punched a five-shot group of 1.15 inches, with the best three in 0.50-inch. The latter measurement would extrapolate to a 2-inch group at a hundred yards!

Most accurate of all was the 158-grain semi-jacketed HP from Black Hills. This excellent ammunition punched a quintet of holes that measured 0.80-inch, with the best three hits in the same half-inch cluster as the best three Silvertips. The .357 is suitable for game such as javelina and small deer, and in the TRR8 delivers accuracy in keeping with the history of its predecessors. Col. Douglas Wesson traveled the world killing big game,

*The scandium frame allowed S&W1911PD to achieve light Commander weight without the perceived weaknesses of an aluminum frame. LaserGrips from Crimson Trace were installed by S&W as a package option.*

such as moose and brown bear, with one of the very first .357 Magnums.

The double action was very smooth, if not necessarily the smoothest we've seen come out of the Performance Center, nor the lightest. I looked in vain for a suitable match in which to shoot it, and couldn't find one whose scheduling coincided with mine. Making do, I put my Bianchi Barricade on the 25-yard line and shot that stage from the Bianchi Cup with the TRR8. That involves six shots from either side, in eight seconds per run. The result: all shots (158-grain .38 Special semi-wadcutter reloads) were inside the ten-ring, and most of them inside the tie-breaking center X-ring within it. It was better than I ever shot the *actual* Bianchi Cup the eleven times I competed there. But as my old friend Tom Campbell used to say, "practice ain't race day." Tom having shot more Bianchi Cups than anyone else I know, I find his comments comforting.

This would be a choice revolver for ICORE (International Congress of Revolver Enthusiasts) matches. It would be great for bowling pin shooting in Open class, giving the six-gunner parity with the .45 autos and a three-shot fudge factor on five-pin competition tables. (Jerry Miculek, pin-shooter *extraordinaire*, had a lot to do with the development of the eight-shot S&W .357 and switched to it for pin shooting as soon as he could get one in hand). If I were to shoot a revolver at Bianchi Cup again, I think this one would be my choice. It's only six-shot sequences there, but the two rounds in reserve can salvage a misfire or similar catastrophe. Along about 1986 at the Cup, I watched a front-runner from the LAPD Pistol Team lose the title because he short-stroked the trigger of his S&W .38, cycling past the chamber. He couldn't pull the trigger six more times to make that shot before the moving target disappeared. With the TRR8, one more stroke of the trigger would have kept him on track for the National Champion title.

Home defense? Bulky as the TRR8 looks, house guns aren't holster guns necessarily. I'd have iron Trijicon sights on top. I'm sold on white light attachments for home defense pistols, but on this revolver, the unit is too far forward for my thumb to reach the toggle switch from a two-hand hold, and if it was long enough, it would be exposed to barrel/cylinder gap gas blast. Still, eight rounds of .357 Magnum are more comforting than six when a potentially armed burglar is climbing through the window.

The flashlight attachment on this particular gun, for me, would only make sense if I was legally shooting at night (raccoon hunting, for example) and could leave the beam locked on. Still, I remember Skeeter Skelton and his favorite 5-inch Model 27 revolver that he carried on duty down near the Border. If we could send him this one back in time – super accurate, with two more shots, and as light as a Combat Magnum – I have no doubt at all that it might find its way into his duty holster.

At $1260 suggested retail, the Smith & Wesson Model 327 TRR8 is priced commensurately with its quality and its fascinating mix of features. It is more useful than it looks at first glance, and will write an interesting chapter in the more than 70-year history of the fabled Smith & Wesson .357 Magnum revolver.

### Awesome Eight-Shooter: S&W Performance Center Model 327

Smith & Wesson started the scandium/titanium revolution in construction of defensive carry handguns. One of their latest works in this *milieu* is the Model 327 snubby from the company's elite Performance Center.

"They sent you an empty gun case," said Gail Pepin, tricked by the revolver's feathery heft. Upon opening the container, another observer remarked, "It's freakish. The barrel looks…*vestigial*." My own reaction was, "It looks and feels like a toy." When I was a child, I owned a plastic toy revolver of the same coloration: gray cylinder, glossy black frame, and if memory serves, about the same weight, too. As my youngest used to say when she was little, "It's ugly, and its mother dressed it funny."

Well, to paraphrase Forrest Gump, "Ugly is as ugly does." The S&W PC327 went into the testing cycle with my southern crew, for a mix of practical shooting and concealed carry. When it was over, the 327 didn't seem so ugly anymore.

Herb Belin, S&W's head of revolver production, explains the metallurgical bouillabaisse that comprises the Model 327. "The frame is scandium," Herb told me. "The cylinder is titanium, and its yoke is steel. The two-piece barrel is comprised of a stainless steel barrel tube and an aluminum shroud. The internal mechanism is carbon steel." The handsome hardwood stocks look like Ahrends, and lack the traditional inset S&W logo medallion.

Like all current S&W revolvers, this one has the internal lock, its keyway located directly above the cylinder release latch. The locking piece rises slightly up and out of the frame on the test sample, but showed no problems in actual shooting or carry.

This is an N-frame gun, and its fat .44-size cylinder is bored with eight chambers for .357 Magnum or .38 Special cartridges. With a typical Performance Center touch, the edges of the chamber mouths have been very lightly chamfered to speed the reloading process, which is done with proprietary S&W full-moon clips. This gun's all-steel big brother, the Model 627, has given awesome accounts of itself in bowling pin matches, ICORE events, and other speed-shooting arenas where a powerful eight-shot revolver comes into its own.

That startlingly incongruous snub-nose barrel, only 1-7/8 inches from forcing cone to muzzle, combines with the exotic high strength/light weight metallurgy to make this revolver amazingly light for its frame size. On a calibrated postal scale, it registered one and three-eighths pounds, or 22 ounces. This is about the weight of a .32-size J-frame S&W Model 60 .38, and two or three ounces less than the all-steel five-shot Chief Special in .357 Magnum. In the hand, it felt exactly like my old S&W Military & Police Airweight, a K-frame .38 snubby, perhaps because it had an identical K-size round butt grip frame. Trigger reach was a good fit for my average size male hand.

The express-style V-notch of the 625-10, basically the same gun rendered as a six-shot .45 ACP, has been abandoned on the 327 in favor of a conventional square notch rear sight milled out of the topstrap. A bright orange front sight, though fixed, is dovetailed and therefore replaceable and presumably crudely adjustable for windage, and for elevation by changing its height.

The double-action trigger was quite good, in the nine-pound range and smoother than most scandium and titanium guns I've shot. The single-action pull was particularly sweet, breaking at between two and three pounds.

The first thing we all noticed in shooting it was that recoil was much milder than expected. I've shot scandium Smiths from the vicious little 11-ounce 340 PD .357 to the torturous Model 329 PD 26-ounce .44 Magnum, and I can tell you they all hurt like hell when they go off, particularly with wooden stocks like these.

The 327 kicked less than the equivalent .45 from the Performance Center, even with hot Winchester 125-grain .357 Magnum loads. That's counter-intuitive, I know. Hell, it's contrary to the laws of physics. I just report the perception, folks; I can't always explain it. It might be that the grips on the 327, being distinctly larger than the shaved-down Eagle "secret service" stocks on the snub .45, were distributing recoil more efficiently to the hand.

With that tiny barrel and only a 3 Ω-inch sight radius, we didn't expect much for accuracy at the standard handgun testing distance of 25 yards, but the Model 327 surprised us. We started with Federal's Gold Medal Match 148-grain mid-range wadcutter in .38 Special. This is the lightest target load in its caliber that you can buy from a major manufacturer. It was fun to shoot, and rewarding: the five shots were in an inch and seven-eighths, and the best three of those – always a good indicator of pure mechanical accuracy potential since it helps factor out human error – were only 5/8-inch apart.

Many seasoned shooters prefer to load .38 Special +P in these super-light .357 Magnums to avoid recoil punishment. Hornady's high-quality XTP 125-grain JHP +P .38s shot softly enough, and delivered a 2 1/2-inch 25-yard group with all five shots, and 1-5/8 inches for the best three.

But the 125-grain .357 Magnum round, even out of a short barrel, has earned a reputation as one of the best "manstoppers" on the street. It was with Winchester 125-grain Magnum semi-jacketed hollowpoints that we discovered how controllable this gun's recoil is. Five of those Winchester screamers hit the target two and a quarter inches apart, with the best three an inch tighter than that. With all ammo, the gun shot distinctly low. This specimen needs a shorter front sight to bring the muzzle up, which with the dovetail arrangement shouldn't be too hard to achieve.

Testing it for its primary mission, I carried the 327 loaded with Winchester Magnum for three consecutive days. Day One: in the left side pocket of a Tropical vest, the lightest that Concealed Carry Clothiers makes. Day Two: The deep left-side pocket of Royal Robbins 5.11 BDU pants was capacious enough to swallow this large-frame snubby, which rode in a size large pocket holster by Bob Mika. Day Three: the 327 dwelt just behind my right hip in a leather belt slide holster by Mitch Rosen. Conclusions: carrying this 22-ounce lightweight, even with eight rounds of live ammo, felt about the same as carrying an all-steel small-frame .38 snub loaded with five rounds. This 22-ounce gun feels like a 22-ounce gun. Duh…

S&W Performance Center guns aren't cheap, but they deliver what they advertise and become lifetime heirlooms and conversation pieces, like Rolex watches. This particular one fills a definite niche. It can also be had with a 5-inch barrel, adjustable rear sight, and gold bead or fiber optic front sight.

The snub-nose version of the Performance Center 327 is a pleasing handgun. For the many who prefer a revolver to an auto for personal defense, it delivers fast, accurate shots smoothly and gives you eight rounds of .357 Magnum with which to protect your family, while carrying at the same weight as older technology that gave you five rounds of .38 Special. Some handgunners, once they've fired one and discover how "shootable" it is, will consider this revolver an answer to a prayer.

### Smith & Wesson's New Military & Police Autoloader

There has been a lot of excitement about Smith & Wesson's latest design, the new Military & Police autoloader. If my memory serves, it's the first S&W handgun since 1957 to have a model *name* instead of a model *number*. And the name is one that S&W fans conjure with.

#### "Military & Police"

Introduced in 1899, Smith & Wesson's Military & Police model became the paradigm of the modern double-action revolver. It remains in production, more

*Federal Classic 155-grain JHP .40, which earned an excellent reputation on the street, proved most accurate in Ayoob's first test sample S&W M&P.*

than a century later, as the Model 10. Over the years, the M&P sobriquet graced revolvers in calibers .22 Long Rifle, .32-20, .38 S&W, .357 Magnum, .41 Magnum, and the favorite by far, .38 Special.

This year, S&W introduces two new guns with the M&P stamp. One is a 223/5.56 rifle in the AR15 format. And the other has been proclaimed by many to be the strongest challenge to the Glock pistol to yet come down the pike.

Passed around to gun writers in the latter half of 2005, the M&P pistol didn't start reaching customers in quantity until 2006. So far, reviews have been mostly positive. That's understandable.

First, this pistol is *sleek*. Finished in Melonite, S&W's answer to Glock's much loved Tenifer finish, the slide sits on a polymer frame with steel insert. The popular interchangeable backstrap grip option, popularized by Walther and copied since by countless others, reaches its highest evolution in the Military & Police. That may be one reason why the first thing most people comment on when they try an M&P is the good feel of the new pistol.

Three inserts are offered. The small one gives tremendously good reach to the trigger. I can very easily get in to where my index finger contacts the trigger at the distal joint, the hold we old double-action revolver shooters learned gave most of us the best control of the trigger pull. It won't be hard for short-fingered people to reach. The medium size still has good trigger reach, and a bit more girth. Most hand-filling of all is the large size, with pronounced palm swells that fit a lot of people's hands better than anything else. I've run across folks with medium-size hands who love the size large M&P insert, and some with truly huge hands who wish there was something still bigger. For most, however, the grip size that will fit them comes in the box with the new M&P.

The grip frame arches back over the web of the hand, resembling a Robar conversion of the Glock pistol. Bore axis is very low in the hand. That feature is one reason why muzzle rise is not bad for the .40 S&W (the M&P's first available chambering), and testers were unanimous that this was a soft-shooting gun, even in extended runs of rapid fire with the high-pressure .40 round.

The magazines are steel. They drop free at a touch, as designed. They even have "positive release." That is, if you turn the pistol upside down and press the release button, the magazine will pop up about half an inch. These steel mags are thinner than plastic mags of similar capacity. In .40 S&W, the M&P's payload is the same as a Glock 22's: 15 in the magazine, one more in the chamber. However, the slimmer S&W magazine rattles around inside a Glock mag pouch. Magazine exchanges are particularly smooth, clean, and fast with the new Smith.

The trigger will be loved or hated, depending upon pre-existing taste. The trigger is hinged, in a fashion similar to the Glock but lacking the latter gun's centrally-located trigger safety lever. This means that the M&P's trigger can be brought back to fire by rearward pressure on the outside edge of the trigger.

The pull itself is…different. There is a short, early take up that seems to grate a little, even after hundreds and hundreds of pulls. Then the finger meets firm resistance, and the grating goes away. There is now a short distance farther to pull, and the "soft-feeling" trigger suddenly releases the shot. At this point, the trigger slaps to the rear of the guard with significant "backlash." S&W seems to have molded vestigial, nubbin-like trigger stops into the rear of the trigger guard, but they don't reach forward far enough to stop the annoying extra rearward movement.

An accessory rail is molded into the front dust cover, as on all polymer duty pistols these days and even some of the .22 "fun guns." An InSight 6X heavy-duty white light/laser unit worked perfectly on the test sample M&P. The test gun had a magazine disconnector safety, and visible loaded-chamber indicator.

Some attributes of this gun did not meet with the universal approval of the test team, all experienced handgunners. The ambidextrous slide release seems a good idea, but on the first M&Ps produced was so flush-fitted and sits so deep inside the little niches built into the frame, that it was literally protected from the digits trying to operate it. "Impossible," some testers snapped in exasperation. When reloading from slidelock, we all had to release the slide forward with a rearward tug.

Now, some say that this is the way it should be done anyway, on the theory that under stress hitting a lever with a thumb is too much of a fine motor skill to count on. I don't entirely buy that, but we could debate it for an hour. One thing you and I probably won't debate is this: you and I, not the designer, should determine how we can most efficiently fire our guns. I discussed this with former National IDPA Champ Ernie Langdon, now head of governmental sales for S&W, and Joe Bergeron, head of auto pistol production for the company. Both assured

*Steve Sager sends brass and lead flying in rapid fire with .40 M&P, but muzzle remains on target. Human engineering is, by and large, excellent.*

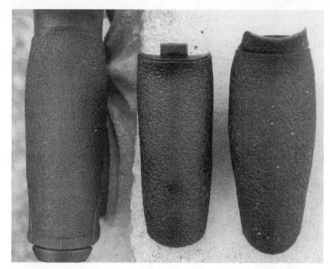

*In Ayoob's opinion, these three M&P grip inserts, packed with every gun, set a new standard for adjustability of grip fit to hand.*

me they were on top of it, and optional oversize ambi slide releases were already in production.

Once those came out, the problem was solved. Who knows but that in fifty years, gun collectors will be seeking rare, unconverted "first run" M&P pistols with the too-small release? Fortunately, today's shooters no longer have to worry about it.

I experienced some problems with the sights. The white insert in the front fell out when the fifth shot was fired from the new-in-the-box pistol. About halfway through the second hundred rounds, we noticed hits drifting to the right. Sure enough, the rear sight had come loose and was sliding to starboard in its dovetail. The gentle kiss of the proper wrench solved that particular problem.

Joe Bergeron had told me the guns were built to deliver 3-inch groups at 25 yards. We put M&P serial number MPA5274 on the bench to see. With Black Hills EXP 165-grain JHP, 3.45 inches was the measurement of the first 5-shot group, with the best three in 1.55 inches. (We later got a group with the same ammo measuring 2.30 inches for all five, and 0.75-inch for the best three, with four of the shots in 0.95-inch. That was more like it for this unusually accurate .40 S&W load!)

Remington's Golden Saber is a high tech evolution of the original .40 S&W duty load, the 180-grain subsonic. Five of the brass jacketed hollowpoint bullets went into 2.45 inches, with the best three clustered in only 1.85 inches. Winchester's street-proven Ranger police round with a 165-grain JHP punched a 2.75-inch cluster at the same 25-yard distance, with the best three snuggled in 0.95-inch.

The single most accurate five-shot group came from Federal Classic 155-grain JHP, a load that has earned its chops with cops on the street. The quintet of bullets formed a wedge-shaped group that measured 1.50 inches on the nose, with the best three in 0.85-inch! All groups were measured center-to-center, to the nearest 0.05-inch, with the "best three" measurement included to help factor out human error.

To shorten the story, the Smith & Wesson Military & Police .40 is even more accurate than its manufacturer says it is. My compliments to the chef! I wonder what sort of accuracy we'll see when people start doing trigger jobs on them to reduce the backlash.

The 9mm followed the .40 in the M&P. Julie Goloski promptly started winning IDPA championships with it, along with Team S&W stablemate Ernest Langdon and others. Todd Kennedy, of the Federal Law Enforcement Training Center, reportedly captured First Expert honors at the prestigious Carolina Cup (IDPA) with a Smith M&P auto. The 9mm and particularly the .357 SIG have, historically, been inherently more accurate cartridges than the .40 S&W. The .357 SIG version of the M&P should be available by the time you read this, having worked very well in testing according to factory insiders, but I haven't been able to get my hands on one yet. And a compact version is to be announced at the SHOT Show of 2007, as this edition of the GUN DIGEST BOOK OF COMBAT HANDGUNNERY makes its way to Krause Publications in manuscript form.

The 9mm, like the .40, is very soft shooting, and the .357 SIG version should be as well.

A bunch of us shot the M&P .40 and later the 9mm when we got our hands on them. Everyone had heard about it and wanted to try it out. It was fired by the big and the small, the short and the tall. So long as we kept our wrists firmly locked, strong hand or weak hand or both hands, it went *bang* and never failed to cycle. We also never experienced a misfire in several hundred rounds.

However, we discovered that the .40 was prone to stoppages with a "limp-wrist" hold. The pattern was always the same: a 6 o'clock misfeed at the bottom edge of the chamber. Invariably, a light backward tug on the slide instantly cleared the stoppage. Now, it is well known that *any* auto pistol can theoretically jam from "limp-wristing." The pistols are designed for the slide to run against the firm abutment of a solidly-held frame. A weak grasp lets the frame recoil with the slide, dissipating rearward slide energy to the point where it runs out before the cycle can be completed. Some guns are less susceptible than others: the Beretta 92 in 9mm and Px4 in .40, for example. Our test sample M&P .40 did seem susceptible. However, when the gun was held the way it was supposed to be held, it ran 100 percent.

Apparently, Bergeron and company were on top of that, too. Subsequent to my early sample, I've not heard of any M&Ps exhibiting problems when fired limp-wristed. My fellow Gun Digest book author Pat Sweeney tested his subsequent sample exactly for that, and reported that it ran without a bobble.

Joe Bergeron led the design team on this gun, and the M&P auto pistol is really pretty much his baby. He has been extremely responsive to constructive criticism. Sergeant Ken Paradise of the Iowa State Patrol, which has adopted the M&P .40, told me, "Of our first three test guns, we had one that would occasionally fail to fire, with light striker hits on our CCI primers. Smith & Wesson redesigned the striker after we reported this to them, and the problem disappeared." Today, says Sgt. Paradise, "They are working out very well so far. We've found that the medium-size grip insert seems to be the favorite among our troopers."

Other departments have also reported satisfaction with the M&P. The North Carolina Department of Corrections bought 5,700 M&P .40s, and their firearms training director, Max Mathews, told me that they're working out very well. The interchangeable grip feature has been beneficial to those NCDOC personnel permanently issued their own weapons (transport officers, dog handlers, escort personnel, and some 1,400 probation officers). They appreciate being able to tailor their new service pistol to fit their hands. The remaining guns are "pool weapons" that will be issued to authorized personnel as needed, and these are all fitted with the size medium insert, in hopes of fitting the most hands adequately.

The Columbus, Ohio police department purchased two thousand of the same .40 S&W M&Ps. "The simple design of the M&P, with no decocker or manual safety, was a plus in its selection, said Officer Ron Barker of the CPD firearms training unit, who also told me, "The ambidextrous slide lever is friendly to our many left-handed officers, and the interchangeable grip units are extremely user-friendly for our wide range of hand sizes, particularly our smaller female officers."

Cincinnati, Ohio has also ordered M&Ps for all their sworn police officers. All 1,500 pistols will be chambered for 9mm, however.

With pricing in the Glock range, the Smith & Wesson Military & Police will give the other polymer pistols a run for their money. "Feel" is a subjective thing, but in this writer's admittedly subjective opinion, the M&P is now the frontrunner in the "Ergonomics Sweepstakes."

The M&P is already evolving. By the time you read this, in addition to the compact models and the .357 SIG version, there should be two .45 ACP versions available, according to Paul Pluff in S&W's marketing division. One will be just like the 9mm and .40 in conception. The other will have a polymer frame of suitable GI hue, and a manual safety, to fit the specs put forth by the government for the next military trials of .45 service pistol candidates.

It is significant to notice that, in a world where lawyers seem to demand integral locks and magazine disconnector safety devices, and enthusiasts almost reflexively rail against them, S&W did a "Burger King" on the M&P pistol and in essence said, "Have it your way." Government agency or gun dealer, policeman or law-abiding armed citizen, you can have the M&P pistol with or without the integral lock and the device that keeps a chambered round from firing if the magazine is out of the gun. Bergeron tells me that the way orders are running right now, 30 percent of M&Ps are going out the shipping room door with the integral lock and mag disconnector in place, and 70 percent are being shipped without them.

Joe Bergeron is a young "wonder child" in the industry, having first earned his reputation at Colt's, a ways downstream from S&W in Gun Valley. His work on this design has impressed me. But what impresses me more is the willingness with which he and Smith & Wesson have solicited constructive criticism, listened to it, and immediately fixed each and every concern the end users have expressed regarding the new pistol.

That is a most refreshing attitude in the gun industry, where the attitude has traditionally been, "We *made* the damn gun, and we know more about it than you, so don't you dare be telling us how to make our product better!" I hope this attitude continues at Smith & Wesson. I hope it spreads across their entire product line. Indeed, I hope it spreads across the entire *industry*.

The Smith & Wesson Military & Police semiautomatic pistol is new, different and worthwhile. It's worth your time to check it out.

### Single-Action SIG-Sauer .45: The P220 SAO

SIGARMS dropped a bomb on all of us in the gun press when they quietly displayed their new single-action-only P220 .45 at the 2006 SHOT Show in Las Vegas. Yes, you read that correctly: single action only, or SAO as they call it in their sales literature, though the pistol itself is simply marked "SIG Sauer P220."

Now, the traditional double-action SIG-Sauer P220 pistol, double action for the first shot and self-cocked to single action thereafter until the operator activates the decocking lever, has been around for 30 or so years. For the last several years, we've had the DAO (double-action-only) model, popular in the Chicago Police Department and elsewhere. More recently we've had the DAK, which stands for Double Action/Kellerman. Named after its designer in Europe, this is a sophisticated double-action-only trigger mechanism – self-decocking, if you will – that gives an excellent, manageable pull that has found great favor with the Border Patrol and other Homeland Security-related law

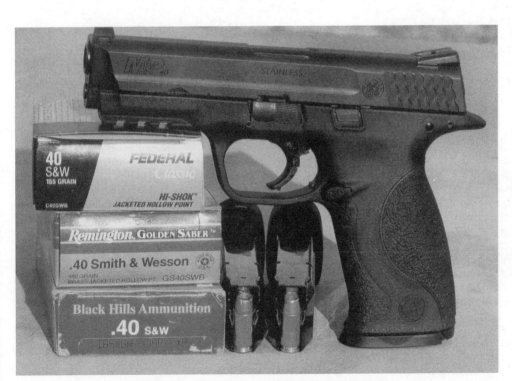

*No matter what the bullet weight, S&W M&P .40 proved very soft-kicking.*

*Left, conventional SIG P220, decocked with hammer at rest. Right, SAO version of same gun, cocked and locked. Note ambi thumb safety.*

enforcement organizations. A number of private citizens have picked up on its advantages, too.

But single action only? We have to ask ourselves why.

It won't be a fruitless quest, because there are indeed some solid answers.

To understand "the tao of the SAO," we have to face certain facts. Some folks just don't like pulling a long, heavy trigger for their first shot. Some even thumb-cock their double action autos for that first round. That's a slow and awkward procedure when done with both hands, and can be a *fatally* slow and awkward procedure when attempted one hand only.

Tradition has it that a cocked pistol should be a *locked* pistol when it's being carried as opposed to being actually fired. In other words, it has a manual safety engaged. The one SIG has fitted to the P220 SAO is comfortable – not too narrow to hit, and not so broad that it conflicts with safety straps or alters your grasp of the pistol – and it's more or less ambidextrous. I say "more or less" for a reason. When firing right-handed, all our testers were

able to off-safe and on-safe easily with their firing hand thumb. They were able to off-safe just as easily when shooting southpaw… but that extra lever on the right side of the frame just didn't want to go back up into the "safe" position. I found that I could turn my left hand on the gun and get the ball of the thumb's median joint on the lever with enough force to on-safe it left hand only, but most of us just used our right hand to perform that function. I submit that a defensive pistol should be able to run using one hand only, with either hand, because that's a distinct real life possibility in a defensive handgun's mission statement.

I thought the lever on the right might just be stiff on our sample, but apparently not. A southpaw friend at SIG told me he's seen the same. "I don't have any trouble with it, but right-handed people seem to, when they work one of these left-handed. My left is my dominant hand, so maybe it's a strength issue," he observed.

Like all late production P-220s, the magazine release button on this one is convertible to right side placement for southpaw shooters, or for those righties who prefer to dump the magazine with their trigger finger instead of their right thumb. Most of the shooters on the test team were right-handed, so we just left the test gun as it was.

Why a cocked and locked SIG? For one thing, it's not a 1911. The classic 1911 pistol set records for military weapon reliability when it was left with its original recoil spring system and loaded with 230-grain full metal jacket round-nose military ammo. For generations, however, American enthusiasts, gunsmiths, and gun designers have messed with it hoping to improve it. They change the springs, they tighten the tolerances, they change the feedway, they load it with gap-mouthed hollowpoints or sharp-edged semi-wadcutters, and guess what? It's not always so reliable any more.

The P220 .45 was built from the ground up for reliability with hollowpoint ammo of the Western world. It has more of a straight-line feed angle than does the 1911. All things considered, many people believe the P220 is a more reliable platform. For those who feel that way, a cocked and locked P220 is a blessing from Heaven and not just from SIGARMS.

*At an Amarillo class, Ayoob shot this virtually one-hole 60-shot group during timed qualification. Pistol is SIG P220 SAO in short 3.9-inch barrel Carry format, drawn from LFI Concealment rig and loaded with Rem-UMC .45 hardball. Target is Texas DPS.*

*Starting with flush bottom (for concealment) older generation 7-round mag, author put eight rounds into this satisfying group from 25 yards, right-hand barricade, with SIG P220 Match with 5-inch barrel.*

Another thing the P220 delivers more readily than most 1911s is accuracy. You're generally looking at spending $2500 with a pistolsmith, minimum, to get a 1911 that will shoot much under two inches at 25 yards and not jam all the time because its tolerances have been choked up too tight. That's just about the level of accuracy that comes out of the box with a SIG P220 .45 ACP. I've shot two of them that put five shots in 7/8-inch at that distance, both pistols in out-of-the-box condition, and both using Federal's fabulously accurate 185-grain Classic hollowpoint. It's not guaranteed, but the accuracy potential is certainly there. This one broke the 2-inch group mark with half of the ammo tested. However, it should be borne in mind that this particular pistol was the Carry model, with a sub-four inch barrel and proportionally shorter sight radius.

As noted, the P220 SAO is not a 1911, and that means some other things. It means that you can leave the manual safety engaged when operating the slide. It means you have the fabulously easy takedown of the SIG-Sauer system.

It means that this is one cocked and locked pistol that *won't* discharge if you *first* pull the trigger and then, while holding it back, release the safety. You'll feel a strong resistance when you try to do this, and will discover that only when you ease up on the trigger and let it move a little forward will you be able to start rearward pressure again, and *then* pull the trigger of the now-off-safe pistol.

Also unlike the 1911, the P220 SAO offers a convertibility factor. Merely by sending your P220 SAO to the SIGARMS plant in Exeter, N.H., you can have it converted to traditional double-action first shot, or double-action-only (DAO), or DAK, SIG's light pull, high-tech DAO system. This is only possible with P220 frames manufactured in the last few years. They are easily distinguished by the size of the window cut in the frame for the trigger. If your pistol has a 10mm wide trigger window in the frame, says SIGARMS engineer Joe Kiesel, you're good to go on the conversion. If you have the older frame, where that window is only 8mm wide, your only options are traditional DA/SA, or the older style of DAO with the heavier pull. The SAO and DAK require the current production frames.

The P220 SAO won't take 1911 magazines, either, but there are so many bad magazines of that type floating around that this fact is probably a blessing. Stick with SIG magazines, and those made by MecGar of Italy, who have produced a huge number of SIG-Sauer's own magazines anyway. A third that I would trust is the Novak, though mine hold only seven rounds. The test pistol worked fine with early generation P220 American magazines, 7-round with a flat bottom that helps concealment in most types of holster. It worked fine with a second-generation 8-shot "DPS" magazine, created by SIG for Texas cops with P220 .45s. And of course, it worked fine with the two 8-round stainless magazines of the type SIG is now supplying with these guns, complete with a bumper pad for positive insertion and my favorite of the pack. About all it *won't* work with are aftermarket junk, or early P220 European and Browning BDA magazines, which were designed for butt-heel release and don't have the proper cutouts for a current SIG.

SIGARMS offers the SAO P220 in three barrel/slide configurations. One is the short 3.9-inch barrel Carry version, like the SAO itself a recently introduced option; another is the standard 4.4-inch barrel length; and a third is a 5-inch target model. SIGARMS sent a Carry configuration SAO to *On Target,* the first of the DAO SIGs I was able to test in depth.

The test pistol's barrel measures 3.9 inches in length. The traditional P220 is listed in the specs as having a 4.4-inch barrel. The .45 ACP cartridge has, over the years,

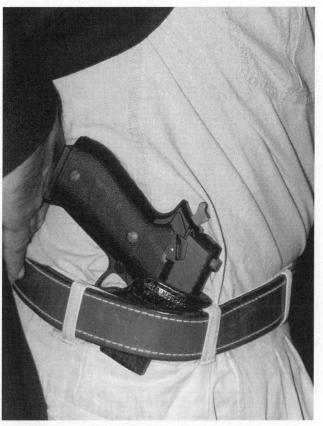

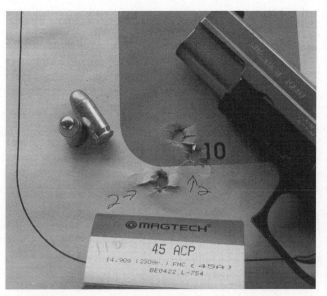

*Five rounds, including two doubles, equal 1-inch group with inexpensive MagTech .45 hardball and SIG SAO P220 match. Distance was 25 yards.*

*Ayoob found the P220 SAO worked fine in this LFI Concealment Rig by Ted Blocker, cut for standard P220.*

been notorious for its sensitive "velocity floor" insofar as conventionally designed hollow-point bullets opening. I did one test with a trio of Colt .45 autos back in the '80s, using 185-grain Federal hollowpoint fired into slaughterhouse animals under humane conditions. The bullet from the 5-inch Colt Government Model mushroomed perfectly and dramatically. The one from the 4.25-inch Lightweight Commander deformed into a distinctly smaller mushroom shape. The one from the 3.5-inch barrel of an Officer's ACP did not deform at all, and probably could have been reloaded into a fresh cartridge if I'd wiped off the blood and flesh.

Today's high-tech hollowpoints are expressly engineered to open at the lower velocities predictable from shorter barrels. These include CCI/Speer's Gold Dot, Federal's Hydra-Shok and particularly their HST series, PMC's Eldorado Starfire, Remington's Golden Saber, and Winchester's SXT and Ranger lines.

We compared the P220 SAO with a regular P220 on a Chrony, using Speer's popular Lawman 230-grain full metal jacket .45 ACP practice load. The standard P220 averaged 786.64 fps. The shorter P220 SAO averaged 769.94 fps. The difference? A mere 16.7 fps. Not anything to worry about. You'll often see more difference than that between two supposedly identical cartridges out of the same lot of ammunition, fired from the same .45 pistol.

We noticed something else: this short, light pistol kicked less than its big brothers. It kicked less than the standard aluminum-frame P220. It kicked a little less than even the heavy, all-steel P220 ST. Not believing our hands, three of us shot those three guns side by side and the verdict was unanimous: less jump, distinctly, in the P220 Carry than either of the others, including the all-steel gun.

This is counter-intuitive. A 16 fps reduction in muzzle velocity does not reduce corresponding recoil enough to notice. Joe Kiesel opines it's the lighter mass of the shorter slide going back and forth that is reducing both the muzzle jump and the rearward kick. Live and learn.

The SIG-Sauer P220 has always been one of my favorite double action .45 autos, and the only thing I would have added to it if I could, would have been a thumb safety. Those things can be life-savers when you're in a struggle for your pistol with the bad guy. Now, I *have* a SIG-Sauer P220 with a thumb safety. Thank you very much, SIGARMS of America and Sauer of Germany! *(My sources tell me the P220 SAO project was 50/50 between the two entities.)*

That P220 SAO Carry wound up with Editor Ben Battles at *On Target.* We might have fought over which one of us was going to send a check to SIGARMS and keep it, but I was holding out until I tried the longer guns. After all, Paul Erhard in SIG marketing was promising 1-inch groups with the 5-inch target model, and I hadn't tried that one yet.

I subsequently got a 5-inch, the configuration they call the Match, and damned if it *didn't* shoot into an inch! Even more impressive, the ammo was cheap Brazilian Mag-Tech hardball, and the "bench rest" was the top of a 55-gallon drum on one of the tactical ranges at Marty and Gila Hayes' excellent training facility, the Firearms Academy of Seattle. This gun, too, shot soft in terms of recoil. The only thing I didn't like about it was the sharp edges on its adjustable sights. After I wrote it up for the cover story in *Guns* magazine (February, 2006 issue), I sent it back. *Almost* bought it, but had a feeling that the standard length gun might be the one for me. I already

*SIG P220 SAO in standard size configuration with 4.4-inch barrel.*

had plenty of leather for the standard size, and as mentioned above, I had been able to achieve that magic one inch at 25 yards twice before with standard size P220s in the double-action configuration.

Then, lo and behold, *American Handgunner* editor Roy Huntington decided he wanted an article on the whole kit and kaboodle, so he sent along one in each length! The 3.9-inch Carry proved functionally identical in every respect to the one tested for *On Target,* including the same accuracy, the same soft recoil and the same high order of reliability. My only beef with it was that the sights weren't spot on. The long-barrel Match model shot direct to point of aim/point of impact right out of the box, though, and proved that it could hit the magic inch with that equally magic Federal 185-grain JHP, which used to be called Match Hollow Point on the box for good reason.

But, at long last, I had a 4.4-inch standard size P220 single action! I was a bit disappointed to discover that it shot distinctly to the left, but I knew that was nothing I couldn't fix with a Brownell's fixed sight moving tool, or the equivalent available through SIGARMS Academy for us armorer's school graduates. And, by golly, the elusive inch didn't prove that elusive at all. You guessed it: Federal Classic 185-grain hollow point was the ticket, though this pistol shot everything else pretty well, too.

I've spent weeks at a time carrying one or another of these guns concealed. Only one, the first P220 Carry, ever accidentally wiped its cocked and locked safety to the down position, doubtless from brushing the outermost of its ambidextrous levers with my forearm while carrying it in an open-top holster. The safety lever works very positively on all these guns. Indeed, the standard model was fitted so tightly I couldn't thumb it back on-safe with the firing hand, and had to do so with a separate movement of the support hand.

I've worn them in the heat of a Texas summer (Amarillo, Carry model, LFI Concealment Rig inside the waistband by Ted Blocker, July '06) and in the chill of a Minnesota winter (Minneapolis, 5-inch Match model, Ted Blocker thumb-break belt-slide, December '06). It worked fine with gloves and cold hands. The thumb-break of the Blocker holster shielded body and clothing alike from the sharp upper corners of the adjustable rear sight.

I've also finally had time to shoot all three of them in IDPA matches. Each time I was shooting against 1911s, in the Custom Defense Pistol category created for cocked and locked .45 autos. Summer, Oak Park, Illinois: Second Master. Illinois State and Midwest CDP Champion Rich DeMondo beat me with his custom 1911, though not by much. I shouldn't complain. He's a hell of a shot, and to salve my ego, he's one of my LFI graduates. I had been shooting my first test Carry model in that event, with Speer Lawman .45 hardball. Autumn, Orlando, Florida: shooting my second test sample Match SAO and Winchester USA .45 hardball, I took First Master. Winter, Jacksonville, Florida: shooting the 4.4-inch configuration SAO with 230-grain match loads developed expressly for CDP-class IDPA shooting by Atlanta Arms and Ammo, I managed to win First Master and CDP category overall.

The matches tell you less about inherent accuracy than they do about handling under stress. What they told me was that this new SIG will, as Bill Jordan used to say, "Do to ride the river with."

If you like the idea of a cocked and locked .45 but for this or that reason are put off by the 1911 design, this is the gun for you. The most expensive, the Match variation, can be had for just under a thousand dollars with fixed night sights, and just over that with the adjustables. If that sounds steep, consider that a 1911 that will give the same 100 percent reliability and one-inch-at-25-yards accuracy would cost between $2500 and $5000, and would probably entail a waiting period of up to five years before the master gunsmith got through his backlog to work his magic on your gun.

I call that a helluva deal, and I call the SIG P220 SAO one of the most noteworthy pistols to make its debut in the last five years.

### SIG P226 DAK .357

SIGARMS' P226 pistol was once the most popular police service auto in this country. Of late, the SIG brand has been Number Two in law enforcement sales, behind the Glock, but the company is surging forward again. SIGARMS and Heckler & Koch share a huge Homeland Security purchasing contract. The SIG pistols approved by Homeland Security include the full size P226, the compact P229, and the subcompact P239, all in calibers 9mm Luger and .40 Smith & Wesson. All are in double-action-only formats, the first two with a relatively new trigger group called the DAK.

The acronym stands for Double Action, Kellerman, named after its European designer. An improved double action only concept, it actually embodies three potential trigger pull modes. It competes directly with HK's LEM (Law Enforcement Module) trigger group, which is slightly different mechanically and in that subjective quality of "feel." For purposes of an article *On Target* provided me with a P226 DAK, serial number UU 605295. I also attended the SIG Armorer's Course for the DAK pistol (specifically, for the functionally identical P229 DAK) in Arlington Heights, IL.

Our test pistol was chambered for the .357 SIG round. Going back a dozen years, this cartridge resembles a .40 S&W casing necked down to 9mm, though engineering-wise, it's much more than that. Ted Rowe, then a prime mover at SIGARMS, wanted to put the lightning-strike power of the most popular .357 Magnum revolver round among police, the 125-grain hollowpoint at 1.450 fps, into

*SIG P226 DAK in .357 SIG.*

the ergonomic SIG pistol. SIG and Federal Cartridge pretty much succeeded, and the .357 SIG round was born.

So, we have here a proven pistol, an excellent and promising fire control system, and a cartridge that has worked out extremely well on the street. Let's look at each of those elements separately, to better see how they come together in the test pistol.

**The P226 Pistol** is essentially a P220 design with its grip frame widened to take a double-stack magazine, and built "American style." The P226 was created more than twenty years ago by the Swiss/German collaboration of SIG and Sauer to compete in the JSSAP trials for selection of the new American 9mm military service pistol. Though it tied and, by some accounts, beat the Beretta 92, the U.S. armed services contract went to the Italian-designed pistol. A more compact version, the SIG P228, was adopted by Army CID, however, and the Navy's SEALs have insisted on the P226 9mm as their sidearm for many years. Over the decades, the P226 was redesigned for greater strength, an upgrade that made the powerful .357 SIG and .40 Smith & Wesson rounds practical in that envelope, and the design has received other timely "tweaks." Among them is the Picatinny rail on the dust cover of the frame of the P226R variation, which encompasses our test sample.

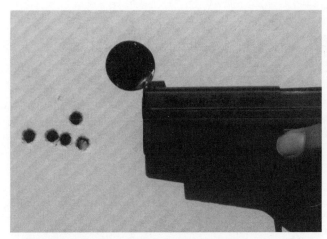

*SIG's manageable "double-action Kellerman" trigger gave this excellent group at 25 yards.*

**The DAK Fire Control Mechanism** is an important breakthrough. Some police departments feel that a trigger pull that works with a long, deliberate stroke for every shot, plus a mechanism that "decocks itself," is safer, more stress-resistant, and less prone to civil liability. SIG's standard DAO pull was adopted in the P226 by Ohio State Patrol (caliber .40) and as an option for NYPD (9mm), among others. However, many officers and instructors wanted something with an easier pull.

It was with this in mind that Kellerman designed the new system, which I first tested in prototype at the SIGARMS facility in Exeter, N.H. in 2003. The initial trigger pull is long, but light and very controllable. The shooter may use this pull for every shot by simply returning the trigger all the way forward each time. However, there is also the option for the skilled user of allowing the trigger to go forward just until it catches its first "link." It is now past the disconnector mechanism and has engaged the sear, and second and subsequent shots can be fired from this position. It requires a shorter stroke of the trigger, but since a shorter pull gives less mechanical advantage, the pull weight increases by a pound and a half or so. Finally, as a fallback, if the hammer goes all the way forward (something it can only do if the trigger has been pulled) but the chambered round doesn't fire, the shooter can take another whack at it by simply pulling the trigger again, though with the longer trigger now moving the hammer farther, the pull weight increases to over three pounds more than the first trigger stroke.

**The .357 SIG Cartridge**, while available in a fairly wide variety of bullet weights, is most widely adopted as a 125-grain JHP at 1325 to 1425 fps. The SIG in .357 has been adopted by a number of agencies, including the Texas Department of Public Safety (P226), and the state troopers of Delaware, Rhode Island, and Virginia, all of whom use the more compact P229. The P229 .357 SIG is

*Ayoob rolls a double-action shot from weak-hand barricade at 25 yards with the SIG SAS P239 .40. He prefers to allow the DAK trigger to reset all the way forward for each shot.*

standard issue for the U.S. Secret Service, and the Sky Marshals. In close to fifteen years on the street, the 125-grain .357 SIG round has earned the same reputation for fast man stopping as its six-gun predecessor.

If you've shot the ubiquitous P226 9mm, picture it honked up with a heavier recoil spring (making the slide somewhat stiffer to manually retract, and the slide stop lever a bit harder to push down when the pistol is at slide-lock). Imagine it a bit snappier in recoil, and distinctly louder. That's what it's like to shoot a P226 in .357. No big deal as far as controllability. Unlike most .357 revolvers with Magnum loads, it won't hurt to shoot unless you have a hand or arm injury.

The DAK is easy to get used to, and easy to like. That first pull, spec'd at just under 7 pounds in the literature, averaged slightly over 7 pounds on a Lyman digital trigger weight scale. "Catching the link" after each cycling of the slide, we experienced a trigger stroke with a shorter throw but an average pull weight of 8 pounds, 15 ounces while 9 pounds, 5.5 ounces was the average weight of the

| \*Accuracy Test: SIG P226 DAK .357 | | | | |
| --- | --- | --- | --- | --- |
| **Brand** | **Load** | **Nominal FPS** | **5-Shot Group** | **Best 3 Shots** |
| **Black Hills Red** | 125-gr BHP\*\* | 1325 fps | 1-1/4" | 9/16" |
| **CCI Speer Gold Dot** | 125-gr BHP | 1350 fps | 2-1/4" | 1.00" |
| **Federal Premium** | 125-gr JHP | 1350 fps | 3-1/4" | 1-1/16" |
| **Wolf** | 230-gr | FMJ | 4-1/2" | 1-13/16" |
| **Winchester USA** | 125-gr JHP | 1350 fps | 2-7/8" | 13/16" |
| \* Hand-held on MTM rest @ 25 yards. | | | | |
| \*\* Bonded (jacketed) Hollow Point | | | | |

*"To the barricades." Author finds SIG SAS compact accurate enough and shootable enough for NRA Service Automatic class of PPC shooting.*

*SIG P239 SAS with DAK trigger.*

default trigger pull designed for misfires. *(We were never able to actually fire it in default mode, since that would require a misfired cartridge, and as with every DAK I've shot since 2003, this gun never misfired.)*

It seems counterintuitive, but I shot a tad better with the long "first shot" pull, and soon learned to let the trigger return all the way forward for each shot. Testing with Winchester USA economy 125-grain JHP, I got a 25-yard group of 3 and 3/8 inches while "riding the link" for each shot, and a tighter 2 7/8-inch cluster (5 shots each) while using the longer "first pull," as a true DAO. The lightness of the longer "first pull" helps.

The SIG P226 is an accurate pistol, and the .357 SIG is an accurate cartridge. Firing single action from a rest at the same 25-yard distance at the Manchester Indoor Firing Line in Manchester, NH, a standard format P226 gave me a one-inch 5-shot group with CCI Speer 125-grain Gold Dots. That was one of the Firing Line's rental SIGs, at that! The DAK gun was almost as tight with its favorite load, delivering five Black Hills rounds (loaded with the 125-grain Gold Dot bullet) into 1-1/4 inches. The Gold Dot group was only an inch bigger with the DAK. The best three-shot clusters (often your best indicator of inherent accuracy when firing hand-held from a rest) went into an inch with the Gold Dot, and an extraordinary 9/16-inch with the Black Hills, which unfortunately is no longer produced in .357 SIG. Federal and Winchester ammo also proved suitably accurate.

There were no malfunctions of any kind. The SIG P226 has earned a reputation for extremely high reliability over more than a score of years in 9mm, and the same seems to be true in .40 S&W and .357 SIG. The latter round, being bottlenecked, feeds into the chamber with a smooth wedge effect that only enhances its feed reliability. Early incidents of case neck separation with some brands of .357 SIG ammo seem to be history.

Extraordinarily reliable, extremely accurate, adaptable to quick-detaching flashlights and laser sights thanks to the front Pic rail and now fitted with the Kellerman trigger for better, safer performance under extreme stress, the P226 DAK seems to have it all. The price is commensurate with its high quality and reflects good value. According to scuttlebutt from SIG, the state of Texas is going with the DAK mechanism while keeping their P226 and the .357 SIG round, both of which have worked extraordinarily well for them on the street.

### Springfield Armory XD In 45 ACP

You can't go on an Internet gun forum anymore – even one dedicated to other brands, such as GlockTalk – without seeing someone singing the praises of Springfield Armory's new XD.45 pistol in .45 ACP.

First, "XD.45 pistol in .45 ACP" is not a redundancy. The XD stands for "X-treme Duty," the Croatian pistol that used to be known as the HS2000 before Springfield Armory cornered the market on its U.S. importation. "XD9" is the 9mm version, "XD.40" is chambered in .40 S&W, and "XD.357" is the same polymer-frame pistol in .357 SIG. However, the first "XD.45," which was introduced in late 2004, was actually chambered for the .45 GAP (**G**lock **A**utomatic **P**istol) cartridge.

I liked the heck out of that gun. Mine, a 5-inch "LE Tactical" version, was the most accurate pistol I had ever fired with the new cartridge, giving phenomenally tight clusters at 25 yards with Winchester's humble USA brand "white box" generic 230-grain hardball load. It fit the hand exactly like one of its 9mm Luger, .40 S&W, or .357 SIG stable-mates… which is to say, it fit the hand superbly.

However, the decision was made in 2005 to tool up to answer the demand for this pistol in caliber .45 ACP. Like Glock, they decided they needed a bigger frame for the longer .45 ACP round. The result is the new XD.45ACP. If you review almost any electronic gun forum on the Internet, you'll see this gun's praises being sung by a variety of end-users, with scant complaints from those who've actually fired the pistol. Is it really that good?

*XD .45ACPs in, top to bottom, Tactical size, Service size, and Compact. First two hold 14 rounds, latter, 11.*

In a word, yes.

We tested two XD.45ACPs, a standard size (4-inch barrel) serial number US605996, and a Tactical version with 5-inch barrel and proportionally lengthened slide, serial number US608092. Each had the standard array of modern XD features. Molded-in frame rail for attaching a tactical light. Ambidextrous magazine release buttons, which are extremely handy for right-handed shooters as well as lefties, as we shall see. Grip safety, which must be depressed to fire the pistol or to operate its slide, ensuring a firm firing grasp during handling. Trigger safety, a la' Glock, intended to require a properly located finger to apply intentional pressure before the pistol can discharge. Fixed Patridge sights with three white dots. Loaded chamber indicator, clearly visible and palpable, rising like a shark fin at the rear of the firing chamber. Melonite finish, to quell complaints of rust on earlier XDs.

The first thing most experienced shooters noticed with these guns was the impressively narrow girth of the grip-frame. By using a steel-bodied magazine instead of one with thicker polymer – and adapting the design to the existing shape of the standard XD, which has been superbly ergonomic from the beginning – the engineers ended up with a very "grasp-able" double-column .45 ACP. There is a user-friendly short trigger reach, which lets the average size adult male get a lot of finger on the trigger, and allows anyone with short fingers to reach the trigger with the pad or tip of the index finger while still keeping a firm hold on the pistol, with its barrel in line with the long bones of the forearm.

The grip safety works as intended. With any sort of firing grasp, it releases itself. It is almost a passive safety in that, so long as the shooter is taking a good hold, no deliberate movement is required to release the safety and allow the pistol to fire.

With a release button low behind the trigger guard – *and one on each side* – the pistol is extremely easy to reload quickly. A shooter can use the index finger instead of the thumb to dump the depleted magazine. This has the safety advantage of guaranteeing the finger is out of the trigger guard at this point. It is also generally faster because the shooter need not shift his or her grip to get the thumb to the release button, as is often the case with many other pistols in many shooters' hands. With the XD, the right-handed shooter works the right button with the trigger finger, and the southpaw shooter, the left button. On each side, the buttons are hidden into recesses in the frame that very effectively shield them from being inadvertently depressed during carry or firing.

Adding to the reloading speed is a wide-mouth magazine well, which combines with an upwardly tapering magazine for a very slick and generally fumble-free insertion. Of course, you get this with most any pistol magazine that is double-stack in design. However, combined with the handy ambi mag release, the XD is particularly fast. For those who prefer the speed method of pressing down on the slide stop to close the slide at the end of a slide-lock reload, the XD presents only one problem: the slide stop lever is a little bit sharp at its upper left corner, and can start chewing on the thumb in a long practice session. Those who prefer the slower but more traditional method of closing the slide by tugging it to the rear and letting it snap forward will avoid that minor discomfort, but at some cost in speed.

The slide stop lever and the takedown lever are the only two parts of this pistol that present undesirable

*Ayoob found the Compact Springfield Armory XD to be uniformly accurate with all bullet weights of .45 ACP.*

sharp contact points to the shooter's hands in routine manipulation and firing. Using the straight thumbs position that has become popular in IDPA and IPSC, a right-hander's thumbs took a definite chewing from these parts, particularly the forward thumb. Being an old revolver shooter, I just curled the thumbs down double-action style and got them out of the way. A southpaw shouldn't have a problem with it, since the offending parts are on the left side of the pistol. Still, I'd like to see Springfield Armory get these parts rounded on the edges.

Recoil was pleasantly mild for a .45 ACP. We passed these guns around to a lot of friends who were .45 fans eager to fire this new iteration. Comments were unanimously positive. One shooter promptly went out and ordered one in each barrel length from his favorite dealer.

There has been a lot of discussion as to how this pistol compares to the gun it appears to be designed to compete with directly, the full-size Glock 21 in the same caliber. Most of the discussion centers around recoil. This is a highly subjective comparison. Personally, I can't see much difference in either rearward "kick" or muzzle rise between the G21 and the XD.45. Several county deputies who were qualifying on my range with their issue Glock 21s took advantage of my offer to try the XD.45ACP. Most

*Springfield Armory XD-.45 LE in .45 GAP with InSight light/laser unit. Five-inch barrel allows muzzle to be parallel with lamp.*

said they felt it kicked less than their department service pistol, and one reportedly went right out and ordered a 4-inch version for off-duty carry. I think it may be that the smaller circumference of the XD.45ACP's grip frame gets proportionally more hand around the gun, giving the shooter more control, or at least a sensation of more control. On the other hand, the bore axis of the Glock in .45 ACP is slightly lower, giving the muzzle less leverage to climb. In my own hands, I think those two factors amount to a wash. Proportionally more hand around the "handle" gives me more leverage on that end, but less muzzle rise from the Glock's lower-axis bore cancels that out on the other end. It's probably why I personally can't find a real difference between the two, but as noted above, that's highly subjective.

We tested these guns with a variety of loads. Surprisingly, the longer-barrel gun did not exceed the shorter in accuracy, despite its greater sight radius. The Tactical felt better balanced with more weight out front, but I couldn't detect any real difference in muzzle climb or rearward recoil between the two. The 4-inch came out of the box shooting spot on, while the 5-inch left the factory shooting a tad high and left.

Off the bench at 25 yards, none of the several loads we tested failed to make the old and generous standard of 4-inch groups. Most did better. The tightest group with the Tactical measured 2.05 inches for all five shots, and a stunning 0.80-inch for the best three. That was with Remington 185-grain +P jacketed hollowpoint, fired by IDPA Five-Gun Master Jon Strayer. With that same ammo, the 4-inch pistol did 2.30 inches (five shots) and 1.35 inches (best three shots).

A handload put together by Steve Sager, consisting of a 230-grain Precision polymer-coated round-nose bullet over 5.5 grains of Universal Clays gunpowder and Winchester Large pistol primers started out to be 1.40 inches, but a single flyer expanded the five-shot group to 2-3/4 inches. It is to factor out such human error that I like to measure the best three shots as well. With this gun and the Sager load, that measurement was an incredible 0.55-inch, which included two bullets in one barely-enlarged hole. Needless to say, the XD.45ACP shows promise of being a very accurate pistol.

*Tactical (top) and Compact Springfield Armory XD .45ACPs.*

I've carried the 4-inch XD.45 considerably. It comes with a plastic double magazine pouch and plastic holster, both made overseas. I found both to lean out a bit from the body. As this gun becomes more popular, more companies are making leather for it. I ordered a carbon fiber CQC and a leather Avenger holster for it from Blackhawk, and was rewarded with better concealment and a more comfortable ride on the hip. When I carried it loaded and concealed, no sharp edges attacked my body or clothing. I later acquired a Blackhawk SERPA, the concealable security holster in the CQC line discussed elsewhere in this book. (And, yes, I liked the XD.45 so much that I bought both test samples from Springfield Armory.)

When testing a hunting gun, it's best to go on a hunt with it, to test its attributes in its intended environment. With a defensive handgun, the closest you can come to that is to shoot a combat match with it, and see how it performs when fast handling and straight shooting are demanded under stress. With this in mind, I took the 4-inch gun with me in the holster it came with to an IDPA match in Orlando, Florida on the first Sunday of March, 2006. I brought some of Sager's handloads.

The provided holster and mag pouch, from the line Springfield Armory calls "XD Gear," proved amply fast. The sights were easy to see against gray or white steel knockdowns, and against buff-colored cardboard silhouettes. Reloads, as testing had predicted, were lightning fast. The gun always came right back on target, and hit point of aim.

IDPA, the International Defensive Pistol Association, allows Glocks to be fired in the Stock Service Pistol category against conventional double-action autos, but requires the XD to vie against the cocked and locked 1911-type autos. This is because, mechanically, the XD is defined as a single-action pistol, even though its smooth, even trigger pull (between six and seven pounds in both test samples) feels more like shooting a Glock than anything else. I entered in the Enhanced Service Pistol (ESP) category, and to make a long story short, nailed First Master there, won the ESP category, and posted the high overall score of the well-attended shoot.

The XD.45 had proven its shootability. With over a thousand rounds through each, there had been a single ejection failure (with the 4-inch gun during its early break-in period, and never repeated). It's not hard to see why the XD.45ACP won NRA's Golden Bullseye award. If you're looking for a high quality, high-tech, high-capacity .45 ACP that doesn't demand a huge hand *or* a huge bank account, check out the Springfield Armory XD.45ACP.

### Springfield Armory X-Treme Duty Tactical .40

With lightweight polymer frame and extreme simplicity of operation, the Glock pistol has become America's most popular. Several imitators have sprung up, but none has caught on quite as well as the Croatian HS 2000, currently imported and advertised as the Springfield Armory XD ("X-treme Duty"). The line has expanded rapidly. There is the XDV10, with integral recoil compensation ports; there are subcompacts to compete with the baby Glock; and now there is a slightly extended-length Tactical version. For the Editor's Choice edition of *On Target* magazine, I tested the latter in caliber .40 S&W. The XD series is also available in 9mm Luger and .357 SIG.

The trigger pull is a smooth, soft press. This helps to achieve the surprise break marksmen appreciate. Sights on the test gun were fixed, with a fiber optic red front that stood out well against any background. Unlike many fiber optic units, this one sits in the center of a solid, square-edged Patridge front sight, giving the shooter the option of raw speed or precise aim.

Distinctively, the Tactical has molding on the front of the polymer frame for snap-on flashlights like the InSight M3 or M6, and at the back, is extended out over the web of the shooter's hand in the manner of a RoBar reshaping of a Glock. As with all XDs, there is ample reach to the trigger. This allows an average size hand to make trigger contact at the distal joint, which many combat shooters feel gives more leverage, and it allows those with the shortest fingers to still get the pad of the index finger solidly onto the trigger without compromising grasp.

At the 25-yard bench, we tested the XD.40 Tactical with all three generations of .40 S&W ammo. Winchester full metal jacket with the first generation formula of a 180-grain bullet at subsonic velocity delivered a 5-shot group that measured three inches even, its best three in a tiny cluster measuring only 1-3/8 inches. Typical of the second generation in ballistics was Black Hills' red box EXP load, comprised of a 165-grain CCI Gold Dot at 1150 fps. It gave a cluster measuring just over three inches for 5 shots, with the best three in 1-14 inches. Third generation is typified by a 135-grain hollowpoint at a roaring 1300 fps, such as Pro-Load's Tactical. The Tactical ammo in the Tactical gun gave us a 5-shot group of just over 4 inches, with its best three in less than 1-1/2 inches.

As a rule, the "best three" measurement factors out human error and gives a good approximation of what the gun would do for five shots in a machine rest. This one indicates high accuracy potential. The forgiving trigger, the good sights, and the overall excellent ergonomics of the XD make this a shooter's gun. Recoil was mild with all loads fired, and we simply couldn't make it malfunction even once.

Functioning in essence like a squared-off Glock with a grip safety, and markedly underselling the Austrian pistol, the Springfield Armory XD is making rapid inroads with American gun owners. The Tactical version is particularly nice. Expect to see more of these guns. It would definitely be worth your while to pick one up and see what all the fuss is about.

### Steyr-Mannlicher M9A1 Pistol

In June of 1999, Willi Bubits visited me in New Hampshire with a pistol he said I would be the first in the United States to fire. I was kind of proud of that... and I thought a lot of the gun. A former Glock engineer, Willi had come up with a "steel inside, polymer outside" pistol that Glock didn't want, but Steyr-Mannlicher did. It was a very promising pistol with some radical design features.

It was out-of-print for a while when Steyr-Mannlicher and its continued imports to the U.S. were both in doubt, and there was a period when remaining stocks of the M-series pistol were sold dirt-cheap. That's over now. Steyr-Mannlicher is back from the dead and ready to party, and they're sending us a new "A1" modification of this controversial sidearm, available in .40 S&W as the M.40A1 and in 9mm Parabellum as the M9A1. We got one of the latter in for testing.

The new series retains the best of the old, and has answered the few complaints with design updates that

*Steyr's sweet-handling new updated design, the M9A1, shot this tight group in rapid fire at seven yards.*

solve the previous concerns, real or imagined. Let's examine it feature by feature.

**Grip.** The grip-frame has been subtly re-shaped, retaining the steep grip angle of approximately 111 degrees. All our wide range of testers liked the feel. Whether the shooter's hands were elfin or elephantine, we kept hearing "It fits perfectly." This specimen doesn't have the currently popular grip inserts to alter size. It doesn't appear to need them. The reach to the trigger is very short. Those with small fingers can easily get the pad of the trigger finger onto the "bang switch" without having to weaken their grasp of the grip-frame itself. Those with medium to long fingers can easily attain the "distal joint of the index finger on the trigger face" placement that double-action revolver shooters have long found gives them the best leverage.

The key to this is a backstrap deeply niched out to bring the web of the hand in closer to the trigger. Bubits called this grip shape a "camel-back" grip. It works.

**Trigger.** Reminiscent of the Glock's trigger in appearance, the A1's is different in feel. There's a short take-up, and a relatively short overall movement. Original M-series pistols had five-pound pulls with a seven-pound option for police departments and other conservative types. Armorer Rick Devoid tested the sample's trigger on an official NRA Referee's pull weight

*Unique Steyr sights will be liked or hated. Author likes them.*

*After a rapid-fire magazine from 10 yards, young Courtland Smith is pleased with the performance of the 9mm Steyr.*

I never heard of one firing from impact or inertia. However, many police departments (and some cautious shooters) insist on an internal firing pin lock, so the A1 is outfitted with one.

**Light rail.** Heckler and Koch pioneered the molded-in attachment rail with their USP series more than a decade ago, and it has become a "must-have" option on modern autos. The A1 comes so equipped. For home defense or police work, I like the idea of a quick-on, quick-off powerful white light unit like the InSight or the SureFire. It can solve target identification problems and prevent tragedies. It can blind opponents at opportune moments. It's *A Good Thing.* Just make sure you use it as a target confirmation and target-blinding device, not a searchlight: anything the gun-mounted light illuminates, will be dead in line with your loaded Steyr pistol and its easy trigger. Keep a conventional flashlight handy for the search function, even if you have a lamp attached to your firearm.

device, and found that it broke at seven and a half pounds. Most who fired it guessed the pull weight at four to four and a half pounds. Those who like to "ride the sear" or "ride the link" when manipulating an auto pistol's trigger will find it easy to do on the Steyr M-A1.

**Manual Safety.** I've always been a proponent of a manual safety on a handgun, but only if it's user-friendly. The one on the original Steyr M wasn't. It was awkward to both engage and take off. They've simply removed it from the M-A1, and that may be for the best. If they want a gun that competes with the Glock, they want a gun that is operated like a Glock.

**Passive firing pin safety.** The original did not have an internal firing pin lock. Bubits had designed the pistol not to need one, and was convinced that it was "drop-safe."

**Trigger finger niche.** Another pioneering feature came from Taurus with their 24/7 series: niches molded into the frame to help the trigger finger stay there "in register," and out of the trigger guard at inappropriate times. I don't see any reason for every new pistol not to have this useful feature, and I'm glad to see it on the Steyr M-A1.

**Trapezoidal sights.** Perhaps the most novel and controversial feature on the original Steyr M, these remain on the new iteration. The rear sight rises up in two matching angles as if to form a bridge that is cut away in the center. What goes in the center instead is the tip of a point-up white triangle that is the front sight. For those accustomed to the conventional post-in-notch sight picture, or three dots in a horizontal row, or the dot-the-"i" von Stavenhagen sighting image, this is a radical departure.

It's worth trying, though. It is *very* fast for a "flash sight picture," and keys in very well with the excellent pointing characteristics afforded by the Steyr's Luger-like grip angle. Once you get the hang of it, the pointy top of the front sight can index very precise shots. The concept is reminiscent of the old silver or gold bead atop the front sight, which led to the phrase, "drawing a fine bead on the target."

**Internal gun-lock.** Continued from the first iteration is an internal lock located on the right side of the frame behind the takedown lever. (Takedown, by the way, is simple and uncomplicated.) The lock is activated by a quarter-turn with the two-pronged key provided in duplicate on "civilian" models, or a handcuff key on "police" models. I think the latter is a brilliant idea, since

*Ayoob found the Nighthawk consistently accurate at 25 yards.*

*Nighthawk is among the most promising new brands of 1911. This is the Predator version in .45 ACP.*

most of the cops I know carry a handcuff key with them at all times, on or off duty. While internal gun-locks provoke the same visceral debates as motorcycle helmet laws, I have no problem with them so long as they don't activate by themselves. I've never heard of that happening on a Steyr pistol.

The first thing every single person on our test team noted once the shooting started was that, even for a 9mm, this was a very soft-shooting gun. Ammo included Federal's hot, police-only 9BPLE load, which spits a 115-grain JHP at 1300 fps, and Remington's public market Golden Saber +P with a 124-grain brass jacket hollowpoint at 1250 fps. Part of the easy recoil can be traced to kick-absorbing flexion in the polymer frame, and part to the very low bore axis of this pistol. Those funny looking sights were back on target *immediately* after the prior shot.

Reloading was fast and smooth. The magazines, which appear to be manufactured by MecGar, have polished metal bodies. They insert cleanly, and drop cleanly when the non-ambidextrous mag release button is pressed. The slide release lever is shaped for easy manipulation, and the frame has thumb-niches to help keep that digit from over-riding the lever and preventing it from doing its job of locking the slide open on an empty magazine. Two magazines come with each pistol.

Accuracy testing was done on a range where 25-yard benches were not readily available, so I shot from the rollover prone position developed by Ray Chapman. Our test M9A1 showed itself to be afflicted with "four plus one" syndrome, commonly seen in popular-price semiautomatic pistols. The first hand-chambered shot always seemed to go to a slightly different point of impact than the subsequent mechanically-cycled shots.

I saw something with this gun that is uncommon: mediocre accuracy with three out of four tested loads, and phenomenally good accuracy with one. Remington 124-grain Golden Saber HP had a 4.70-inch group in the center ring of the IDPA target, due largely to that first shot. Rounds #2 through #5 grouped in 3.60 inches. The best three shots, which help factor out human error – present here to a larger degree, since I was shooting without a bench rest – formed a 2.70-inch group. All measurements were to the nearest 0.05-inch, center-to-center between the bullet holes.

Winchester's 147-grain subsonic JHP, famous for accuracy, put five shots in a disappointing 5.50 inches; without the first shot, that group would have measured only 3-1/2 inches. The best three hits were in 2-1/4 inches. Another famously accurate load is Federal's 9BP, a standard pressure 115-grain JHP. This one gave a 5-shot group that measured a sub-standard 5 inches even, but without the first errant shot would have been 2.85 inches. The best three were in an even tighter 1.70-inch cluster.

However, the star of the show was a surprise. The humble, inexpensive, steel-case Wolf 115-grain FMJ practice load gave awesome accuracy, even though it shot low and right from point of aim. All five shots were in 1.10 inches. That included the slightly errant first shot. Rounds #2 through #5 punched a single, connected hole measuring only 0.45-inch! The best three of those were in about a quarter inch! Every shot could have been covered with a 25-cent piece.

I don't usually use that many exclamation points in one paragraph. But I don't usually see a group like that, either.

Suffice it to say that the M9A1 has awesome accuracy potential. It's also safe to say that one will have to grow accustomed to the unusual sight picture to extract that accuracy. It might be well worth the effort. A small coterie of IDPA shooters have

*Taurus continues to be a major player in the combat handgun market. This is the excellent five-shot Tracker, which uses .45 ACP ammo with proprietary full moon clips.*

become dedicated fans of the M-series Steyr-Mannlicher because they've found it *very* fast to achieve hits with in "combat shooting," thanks to its combination of excellent pointing characteristics, those quick-to-the-eye trapezoidal sights, and the user-friendly trigger pull and reset.

Willi Bubits' original design had a great deal to recommend it. The A1 modifications are all good, and a definite overall improvement. Light and comfortable to carry, packing fifteen 9mm Parabellum rounds in its double-stack magazine, and offering very low recoil and muzzle jump for quick shot-to-shot recovery, the Steyr-Mannlicher M-A1 series is full of potential for the serious *pistolero* or *pistolera*.

I for one am looking forward to shooting the M9A1 in an IDPA match.

### Taurus

The last five years have seen a quantum leap in improving the quality of polymer frame Taurus defensive autoloaders. The egregious Millennium has been upgraded into the Millennium Pro, which actually *works*. Better is the slightly larger, but still concealed carry size, Model 24/7. An excellent amalgam of features – striker fired, double action only, ergonomic manual safety – it has a feature I'd like to see on all pistols. This is a well-thought-out fingertip niche on each side of the frame, above the trigger, in which to "register" the trigger finger by feel and help keep it off the trigger when it shouldn't be there. I've had good luck with the 24/7 in all three of its calibers: 9mm, .40 S&W and .45 ACP.

Put on the market shortly before this Sixth Edition went to press, the PT1911 is a well-conceived 1911 with many expensive pistol features, but a sub-$500 retail price. Only complaints I've heard so far are sharp edges, and a rather fragile finish on the blue guns. You might want to hold out for the stainless.

### In Summation

It has been an interesting half-decade between the fifth and the sixth edition of this book. The hardware, certainly, has kept pace. What does the next half-decade hold? I would expect to be seeing a lot more .45 GAPs, and more .357 SIG pistols. These guns have found their respective niches, and are proving themselves.

I think we've got the small revolvers as light and high-powered as they're going to go, but there may be a little room to go farther in the same direction with small autos. We'll see. The 1911 is in more police holsters by far than when the fifth edition was written, and I think that's going to continue. The notoriously conservative Boston Police Department has ordered SIG GSR 1911s for their tactical teams, and the San Diego Police Department approved cocked-and-locked 1911s and saw the troops

*Seen at Bill's Gun Shop outside Minneapolis in late '06, the Taurus 1911 combines high-priced features with extremely low suggested retail, and could become a best-seller among 1911s. They're working well in the field so far, though Ayoob has had reports of blue wearing off quickly, and suggests the stainless variation.*

flock to buy them. Coast to coast, I'm seeing more 1911s *On The Job*.

The military? It's been up and down, but don't be surprised to see a large caliber pistol back in the hands of our troops by the time the seventh edition of *Gun Digest Book of Combat Handgunnery* rolls around.

Armed citizens? When the very first edition came out, there were seven states where there was no provision to carry, and now we're down to two. One of those, Wisconsin, has come achingly close to achieving *Shall Issue*, losing only by a vote or two in the over-ride attempt on the anti-gun governor's veto after passing by a clear majority in the state house in Madison. The Wisconsin stalwarts for gun owners' civil rights will stay in the fight, and I think they'll ultimately prevail. Illinois will be the last anti-self-defense bastion to fall, but a national concealed-carry option that would over-ride their home rule as the Law Enforcement Officer Safety Act did for cops nationwide is less of a pipe dream than ever. In extremely restrictive shall-issue states, the best option may be test cases selectively brought before the states' Supreme Courts. In Hawaii, where for years police chiefs by mutual agreement chose not to issue as state law allowed them to, we are now seeing permits issued for security personnel. The right lawyer with the right clients bringing the right class action suit might just fold that arbitrary and capricious ban on issuing self-protection permits like the fragile house of cards it is.

It's been an interesting five years since the last edition.

But not, I suspect, as interesting as the next five years may be.

# CHAPTER FIFTEEN

# Parting Words

As I was putting the foregoing chapters together, I leafed through the first edition of *Combat Handgunnery* written by Jack Lewis and Jack Mitchell in 1983. I remembered how much I had enjoyed reading it when it came out. Their incisive commentary has stood the test of time.

There were a few pictures of me in it. It's good to be reminded that there was a time when I didn't have a potbelly and only had one chin and nothing had gone gray yet. But that sort of thing reminds us all of how much can happen in 20 years.

The input of physiologists and kinesiologists into both the shooting sports and scientific firearms training has brought things forward in quantum leaps. Technology has evolved, but technique has evolved more. It's not about more high-tech "space guns." The shooters of today, using stock guns of a kind available a score of years ago, are shooting faster and straighter than the champions of two decades ago did with tricked-out specialty target guns.

It's not about the gun so much as it is about the shooter. It's not even about the shooter so much as it's about consistent application of proven tactics and techniques.

There's simply too much to put into any one book. Things have to be prioritized. Some of the topics of previous editions – malfunction clearing, for example,

*Make it a plan to get behind cover before the shooting starts.*

and night shooting – had to be left on the cutting room floor when we ran out of space in this edition. It was more important to nail down advances in shooting technique, how to pick the most suitable tools for the task, and how to avoid doing the wrong thing in an increasingly complex tactical environment. In any case, malfunction clearing and night shooting have been covered very well in past editions.

In the very short space that remains, let's talk about priorities. Training is always a better investment than equipment. Software in your brain is always with you, and there's only so much hardware you can carry. And there are places where you can't carry this kind of

*Get experience beforehand in shooting from awkward, "downed" positions.*

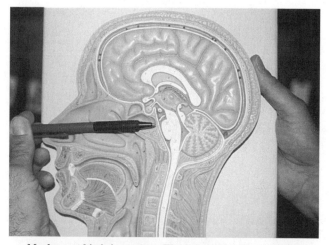

*Marksmanship is important. The pen of an LFI consulting physician shows how small the target is for a hit in the part of the brain that will collapse an opponent without him pulling his trigger even reflexively.*

Think about handgun retention. An open-top holster does nothing to protect this Ruger .45, which is fortunately on safe…

Underlying all this hi-tech kit is a Second Chance Ultima ballistic vest. Any situation where you want a defense gun is a situation where you want body armor.

A thumb-break holster buys you more time…

hardware at all. I take at least a week of training a year for myself, and would recommend the same regimen to you. I can recommend without reservation schools like Chuck Taylor's ASAA, Chapman Academy, the Critical Reaction Training Center near Milwaukee, John Farnam's DTI, Firearms Academy of Seattle, Front Sight, Gunsite, the Midwest Training Group, Clint Smith's Thunder Ranch, and more. You're also welcome to inquire about my own school, Lethal Force Institute, at PO Box 122, Concord, NH 03302 or on the Web at www.ayoob.com.

Remember that awareness and alertness are more important than combat tactics, because they can keep you out of combat to begin with. Tactics are more important than marksmanship, because they can often keep you out of danger without you having to fire a shot. Skill with your safety equipment, including your weapons, is more important than what type of weapon you have. With all those things accomplished, your choice of equipment is one of the few things you can work out before the fight, so it makes sense to have the best quality gear of a kind ideally suited for your predictable threat situation.

Don't just drill on drawing and firing. Drill on movement. Make the use of cover a high priority. Take a

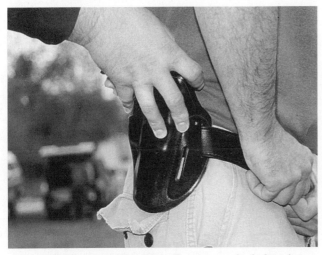

…and this concealable Piece-Keeper security holster is even more snatch-resistant, and only slightly slower on the draw.

The author seconds the advice about awareness on this "tombstone."

*"If you need a gun," said street-wise commentator Phil Engeldrum, "you probably need two." NAA Guardian .380, left, and Kahr MK40 are both popular backup pistols.*

*Your plans should include what your partners are going to do. These Lake County, Mont., deputies prepare for the day they may have to drag a wounded brother to safety under fire.*

class in handgun retention, the art and science of defeating a disarming attempt. Learn to shoot from downed positions and with either hand. Learn from the cops: More than 2,500 officers at this writing have been saved by the concealed body armor that armed citizen Rich Davis invented in the early 1970s. As Kevlar Survivors' Club member #1946 and Second Chance Save #682, I can tell you that the stuff works. If your local dealers won't sell it to law-abiding private citizens, look up the LFI Web site, but be prepared to show proof of a clean criminal record.

If you need to carry a gun, you probably need to carry two. Invest in a backup gun if you're licensed to carry. Backups have saved countless police officers, and could have saved countless more if those slain officers had had recourse to a second weapon.

Make sure your loved ones and your regular companions know what the plan is going to be if this particular kind of danger strikes. That "fight or flight" thing is really "fight, flight, or freeze." The ones who freeze are the ones who don't have a plan. If you have something in your mind that says, "Given stimulus A, I *will* carry out response A," you've made the best possible investment in survival. You want to share the same concept with people you care about, who might be with you when a crisis strikes.

Thanks for taking the time to read this book. The plan is to update this book on a fairly regular basis. I don't know who's going to write the next one…but I'm going to do everything I can to make sure I'm around to read it.

Good luck. Stay safe.

Massad Ayoob
Live Oak, FL
2007

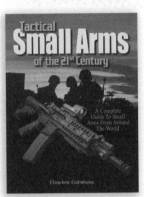

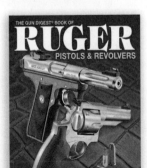
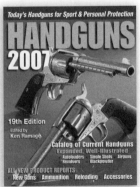